D1278592

A Montage of Media Items

Life (and Death) in the
`YOONITED STATES
of UHMURICA´

A Montage of Media Items

Life (and Death) in the
'YOONITED STATES
of UHMURICA'

Collection by GORD DEVAL
Cartoons by: ED FRANKLIN

Simon & Pierre
Toronto, Ontario, Canada

1 2 3 4 5 • 8 7 6 5 4

Canadian Cataloguing in Publication Data
Main entry under title:
Life (and death) in the Yoonited States of Uhmurica

ISBN 0-88924-135-X

1. United States — Social life and customs — Miscellanea. I. Deval, Gord, 1930-

HN78—L53   973   C83-098542-5

Designer: Newton Frank/Cundari
Printer: Imprimerie Gagné Ltée
Printed and Bound in Canada

Simon & Pierre Publishing Company Limited
Order Department
P.O. Box 280 Adelaide Street Postal Station
Toronto, Ontario
Canada M5C 2J4

CLASSIFIED

Dedicated to my wife, Britta
who had to cope with trying
to read all those cut-up
newspapers.

Table of Contents

Preface

This collection of newspaper-reported incidents describing much of what is occurring in the U.S. of A. now and over the past several years becomes a viable idea for a book only because of Americans' fantastic ability to look at, laugh at, and criticize themselves.

I started collecting these clippings out of curiosity and can honestly state that they are simply the result of reading the daily newspaper. At no time did I make any effort to look elsewhere for material. I wish to express a special thank you to the Toronto Star newspaper and the various wire services, Associated Press, Reuters, Toronto Star Limited, United Press Canada, for their co-operation. Without their support this publication would, of course, have been impossible.

The book, newspaper clippings all, requires no personal individual comment from me! Some of the items are painful to read. Some of them are incredible and others are guaranteed to make you laugh. I simply offer it up in book form, for perusal, soul-searching, laughter, and discussion.

Toronto, Canada

Gord Deval

Money

Oil-rig firm pays $53 million to its workers

KILGORE, Texas (AP) — Texas oil created 13 more millionaires yesterday.

In an unorthodox employee-participation payoff, Delta Drilling Co. of Kilgore paid out $53 million to 87 employees. The average payout was $612,000 but 13 workers received more than $1 million.

Struggling operation

The plan was conceived in 1974 as a way to protect loyal employees. For years Delta had been a struggling oil-rig operation but in the mid-'70s, following the Arab oil embargo and the subsequent restructuring of oil prices, business boomed.

One of the "instant millionaires" a truck supervisor Jack Elkins, said "I told my wife to book us a flight to Las Vegas. For the first time in my life I can have a vacation where I didn't have to worry about how much I was spending."

Mystery woman gives $13,000 to feed needy

MIDLAND, Pa. (AP) — The mysterious gray-haired woman, affectionately dubbed Mrs. Calabash, has struck again — giving away another $2,000 to help feed unemployed workers in this struggling steel town.

She has now given $13,000 — all in $50 and $20 bills — to help the food bank run by United Steelworkers Local 1212 feed about 1,600 families who line up each month for bags of free groceries. It is one of dozens of food funds in Beaver County, where one in four workers is unemployed.

Her most recent appearance was Thursday night. This time, $2,000 in cash came in an envelope with "Happy St. Patrick's Day" scrawled on the outside.

"People ask every day, 'Who is she? Who is she?' " said Jesse Torres, co-director of the food bank. "What she wants is her privacy."

After her first contribution last August, union director Dick Fink dubbed the woman Mrs. Calabash after the sign-off by the late comedian Jimmy Durante on his television shows.

That's what Durante called his first wife, Maude Jean Olson, after a small town they drove through on their way from New York to California.

Fascination has grown around the identity of the benefactress since she first walked into the union local office and the food bank workers are protective of her.

"I don't know what she looks like and if I did I wouldn't tell," said Alex de la Cruz, a former shop steward at the Crucible steel plant, where most off Local 1212's members once worked.

"It's the big thing the day after she's been here," de la Cruz said. "Everyone talks about it, saying, 'where was she? Why wasn't I here?' "

"Mrs. Calabash" has come at Thanksgiving, Christmas and Valentine's Day. times when the food bank seems to need her most.

"She's pulled us out of some tight times," Torres said. "It was like the tooth fairy coming and saying, 'Don't worry, I've got you covered.' "

Wife kept alive as he worries about tax year

CHICAGO (UPI) — This letter came to columnist Carol Mathews of the Chicago Sun-Times:

"My wife is being kept alive artificially by those machines hospitals have these days. She could be kept alive this way for another two months, the doctors tell me.

"That would mean that she would not die until sometime in 1979. If I decide to let them continue with the present treatment, and she dies in 1979, what difference will this have on my income tax liabilities? Do I get to deduct her?"

Ms. Mathews, in her column "Your Money," replied:

"Frankly, I don't know how to answer. Simple humanity would suggest that your wife's needs come way ahead of yours ... Anyone alive for even one day of a new tax year is considered to have been alive for the entire tax year."

The newspaper did not print the name of the husband.

Lottery fortune awaits a winner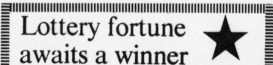

TRENTON, N.J. (UPI) — The largest prize ever offered by a state lottery in the United States — about $8.6 million — will be won in Thursday's "Pick-6 Lotto" weekly numbers game.

Lottery Director Hazel Gluck says the record prize continued to grow because there was no six-out-of-six winner for drawing this week for the fifth consecutive week.

Cost of soap-box car reported up to $20,000

BOULDER, Colo. (UPI) — The car that won the 1972 Soap Box Derby cost $10,000 to $20,000 to build, says a spokesman for the Boulder County district-attorney's office.

Assistant district-attorney William Wise said the cost included shipping the car to the California Institute of Technology for wind-tunnel tests.

Another factor in the cost, Wise said, was the time technicians spent advising the builder. The car was built at the Lange Ski Boot Co. in Boulder.

The 1972 derby was won by Robert Lange Jr., 15. His cousin, James Gronen, 14, won the 1973 derby but was later disqualified for having an electromagnetic system in his racer.

The magnetic system, which gave Gronen's car an added push at the starting line, caused the youth to forfeit the $7,500 first-place scholarship.

Entrants in the derby at Akron, Ohio, are forbidden to spend more than $40 on parts to build their racers.

Bank cuts its prices —$1,000 goes for $800

BEVERLY HILLS, Calif. (UPI) — Some banks give away pens to lure customers, but the drawing card yesterday was the real thing — money — in a giveaway that triggered a near-stampede at the new branch of California First Bank.

Some 200 people lined up at the doors of the bank in the morning, but only about half of them got inside for the "money sale" in which $5,000 was given away in discounted bills during a 45-minute span.

For example, a $2 bill sold for $1, a $1,000 bill went for $800. Other bargains included $100 bills for $80 and $50s for $40.

Stuff this one, Santa Claus

FALLS CITY, Ore. (UPI) — Want to buy a pothole for Christmas?

For some shoppers, the idea apparently fills the bill — or hole.

City recorder Velta Mack said in the last few weeks dozens of calls and letters have come in from around the nation, asking to buy a pothole in someone's name.

The city has sold about 50 in recent weeks and "lately I've been getting some panicky calls from people wanting to know if they can still get them for Christmas," she said.

The scheme was the brainstorm of city officials faced with a mounting pothole problem and no cash. Their solution was a simple one: Sell the pot-

holes; $10 for a regular job, $20 for the deluxe model, which comes with the recipient's name embossed in fluorescent orange paint on top of the repaired hole.

Buyers also receive a certificate that describes the pothole's location, the date it was filled and a pledge that the money was used only to fill the pothole.

The city has raised $860 and, with only a handful of potholes left, Mayor John McGee said any additional money received will go into a special reserve fund until more holes become available.

"We have really sold almost all the potholes," Mack said.

Wife by hour

Wives — as even the most rabid male chauvinist would concede — do have a role, but, in the total context of a marriage, it sometimes becomes ill-defined. Well, a 38-year-old divorcee, Karen Donovan of Petaluma, Calif., has brought it back into focus.

A few weeks ago she started Rent-A-Wife, a service providing part-time wives for single, divorced or separated men who nonetheless find themselves with domestic responsibilities. The rentee will decorate the house, run errands, take care of the kids — in a word, do everything but. "Sex," says Donovan, "is not part of being a wife."

That somewhat arguable point aside, Rent-A-Wife's fees must give a less-than-considerate husband pause: $25 an hour; $150 a day; $600 a week. What's more, within the first week of business, Donovan had received 200 calls.

Let's see now — $600 a week — why, that's over $30,000 a year. Gladys, would you get my wife on the phone and tell her we're going out for dinner. No, not McDonald's!

Turner sells for $7 million

NEW YORK (UPI) — A painting by 19th-century British artist J. M. W. Turner, Juliet and Her Nurse, has fetched a record $7.4 million at auction — $1 million more than has ever been paid for a work of art.

Five bidders at the Sotheby Parke Bernet auction house took less than 7 minutes to boost the minimum price of the painting from $579,-000 to the $7.4 million that an unidentified buyer paid for it.

The painting, which Turner created in Venice in 1836, has been in the Paine and Whitney families since 1901.

Rare wine sold for $35,960

SAN FRANCISCO (AP) — A restaurant owner who vowed to get "the finest bottle of wine in the world," has spent a record $35,960 for an 1822 Chateau Lafite.

John Grisanti, 51, outbid two others in a brisk, three-minute competition to capture the prized wine. Two years ago Grisanti, who operates an Italian eatery in Memphis, Tenn., paid $20,880 for an 1864 Lafite.

"I wanted the finest bottle of wine in the world and I got it," said Grisanti.

Earlier in the day, bidders spent about $65,700 for a variety of California wines.

The wine buyers gathered at the 12th annual Heublein Rare Wine Auction. It is the largest one-day sale of fine wines in the world.

Pair bumped by airline get $208,000

CHICAGO (AP) — A retired judge and his wife who complained Delta Airlines wasn't ready when they were has been awarded $208,000 for being "bumped" from a flight — believed to be the largest award ever made to airline passengers denied their seats.

A jury agreed with former Illinois Supreme Court justice Thomas Kluczynski, 78, and his wife, Melanie, that they suffered "humiliation, indignity and outrage" when they were told all seats were filled because of overbooking on their Delta flight to Florida on Feb. 19, 1976.

The award against the airlines, whose advertising slogan is "Delta is ready when you are," was more than twice the amount requested in the lawsuit. Delta said it will appeal the award.

Not-guilty murderer gets million

LOS ANGELES (AP) — A cook on an offshore drilling platform has been awarded $1 million because he served 2½ years in prison for a murder he didn't commit.

"It has been a long time," said Juan Vanegas, who hugged jurors outside the courtroom after the civil damage verdict was announced.

Jurors voted unanimously for the verdict against the city of Long Beach and three of its police officers who investigated the murder.

Vanegas was convicted in May 1972, along with friend and co-defendant Lawrence Reyes, for the Christmas Day murder of Bill Staga, of Long Beach.

The state Supreme Court released Vanegas on Oct. 28, 1974, ruling there had been insufficient evidence to find him guilty.

The court upheld the conviction of Reyes.

$5 million divorce Sassoon style

BEVERLY HILLS, Calif. (UPI) — Celebrity hairdresser Vidal Sassoon will pay his former wife of 13 years, Beverly Sassoon, about $5 million over 10 years in a divorce settlement — $30,000 a month to his wife and $4,000 a month for their four children.

Lil's coining it

"Miss Lillian" Carter caused a bit of a furor in the United States when she suggested that if she had $1 million she'd hire a "hit man" to assassinate the Ayatollah Ruhollah Khomeini in Iran.

Then last week the U.S. president's mom confided, "Honey, I'm gettin' more money than you ever saw . . ." from people angry at the Khomeini regime keeping 50 Americans hostage in Tehran.

She wouldn't say how much. But now Honest Lil has made a full disclosure: She admits someone mailed her a dime!

Man wed for cash is short changed

Toronto Star special
SANTA FE, N.M. — A man who claimed he married a terminally-ill woman on the understanding he would become her sole heir ended up a loser.

Robert W. Lord told a court he made an oral agreement to marry 64-year-old Bernice Jarrott and "take care of her like a husband would."

She was to leave him her entire estate — but the day after they got married, she made a will making her sister the beneficiary and leaving her husband just $10,000. She died of cancer, after three years, in 1977.

Now the state supreme court has rejected Lord's claim that he should inherit the estate. The court ruled it would violate a public policy against marrying for money.

Legless beggar lived in luxury on his $691,000

WASHINGTON — Eddie the Monkey Man sure made a monkey out of me.

His real name was Eddie Bernstein, a legless beggar who rattled his tin cup from dawn to dusk on a busy Washington shopping street while his pet monkey Gypsy did tricks.

Yesterday it was revealed the smiling panhandler had duped me and tens of thousands of others who regularly dropped loose change into his cup.

For he led a bizarre double life — a pathetic beggar in Washington for half the year and an affluent businessman in Florida the rest of the time.

When he died last month, aged, 79, his estate was worth $691,676.

Each spring and summer for the last 40 years, Eddie begged on the sidewalk a couple of blocks from my office.

He lived a pauper's life dragging himself on his muscular arms after a hard day's begging to the tiny foul-smelling apartment he rented for $105 a month.

But each fall Eddie would return to Pensacola, Fla., where he lived in a $45,000 home in a middle-class neighborhood and owned an $80,000 topless bar, lounge and delicatessen.

In Pensacola he walked on artificial legs with the aid of a cane, dressed smartly, read the Wall Street Journal and Newsweek magazine, and took frequent vacations in Spain, Greece and Israel.

The revelation of Eddie's amazing double life has not only astonished his regular contributors but upset fellow panhandlers who ply the streets of the U.S. capital.

"It's guys like that who give begging a bad name," one banjo-playing beggar in a ragged topcoat and lace-less sneakers told The Star yesterday.

$6,000 a comic investment

SALEM, Ore. (UPI) — Darrell Grimes keeps his own "piece of American history" wrapped in plastic in a safe deposit box. It is a comic book.

His Action comic No. 1 — the book that brought Superman to the world — boasts a $6,000 price tag. Grimes says it is worth more like $7,500 now.

"It's certainly an investment," said Grimes, 26, who owns a comic book store in Eugene, Ore., called Fantasy Shop. "It's gone up $1,000 a year every year since 1974.

"It's something I've always wanted, something people who collect comics want. It's a piece of history."

Grimes bought Action No. 1 through a mail auction held in Los Angeles in April. "I placed a bid for $6,000. I'm really fortunate to win."

The 168-page book carries a June 1938 date. While some 100,000 were produced, he said only 12 known copies remain.

Get-rich-quick ★ ★ 'pyramids' start to ★ crack in California

By Terrance McGarry

LOS ANGELES (UPI) — Like speakeasies in the Prohibition era, they are everywhere — underground get-rich-quick parties in shuttered shops, church basements, hotel rooms, warehouses, suburban homes.

Security precautions are intensifying under growing police efforts to stamp out the illegal "pyramid club" or "business list" craze.

But the fortune hunters turn out by the thousands, drawn by the tales of instant wealth.

The scheme, a variation of the chain-letter scam requires an "investment" of $1,000, with each participant recruiting at least two more investors until there are 32. The senior participant takes $16,-000 in cash then drops out, turning over the lucrative top of the pyramid to the next in line.

The chain continues until the supply of new players cannot meet the needs of those above them. The pyramid goes broke with at least half the players losing their investment.

Federal and local law enforcement officers say they do not have the manpower to combat the "pyramid madness" sweeping Southern California, enriching hundreds of players but ensnaring thousands of potential losers.

In Los Angeles alone there are at least 30 to 50 "pyramid club" meetings a night, each with 50 to 100 participants.

Prizes run to $80,000 and more. Losses usually amount to $1,000 per player.

A man entered a downtown restaurant Wednesday and showed off a suitcase filled with $40,000 in cash, the owner said. "He told me he got it in a new pyramid in Newport Beach, where you pay $5,000 to get in and get $40,000 back in less than a week."

The restaurant owner wound up borrowing a $5,000 stake from the winner to enter the pyramid.

Six "generations" of the game would require participation by more than 33 million people, or the entire population of California and some surrounding states.

Because the laws of mathematics require that the scheme inevitably fail, police may decide to back off and wait for the chains to die of their own accord.

Already, shaken by the laws of mathematics, government and human nature, the pyramids are starting to crack.

Participants say the atmosphere has turned ugly within many pyramid groups, with some of the many losers threatening violence against the few winners to get their money back.

"My pyramid collapsed," one participant reported this week. "It's starting to come tumbling down all over and I'm afraid this is the week all hell breaks loose."

On your way to Heaven? Take message with you

CHICAGO (UPI) — A California company has come up with a new version of the seance — it pays terminally ill patients to carry messages from the living to the dead.

Heaven's Union Messages charges its clients $40 for the service and pays $10 to its terminally ill messengers to relay them. Clients are notified of the "exact time and place of departure" of the messengers, says Gabe Gabor of Grenada Hills, Calif.

He told a Chicago columnist about 500 people have paid for 50-word transcendental telegrams in the company's first few months.

Many of the messages are not to relatives, but to public figures like John F. Kennedy and John Lennon.

'I think people thought they were beyond approach when they were on earth," Gabor said.

Lola rescues hotel staff

LAS VEGAS, Nev. (UPI) — For the first time in Las Vegas entertainment history, a major performer has agreed to work for free.

Entertainer Lola Falana said yesterday she will give up $500,000 and work her four-week engagement at the financially-troubled Aladdin Hotel without pay.

She waived a guaranteed $125,000 a week and said the show would open tonight as scheduled, preventing the layoff of more than 60 Aladdin showroom waiters, waitresses, busboys, cooks and musicians.

"I feel it is my responsibility as a performer to go ahead with the show. There are a lot of people who have booked far in advance. It is not fair they should be turned away," Falana said.

"I know employees' job are important to them, especially during these inflationary times."

Hotel president Richard Daly said the announcement by Falana was a "tremendous boost" for employees.

The casino at the Alladin Hotel was closed by the Nevada Gaming Commission earlier this month, forcing hundreds of employees out of work.

It marked the first time in Las Vegas entertainment history that a major performer agreed to work without salary, other than for charity appearances.

Having 70 kids help in $250,000 swindle

COMPTON, Calif. (UPI) — Barbara Williams was convicted of swindling almost $250,000 in the biggest welfare fraud in the history of the United States. Then she drove her silver-colored Cadillac to her $170,000 home.

A judge who heard the case without a jury reviewed the evidence for 45 minutes yesterday before pronouncing Mrs. Williams, 33, guilty on 22 counts of welfare fraud and one of perjury. She remained free on $50,000 bail for sentencing Dec. 28. She could get eight years.

She drove to court each day in her silver Cadillac and returned to her home in Ladera Heights, which authorities are trying to seize for repayment, along with a four-unit apartment building allegedly bought with the welfare payments.

Between September 1971 and last February, she allegedly collected $239,587.50 in welfare cheques from 10 different names, claiming more than 70 children. She actually has four.

She also allegedly collected another $50,000 in food stamps and medical aid.

She was discovered only after an anonymous caller told authorities to check one of her aliases. Although she used many names, authorities said, the computer check revealed what appeared to be 10 women with almost identical families — children of the same sexes, ages and names.

Prosecutor James Cooper said during the trial that Mrs. Williams showed "tremendous sophistication" in collecting the money, using photostated copies of fake driver's licenses, social security cards and birth certificates to file for aid at different offices.

Defence lawyer Carl Jones said he planned to appeal any conviction on grounds of a state Supreme Court ruling requiring authorities to seek restitution from a defendant before filling charges.

Asked if she would pay back the money if given that option, Jones said. "She would make a very good stab at it."

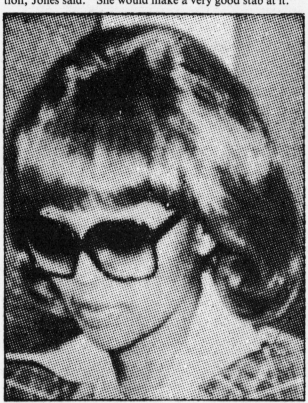

Williams: To court in a Cadillac

Thanks for meals comes 49 years later

OWATONNA, Minn. (AP) — A special Christmas card and three $1 bills arrived at the home of George Boosalis, an 84-year-old retired restaurant owner.

The sender didn't identify herself but wrote that she had skipped out without paying for a couple of meals at Boosalis' restaurant 49 years ago.

"I suppose 1930 was not a good year for a lot of people," said Boosalis, who long ago retired from the restaurant and candy-making business he operated for more than 50 years.

"I thank the lady for making my Christmas a little more special," he said.

$10 million for beating victims

CHICAGO (Special) — A former marine from Chicago has been awarded more than $10 million by a jury for injuries caused by police brutality — the largest award in U.S. history.

Louis Jennings, 29, a former Chicago resident, paralyzed from the chest down, has been in hospital nearly six years since he was allegedly hit in the spine by Detriot police in September, 1973.

The jury ruled against the city of Detroit and all nine policemen named in the lawsuit. Jennings was awarded $8 million, plus 6 per cent interest for the $4^{1/2}$ years the case has been pending.

Detroit police denied that Jennings, then a marine on leave, was struck while in their custody. The city's defence was: "The marines did it."

Rich woman bilked welfare of $377,500

LOS ANGELES (AP) — A stylishly dressed woman who lived in an 18-room mansion with a Rolls-Royce and five other luxury cars in her garage has pleaded guilty to bilking the government of a record $377,500 in welfare payments.

Dorothy Woods, 40, the mother of 12 children, pleaded guilty Tuesday to opening 12 welfare claims under phony names and claiming to have a total of 49 children.

"It's the biggest case by an individual that we've heard of in the country," said police Lieut. Edmund Aleks.

While helping her husband and co-defendant manage a string of apartments, she collected welfare, food stamps and medical benefits by moving into various apartments with phony ID, he said.

"She would stay there long enough to meet the social worker for their one visit, then move back to her residence," Aleks said.

Buy penthouse get free Rolls

LOS ANGELES (Reuter) — Penthouses being sold here for $8 million have a little something extra in the garage for the person who has everything — a free Rolls-Royce.

But the first person to buy one of the two penthouses refused the $170,000 car.

"He already has four, one in each city in which he has a home," said Jody Sherman, the project developer.

"The penthouses are probably the most expensive in the world," Mrs. Sherman said. They will be atop a 21-storey Beverly Hills condominium complex, where units will sell for an average of $2 million each.

In the millionaires' world of Beverly Hills, the condominiums are going fast.

Half sold already

"There will be 67, and we have already sold 45," Mrs. Sherman said. Building does not even start until the end of this month.

Mrs. Sherman said she never doubted the building, to be known as Wilshire House, would be a fast seller.

"We will give the owners luxury without the usual Beverly Hills worries of mudslides and brush fires, complete privacy and the finest security," she said.

"People here will not have to put their Picassos under lock and key for fear of burglaries," Mrs. Sherman said. "Our building will be a fortress."

Each condominium will have emergency "panic" buttons.

Elevators will come up into the condominiums and only people with keys will be able to open the elevator doors.

Mrs. Sherman does not merely show prospective buyers her plans, she entertains them to meals. Business is discussed over champagne.

Chad's father denies demand for $1 million

HASTINGS, Neb. (UPI) — The father of 3-year-old leukemia victim Chad Green has denied a report he and his wife want $1 million for a book about their flight to Mexico so the boy could be treated with Laetrile.

Gerald Green, of Hastings, referred to a Boston Globe story quoting him as saying he and his wife, Diana, rejected $100,000 from one of the publishers competing for book rights because "it's worth a million."

"As far as we're concerned we're not interested in any money. We want Chad's story to be told because we think it is important to the public — they need to know what's going on," Green said.

Chad died last month in Tijuana, Mexico.

Big raise for top Teamsters

LAS VEGAS (AP) — Leaders of the Teamsters union have won whopping pay hikes, giving president Roy Lee Williams a salary surpassing U.S. President Ronald Reagan's.

The 2,000 delegates to the union's 22nd international convention endorsed with little dissent yesterday a constitutional change under which Williams' annual salary will jump from $156,250 to $225,000.

The union's second-ranking officer, secretary-treasurer Ray Schoessling, gets an increase of $75,000 to bring his salary to $200,000.

Approval of the pay hikes elicited some cat-calls from people in the convention hall.

Williams responded by stating "I wish the sergeants of arm on the right would put two or three sergeants of arm up there, and the first one in the gallery that starts hollering and whooping, throw them out."

Man plans to pay debts with $5 million lottery

NEW YORK (UPI) — Curtis Sharp Jr. has just won $5 million in a state lottery — and he says he hopes he'll be able to pay off his debts with enough left over to buy a new car.

"I've got two women out there who are ready to take it," Sharp, 44, told a news conference where he was introduced as the fourth $5-million winner in the history of the New York Lotto game.

Sharp is in the process of divorcing one woman and already plans to marry another.

After paying off his wife's bills and buying a house for himself and his new family, Sharp said he hopes to have enough left to replace his 1971 green station wagon.

Cosmetic Gift

Looking for that special Christmas gift?

The Cosmetic Surgery Centre of New York is offering "head-to-toe face and body cosmetic remodelling" for the man, or woman who has too much of everything.

The whole job — face and neck, eyelids, buttocks, stomach, etc. — takes about a year and costs $20,000.

Touch of genius worth a million

By Jack Smith
Toronto Star special

LOS ANGELES — An entertainment reminiscent of that romantic old television series The Millionaire will soon be launched for real — a new foundation is to spend $750 million to find and encourage geniuses.

The foundation, set up by the late John MacArthur, an eccentric and obscure billionaire who ran his financial empire from a coffee shop in Florida, was left to his son Roderick and other directors to administer without specific instructions.

It will be the fifth richest philanthropic foundation in the United States, and "it could become either the biggest boon to creative enterprise since the Medicis," says Newsweek magazine, "or the biggest boondoggle in history."

The reason is easy to see. Under the plan conceived by Roderick but never contemplated by his father, the foundation will give away $37.5 million a year to free geniuses from humdrum jobs and bureaucratic or academic tyranny so they can think and work in peace and perhaps come up with an idea that will make life on earth a little bit better.

Unlike other foundations, this one will not require candidates to apply for grants, prepare proposals, make progress reports, or say where the money went. No strings at all.

As the younger MacArthur puts it, there was no management team looking over Michelangelo's shoulder and asking for progress reports in triplicate, and how could Einstein have written a grant application saying he was going to discover the theory of relativity? Who would have believed it?

Geniuses will be picked out of the crowd by Nobel laureates and other acknowledged experts in various fields, much as assistant producers pick promising personalities from the studio audience to participate in TV game shows.

All of a sudden some unassuming genius will find himself singled out and handed $1 million (more or less) to be spent in the release and nourishment of his superior intellect.

LOS ANGELES TIMES

Treasure hunters 'hit jackpot' in wreck of Spanish galleon

WABASSO, Fla. (UPI) — Treasure hunters have recovered 1,300 coins, cookware, pieces of china and olive jars from what may be the oldest wreck of a Spanish galleon in Florida waters.

Researchers believe the ship may be the Almirante de Honduras, which sank in 1618 returning to Spain from Mexico. That would make the wreck four years older than Our Lady of Atocha, which Florida Keys treasure hunters have found off Marquessa Key.

The state has leased the wreck site off Vero Beach to a salvage team headed by John Brandon and will share the treasure.

Brandon said the wreck site was discovered by two lobster divers in 1958, but treasure divers had given up when they determined it was not one of several gold-carrying galleons that sank during a 1715 hurricane. His operation began about a month ago.

"Everybody else sort of gave up on it when they didn't find much," he said. "We started searching in another direction and hit the jackpot."

Lonely spinster dies in squalor -- a millionaire

CINCINNATI (UPI) — It reads like a television script: An 81-year-old spinster dies, and her house is found strewn with dirt and garbage. Then she is found to be a millionaire.

But, to whom does the money go? No one knows.

Genette Lemmon died last April. Her home had been without hot water for 15 years and without any water at all for five months. Only one light bulb in the house worked. She kept to herself and neighbors say they were unaware of her plight.

Investigators said she had $112,000 in cash — $42,000 in the house and the rest in a bank safety deposit box. And, at seven banks and savings and loan associations, she had more than $580,000 in accounts. She also owned $400,000 in stocks, making her worth more than $1.1 million.

All Miss Lemmon's close relatives are dead, but about a dozen cousins survive. Now a court must decide what to do with the money.

$7 million taken in biggest-ever gold theft

MIAMI, Fla. (AP) — Gold and jewelry worth between $7 million and $8 million has been stolen from a Miami jewelry store, an insurance investigator said today.

Richard Andrews said the store's owner also owns the company that suffered the loss last month of a $790,000 consignment of precious-metal bound for Brampton, Ont.

Andrews, an investigator of the Jewelers' Mutualo Co., called the latest disappearance the largest single gold theft in history.

Police said the store owner reported the burglary Sunday.

Andrews said 800 pounds of gold and "literally thousands" of ring mountings, bracelets and other jewelry were taken from Trendline Jewelry during the weekend theft.

Trendline owner Al Weinberg owns several other gold and jewelry companies, including Precious Metals Inc. That company lost an aluminum container filled with $790,000 in scrap gold and silver last week at Miami International Airport. The container was en route to Johnson Matthey Ltd., a Brampton refinery.

"They got the mother lode in this one," Andrews said. "I've never seen or heard about a bigger gold theft anywhere. They walked out with 800 pounds of pure gold alone, not counting all the rest of the stuff. It's incredible."

A $100,000 reward has been offered for information leading to arrests.

Ladd Jr.'s fat bonus makes him millionaire

Have you ever received a bonus from the boss? Maybe $100 or even $500?

Well, that's peanuts to Alan Ladd Jr., 41-year-old son of the movie star and husband of Charlie's Angel **Cheryl**, who gets a salary of about $336,000 a year as president of Twentieth Century-Fox.

Of course, you can't expect a Hollywood mogul to get by on those wages, so Alan Jr. has devised a little incentive bonus scheme for himself and the other execs.

Seems the studio's shareholders have just received a financial report on Ladd's bonus for 1978 — a cool $1,581,381.92.

Luxury for the birds

TULSA, Okla. (UPI) — The U.S. army corps of engineers plans to build a $10 million private resort in Oklahoma just for the whooping crane. The multi-million-dollar bird bath would be a rest stop for the 100 remaining birds during their annual migration.

Hear the sheik shriek:

Sheik Mohammed al-Fassi, who has been touring the United States, handing out money to help beautify financially troubled cities, has been accused of doing $10,000 damage to a Miami Beach park.

Al-Fassi, it seems, has been using a public park next to his multi-million dollar estate as a parking lot for construction workers' cars and trucks.

Perhaps the sheik misunderstood the term 'public park'.

Al-Fassi also has been slapped with a zoning citation for erecting a 15-foot-high family crest on his estate grounds. Miami law limits signs to one square foot.

How's al-Fassi taking all this attention?

"I'm going to fight it," the sheik shrieked. "I will sue the city for 10 trillion dollars — $10 trillion, at least!"

At least!

Hollywood sharpie ups ante to $1 million

We now present The Killing, a lucrative drama in five acts starring **Farrah Fawcett** and her ex-manager, **Jay Bernstein**, in the true story of how a Hollywood sharpie enabled Farrah to earn $1 million for 3½ hours of work.

Act I: Bernstein receives a call from Farrah's attorney, **Charles Silverberg,** who says a group of three wealthy businessmen want to put out a miniature gold faucet on a necklace, called the Farrah faucet. Would Farrah endorse the project for $250,000?

Act II: "I went to Farrah and she wasn't interested," recalls Bernstein. But "instead of telling Silverberg no, I said, 'Look, why don't you see if you can get double. Try.' So Silverberg came back and said, 'I got $500,000.' I said, 'That's incredible!' I didn't tell Farrah. I waited about two days, called him back and said, 'Charles, I hate to do this to you, but for $750,000 I think she'll do it.' "

Act III: Bernstein manages to get the ante up to $750,000. Only then does he tell Farrah what he's been up to. She agrees to the deal. Bernstein arranges for the three businessmen to meet Farrah at his house to finalize the matter, but she doesn't show. The phone rings.

Act IV: "She calls and says she's going to be late," says Bernstein. "I say, 'I got an idea. Just follow my lead. I don't want to tell you, 'cause I can't talk now.' I got off the phone and made myself look ashen, which is a good look for a manager. And I said, 'I don't know how to tell you this, but we've got a problem with the deal. And they all panicked, so I didn't have to lie. I mean, I don't lie. I omit sometimes, but I don't lie.' "

Act V: When Farrah arrives, says Bernstein, "they were all really upset." A long session ensues in which Bernstein does most of the talking, claiming Farrah is loath to endorse commercial products because it could hurt her image as an actress. But, eventually, Bernstein says Farrah will agree to be photographed with the necklace, a job which involved 3½ hours work. He makes one last request: "Let's just do one thing. Let's just make it an even million." They agree.

Postscript: The necklace was not a big success.

37 minutes cheats widow of $358

DAVID CITY, Neb. (UPI) — Roy Gillespie died at 11.23 p.m. on May 31 but the Social Security administration said that was 37 minutes too soon for him to collect his May benefits.

Since his heart attack did not allow Gillespie, 72, to live past midnight, the government wants his widow to repay $358.60 — the amount of his May social security cheque.

Kay Gillespie, also 72, said she spent the money on her husband's funeral and will not give the government a cent.

"Thirty-seven minutes," she said. "That's incredible."

But officials say it's the law.

"He would have had to live until 12.01 to qualify for May," said Darrell Gray, district manager at Council Bluffs, Iowa.

Gray said a person must be alive every second of a month to qualify for that month's Social Security payment. Officials said the regulation has been in effect since Social Security began and has drawn frequent criticism.

One-arm bandit rings bell for $300,000

LAS VEGAS (Reuter) — Jerry Sommer, a 68-year-old semi-retired salesman from Ocean City, N.J., has won $300,000 — the biggest slot machine jackpot in Las Vegas history.

Sommer was on his way back to his hotel when he decided to call into the Flamingo Hilton casino. He and his son, Paul, each put $15 into a pool and put $3 a time into the machine.

On his fifth pull of the handle, Sommer had jackpots on all three lines of digits on the machine, including five sevens on the bottom line, needed for the major jackpot.

The jackpots set bells ringing and lights flashing and, when they stopped, the machine had rung up $300,000. The prize was presented to Sommer by cheque.

Navy man wins record dough on TV

LOS ANGELES (AP) — Back when young Tom McKee used to scrawl X's between crossed lines to try and beat the other kids at tic-tac-toe, he didn't realize he was training for the Big Time.

Now, according to the people at the Guinness Book Of World Records, U.S. Navy Lieutenant McKee's winnings of almost $230,000 from the Tic Tac Dough television game show have made him the all-time top winner on a single series.

And no one has stopped him yet. (The show's on Channel 3 at 6 p.m. and Channel 7 at 7 p.m. each day.)

When filming for the show cut off for the summer last month, McKee, 24, had defeated 30 opponents and raked in $141,000 in cash, six Buick Centuries, two sailboats, motorized water skis, camera equipment, a hot tub and 11 vacation trips to places such as Rome, Paris, London, Tahiti and Fiji.

But McKee, who in a month won almost 20 times what he and his wife, Jenny, earned in all of 1979, says their lifestyle remains simple.

"The only thing that's changed is we got the down payment on the house and a dog and a cat, and the dog just pooped on the carpet."

McKee, a pilot trainee at Miramar Naval Air Station in San Diego, has already donated one sailboat to a relief fund that helps navy families, and he gives 10 per cent of his winnings off the top to the Baptist Church and his missionary brother in Africa.

As for the six cars, he says he plans to sell them. "They just don't get the mileage we want."

Step right up for perfect gift

NASHVILLE (AP) — At last, the perfect Christmas present has been found.

You don't have to wrap it, worry about the correct size or the right color, nor even fight frenzied shoppers at the crowded department store to buy one. You can order it by mail.

You can turn your Christmas into a three-ring circus — literally.

For a private performance of the Clyde Beatty-Cale Brothers Circus, just send your order to Irwin Kirby, post office box 24281, Nashville, Tenn., 37202. The price of this Christmas special? Only $35,000 (cheque or money order only, please).

Gas gouger jailed

BOSTON (UPI) — Glenn Heller, the service station owner who charged the highest gasoline prices in the United States last summer, has been sentenced to 30 days in prison and fined more than $9,000 for price gouging. Heller, 30, charged up to $1.56 per U.S. gallon (equivalent to around $2 Canadian per Imperial gallon) at his pumps — 70 cents above the ceiling imposed by federal regulations.

HOUSTON, Tex. (UPI) — Want to buy your wife something special for Christmas? A store here is offering a city park, named in her honor and complete with an opening ceremony to be attended by the mayor. The price? A mere $800,000.

Dollar windfall becomes $391,000

NEW YORK (UPI) — A Colombian woman visiting New York city found a dollar bill on the street and parlayed it into a $391,000 windfall.

The woman, Melina Chica de Zapata, 42, of Cali, Colombia, decided her find must be a lucky omen and played some combinations from the dollar's serial number in the state's Lotto game, state lottery officials said.

As a result, Mrs. Zapata will be returning home in two weeks to her husband, two daughters and three sons with more than $391,000 from Lotto's first prize jackpot.

It was the first time she had ever played a Lotto game and the jackpot was the first time she ever won anything.

When bank made mistake Gus took $700,000 and ran

Special to The Star

WARREN, Ohio — A lot of people are cheering for Gus Delinikos.

Delinikos asked that $774.75 be transferred from his Greek account to a Warren bank so he could send his wife and two children to their native Greece for a summer vacation.

But when the bank mistakenly gave him $774,750, he took a huge chunk of the money and ran.

Officials of a French bank in Paris are not laughing. They are trying to find Delinikos and the money.

"He was made a hero locally because he's beaten the establishment out of all this money," said Doug Neuman, attorney for the Warren bank.

On June 18, the French American Bank in New York, which handles transfers between international and domestic accounts, received instructions from the Banque Francaise de Credit Internacional in Paris.

Misplaced decimal

The $774.75 that was in a branch of the French bank in Greece was to be transferred to Delinikos' account in the Second National Bank in Warren.

Somewhere between New York and Warren, a decimal point was misplaced.

According to court records, Second National received a wire telling it that $774,750 had been credited to Delinikos' account there. The account had $456 in it before the windfall.

Second National called Delinikos to tell him his money had arrived. Delinikos came in, looked at the account and said nothing.

Two days later, on June 23, Delinikos withdrew $490,000. Of that, $165,000 was in cash and $325,000 was in three cashier's cheques made payable to Delinikos.

On June 25, he withdrew another $33,228 in cashier's cheques.

On June 30, he withdrew $25,000 in cash and still more in cashier's cheques.

All told, according to court records, Delinikos withdrew all except about $32,000.

Account frozen

On June 30, a clerk at French American matching orders with actual transfers found the error. Second National was instructed to freeze the money in Delinikos' account.

Robert Hoy, a branch manager, called Delinikos to tell him something was amiss and that he might have to return the money.

Delinikos told him the money was "all gone."

Hoy said no, the computer showed he had $232,000 in his account and suggested Delinikos come to the bank to straighten things out.

But Delinikos didn't show. Hoy called but got no answer. He went to Delinikos' house and found no one home.

Delinikos faces a federal charge of interstate transportation of stolen property, and Warren police have charged him with three counts of theft.

Members of Warren's large Greek community say Delinikos has been seen in Greece.

KNIGHT-RIDDER NEWSPAPERS

'Church' ruler sets up as 'pope' of dope

NEW YORK (UPI) — Enterprising dope pushers, banding together in the name of their own "church" and answering telephone orders, are supplying New York's posh Upper East Side with marijuana on a home-delivery basis under the noses of police.

The Manhattan operation, which deals only in marijuana and calls itself the "Church of the Realized Fantasies," can be reached at an advertised number, day or night. Its founder claims to be doing business to the tune of $30,000 a day.

"Sitting down on a Saturday night and watching TV, you don't want to go out and buy, so you call up," said one of the "church's" door-to-door deliverers, who called himself John Doe. "I make a lot of money. And I've met some neat people."

Chicago transit strike over

CHICAGO (UPI) — Chicago Transit Authority and striking workers agreed to end a four-day strike that created a nightmare for a million commuters and cost the area's economy $80 million a day.

PINCHING PENNIES PAYS OFF

PAWTUCKET, R.I. (UPI) — A penny here and a penny there adds up.

Pharmacist Norman Rondeau bought a new car yesterday with 433,000 pennies. He took 1 1/2 tons of coins in 86 cloth sacks to the auto dealer in a pick-up truck.

Rondeau, who saved pennies paid to him by his customers for four years, said it's easier than saving dollars.

"When you have a dollar, you're going to spend it," he said.

Stars hype anything if the price is right

I t may be lonely at the top — but the endorsement money is a lot better than here on the bottom.

Consider these examples:

☐ Brooke Shields will earn $5 million U.S. over the next three years for hyping Calvin Klein Jeans. And she once picked up $900,000 for a one-minute TV spot advertising Japanese cosmetics.

Even after mother Terri takes her cut, Brooke should have enough left over for a cherry Coke and fries (and the end justifies the jeans).

☐ Ever wonder why former actor Orson Welles goes on TV saying Paul Masson "will sell no wine before its time?" Could it be because he earns $850,000 for two minutes of saying just that?

☐ Johnny Carson makes $2.5 million a year for two minutes of plugging Johnny Carson suits, while Jaclyn Smith grabbed half-a-million for claiming to drink Dubonnet.

☐ When it comes to easy bucks, actor James Coburn has them all beat: In 1977, he brought down $500,000 for saying two words: "Schlitz Light". That — for the less mathematically inclined — is $250,000 a word. Lets' see? What's that work out to per hour?

Looking for the special Christmas gift?

The Cosmetic Surgery Centre of New York is offering "head-to-toe face and body cosmetic remodelling" for the man, or woman who has too much of everything.

The whole job — face and neck, eye-lids, buttocks, stomach, etc. — takes about a year and costs $20,000.

Jobless man offers an eye for $10,000

OMAHA, Neb. (UPI) — Dan Hebert is out of work, two months behind in rent and $7,000 in debt. To get out of hock, he's willing to sell one of his eyes for $10,000.

"Ten thousand dollars is a lot of money to us," said the 31-year-old father, "but I thought for somebody without eyesight, it wouldn't be much if they could afford it."

Hebert wanted to place an advertisement in an Omaha newspaper, The World-Herald, but attorneys advised the paper such an ad would be illegal.

"When I got the letter back that they wouldn't run the ad, I was just shot," Hebert said. "I was just positive this was going to work."

Cornea transplant

Hebert said he first thought of selling his cornea to get out of hock after watching a television report about a woman waiting for a cornea transplant.

He said he would be willing to donate an eye for $10,000, provided the fee is tax free and the recipient pays hospital costs.

He waited several days before telling his wife, who initially was against it but finally agreed.

"I would sit here and watch TV with a hand over one eye to see what it was like," Hebert said. "I shaved with one eye closed and manoeuvered around the apartment with a hand over my eye."

Hard time

He said he had a hard time explaining his plan to his 8-year-old son, Shane, but the child finally understood.

"I told him I'd be like a pirate and have a patch over one eye," Hebert said.

He and his wife looked for work in California for a time. Last winter she worked as a hotel maid in Florida while he picked oranges.

After returning to Omaha last February, Hebert worked at a grocery store but was laid off. His wife lost her job as a maid in a hospital through absenteeism.

Hebert drove a cab until a few weeks ago, quitting because, he said,: "I'd work from 7 in the morning until 10 or 11 at night and only make $10 or $15."

The apartment building they live in has been sold and the new owner wants them out by Nov. 10, Hebert said.

Ford Overreaction

DEARBORN, Mich. (AP) — Ford Motor Co., which expects to lose $1.6 billion in 1980, has spent $350 to fly an engineer to New York to fix a bent license plate frame on a company director's new car. "It's an overreaction, no doubt about it," a Ford spokesman admitted.

Gambler's $690,000 night

LAS VEGAS (Reuter) — Professional gambler Jimmy Chagra built up a bankroll of $390,000 shooting craps here, then on impulse bet $100,000 of it on a blackjack hand. He was dealt cards totalling 12, asked for one more card — and drew a nine to make 21, which paid him even money. Then he placed some basketball bets, which earned him $200,000 more.

Alaska gets no thanks for $1,000 giveaways

By Jay Mathews
Star special news services

ANCHORAGE, Alaska — This U.S. state government, deciding to see if money really will buy happiness, has been getting only flak for its generosity.

In a scheme to share its oil taxes and royalties with its estimated 415,000 people, Alaska has been sending out $1,000 cheques this month to every man, woman and child in the oil-rich state.

So far, few of the recipients have even bothered to say thank-you.

In the state revenue department at Juneau, Colleen Brown reports that givers are not blessed by receivers, who call only to complain if their cheques have not arrived.

"We have received enraged and irate calls from just about everybody," Brown says. "You've never seen so many greedy people in your life."

"I almost feel that I'm on welfare," grumbles Ron Moore, a 36-year-old realtor from Soldotna. "I've lived here 30 years and I don't see why I should rely on the state for subsistence."

The giveaway "was very poorly planned," says Kathy Potter, an office supply sales supervisor here who plans to buy drapes with her money. "There should have been a better way to do it."

So goes the early days of Alaska's "permanent fund dividends," in which its oil taxes and royalties are shared — not through new roads or deeper harbors or any of the other projects government are familiar with — but with blue and yellow cheques instantly cashable at any bank. This northernmost state's experience with the idea so far may frighten away any future leaders elsewhere so bold and so rich as to attempt such generosity.

The giveaway has sent many Alaskan brains churning, not with sweet thoughts for Gov. Jay M. Hammond and the state legislature but with schemes to separate other Alaskans from their money.

Police have reported several cheques stolen from mail boxes. A full-page ad for the Alaska Bank of Commerce in the Anchorage Daily News said: "One thousand dollars! We'll help you make the most of it." A furniture store announced a "cheque's in the mail" sale: "Turn your permanent fund dividend into a water bed that you will enjoy for years to come."

Anchorage Times political reporter Ralph Nichols concluded after many discussions with his fellow Alaskans that "with few exceptions they think it's the dumbest thing in the world, the only thing dumber being not to apply for it as long as they are giving it away."

This philosophy extends to the young and the unborn. The state's vital statistics bureau has been swamped with 1,000 requests a day for certified copies of birth certificates, necessary if parents are to claim $1,000 for each of their children. Any resident's child born before midnight Oct. 15 may claim a cheque, prompting speculation that women with babies due about that time will flood hospital maternity wards and induce labor in order to make sure.

The Revenue Department has sent out 87,901 cheques so far, each decorated with the state flag, which shows, appropriately enough, the stars forming the Big Dipper.

Few benefit

But Alaskans don't seem quick to ladle out their new riches. Automobile and snowmobile dealers say there has been little upturn in business so far, and few charities claim to have benefitted from the giveaway, though in some cases not for lack of trying.

Alaskan politicians who conceived the giveaway years ago wanted to demonstrate their faith in the people's ability to decide themselves how their money should be spent rather than building the usual political pet projects.

Jay Hammond:
Alaska governor wants to give more money away.

Hammond wants to give away even more. He has argued that all of the oil money, now about $4 billion a year, ought to go into the permanent fund.

Since the state income tax has been abolished, Hammond says, there is no other way to keep voters interested in the old question, "What are you idiots doing with my money?"

WASHINGTON POST

GRAND RAPIDS, Mich. (UPI) — The lure of lucre apparently is stronger than the fear of frostbite. Some 20 women, a man and a boy showed up in bikinis at a local radio station at 7 a.m. in sub-zero temperatures hoping to win $100 offered by the station in a "Think Summer" promotion. It was the coldest Michigan night this year.

NEW YORK (Reuter) — The top hat Abraham Lincoln wore to Ford's Theatre the night he was assassinated and the opera glasses he had with him fetched a total of $34,000 at an auction here yesterday.

Logger can't spend his injury money fast enough

ST. LOUIS (AP) — Joe Dwyer has two Rolls-Royces, a Ferrari, a Porsche, a sporty Datsun and a $500,000 vintage Duesenberg. And a Ford for his dog.

The former logger, whose undisclosed multi-million dollar fortune come from the 1974 on-the-job accident that disabled him, says he can't spend his money fast enough.

"I don't want my money to gather dust in a bank somewhere," Dwyer said from a hospital bed in Hialeah, Fla., where he is undergoing his 66th operation. "I'm trying to spend it and enjoy myself.

"With the kind of money I've got, it's coming in faster than I can spend it — money markets and second mortgage investments, stuff like that."

Dwyer, 49, a former U.S. Army helicopter pilot and reformed alcoholic, won the court settlement from four companies 16 months ago after he was run over by a front end loader several times.

His pelvis was crushed, his right side pushed downward about an inch, and just about every bone in both legs was broken, forcing dozens of operations.

Soon after the settlement, Dwyer bought a 1979 Silver Wraith II Rolls-Royce for $96,000. He then bought a 12-cylinder 1972 Model 365 GTC4 Ferrari for $50,000. Then a white 1958 Rolls-Royce Silver Cloud I for $36,000. Then a 1979 Datsun 280ZX for $10,000. Then a 1979 Porsche 924 for $17,500. And recently, the $500,000 SJ Supercharged 1933 Duesenberg.

And the Ford Pinto station wagon his wife had before they were married has become their "dog car," used to transport their Doberman pinscher.

No cash, no treatment MDs tell stab victim

ST. LOUIS, Mo. (UPI) — A man with a steak knife stuck in his back was refused treatment at Barnes Hospital here because he had no insurance — a policy on indigent patients the hospital was defending today.

Theotis Little, 36, was rushed to Barnes two weeks ago, after he was stabbed with a steak knife during a quarrel, officials said. The handle broke off and the blade was imbedded in Little's back, wedged against his spinal cord.

He had x-rays and other tests for three hours at Barnes. But Little's stepfather, Eddie Bostic, said doctors refused to remove the knife unless Little could pay for the surgery.

"They came to me and said I'd have to put up $1,000 cash before they'd take the knife out," Bostic said.

"The only thing I could do was write a cheque, but they said no,

there was no way to see if the cheque was good."

A Barnes hospital spokeswoman said the policy of not admitting patients who cannot pay their bills may seem "cold-hearted," but she said the hospital does provide emergency care.

"If the man was dying or needed something done right away, we would have done it," she said. "Our feeling is that's why City Hospital exists — so indigent people can have health care."

Little, whose left leg was paralyzed by the injury, was transferred to City Hospital. The knife was removed and he is undergoing physical therapy as an outpatient.

Barnes officials said a neurosurgeon approved Little's transfer and City Hospital personnel were waiting for the patient. A Barnes nurse supervised the ambulance ride.

Pocketful of jewels returned to owner

FOUNTAIN VALLEY, Calif. (UPI) — When Dottie Zuvela thrust her hand in the pocket of a jogging suit she had bought for $2 at a garage sale, she pulled out a leather pouch filled with $10,000 worth of diamond jewelry.

She knew immediately who it belonged to.

A week earlier, she had watched a television newscast about an unfortunate woman, Janice Snowden, who lost a lot of jewelry she had tucked in the pocket of an old jogging suit for safekeeping. She had sold the suit at her Nov. 6 garage sale, and didn't realize until a week later that it still held four diamond rings and a pendant.

Zuvela called Bob Snowden, who quickly set up a surprise dinner party for his wife.

When Mrs. Snowden opened the door Zuvela, trying to look angry, handed her a brown paper bag and complained, "I bought this from you and the merchandise is inferior, so I brought it back."

Inside was the jogging suit and inside the suit's pocket was the jewelry.

Zuvela said she never thought about keeping the valuables.

Look who's gone broke -- the bankruptcy court

DETROIT (UPI) — The federal bankruptcy court here is in receivership.

Its chief clerk has been indicted, its judges are under investigation and its reputation has been sullied amid charges of sexual misconduct, cronyism and on-the-job drunkenness.

The ultimate irony is really the receivership, ordered by the Court of Appeals for the bankruptcy court — which was responsible for taking over the financial disasters of people and business.

The takeover move comes amid an FBI and a grand jury investigation of a series of allegations.

These include:

☐ Promotions for some female court clerks depended on sexual favors.

☐ The blind-draw system of assigning cases to bankruptcy judges — crucial to the court's integrity — was tampered with to benefit certain lawyers.

☐ Senior bankruptcy Judge Harry Hackett awarded extraordinary fees to a lawyer with whom he had an illicit financial partnership.

☐ Chief clerk William Harper bought items from the estate of a bankrupt man.

His fare couldn't pay so cabby took wheelchair

DETROIT (AP) — A cabdriver who had given a ride to a 61-year-old stroke victim seized her wheelchair because she could not pay all of her $3 fare.

Isabel Woodson said the driver took her to her doctor's office and became angry when she could pay only $2 of a $3 fare.

"I said I don't have no $3 but I have $2 and I'll give you the rest if you'll take me to the bank," said Mrs. Woodson, who lives in a senior-citizens' housing project."

The driver, David Walter, wheeled her into the office, forced her out of the chair, then folded it up and carried it away, she said.

★ ★ ★ ★ ★

Radio offers pennies from heaven

COLUMBUS, Ohio (UPI — Many people fear a knock on the noggin from Skylab's re-entry into the earth's atmosphere, but a radio station in central Ohio says it will make such a bruise worthwhile.

WNCI will give $98,000 to the first person in the state who brings a piece of Skylab to the studio within 98 hours after it hits Ohio.

PHILADELPHIA (UPI) — Father-of-four Ron Bunch had 68 cents in his pocket when he saw a bag containing $205,000 drop from an armored car.

He still had only 60 cents after he returned the money intact to Brooks Armored Car Service.

The firm, piqued at publicity, said there would be no reward. Hours later it relented and sent Bunch a $5,125.

Tailor-made casket for your pet?

EAST RIDGE, Tenn. (UPI) — Pets, Haskell Castleberry thinks, should have a proper burial.

The former restaurateur, deciding something should be done, opened Pet Caskets Inc. yesterday to give people a dignified way to bury their pets.

Castleberry has "caskets to fit everything from a white mouse to a lion or tiger, parakeets or snakes."

His "really beautiful" plastic coffins — $75 to $360 U.S. — are covered in white, pink and blue satin or velvet.

Noting "price is really no object for most people," Castleberry said "if they think enough of their pet they don't mind paying the price."

MUNCIE, Ind. (AP) — For 20 years, Daisy Cook had been paying a dime a week for a $1,500 insurance policy on her grandson's life. When he died, she collected only 80 cents.

Her grandson, Keno Lewis, 21, was shot and killed at random by two youths as he walked down a Muncie street last February, and the fine print in the 20-year-old policy said it would not cover homicide — unless caused during a burglary or robbery.

"The two people that we have under arrest apparently had no motive at all," a police spokesman said. "They just did it."

Commonwealth Life Insurance Co. of Louisville, Ky., which holds the policy, has since updated its definitions of homicide, president Duane Murner said.

"In fact, now we would pay off unless the death was provoked by the insured," he said.

But he has no intention of applying the new definition in Cook's case.

So his firm sent Cook a cheque for 80 cents — the amount she had paid in advance on the policy.

Toilet trouble is money down the drain

NARRAGANSETT, R.I. (UPI) — The price was right, so Narragansett officials bought 2,640 rolls of toilet paper.

But now cases of tissue are stacked 8 feet deep in the recreation centre basement and the deal doesn't look so good.

When officials were offered toilet paper last month at $10 a case — one-third of the normal price — town manager Donald J. Martin rolled into action.

He snapped up 33 of the 80-roll cases.

"That's a lot of toilet paper, but it was too good a deal to pass up," Martin said.

Problems set in. The toilet paper doesn't fit dispensers at the town beach, the biggest municipal tissue user.

Now, town officials say they'll resolve the issue by spending the $500 they saved to buy new dispensers for the town beach that fit the rolls they bought. Abrams says he'll think twice before he offers the town a good deal again.

Talking tombstone has grave undertones

SUNNYVALE, Calif. (UPI) — For those who wish to speak to their loved ones in the great hereafter, engineer Stanley Zelazny has come up with a $10,000, "electronic tombstone" operated by solar energy.

Zelazny, 37, of Sunnyvale, a senior manufacturing engineer at a major electronics firm, invented the tombstone which transmits muted recordings of the voice of the deceased.

Small speaker

Zelazny and his partner in invention Michael O'Piela of Topeka, Kans., have acquired a patent on the plexiglass enclosure with a solar collector placed in a hollowed-out tombstone. The tombstone contains a small speaker and a three-inch-square solar panel.

"This can play up to 90 minutes of pre-recorded gab from the grave, and the solar device operates under all extremes of weather — even buried under snow," Zelazny said.

"Every single rock star will want one — it's an ego trip."

'It's good'

The sound level of the voice of the deceased is muted so that only mourners standing close to the tombstone can hear it, he said.

"A gravesite is personal property. There will be no charges of disturbing the peace.

"We're going to change the course of the world. I love it, and it's good, and America and the world wants it," Zelazny said.

COUPLE TOLD SON HE WAS DYING — TO RAISE CASH

MARNIA, Calif. (AP) — Warrants charging grand theft and cruelty to a child were issued yesterday for the arrest of a man and his wife who were showered with public sympathy — and cash — after they reported their 9-year-old son was dying of leukemia.

Police Sgt. George Simon said tests conducted last week disclosed that the boy, Ronnie Welts, does not have the disease.

Ronnie, who with his 11-year-old brother was placed in protective custody after the tests, "apparently believed he had leukemia and was going to die," Simon said.

The parents — Jim Wels, 43, and his wife, Frances, 31, provided a list of doctors they said had treated their son. But Simon said the doctors either do not exist or have never treated the child.

The local American Legion post launched a campaign to help the family and donated a wheelchair and food. Police said they do not know how much was donated.

Red carpet turned into 'royal mats'

Special to The Star

LOS ANGELES — Hayward's, a Santa Barbara, Calif., home furnishings store, has filled a lot of orders for carpet in the 100 years that it has been in business but none was as memorable as one it handled late last month.

The company supplied the red carpet rolled out for the arrival of England's Queen Elizabeth II in Santa Barbara.

After the welcoming ceremony at the airport, Hayward officials wondered what to do with the used carpet that had been trod upon by the Queen.

One person wanted to make pieces of the carpet into souvenir coasters, another suggested renting it out for parties. The mayor of Baltimore wanted to borrow it for official functions and one woman wanted a segment to put under her kitchen sink.

But Hayward's decided to donate 25 feet of the carpet to the City of Santa Barbara for official functions and to cut the rest into doormats 3 feet wide and 2 feet long. They are selling the "Royal Welcome Mats" for $250 apiece.

Kidnap ransom: Two Big Macs

LONGWOOD, Fla. (UPI) — Kidnappers of a statue of Ronald MacDonald yesterday failed to pick up their ransom — two Big Macs and a Quarter Pounder.

The $500, six-foot plastic statue of the hamburger clown was sawed off at the feet and snatched from a McDonald's restaurant earlier this week.

---

25 cents a day pulls in pupils

SAN DIEGO, Calif. (AP) — A plan to entice pupils to attend a San Diego school by paying them 25 cents a day is working.

"They're showing great interest," says Dr. Robert Amparan, principal of Memorial junior high school.

"Absenteeism is running slightly under 6 per cent compared with 9 per cent last year, and we think it's holding its own or going down slowly."

The San Diego Unified School District approved the experiment, starting last Wednesday. If it cuts truancy, trustees said it may be extended to other San Diego public schools.

Memorial junior high lost $132,000 in state per-pupil attendance funds because of its high absentee figures last year.

Almost 900 boys and girls who showed up for school last Wednesday were given "privilege cards" retroactive for a month. It shows the figure 25 cents for every day they were in school, and each 25 cents is punched out when they buy school-related items.

Amparan, who earlier wanted the pupils to buy milk and other "non-junk" food as well as school supplies, decided to exclude food items because "we were having difficulty deciding what was junk food and what wasn't."

Ancient gallows go on the block

Toronto Star special

WILMINGTON, Del. — And now, something for the discriminating collector: a much-used turn-of-the-century gallows, complete with new noose.

It's destined for the auction block in Delaware to help pay off a $21,000 debt the state owes to a group of civil rights lawyers.

Delaware lost a lawsuit involving overcrowding at its largest prison, and was ordered to pay legal fees to the victors. But the state said it couldn't come up with the money.

The unsatisfied creditors moved to take possession of the prison chief's office furniture, his state car, other items and the gallows.

An expert at New York's Sotheby Parke-Bernet, auctioneer to the wealthy, had this to say of the possible sale: 'A gallows? Wonderful . . . yecchhh."

Delaware Deputy Attorney General John Parkins, who is trying to save the state property, has mixed feelings about the gallows.

"I say with tongue in cheek, I'm not sure what it means to us if we lose it . . . but we're not going to let it go without some defence," he said.

Delaware has a capital punishment law, and hanging is still the official means of execution. But the old gallows, built in 1901, and used to hang 25 people, is unfit for any more executions. It was last used in 1946.

Last big spender?

NEW YORK (AP-Special) — F. Masood Khan was quietly eating in a cafeteria when four bandits ordered him to write a cheque for $1 million. He escaped and told police, who discovered the Pakistani himself was wanted on a charge of threatening several people.

Khan, who owns a construction company, is famous for writing $1 million cheques — and for reneging on them. Last month he wrote cheques for $2 million in a Dallas disco but stopped payment. A $2,300 cheque for his dinner and champagne for everyone did clear the bank. "He's got the money," a police sergeant said. Even so, the big spender spent Friday night in the Manhattan Correction Centre — without champagne.

He loves to be insulted — for profit

SAN FRANCISCO (UPI) — Jay Stuart is a self-styled verbal whipping post who makes a few bucks a day at it.

A sign he hangs around his neck says: "Abuse Me Verbally, 25 cents, 3 minutes. Call me anything, but call me."

The other day a group of punk-rock types passed him at an outpost on Market St., and Stuart offered them a wholesale rate, six minutes for 65 cents.

He said he has developed a taste for quality abuse, and these fellows didn't heap anything inspired on him.

His profession comes naturally to him, Stuart said, "I have been abused since Day One." So, he figured, why not make a buck from it?

The business isn't for everyone, he concedes. You have to be able to absorb the slings and arrows people want to pour on you. But everybody's better off afterwards.

Robin Hood pair stole $400,000

ROCHESTER, N.Y. (AP) — Rochester police and FBI agents early today captured a father and son employed by Wells Fargo who are alleged to have taken $400,000 in an armed robbery of one of the company's armored trucks because of dissatisfaction over wages.

A long letter, pierced with an arrow and called Geronimo's Revenge, was left on the front seat of the truck complaining that $4 an hour was not an adequate wage for Wells Fargo employees.

Bumbling thief gets year off to a bad start

LITTLE ROCK, Ark. (UPI) — The new year got off to a bad start for a bumbling robber who was ignored and beaten by several of his intended victims, and collected only about $75 in four robbery attempts.

Harold Stivers, 33, ended the disastrous first day of the year in jail.

A man with a knife tried to hold up a service station about dawn, but when the attendant refused to give him any money, he left.

Next, police said, he tried to rob a self-service station attended by a slight, white-haired woman. He began pleasantly enough, asking for change for a dollar.

"Just as I turned to open the cash register," the cashier, Harriet Starkey, said, "I saw some quick movement to my side. I turned and it was a knife. As I turned . . . I caught his arm in the window and I wouldn't let go. He swore at me. He was drunk."

The knife hit the floor when she slammed the window.

"I picked it up and threw it out, thinking he would chase it," she said. "When he did, I ran in the back and shut the door. He didn't get nothing."

Police said Stivers next went to a convenience store. He was not refused money and apparently was not attacked, but the store kept no more than $50 in the cash register.

With his partial success apparently fresh in his mind, he tried a second convenience store, authorities said. The second convenience store robbery netted $25. Stivers was arrested later and charged in all four incidents.

Couple sold sons for $600 to pay the rent, police say

FORT MYERS, Fla. (UPI) — An indigent couple, three months behind on their rent, were arrested for selling their two sons for $300 each so they would not be kicked out of their apartment, police say.

Six people — the parents and the buyers — were arrested when Miguel Angel Ocasio, 28, confessed to authorities that he and his wife, Luce Nilda Ocasio, 21, sold 17-month-old Oscar and 9-month-old Miguel out of desperation, officials said.

The Ocasios were charged with unlawful sale of children.

Charged with receiving a child for pay were Aida Esther Gonzalez, 43, and her husband, Juan Jose Gonzalez, 31, and Ann Margarita Williams, 26, and her husband, Gary Williams, 23, police said.

Police said they received a tip from a neighbor that the Ocasios might have sold their children.

At police headquarters, the father confessed he sold the children because he did not have a job and the family was going to be thrown out of their apartment, authorities said.

The mother wrote a note surrendering custody of the children to the couples who bought them, police said. Birth certificates, social security cards and other records were reportedly provided with each child. State officials are now looking after the two babies.

★ ★ ★ ★ ★ ★ ★

Hurricane city hit by price gougers

By Jeff Prugh Toronto Star special

MOBILE, Ala. — Tempers remained short and lines for ice and gasoline got longer as price-gougers sold $150 chain saws for as much as $650 and $400 power generators for $1,200 in hurricane-scarred Mobile.

The city's board of commissioners passed an emergency bylaw that banned setting prices for any merchandise higher than prices that prevailed during the 90 days before hurricane Frederic left the Gulf Coast city in shambles. Despite this truck drivers were peddling 10-pound bags of ice for $5 each to people without power for fridges.

Forced to live in shed old man says landlady treated him 'all right'

MIAMI (AP) — An 85-year-old man who police say was held against his will for more than six monts in the swimming-pool pump house, says he didn't mind living in the tiny, mosquito-infested building.

After police found Victor Hartman last Thursday, they arrested Bonnie Wilkie Blanchard — who lived in an $85,000 home in front of the pump house — on a charge of false imprisonment.

But Hartman, who was taken to a hospital, said later that Mrs. Blanchard, 55, treated him "all right."

"Sometimes I lived in the big house, sometimes in my own house — I liked it just the same," he said.

Police said they had no intention of dropping the charges against Mrs. Blanchard.

Police said Hartman was kept in a padlocked pump house surrounded by a chain-link fence that was topped with barbed wire.

Police said Mrs. Blanchard had been drawing Hartman's $186-a-month Social Security cheque as payment for room and board.

Oh, what a half-baked honeymoon

CHICAGO (UPI) — A couple whose wedding cake went missing were so upset they couldn't consummate the marriage for three days, they told a judge.

They paid $95 for the 3-tiered cake — complete with special glass top — to be delivered at their nuptials Aug. 30, 1980.

But at the reception, they found no cake. The baker confirmed it never made it into the oven. He offered to provide a small substitute and a $95 refund.

But the bride said she wanted her own cake or nothing at all. Court records said she "began to cry uncontrollably." She was "extremely shaken and emotionally upset."

The couple got through dinner and dancing, but the groom said he was unable to enjoy his wedding day, couldn't sleep that night and couldn't consummate the marriage for three days.

The bride said she couldn't sleep on her wedding night, lost her appetite, dropped more than 10 pounds and "did not actively participate in her marriage for approximately two weeks."

The couple stewed until January 1981 then filed a lawsuit against the baker asking $5,000 in damages.

The bakery's attorney claimed that waiting so long they had in effect accepted the bakery's offer of compensation.

The judge agreed, and dismissed the suit this week.

The lawyer reported they had since become parents.

These messages get great exposure

NEW YORK (AP) — The executive was flustered when the applicant who said she'd "do anything" for a job began unbottoning her blouse in his office. It got worse when he told her to leave.

She turned on a portable tape recorder and, to the sound of striptease music, peeled down to her G-string and bikini top and read him a Happy Birthday message.

New Yorkers have begun saying it with Strip-A-Grams, the newest alternative to singing telegrams, and the entrepreneurs who started the company four months ago say franchiese are expected to open within a few months in Boston, Los Angeles, Chicago and even London.

Strip-A-Grams have been delivered to offices, parties, even hospitals. But Gregory Fibble, who owns the service with Gary Blumsack, says they have to be careful.

"We always have to investigate who else is in the room. If there's a 90-year-old guy with a pacemaker in the next bed, we have to draw the curtainso we don't end up with a liability suit."

For $80, Strip-A-Gram will send a man or woman dressed as an office worker, party guest or some other character to deliver a surprise greeting.

For $150, customers can get a male-female combination or two strippers of the same sex. A full burlesque routine of three to five strippers can be had for an undisclosed price.

The six women and four men who deliver the Strip-A-Grams — actors and dancers earning some extra money — show no full nudity and offer no sexual services, the owners say.

"We show that burlesque can be fun, classy and clean," Fibble says. "A secretary who would never go out to see burlesque can receive a Strip-A-Gram and talk about it for 20 years.

The service, which the partners established with $80, now delivers 35 to 60 Strip-A-Grams a week.

One of the strippers, armed with a bogus resume saying she had studied at Harvard, was offered a job during an interview at an advertising agency before she began taking off her clothes.

The actress, who uses only the name Lyndsy, earns $300 to $400 a week for deliveri about seven Strip-A-Grams.

★ ★ ★ ★

You may be paid to have a baby professor says

NEW YORK (UPI) — Women in the United States and Europe one day might be paid by their governments to marry and bear children, says a Princeton University professor.

The incentive is shrinking populations that have already pushed some countries past the point of zero-population growth, Dr. Charles F. Westoff says in the new Scientific American magazine.

According to projections by the professor of sociology and demographic study, populations in the United States and the Soviet Union will record more deaths than births by the year 2015.

"An industrial nation that decides not to tolerate negative growth may have to subsidize production on a large scale with a serious investment of public funds," Westoff says.

NEW BOSS TO GET $1.5 MILLION BONUS

Special to The Star

CHICAGO — Who says professional athletes are getting all the big signing-on bonuses?

Truck and farm equipment manufacturer International Harvester Co. is paying a $1.5 million bonus to its new president, Archie R. McCardell, to entice him from the chief executive's suite at Xerox Corp. His salary, according to a five-year contract, will be $460,000 a year.

Another sweetener is a $1.8 million loan, at 6 per cent annual interest, to enable McCardell to buy 60,000 shares of International Harvester stock. If the company reaches certain financial objectives under McCardell's leadership, the loan will be written off.

Oh, yes. The company is also paying McCardell's moving expenses.

This cheque didn't bounce

DOVER, Del. (AP) — The clerk of Dover magistrate's court paid James McBride's $30.50 speeding ticket after deciding his cheque — etched on a 40-pound slab of pink granite — would make a good conversation piece.

McBride, a tombstone maker, said the $5.40 postage was well worth the satisfaction he gained protesting the ticket.

Town buys man a new heart

FRAMINGHAM, Mass. (UPI) — Most New England town meetings concern themselves with items like the purchase of new sidewalks, new snowplows or new jails.

Framingham is buying a new heart.

Dipping into the town treasure, residents have voted 104-13 to spend $30,000 for a transplant operation for 39-year-old firefighter Fred Kelley, who doctors say won't live another year otherwise.

Baby firm expecting first product

LOUISVILLE, Ky. (AP) — Surrogate Parenting Associates Inc. is expecting its first finished product this fall.

It will be a baby boy, due sometime around the week of Nov. 15.

Surrogate Parenting is a baby-making business, signing up women willing to bear children for couples who themselves cannot produce offspring.

Katie Brophy, the organization's lawyer, said this first surrogate mother — who does not give her real name but goes by Elizabeth Kane in connection with her surrogate mother activities — is a 37-year-old Illinois woman with three children of her own.

She was impregnated with sperm from the male partner of a couple who cannot bear children.

Couple traded in their baby for a used sports car

FLEMINGTON, N.J. (UPI) — A couple offered car salesman Italo Patinella an unusual deal — their 14-month-old son for 1977 Corvette. He almost accepted.

Patinella, who lost his son, daughter-in-law and grandchild in a fire two years ago, agonized over it. But eventually he notified police who arrested the couple, James Green, 29, and his wife, Pamela, 21. The child, whose name was not revealed, was placed in a foster home.

Patinella said the incident hit very close to home. "I can't find it easy to talk about. I lost three of my own children and this feels like I've almost seen another child lost.

"My first impression was to swap the car for the kid," he said.

"(But) I knew moments later that it would be wrong. Not so much wrong for me or the expense of it, but what would this baby do when he's not a baby any more? How could this boy cope with life knowing he was traded for a car?"

The Greens were arraigned yesterday on charges of endangering the welfare of a child and offering an illegal adoption.

Judge Jeffrey Martin ordered them held in the county jail on bail of $100,000 each. They could be sentenced to up to five years in jail and fined $7,500 on each offence.

Patinella said the bizarre case began last week when the Greens allegedly walked into his showroom and proposed the swap for the $8,000 sports car.

He recalled a "feeling of shock," which quickly turned to anger as the full import of the offer sunk in.

He notified the authorities.

When the Greens returned to complete the deal, Patinella pretended to go through with. The two were arrested as they left the showroom, keys and ownership papers to the Corvette in hand. They were arrested beside the car as mechanics were putting on the license plates.

"They left the baby in the showroom on the floor, just turned around and walked out. They didn't even kiss it."

Three strikes and he's out

DES MOINES, Iowa (UPI) — Instead of vacationing in Hawaii, Elton Adams spent yesterday looking over police mug shots, trying to find the people who robbed him, and robbed him, and robbed him.

Adams, 65, told police a woman jumped into his car while he was stopped at an intersection. He said she wrestled away his wallet containing $150 and fled.

In an attempt to learn her identity, he stopped in a nearby pool hall — only to be robbed again by a man who took $300 in travellers cheques the woman robber had left behind.

Adams returned home to find his house had been burglarized

Everyone will be a millionaire by 2050!

WASHINGTON (AP) — How far will your income go in the mid-21st century?

Nobody knows for sure, but if the U.S. Social Security Administration's projections hold true, the average U.S. worker will be making $656,000 a year. Millionaires will be a dime a dozen.

GOODLAND, Kan. (UPI) — Dozens of friends and acquaintances today buried centenarian Jim Gernhart in his well-worn copper coffin beneath a tombstone that read: "He held his own funeral in 1951." Over the past three decades, Gernhart, 103, had climbed into his coffin 26 times and smiled through a mock funeral staged for his own enjoyment and that of his friends. A funeral, he always said, was one party a person shouldn't have to miss by being confined to a grave. In the first funeral, Gernhart doubled as corpse, chief mourner, stage manager and maitre d'. There were eight pallbearers, 18 honorary pallbearers and Gernhart personally prepared a large meal for all of the 1,200 mourners. It cost him $15,000.

She bears their child for $10,000 ★ ★ ★ ★

NEW YORK (UPI) — A 37-year-old Illinois housewife and mother of three who answered a newspaper ad for a surrogate mother is now carrying a childless couple's baby for $10,000, People magazine says.

The woman, who was not identified, is due to give birth in November to the child of a man she never met, the magazine said yesterday.

The baby was conceived by artificial insemination and will be handed over to an anonymous Louisville, Ky., couple at birth.

A Louisville fertility specialist, Dr. Richard Levin, arranged the pregnancy and has also arranged three others in Kentucky, the magazine said. "This is the best and quickest way to produce a child genetically most like the couple," he said.

Most states, Levin said, prohibit surrogate mothers to prevent black market babies. But after researching legal and medical precedents, he said he took out advertisements for a surrogate in six major newspapers.

Above average

He said the adoptive parents specified the woman "be tall and have above average intelligence."

Lawyers drew up a "loophole-free contract (if there are twins, for example, the parents will have to take both)," the magazine reported. The mother also agreed not to smoke, drink or use drugs

The surrogate mother said at first her husband, a 45-year-old business executive, opposed the idea, but finally agreed to it, People said. She said although she "would do this for free," her husband urged her to take the payment of $10,000.

The surrogate mother and her husband have three children of their own.

Chapter 2

Law Suits

Wife can sue her mate for not shovelling snow

BOSTON (AP) — The Massachusetts Supreme Court says a woman can sue her husband if she slips and falls on an icy sidewalk that he has failed to shovel and sand.

The unanimous ruling this week sent the case of Shirley Brown v William Brown back for trial in a lower court where it was dismissed last year.

At that time, Superior Court Judge George Hayer dismissed the suit on the ground that the old common-law rule prohibiting husbands and wives from suing each other applied in Mrs. Brown's claim.

But the high court said it was time to change the "antediluvian assumptions concerning the role and status of women in marriage," which led to the development of the legal principle that husband and wife were one person and could not sue each other.

The court said its own 1976 decision allowing a woman to sue her husband for injuries suffered in an auto accident opened the way for the first time in Massachusetts for lawsuits between spouses.

Noting that other states allow spouses to sue each other in certain types of accident claims, the court said Mrs. Brown should at least get a chance to prove her case in court.

Mrs. Brown slipped and broke two pelvic bones while walking from her Wakefield home to a driveway, court papers say. Her husband had left home an hour earlier, 7 a.m., to go to his construction job in Boston.

Her $35,000 suit claimed Mr. Brown was "careless and negligent in his maintenance" of the walks and failed to leave them in a safe condition for his wife.

Mr. Brown's lawyers said it was unreasonable to expect a husband leaving for work that early to take care of the sidewalks.

Don't monkey with Tarzan's reputation

NEW YORK (AP) — High Society magazine has "besmirched, tarnished and debased" the image of Tarzan and Jane in showing them "purportedly engaged in explicit sexual activities and conversation," a U.S. judge said in ordering the magazine's July issue recalled from distribution.

High Society faces a $3-million damage suit for its 10-page article, Monkeying Around With Tarzan and Jane.

The two characters are trademarks of Edgar Rice Burroughs Inc. of Tarzana, Calif. — the firm is named after Tarzan's creator — which licenses their use only to those who will portray them as persons of high moral character.

He stabbed himself to prove his point...

SOMERVILLE, Mass. (AP) — Sometimes it takes more than complaining to get people to listen to you. You've just got to take the matter in hand.

A jury has awarded $350,000 in damages to a man who said he tried to commit suicide because nobody would believe that a cloth pad had been left in his stomach after a gall bladder operation.

The jury was told that George Bonin, 64, repeatedly complained of stomach pains following the 1974 operation, but the pad wasn't discovered until Bonin tried to commit suicide by stabbing himself in the stomach 18 months later.

Hugh O'Brien, Bonin's lawyer, said his client stabbed himself because he was depressed by the fact that his repeated complaints about stomach pains were ignored.

Dr. William Croskery, the surgeon who performed the operation, and other medical personnel were named in the suit. The hospital is no longer in existence.

MAN LOSES HIS PENIS GETS $9,000

VENTURA, Calif. (UPI) Ancel Lesley, 43, of Santa Paula, has accepted $9,000 for his lost penis.

Lesley brought a $3 million malpractice suit against three doctors, but settled out of court for $9,000, superior court records disclosed yesterday.

He said that when the doctors took skin grafts from his left thigh in April, 1973, they accidentally nicked his penis with a scalpel. Gangrene set in and the organ had to be amputated, he complained.

Lady and the tramp: $20,000 sought in puppy paternity suit

Star special news services

WARMISTER, Pa. — The owner of Ice Princess, a purebred Alaskan malamute, has taken the owner of Bear, a black Labrador retriever, to Bucks County Court in what both sides agree is essentially a puppy paternity suit.

According to the suit, filed by Linda A. Leavens of this Philadelphia suburb, Bear leaped over a four-foot fence and into her backyard on the night of Jan. 6, and the ensuing romantic interlude produced 13 puppies.

Leavens contends in the suit that Leonard Blazick, the owner of Bear, was negligent in allowing his dog to "run loose and at large." She is seeking damages of nearly $20,000, because, the suit said, the pregnancy and subsequent complications ruined Ice Princess' earning potential as a breeding animal.

"It's a wrongful-birth action," said Richard J. Molish, the attorney who filed the suit last week. "That's a good way to describe it — the lady and the tramp."

$556 in support

Leavens said she is also seeking $556 in "puppy support" to cover expenses that include veterinarian bills and $119 worth of puppy food. All 13 of the black, furry pups have been given to good homes, she said.

Leavens said she had left Ice Princess unattended in her backyard for "only a minute to answer the telephone." When she returned, she said, she caught Bear in the act.

"It's only nature; dogs will be dogs," Blazick responded in a telephone interview. She left her dog in the backyard, and she knew it was in heat. She was taking a chance there."

He said that he kept Bear chained in his backyard but that the dog apparently broke loose and ran half a mile to Leavens' home. Although Blazick did not deny that Bear was there, "they're going to have to prove beyond a shadow of a doubt that he was the father," he said.

Appealed ruling

The case was taken to Bucks County Court after Blazick appealed a ruling by a district justice in Leavens' favor in April.

"It's snowballing, all this suing business in our country," he said. "It's ridiculous because it's just as much her fault as ours. You don't leave a dog in heat in a backyard in the middle of Warminster. The male dogs go crazy."

Said Leavens: "It's always the woman's fault for being pregnant. That's the typical male attitude."

KNIGHT-RIDDER NEWSPAPERS

Language of love: $167,000

FORT LAUDERDALE, Fla. (UPI) — Never take the language of lovers literally, said a judge who slashed a $6 million palimony claim against Avon heir Douglas Henderson to $167,000.

Judge Miette Burnstein conceded that Henderson may have promised Rosemary Lepera, "I will provide for you and I will take care of you forever."

However, she said, "hyperbole is the language of lovers. Adults have to view such language as momentarily expressive of intense and immediate emotion and desire.

"The plaintiff was a sophisticated woman, a divorcee and a mother. Such language alone cannot be said to form the basis for any contractual obligations. What a pallor the courts would cast on courtship if they were able to hold otherwise."

Mrs. Lepera, now 40, sells luxury cars in San Marino, Calif.

Rod Stewart sues ex-manager for $70 million

LOS ANGELES (Reuter) — British rock star Rod Steward has sued his former manager, Billy Gaff, for $70 million in a suit alleging breach of contract, Stewart's lawyer, Barry Tyerman, said in Los Angeles yesterday.

He said the suit was in reply to a suit filed by Gaff last May seeking $5 million in compensatory damages and an unspecified amount in punitive damages from Stewart.

Gaff, who is also British, accused Stewart of the wrongful termination of their business relationship.

Tyerman said the Stewart suit alleged Gaff made deals and commitments on behalf of Stewart without consulting the rock star. The suits seeks $20 million in compensatory damages and $50 million in punitive damages, Tyerman said.

The relationship between Stewart and Gaff ended last March in what Stewart's press agent described at the time as an amicable arrangement.

Woman files $4.5 million drug lawsuit

ST. LOUIS (UPI) — The daughter of a woman who took the drug DES has filed a lawsuit seeking $4.5 million from companies that manufactured or distributed the drug.

Hope Levinson and her husband, Mark, filed the suit in St. Louis Circuit Court against 96 companies in 17 states and Great Britain, all the known manufacturers and distributors of the drug, a derivative of the chemical stilbene.

The drug was prescribed for many pregnant women from the '40s to '60s as a means of preventing miscarriages. Mrs. Levinson, 28, said her mother had taken DES. The suit claims Mrs. Levinson has suffered cell and tissue changes and an increased risk of cancer and will require extensive medical treatment.

Fetus swapped for stolen infant

LOS ANGELES (UPI) — Testimony has begun in a bizarre $24 million baby-swap suit brought by a woman whose healthy infant daughter was replaced moments after birth with a stillborn male fetus.

The swap was uncovered only after a grisly murder eight months later.

Mary Childs, 41, a grocery store clerk from Duarte, Calif., has charged Kaiser Foundation Hospital in Hollywood and three doctors with negligence, malpractice and fraud in the kidnapping.

In 1974, Norma Armistead, a registered nurse employed by Kaiser, replaced Mrs. Child's baby Daughter with a stillborn baby boy she had stolen from the hospital nine days earlier and kept in her apartment freezer.

The suit charges that Kaiser Hospital and the three doctors — Jack Kartel, Eugene Bagley and Jerry Lawson — were negligent in not noticing the switch.

Mrs. Childs and her daughter are seeking a total of $24 million from all defendants.

After Mrs. Childs gave birth, Mrs. Armistead switched the babies and called Dr. Kartel, who testified yesterday that he found Mrs. Childs with the dead baby in a birth position between her legs and he assumed she had delivered a stillborn boy.

The kidnapping was eventually uncovered when Mrs. Armistead was arrested for the murder of a 28-year-old pregnant woman, whose throat she slit and whose baby she then took from the dead body by Caesarean section. Mrs. Armistead, 49, is serving a life prison term for that murder.

Man wins $85,000 sex drive suit

WICHITA, Kan. (UPI) — Society's view of the worth of an older man's sexual drive — that's the crux of the settlement reached by an elderly farmer who filed suit against a doctor for mistakenly removing his testicles.

Harris Stevens, 68, settled for $85,000 to compensate him for the loss. His doctor mistakenly thought the testicles were cancer-ridden.

"It's just a question of what your testicles are worth at age 67," said Stevens' attorney, Gerald L. Michaud.

"If this man would have been 22, he would have got a lot more — maybe a million (dollars)."

Stevens' suit against Dr. Elliot A. Magidson of Wichita, Kan., said that after the operation he was less able to function sexually, suffered mental anguish and side affects related to diminished hormones.

It was discovered some time later that Stevens did not have cancer.

"When I talk to young people, they don't think it should be worth much," Michaud said. "But older persons seem to think it should be worth more. Young people don't think they'll even live to be 67 and don't think they'll need testicles at that age."

EVEN A SPOUSE OF 90 LIKES SOME EXTRA LOVE

CHICAGO (AP) — Two women and a man whose combined ages total 253 years have become involved in the eternal triangle.

Louise Kubiniec, 82, filed a $250,000 alienation-of-affection suit on Thursday against Mary Rieser, 81.

Mrs. Kubiniec's suit accuses Mrs. Reiser of "openly and maliciously carrying on an illicit affair in Chicago and in Hot Springs, Ark.," with Mrs. Kubiniec's husband, Albert, 90.

Mrs. Kubiniec said Albert, a retired cemetery worker, has been trying to stay young by taking annual trips to the health spa in Hot Springs.

She said Mrs. Reiser accompanied Albert on his trips.

Regarding the suit's charge of illicit conduct, Mrs. Kubiniec said: "Age don't mean nothin' to Albert."

Murderess can't sue

DES MOINES, Iowa (UPI) — The Iowa Supreme Court has ruled a woman cannot sue her psychiatrist because he failed to prevent her from murdering her ex-husband.

The justices pointed to "Public policy" and "established social mores" in overturning a lower court ruling that allowed Mary Kathleen Cole and her current husband to sue psychiatrist Michael Taylor.

Cole was convicted of first-degree murder about four years ago for the 1977 shooting death of her ex-husband, Alan Taylor, a Des Moines physcian.

The Supreme Court upheld the conviction last year.

Bungled sex change alleged in $7 million lawsuit

SAN FRANCISCO (AP) — A person who claims a bungled sex-change operation left her neither man nor woman is suing a doctor for $7 million damages.

Julie Phillips, 38, wept yesterday as eight men and four women were chosen for the jury trial which begins next week.

The suit said Miss Phillips was led to believe the operation would result in "fully functioning female genitalia."

But "I don't know where I belong," she told a reporter. "I can't have sex. I don't belong in the gay life. I don't belong in the straight life . . . it isn't the money; I want peace of mind."

The defendants, who were not in court, are Dr. John Brown, said by his lawyer to be practising medicine in Mexico, and James Spence of San Jose, Calif. Brown's license to practise medicine in California has been revoked.

Miss Phillips' lawyers, Melvin Belli and Salle Soladay, said their client wants $2 million general damages and $5 million puni-

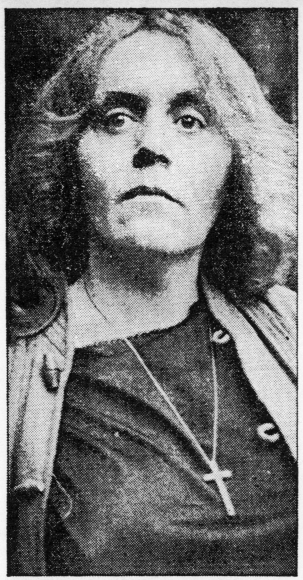

Julie Phillips: Neither man nor woman

tive damages for alleged suffering.

Miss Phillips claimed Brown charged $5,000 for operations in December, 1973, and January, 1974.

The suit says Brown used "his agent," Spence, as a medical assistant although Spence was no doctor, and employed Spence to drum up business from persons who wanted sex-change operations.

Surgeon makes a wrong cut

CEDAR RAPIDS, Iowa (UPI) — A brain surgeon suing hospital anesthesiologists for refusing to assist him testified he made an "unbelievable mistake" when he cut into the wrong side of a patient's head.

"It was the worst moment of my whole life . . . an unbelievable mistake," Dr. Herbert Locksley told a five-man, three-woman jury in a soft voice yesterday.

"No one will ever know the hours of soul-searching and debriefing I have done to try to understand how I could make such a mistake," he said, adding with emphasis: "How could I make such a mistake?"

Locksley was called to testify on 19 alleged acts of incompetence that attorneys for the city's anesthesiologists and two hospitals — Mercy and St. Luke's — have cited in their defence of his $9 million breach-of-services suit.

He said he accepts full responsibility for one mistake, in which he cut into the wrong side of a patient's head in an attempt to repair an aneurism in the carotid artery.

The patient recovered but lost his sense of smell because of the mistake, Locksley said.

A malpractice suit filed by the patient was settled out of court for an undisclosed amount.

Organ donor sues after kidney dies with mother

ROCHESTER, Minn. (UPI) — A kidney donor is suing the Mayo Clinic for $300,000 in damages for the death of his kidney because its recipient — his mother — died after allegedly falling out of her hospital bed.

Michael Durell is also seeking another $300,000 damages for what he claims to be negligence, malpractice, intentional death and breach of contract in the death of his mother, Rose Durell, who died in February 1981.

Deflated woman wants $200,000 for breastwork

ST.LOUIS (UPI) — A 29-year-old woman is suing a medical supply company for $200,000 because breast implants she received nine years ago have deflated.

Pamela Kidd says the implants, made by American Heyer-Schulte, were "unreasonably dangerous" because the implant solution would eventually leak into surrounding tissue.

She was left with scars when the implants were replaced last year after the first ones suddenly went flat, the suit says. "We manufacture excellent products," a Heyer-Schulte spokesman said.

Woman awarded $4.6 million

SAN DIEGO, Calif. (AP) — A court has awarded a record $4.6 million to a woman who testified she suffered mental damage after being seduced by her psychiatrist.

A 10-women, two-men, Superior Court jury deliberated four hours before returning a unanimous verdict in favor of Evelyn Walker, 41, of San Diego, plaintiff in the civil suit against Dr. Zane Parzen of La Jolla.

Marvin Lewis, Walker's lawyer, said the award was the largest malpractice award in San Diego County history and possibly the largest award of its kind in the U.S.

Lost family

Lewis, who had asked the jury for a $6.9-million judgment, argued that Walker lost her first husband, the custody of her two children and her share of the community property because of Parzen.

Her mental condition had worsened and she attempted suicide more than 30 times since Parzen broke off relations with her, Lewis said.

Parzen admitted during the trial he had committed "medical and ethical malpractice" by having sexual relations with Walker.

When he referred her to another psychiatrist in January, 1977, after 2½ years of sessions, he said she was a "borderline psychotic."

Michael Neil, lawyer for Parzen, said he will ask for a new trial or ask the judge to reduce the award.

Parzen's licence was suspended by the state last year after he admitted engaging in sex with Walker.

Girl awarded $7.6 million

SAN FRANCISCO (AP) — A teenager who was paralyzed after a "double dose" of cancer-fighting radiation destroyed her spinal cord has been awarded $7.6 million in damages — thought to be the biggest single malpractice award in U.S. history.

Laurie Necochea, now 18, is confined to a wheelchair for the rest of her life. She needs round-the-clock nursing and her medical bills run to $55,000 a year, a jury was told. Lawyers for the Mount Zion Hospital where the girl became paralyzed in 1972 plan an appeal.

Al fails to get the bird

MIAMI, Fla. (UPI) — Policeman Al Sturtz had three tries at silencing a rooster greeting the dawn too vigorously. He missed, but was suspended for four days after citizens, the Audobon Society and a local clergyman protested.

Other citizens were angry because he missed the bird, and the Civil Service Board decided the penalty for bad marksmanship was too severe. Al will get back $300 in wages he lost due to the suspension.

$9 million

CHICAGO (AP) — A woman left a speechless quadraplegic after cosmetic surgery on her nose has been awarded $6.5 million. Her husband was awarded $2.5 million to look after her.

The 12 jurors never heard Eileen Tannebaum, 46, describe her condition aloud. She testified for a total of five minutes, flat on her back in a bed, making high-pitched sounds meaning "yes" or "no" as a therapist pointed to a board with 64 words.

Doctors said her arms and legs are permanently paralyzed after her brain was deprived of oxygen during surgery in 1975 at Northwest Hospital here.

Her husband, Louis, 51, was awarded the $2.5 million for her medical care. The $9 million amount is the largest personal injury award in Illinois.

The woman, who has a 19-year-old son and two married daughters, has been confined to bed since the nose surgery.

At one point during her court appearance, Tannebaum was asked: "If you could have one thing in the world, what would it be?"

With the help of the words on the board, she replied: "Stop pain."

The jury's decision follows a 57-day trial in the suit against the hospital, a plastic surgeon, an anesthesiologist, and a nurse. The nurse was found innocent.

Her lawyer, John Hayes, told court the medical error occurred near the completion of the nose surgery. "She has a beautiful nose and that's about the only beautiful thing left," he told the jury.

He called the incident "a clear case of malpractice which has destroyed a woman's life."

The family has spent about $300,000 on medical bills, Hayes said, adding the paralysis makes Tannebaum subject to frequent, painful spasms. Her mental facilities are, however, unaffected.

Bellybutton battle all sewn up

NEW YORK (UPI) — A Florida woman awarded $854,000 because her bellybutton was placed off centre during plastic surgery has agreed to settle for $200,000, it was learned yesterday.

Virginia O'Hare, 42, who flew up from her Fort Lauderdale, Fla., home to have a "tummy tuck" performed by plastic surgeon Dr. Howard Bellin, agreed to the lower sum after her attorney and Bellin's insurance representative met behind closed doors in the chambers of state Supreme Court Justice Alvin Klein.

Both sides apparently decided to end the case quickly rather than go through a prolonged legal battle on appeal.

The jury awarded O'Hare the sum May 2. She claimed she suffered pscyhological damages and her sex life suffered because the surgery left her abdomen scarred, and her navel 1½ inches off centre.

Man awarded $825,000 for surgeon's unkind cut

PITTSBURGH (UPI) — A large out-of-court settlement has been awarded to a man whose penis was amputated accidentally at a hospital during surgery four months before he was married.

Harold Michael, 26, was believed to have been awarded $825,000.

The settlement was reached this week under the supervision of Allegheny County Common Pleas Judge Francis A. Barry, who declined to disclose the amount involved.

"My hands are tied in this case," the judge said. "This matter is just too sensitive."

Reports said the figure totalled $825,-000. Last year, Michael rejected a $300,-000 offer and reportedly asked for several million dollars in damages.

In May 1974, Michael, then 21, was admitted to North Hills Passavant Hospital for surgery to correct a recessed testicle.

During the relatively routine surgery, Dr. Walter S. Nettrour Sr. accidently amputated the penis, Michael's attorney told the court.

Hospital officials immediately advised the insurer, the Hartford Insurance Group. The operating privileges of Nettrour, then 70, were revoked and the physician retired Jan. 1, 1975.

"It's a shame about the boy," the doctor was quoted as saying in an interview following the settlement. "I don't want to say any more than that. My attorney doesn't want me to talk about the case."

Michael, who married on Sept. 7, 1974, filed a negligence suit in March 1976.

Named as defendants were Nettrour, the hospital and Tri-Rivers Surgical Associates, a group to which Nettrour had belonged.

Staple diet a big loss

EDWARDSVILLE, Ill. (UPI) — A woman who had her ears stapled in a weight reduction effort but gained weight and an infected ear has been awarded $9,333.

Rose A. Chadeayne, of East Carondelet, Ill., filed a lawsuit in circuit court in 1977 against chiropractor Thomas J. Clay when she developed an infection from the ear-stapling procedure.

Clay had performed "auricular therapy" on Chadeayne by placing staples in the upper inside of the ears to reduce appetite. It was not explained how it worked.

Chadeayne said she gained weight and an infection that required two minor operations.

A Madison County Circuit Court jury rejected Chadeayne's charges that Clay acted improperly and dismissed a settlement she had sought "in excess of $15,000."

The $9,333 settlement was for medical treatment for the infection.

★★★★★★★★★★★★★★

HACKENSACK, N.J. (UPI) — After examining the evidence for more than a month, a judge upheld Eastman Kodak Corp.'s right to refuse to return nude photographs of Penthouse Magazine's Pet of the Year to avoid possible violation of federal obscenity statutes. A Kodak attorney said the unpublished pictures "are obscene, to say the least." Penthouse complained one of the photos was of an empty chair, with no sign of the Pet of the Year. Kodak agreed to return the slide.

★★★★★★★★★★★★★★

Girl, 16 sues parents for $3 million

SANTA ANA, Calif. (UPI) — A 16-year-old girl who claims her parents had her locked up in a mental hospital in an effort to force their values and lifestyle on her has filed a $3-million false imprisonment lawsuit against them and the hospital.

The suit also seeks to establish two legal precedents: That parents cannot involuntarily commit minor children to a private mental hospital without a prior hearing; and that doctors affiliated with profit-making hospitals cannot make neutral decisions on whether patients should be admitted or released.

Judy Reeds claims her parents, Robert and Elizabeth Reeds, knew she was not mentally ill when they decided to have her locked up against her will last March 12.

Instead, she claimed, they hoped to modify her thinking and behavior so she would embrace their values and stop seeing her boyfriend. The boyfriend, Dan Sherbondy, 20, secured her release April 17 with help from a local chapter of the American Civil Liberties Union.

Restaurant chokes on necktie rule

VENTURA, Calif. (UPI) — Two men who were refused dinner in a posh hotel restaurant because they were not wearing neckties have been awarded $18,000 in a sex discrimination suit.

A California Superior Court jury awarded Robert Hales $13,000 in damages against the Ojai Valley Inn while Dr. Irving Losner was awarded $5,000.

The two men had charged sex discrimination under civil rights legislation on the grounds that women were not required to wear ties in the hotel restaurant.

The men went with their wives to the hotel, about 75 miles northwest of Los Angeles, wearing leisure suits.

Although both eventually did put on ties and were served meals, they claimed during the trial they had been publicly harassed.

Hustler to pay $39 million for libel

COLUMBUS, Ohio (UPI) — A Franklin County Common Pleas Court jury has awarded Penthouse Magazine publisher Robert Guccione $39,300,000 in his libel and invasion of privacy suit against Hustler Magazine and its publisher, Larry Flynt.

The jury of five women and three men deliberated for 10½ hours over two days before determining the award, believed to be one of the largest ever made in such a case.

Larry Sturtz, Flynt's attorney, said he would appeal and termed the award "ridiculous."

Guccione had asked for $80 million in damages.

During a pornography trial in Georgia in 1978, Flynt was shot in a murder attempt and remains partially paralyzed.

Guccione maintained during the trial that Flynt has attacked him in Hustler since the first issue of the magazine in 1974. But the jury considered damages on just one issue — publication of a picture in which Guccione's head was superimposed on the body of a nude man engaging in a homosexual act.

Fleming's lawyer vows to fight on

SANTA MONICA, Calif.

THE OFTEN theatrical Groucho Marx estate trial ended when jurors awarded $471,000 to the Bank of America but praised Erin Fleming for giving the aging comedian "a lot of love" in his sunset years.

The jury foreman said most of the panelists believed that Miss Fleming violated the trust that Marx placed in her and took advantage of him for financial gain.

But Miss Fleming's lawyer, David Sabih, promised a quick encore in court as he seeks to have Wednesday's verdict thrown out. Failing that, he said, he will appeal.

Sabih, interviewed yesterday on ABC-TV's Good Morning America, said a juror told him late Wednesday that one of the jurors who voted against Miss Fleming was married to a Bank of America employee. Sabih said he would subpoena payroll records of the bank and also its telephone bills and lawyers to "see if there were any conversations between the wife of the juror and the bank attorneys."

Sabih said he was putting the former actress under round-the-clock guard because he feared a suicide attempt. Miss Fleming was not in court for the verdict, but later said there was "absolutely no way" she could have cheated Marx and vowed to clear her name.

The bank, executor of Marx's estate, sued for return of $428,000 in cash and gifts which it said the 42-year-old Miss Fleming received through threats, menace and physical abuse. It also sought punitive damages of $500,000, calling her "a gold digger" who exploited Marx for his money.

But the divided jury voted nine to three to award only $221,000 in compensatory damages and $250,000 punitive damages.

Jury foreman Eugene McCarthy said the jury never believed there was outright fraud on Miss Fleming's part but felt she did exert "undue influence" over Marx, who died in 1977 at the age of 86.   —AP

$133,000 for crooked toe

HAYWARD, Calif. (UPI) — A judge has awarded $133,000 to a woman who suffers from a crooked toe as a result of three operations to correct bunions and a fungus infection.

Superior Court Judge John Purchio made the award to Susan L. Blake, 32, of Fremont, a merchandise clerk at a Hayward warehouse, who charged her podiatrist negligent.

The podiatrist, Myron Mintz of Fremont, performed three operations to correct bunions and a fungus infection under two toenails. When the cast was removed from her left foot the big toe stuck straight up.

Strip-searched woman awarded $60,000

CHICAGO (Special) A federal court jury has awarded $60,000 to a Chicago woman who was strip-searched by police in 1977 after she was stopped for a minor traffic violation.

The award to Hinda Hoffman, 29, who works as a court reporter in Chicago, was made by a four-member jury in U.S. district court.

During trial in the Hoffman complaint, evidence revealed she was stopped by traffic policemen for making an illegal left turn on Aug. 8, 1977.

She subsequently was given a ticket, and taken to the Belmont District, where police ordered her to disrobe. Hoffman initially refused to disrobe, but then did so under threat of being forcibly disrobed by a police matron.

Two policemen watched Hoffman disrobe through an open door.

Miami Dolphins sued by male 'cheerleader'

MIAMI (UPI) — The San Diego Chargers may have a Big Chicken, the New England Patriots a male cheerleader, and the Los Angeles Rams a Little Old Lady, but the Miami Dolphins' cheerleaders, the Starbrites, want no part of Glenn Welt.

"He's just not built like a girl," said Starbrites choreographer June Taylor. "I was not about to put him in pantyhose and leotards and have him waving hankies and pompons.

The Starbrites have all-American girl appeal."

Welt, 31, an electronics executive, said he thinks the Dolphins' female fans "deserve a little stimulation too."

He filed a sex-discrimination suit against the Dolphins.

Ms Taylor, the onetime choreographer for the June Taylor Dancers who appeared on the Jackie Gleason show for many years, said Welt "just wouldn't fit in with the girls."

'This kid's got a million dollars' worth of brains'

SCHOOL IS SUED FOR BORING BOY

CHICAGO (UPI) — The parents of a fifth-grader with an IQ of 170 say regular school classes bore the young genius. So they've filed a $1 million lawsuit against the school board.

Ronald and Janet Irwin say the elementary school district in suburban McHenry caused their 10-year-old son, Thomas, to become bored and indifferent to school, denied him adequate mental stimulation and hindered his educational development.

Since the boy began school, his mother said, teachers have accused him of being a class disruption. In one instance, he was suspected of having a learning disability. Now he talks with a school worker and brings home a behavior performance card each day.

When the family moved to McHenry two years ago, school officials gave the youth an IQ test to determine if he had a learning problem. He came out with a 170 IQ — which puts him at the genius level.

Mrs. Irwin said Thomas talked only at the age of 2 — but then, in full sentences. At 4, he knew the functions of every part of human anatomy and how to play chess, but the family had no indication of his high intellegence levels, she said.

But in the years since the testing, Mrs. Irwin said, McHenry elementary school officials have not bowed to the family's request to set up a program for her gifted son. And they refused to allow him to attend a high school Spanish class in addition to his fifth-grade studies, she said.

"That was the straw that broke the camel's back," she said. "It's not fair. Much more money is spent on handicapped education than education for gifted children. It's terribly frustrating. We're paying hefty school taxes and we're not getting anything for our child."

Thomas, who said he gets along with most kids his age, even though he has the verbal ability of a 19-year-old, is not bitter over not being recognized as gifted. He said he definitely wants a better education.

"It's rather boring in the regular classes," said the 4-foot-8, 80-pounder who wants to be a nuclear physicist.

'Dog Day' muzzled by court

MEDICINE BOW, Wyo. (UPI) — Medicine Bow's "Dog Day" — what animal lovers feared might be a slaughter of stray dogs — fizzled yesterday under a court order and the sheltering of pooches by dog lovers.

As policemen and volunteers patrolled streets in the town of 1,000, Police Chief Gene Combs said the dogs were conspicuous by their absence.

"There just aren't any dogs out today," Combs said. "Apparently a lot of people have taken the dogs into their homes."

Police were also empowered to tranquilize, disable or shoot any animals that eluded captors.

But the Humane Federation of Wyoming won an 11th-hour restraining order in district court Saturday that permitted only the capture of stray dogs.

Leukemia victims file $2-billion suit

SALT LAKE CITY (AP) — People living downwind from aboveground atomic tests in the 1950s and '60s developed leukemia at a rate up to 20 times the normal incidence of the illness, plaintiffs in a $2-billion lawsuit are expected to argue tomorrow.

In their proposed pre-trial statement, lawyers representing about 1,000 people suing the U.S. government cite studies conducted in the late 1960s in Atlanta, which show that the incidence of leukemia in Fredonia, Ariz., was 20 times the "expected rate."

They will ask the court to accept the evidence as uncontested fact in the suit which comes to trial Sept. 13, said Ralph Hunsaker, one of the lawyers.

The plaintiffs contend they or their relatives suffered illness because of exposure to fallout from the tests at the Nevada Test Site.

The plaintiff's statement said the study found the rate of leukemia in Pleasant Grove, Utah, to be 5.7 times higher than would have been expected, while the rates in Parawan and Pagonah, Utah, were two to three times above expectations.

The incidence of leukemia among soldiers who witnessed a test called Smoky was three times the expected rate, the study says.

The study "could not identify any cause" for the high rate in Fredonia, "excluding that these people lived in the fallout area," the proposed statement said.

Dead child's parents file $200 million suit

Associated Press

LOS ANGELES — A lawsuit seeking damages of more than $200 million was filed yesterday against five companies and nine individuals — including Warner Bros. Inc. and producer Steven Spielberg — in the helicopter crash that killed actor Vic Morrow and two children.

The lawsuit was filed in Van Nuys Superior Court on behalf of the parents of 6-year-old Renee Shin-Yi Chen of Pasadena, who died of trauma after the accident at 2:30 a.m. on July 23.

Morrow and 7-year-old My-ca Dihn Le of Cerritos were decapitated when explosions below the helicopter apparently caused it to go out of control during filming of the movie "The Twilight Zone." The helicopter fell onto the actor and children.

On Friday, Warner Bros. and three individuals were assessed $5,000 civil fines for exposing children to hazardous conditions, for not having work permits for them and for allowing them to work in the early morning. Under state rules, children cannot work after 6:30 p.m.

State labor officials are to turn their findings over to the Los Angeles district attorney to determine if criminal charges should be brought. District attorney's spokesman Al Albergate said yesterday that his office did not expect to receive the evidence for two weeks.

The civil lawsuit brought on behalf of Mark Wei-chun Chen and Shayah-huei Chen, father and mother of the dead 6-year-old, alleges "negligent misrepresentation" of the dangers of shooting the movie. It seeks $100 million in general damages and $100 million in exemplary and punitive damages.

$75-million tampon suit is launched

DAYTON, Ohio (UPI) — A $75-million class action suit filed against Procter & Gamble Co. seeks damages for all women in Ohio who have "suffered significant injury from the use of tampons.

The suit filed yesterday in a Montgomery County court accuses the Cincinnati-based makers of Rely tampons of negligence "in the design, inspection, testing, manufacture, distribution, and sale" of teh tampons.

Two couples named as plaintiffs in the suit, Helen and Leslie George of Kettering and Loma and Ernie Langdon of Miamisburg, charge that the women were stricken with toxic shock syndrome as a result of using Rely tampons.

Rockets Suing Lakers

Rudy Tomjanovich got more than he asked for yesterday from a federal court jury in Houston, Tex.

The star forward with Houston Rockets of the National Basketball Association was awarded $3.3 million in damages for the injuries he suffered when struck by former Los Angeles Lakers' player **Kermit Washington** during a 1977 game.

The five-man, one-woman jury gave Tomjanovich $1.8 million in actual damages and $1.5 million in punitive damages. Tomjanovich had asked for $2.65 million.

The jury found that Washington, now with San Diego Clippers, committed a battery on Tomjanovich; acted with wreckless disregard for the safety of others and did not act in self-defence.

The jury also ruled the Lakers were negligent in training Washington and were negligent in keeping the player on their roster when "they became aware that he had a tendency for violence while playing basketball."

Washington was fined $10,000 by NBA commissioner **Lawrence O'Brien** after the incident and suspended for 60 days.

Lakers' troubles aren't over yet. The Rockets are suing the Lakers for $1.4 million for the loss of Tomjanovich's services during most of the 1977-78 season. That phase of the trial will be heard by the same jury next week.

$113.8 million suit after 3 die in Ford

BROWNSVILLE, Texas (UPI) — Three youths burned to death in a fiery auto crash because Ford Motor Co. wanted to save $8 in assembly line costs, lawyers for their families have told court.

Presenting opening arguments in a $113.8 million lawsuit against Ford Motor Co., lawyer Larry Watts said the auto maker knew the fuel tank design selected for 1965 Mustangs was unsafe.

"They (the youths) didn't have to be sacrificed for that $8 (cost per car)," Watts told a federal court jury. "They spent the lives of these boys."

Watts' remarks came during the opening of a federal civil lawsuit in which families of three youths killed in a rear-end collision allege Ford knew of nine safety defects in the company's 1965 Mustang model.

$2.7 million awarded for unnecessary mastectomy

NEW YORK (AP) — A jury has awarded $2.7 million to the family of a woman who had both breasts removed because her surgeon erroneously thought she had cancer.

Mary Williams, of Queens, was 40 years old when the operation was performed June 13, 1973, in Hillcrest General Hospital by Dr. John Cordice.

She died last year of unrelated causes and the money will be shared by her sons, Reginald, 24, of Queens, and Peter, 14, who is living with relatives in Virginia.

Her husband, Henry, died a few months after his wife's operation.

Dr. Cordice testified at the trial that he performed the operation after the report of biopsies said she had cancer in both breasts.

Mrs. Williams discovered the error several months later when she went to Sloan-Kettering Institute for treatment and was told she never had cancer of the breasts.

Woman sues tampon makers

ST. LOUIS (UPI) — A young woman has filed a $25 million suit agains Procter & Gamble charging she suffered toxic shock because she used the company's Rely tampons.

The suit, filed by Sheryl Fox, 20, of St. Ann, Mo., says the company failed to warn her about the allegedly defective and unsafe nature of the tampons.

Judge chips in to free 'hostage' doll

Toronto Star special

SAN DIEGO — Sandy, a chubby-cheeked doll seized as ransom in a row over a babysitting fee, was back in the arms of her young owner yesterday after a bizarre courtroom melodrama.

"She feels real good," sighed 8-year-old Stephanie Dressin, as a bailiff returned her doll. "We're going to have a party with all my other dolls, then we're going to sleep."

Sandy the doll's 10-months as a "hostage" ended after two benefactors came to the rescue.

Harvey Massey, of Ripley, Ohio, who had read of the incident in his local newspaper paid the $52 in fees that babysitter Sharon Russell said she

must have if Stephanie was to ever see her doll again.

And judge Ronald Mayo put up the remaining $8.50 to clear the court costs off the docket.

"Jeez, wouldn't you?" asked the weary judge, who had watched Stephanie weeping in his small claims court as her mother, Michele Dressin, and Sharon Russell exchanged brickbats. All the time, the doll was concealed in a paper bag in court so Stephanie would not see it.

Before Massey stepped in, both parents had baulked at Mayo's order — that Stephanie's mother pay the disputed $52, plus costs, and Russell return the doll.

Judge handling Liberace suit refused to believe it was brown

LOS ANGELES (Reuter) — A judge yesterday ordered that a summons against Liberace in a $113-million lawsuit be served again because the process server reported the flamboyant entertainer was wearing a brown suit.

Los Angeles Superior Court Judge Irving Shimer, amid laughter from spectators, declared that the entertainer "would not be caught dead in a brown suit."

By quashing the summons, the judge indicated he was not satisfied the man served with the summons was necessarily Liberace, who likes to dress up in furs, sequins and vivid flowing cloaks.

The summons must be served again.

Scott Thorson, 23, alleged in the suit he had a six-year "sexual, emotional and business relationship" with Liberace. Thorson said the relationship ended when four representatives of Liberace forcibly evicted him from the 63-year-old entertainer's penthouse in Los Angeles last April.

Thorson is seeking $113 million, mainly in punitive damages.

After the hearing, Thorson's lawyer, Michael Rosenthal, said, "All this means is that we'll have to serve again, probably in Las Vegas." Liberace is starring on the Las Vegas Strip.

Beauty Queen wins sex libel case

CHEYENNE, Wyo. (UPI) — A former Miss Wyoming has won a $26.5 million damage award from Penthouse magazine because of a story about the sexual fantasy of a beauty queen. Her lawyer called it the largest such award ever.

A federal jury awarded Kimerli Jayne Pring, the 1978 Miss Wyoming $1.5 million in actual damages and $25 million in punitive damages.

Pring called the judgment "more than fair," and said she did not have

"any animosity toward Penthouse magazine. I just think it was really unfortunate the way things happened. They should have been more careful."

The story, billed in the magazine as humor, concerned a baton-twirling Miss Wyoming at the Miss America pageant who could levitate men and her baton by oral sex. Pring, the former women's national champion baton twirler, performed a baton routine at the 1978 Miss America pageant.

Women get each other's operations in mix-up

PHILADELPHIA (AP-UPI) — Pennsylvania health authorities are investigating a bizarre hospital mixup in which two women underwent an operation intended for the other.

Graduate Hospital in Philadelphia would not comment on the incident, except to say that it was "horribly regretful."

Annie Robinson, 50, was admitted to the hospital last week for a back operation. Virginia Edmondson, 54, was there for surgery to remove her parathyroid glands in her neck. Each went under the knife for the other's ailment.

The state health department and other medical agencies said they are conducting an investigation to learn how the foul-up occurred.

The two women reportedly were in fair condition.

No surgery was scheduled to give the women the proper operations.

Murray Levin, a hospital board member, said neither woman was harmed. He said the doctor who operated on Mrs. Robinson stopped as soon as he found nothing wrong.

"I understand the surgeon said, 'This is about as close to having a non-operation as you can have,' " Levin said.

Levin said the doctor who operated on Mrs. Edmondson removed a nodule on the parathyroid but did not remove the gland.

Levin added: "Luckily both patients are in good condition and they understand what happened."

Alfred Edmondson said he's planning legal action against the surgeon. He said his wife went into hospital for back surgery last Thursday, but when he went to see her afterward he was summoned to a room down the hall by a staff physician.

"He told me they had made a mistake," Edmondson said. "He said the doctor who was to have operated on my wife operated on the other woman.

"But you don't just cross people up like that.

Mom sued — for paternity

CHICAGO (UPI) — In what may be the first case of its kind, a man has filed a paternity suit against a woman. He wants to prove he is the father of a child born to his former girl-friend, now married to another man. The man seeks visitation rights for the child. The parties were not identified.

Tales of lesbianism face scrutiny at Pulitzer trial

WEST PALM BEACH, Fla. (UPI) — The elderly heir to the Kleenex fortune is expected to take the stand in the sensational Pulitzer divorce trial today to defend his young wife against charges of lesbianism.

The two principals, Peter Pulitzer, 52, and his wife, Roxanne, 31, have levelled bitter charges and countercharges against each other, including incest, lesbianism, infidelity, cocaine abuse and occultism.

The trial was in recess yesterday to allow Judge Carl Harper time to attend to other business.

James Kimberly, 76, an heir to the Klennex fortune, is expected to testify on behalf of his wife, Jacqueline, 32, whom Pulitzer charged had a lesbian affair with Roxanne. He also said he joined the pair in bed.

Witnesses have also said Mrs. Pulitzer once went to bed with a cape and a trumpet.

Mrs. Kimberly has scoffed at the charges, calling them "disgusting." Mrs. Pulitzer also denied them.

Another unresolved issue involving the Kimberlys is whether it was Pulitzer or his wife who gave Mrs. Kimberly a gift-wrapped ounce of cocaine for Christmas two years ago.

Pulitzer, grandson of publishing magnate Joseph Pulitzer, and Roxanne are battling over custody of their twin 5-year-old sons, Mack and Zack. She has also laid claim to half of his fortune she says totals $25 million. He insists he's worth only $2.5 million.

After 15 days of testimony, virtually no part of the Pulitzers' private lives during their six-year marriage has been left unexposed.

Drug dealer

Mrs. Pulitzer testified Wednesday, that her husband had a sexual relationship with one of his daughters, Liza Leidy, from his first marriage. Mrs. Leidy and Pulitzer have denied it. The judge labelled the charge "pure conjecture."

Mrs. Pulitzer also portrayed her estranged husband as a drug dealer who smuggled marijuana and cocaine into the country.

Those allegations have not been corroborated by other witnesses.

Pulitzer has made his own charges, saying his wife had numerous lovers, including a Grand Prix race car driver, a French baker and an unemployed handyman, as well as Mrs. Kimberly. He has also charged his wife dabbled in the occult and had a serious drug problem.

Pregnant star 'Shirley' sues Paramount

LOS ANGELES (UPI) — Laverne And Shirley star Cindy Williams has filed a $20 million suit accusing the show's producers of trying to force her our of the long-running ABC-TV series because she is pregnant.

The suit alleges that Paramount Pictures executive producer Garry Marshall, brother of co-star Penny Marshall, tried to exclude Williams from the show after making oral commitments to her that she would continue to appear on the comedy program.

The suit says the problems started last May when Williams (who plays Shirley) told Paramount she was pregnant. In an oral agreement, the studio allegedly told Williams that her pregnancy would be written into the show, and agreed to let her work through mid-October. Her baby is due in November.

It's the $188,000 stomach ache!

MINEOLA, N.Y. (UPI) — A physician yesterday was ordered to pay $188,233 in damages for causing a gas explosion in the intestinal tract of a patient during an operation.

A state Supreme Court jury ordered the damages paid to Richard Schwarz, 54, whose colon was punctured by the explosion the during the operation by Dr. Howard Jay Eddy Jr.

According to court papers, on June 28, 1974, Dr. Eddy was using an electrically powered instrument to destroy two polyps in Schwarz' colon when a spark from it ignited gas in the intestinal tract.

The blast blew two holes in Schwarz's colon, and he was rushed by ambulance from Eddy's Garden City, N.Y., office to a hospital where surgery was immediately performed to repair the damage.

Schwarz, of Westbury, N.Y., remained in the hospital for more than a month and claimed that he still suffers discomfort as a result of the accident.

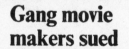

Gang movie makers sued

VENTURA, Calif. (AP) — The family and friends of a youth who was stabbed to death between screenings of the controversial gang-violence film The Warriors have filed a damage suit against the film's producers, Paramount Pictures.

Other defendants named in the superior court suit include the Motion Picture Association of America, Mann Theatres Corp., owner of the theatre where the fatal stabbing occurred, and the Esplanade shopping centre, where the theatre is located.

COUPEVILLE, Wash. (AP) — A judge has found the stae of Washington negligent in the case of a man who fell through the rotten floor of an outhouse into a tank of human waste. Francis Smythe, 55, told an Island county court that he repeatedly slipped back into the effluent. "I was fighting for my life." Judge Howard A. Patrick ordered the jury to determine the amount of damages. Smythe wants $100,000.

Chrysler sued for $3.2 billion

WEST ALLENHURST, N.J. (UPI) — Neal Cowe bought what he thought was a new Dodge van in 1978. Now he's suing Chrysler Corp. for $3.2 billion, claiming the vehicle actually was used and reconditioned.

Cowe bought the van for $7,310.10, but he is asking high damages because that's the amount Chrysler originally sought in loan guarantees from the federal government.

The clue to his having bought a lemon came when he was issued a traffic summons and police found the vehicle number in their records did not match the number on his registration.

His suit charges that Chrysler sold a damaged and repaired vehicle as new.

Homosexual adopts lover as a son

NEW YORK (Special) — A man may legally adopt his homosexual lover as a son, the appellate division of New York State Supreme Court has ruled. The 4-1 decision reversed a Family Court decision that denied the adoption of "Mr. H.," 43, by his homosexual lover "Mr. S.," 32, on the basis that it would not "result in the creation of a parent-child relation," and was against the public policy. The identities of the men were not disclosed.

Sterilization fails but deformed girl can't sue

PITTSBURGH (UPI) — A young girl severely crippled by a hereditary disease cannot sue for "wrongful birth" doctors who said they sterilized her father and performed an abortion on her mother, the state Supreme Court ruled.

The decision was blasted as a "calloused and unjust act" by justices who supported the suit.

But in a separate decision, the high court said the child's parents could sue the doctors.

One justice called the girl an "incurably diseased, deformed and suffering human being."

The child, 6-year-old Francine Speck, was born with genetic neurofibromatosis, a hereditary nerve disease also suffered by her older brother and sister.

Her parents, Frank and Dorothy Speck, had tried to avert her birth by having Speck, the apparent carrier of the disease, undergo a vasectomy in 1974.

According to the Specks' suit, Dr. Richard Finegold, who performed the vasectomy, told Speck it had made him sterile. However, Mrs. Speck later became pregnant.

She underwent an abortion in December 1974, but later told her doctor, Henry Schwartz, that she thought she was still pregnant. Schwartz repeatedly insisted that she was not, the suit said.

Francine was born prematurely in April 1975.

Ali challenges Playgirl

Heavyweight boxing champion Muhammad Ali is peeved at Playgirl magazine for printing an "obscene likeness" of him in the nude in its February issue.

Ali, in fact, has sued the magazine for $4 million, claiming he has had "mental suffering and distress" that interferes with his boxing and his religious work. (Ali describes himself as a minister of the World Community of Islam.)

$5 million Chinese puzzle

CHICAGO (Reuter) — A $5-million lawsuit was filed here yesterday on behalf of a Chinese immigrant reportedly kept in mental institutions for the last 28 years simply because doctors could not communicate with him.

The suit charges that a succession of mental hospitals did not bother to try to get a Tisonese dialect interpreter capable of finding out what was wrong with the man. Tisonese is widely spoken by Chicago's Chinese community.

Cook County Public Guardian Patrick Murphy said in the suit filed in federal court that the patient — identified only as David T. in his 50s — was never treated for any mental illness.

The suit claims the man, who came to the United States from China in 1949 and was involuntarily committed to a mental hospital in June 1952, was wrongfully incarcerated because he was neither dangerous nor retarded.

Murphy said that when the patient was given a chance to talk to workers at a Chinese restaurant last November, they said he was of at least average intelligence.

Diet victim's family wins $230,000

MILLVILLE, N.J. (UPI) — The family of a woman who lost 100 pounds on a liquid protein diet and then suddenly died, has received $230,000 in an out-of-court settlement.

Gladys Wyckoff of Millville died in September 1977, seven months after being placed on the diet by a doctor at the Vineland Obstetrical and Gynecological Professional Association.

Mrs. Wyckoff's weight reportedly dropped from about 239 pounds to 139 pounds.

The tax-free settlement will go to Richard Wyckoff Sr., 39, the woman's husband, and the couple's son, Richard Jr., 13.

The settlement, announced this week, was reached between the family's attorney, Carl Valore, and the association's insurance carrier, Medical Inter Insurance Exchange of Mount Laurel.

Mrs. Wyckoff had been named by the U.S. Food and Drug Administration as one of 15 women in the country who died from the effects of a liquid protein diet.

Valore had charged Vineland Obstetrical with failure to conduct proper tests on Mrs. Wyckoff. He said she died of cardiac arrythmia caused by a loss of potassium.

Jury rules on value of housewife's work

JACKSONVILLE, Fla. (UPI) — How much is a housewife's work worth?

A Florida State University economist, testifying in a circuit court civil case, suggested the "rock bottom" value of a Live Oak housewife's work was about $14,500 a year.

The jury, three men and three women, considering the value of housework among other things, ruled the woman and her husband should receive $556,205 for injuries she suffered when a stack of plywood fell on her.

"In the world of the economist, it (housework) has always been considered as valuable," said professor Robert G. Turner. "What is beginning to occur is that the juries are beginning to believe it."

The claimants in the case were Norma Walter Lawson, who were in a Jacksonville home supplies store when plywood paneling stacked on end fell on Mrs. Lawson, knocking her to the floor and injuring her shoulder and neck.

Mrs. Lawson, the mother of two children, has to wear a brace and has had surgery to correct a related back injury. She said she suffers pain.

Bizarre crib accident costs firms millions

PHILADELPHIA (UPI) — A Philadelphia family will get up to $10 million for a bizarre accident in which the combination of a crib post and a clothing cord choked a baby.

Ronald Lewis Jr. was left permanently brain damaged and partially paralyzed by the November 1979 accident in which he stopped breathing for several minutes.

Smith Furniture Co. of Fort Smith, Ark., the crib manufacturer, and Hatboro Industrial Park Industries Inc., of Hatboro in suburban Philadelphia, agreed to pay the boy, now 4, $21,000 annually for life with a 5 per cent cost of living increase each year.

They also agreed to pay the parents, Helen and Ronald Lewis, an $18,000-a-year income for life and a $650,000 to the faimly immediately for medical bills.

The firms also agreed to make a series of cash payments totalling $650,000 to the family over the next 50 years.

The boy was wearing a sailor suit, with a nylon whistle cord when he attempted to climb out of the crib. The cord wrapped around a crib post, strangling the child for 20 minutes until his mother found him.

CHASTITY BELT SPARKS SUIT

ALGONA, Iowa (Reuter) — A 26-year-old woman has filed a $100,000 damage suit against her former boyfriend for burns and scars she says she received when he welded a chastity belt about her body.

Geraldine Hauenstein claims Leonard Tripp, 33, look her to his welding shop last September, tied her to a board and welded the chastity belt in place.

Shortly afterward. Tripp, apparently prompted by Miss Hauenstein's cries, again used his welding torch to free her. She suffered second and third degree burns.

TIFTON, Ca. (UPI) — Albert August claims he was awakened by a rat gnawing on his ear. So now, he has filed a $1-million damage suit against a major motel chain. August was treated in hospital following the incident. He contends the motel was negligent in that it allowed rats to nest in the box springs of the bed.

Fetus given right to sue in beating case

HARTFORD, Conn. (AP) — A 5-month-old fetus has been given the right to sue in a ruling one legal expert said might be an important victory for anti-abortion forces should the precedent stand.

U.S. District Judge Emmet Clarie, Connecticut's chief federal judge, ruled in a police brutality case that Paul Douglas, now 9 months old, has an equal and independent right with his mother, Rosalee Douglas, to sue the Hartford Police Department and two city policemen.

It is the first time a federal judge has recognized a fetus as a person with the right to sue for damages under the 1871 federal civil rights law.

Douglas was 5-months pregnant in July, 1981, when she was allegedly beaten in the backyard of her Hartford home by one of the policemen while the other stood by. Police were in the area investigating a car theft.

The lawsuit, not expected to reach trial until next year, seeks $250,000 in damages without specifying an allocation between mother and child.

Wife jailed

MOUNT CLEMENS, Mich. (UPI) — Macomb County Circuit Judge Raymond Cashen says he never dreamed he'd send a woman to jail for failing to pay her husband child support. But he did it this week for the first time in his six years on the bench.

Cashen sentenced Susan Barr, a 36-year-old machinist from Clinton Township, to 90 days for failing to pay $29 a week to her former husband, Robert, for support of their two children. Barr was awarded custody of the children when the couple divorced last October.

Ad has woman all burned up

CHICAGO (AP) — A woman who says she never gave permission for a television and magazine advertisement showing a model of her home on fire has filed a $2.2 million suit.

Michele Miner says in the suit against Allstate Insurance Co., its advertising agency and a photographer that the ad has led to telephoned threats of arson at her home.

Jordache files $100-million jeans war suit

NEW YORK (UPI) — Jordache Enterprises Inc. has gone on the defensive in its blue jeans war with K mart Corp., calling the retail discount firm's allegations of antitrust violations "absurd and without any justification."

Jordache has filed a $100-million triple damages suit accusing K mart, the second largest retailer in the U.S., of selling thousands of pairs of counterfeit jeans in its 2,000 discount stores nationwide.

In response, K mart chairman Bernard M. Fauber said the Michigan-based company has been assured by its suppliers that the Jordache jeans were, in fact, genuine.

"Jordache refuses to sell to K mart directly, but K mart is able to buy Jordache jeans from reputable sources that supply genuine Jordache merchandise," Fauber said.

Fauber said Jordache filed the suit in an attempt "to prevent its purchasers from reselling to K mart and other discounters so that it may maintain resale prices and distribution control."

He said K mart "intends to file and answer and counter-claims alleging intentional interference with business relationships and violation of antitrust laws by Jordache," Fauber said.

Last week, a federal judge in Los Angeles issued a temporary restraining order barring K mart from selling the jeans.

Bubbly makers sued

BUFFALO (UPI) — A Connecticut man who was hit in the eye by a champagne bottle cork at his wedding is suing the Taylor Wine Co. for $2 million. Attorneys for Robert Hurwitt, 25, said Hurwitt has suffered "permanent eye damage."

Stolen girdle nets inventor $31 million

LOS ANGELES (UPI) — A Norwegian immigrant who invented a garterless girdle to keep his wife's stockings from running has been awarded $31 million by jurors who found that a manufacturer stole his idea.

The jury heard six weeks of testimony and deliberated two days before awarding the huge judgment to Knut L. Bjorn-Lersen, 58, of Carpinteria, Calf.

"It's fantastic," said Bjorn-Lersen, who immigrated from Norway in 1946. "This has taken a very long time. I believe in the American system and I believe in the American people."

The jury found that Munsingwear Inc. infringed on the inventor's patent when it began marketing the "Hollywood Vassarette," a garterless girdle still on the market.

Bjorn-Lersen was awarded $15 million for fraud, $500,000 for violation of trade secrets, $500,000 by reason of unfair competition and $15 million in punitive damages from the Minneapolis-based clothing manufacturer.

A better way

U.S. District Judge Jesse W. Curtis Jr. presided over the case, which has been pending in various courts since 1972. It was not known if Munsingwear would appeal the judgment.

John Wagner, one of three attorneys who handled the case for the inventor, said Bjorn-Lersen recognized in the early 1906s there was a need for a better way for women to hold up their stockings.

"He was the classic garage inventor," Wagner said. "He tinkered around and came up with a concept that involved putting plastisol on the inner surface of the bottom of the girdle to create friction and hold up the stockings.

Knut Bjorn-Lersen: Patented girdle kept his wife's stockings from running.

"And that was long before pantyhose were invented," he added.

Wagner said the inventor was introduced to Munsingwear executives by the retired chairman of the board and the company signed an agreement with Bjorn-Lersen, who held the patent, within 24 hours.

The lawyer said the company later told Bjorn-Lersen it was dropping the idea, but soon introduced the garterless girdle as the "Hollywood Vassarette."

"My wife used to complain about those bloody garters ruining her stockings back in the days when the hemline was below the knee," Bjorn-Lersen said. "I just dreamed up the idea."

Shake a hand, file a lawsuit

PORTAGE, Wis. (UPI) — A handshake during a "greeting of peace" ceremony in a church service has resulted in a $100,000 lawsuit.

Catherine Fritz, a Columbus real estate broker, said the handshake of William Schleicher Jr., of Marshall, was not friendly. Her suit contended Schleicher "did willfully, wantonly, with malice intent and with great force so grasp and seize" her right hand that she suffered "great pain and discomfort."

The March 22, 1977 rite at St. Jerome's Church in Columbus called for members to shake hands with people sitting near them.

Parents sued for $33 million

DETROIT (AP) — A 27-year-old woman born with a defective spine is suing her parents for $33 million, claiming they abandoned her in a home for the retarded and told relatives she was dead.

In a suit filed in Detroit, Karen Multack Boldt alleged that her parents, Hyman and Lorayne Multack, of East Chicago, Ind., abandoned her shortly after birth because she suffered from spina bifida.

Doctors say the condition, in which the spinal cord is exposed without a bone covering, can leave the victim crippled. If untreated, it can result in death.

Mrs. Boldt, who walks with crutches, said she was 14 when she saw her mother again.

"'You're dead,' Mrs. Boldt quoted her mother as saying in that encounter, "Your father and I are the only two people in the family who know you are alive. You're dead.'"

Mrs. Boldt accused her parents of depriving her of the love and affection of a family and of unlawfully placing her in a home for the mentally retarded.

Named as defendants in the suit, in addition to her parents, are in home, the physician who delivered her, the hospital where she was born, and the state of Illinois.

While she was in the home, from infancy until age 7, she was not trained to speak or care for herself and was never tested to determine her level of intelligence, the suit says.

She also was beaten while at the home and sexually abused by retarded women patients, Mrs. Boldt said in the suit.

She was released and placed in a foster home after a nurse noticed she had taught herself basic speech and could feed herself, Mrs. Boldt's lawyer said.

Tut! Boy-king blamed for policeman's stroke

SAN FRANCISCO (UPI) — A police officer has filed suit for $18,400 in disability pay, saying the curse of King Tut may have caused the stroke he suffered while guarding the boy king's golden funeral mask two years ago.

George E. LaBrash, a police lieutenant, said in a 15-page brief that there have been untimely, often abrupt deaths of more than a dozen people involved with discoverers of King Tut's tomb in 1923 and in the public display of items from the find.

LaBrash, who helped guard the priceless Egyptian treasures in San Francisco during the King Tut exhibit's tour, suffered a stroke in September, 1979, and has asked disability pay for the eight months of recuperation.

"Egyptians believed in a curse, pronounced by Osiris, god of the dead, on all who should disturb the dead," LaBrash's attorney said yesterday in a supplement to the lawsuit.

★ ★ ★ Pet tries to bar Penthouse

NEW YORK (Reuter) — A judge has ruled that sales of the November Penthouse magazine cannot be stopped because a reluctant Italian model is unhappy with a picture spread depicting her as Pet of the Year. The model, Isable Lanza of Rome, sought to bar the issue's sale yesterday because it contains a 10-page section showing her in explicit nude poses. Last week Miss Lanza stormed out of an awards dinner and refused to accept the Pet title.

She charged in court that she was "victim of a disgusting fraud" because she did not give her consent for the photos to be used and she renounced the title of Pet of the Year and $300,000 in prizes that go with it.

Supreme Court Judge Michael Dontzin refused to order sales of the magazine stopped and set Oct. 20 as the date for trial.

Drug firm sued for $10 million

AUSTIN, Texas (UPI) — A Texas man is suing a drugstore chain for $10 million, claiming a pharmacist's mistake in filling a prescription resulted in sexual problems, possible brain damage, and a loss of interest in such activities as boating and yard work.

Francis Patranella and his wife, Elizabeth, filed suit last week charging a druggist gave Patranella a powerful tranquilizer instead of kidney medication.

Patranella also charged he suffered depression, sleep disorders, tension, visual problems and loss of motor skills as a result.

Drain cleaner on her salad?

GLENWOOD SPRINGS, Colo. (UPI) — A woman who claims a local restaurant served her drain cleaner in place of salad dressing has filed a $20,000 suit.

Jo Ann Temple said she suffered from vomiting, bleeding of the mouth and lost her sense of taste for more than five months as a result of the March 24 incident.

The $2.5 million baby

The $2.5 million baby — that's what the New York headline writers have dubbed the child born to Sunday school teacher **Kathy Jetter**.

Kathy, 24, recently won a court fight to prove that **Engelbert Humperdinck** was the father of her 3-year-old girl. Court accountants say the judge's order for the singer to support Kathy and Jennifer will cost him more than $2.5 million.

Last week Kathy talked about how she met Engelbert when she tood red roses to him on stage in New York. He kissed her, then invited her backstage.

The following week, she says, he invited her to Philadelphia and they booked into a hotel. The "deeply religious" Kathy was just 18.

She waxes positively lyrical in describing that first weekend.

"I fell deeply and truly in love with him. He took me from schoolbooks and crayons and put lipstick on my mouth and perfume on my body and made me a woman.

"The night I lost my virginity he was so gentle, yet so strong. I will always be grateful to Engelbert for that. it was so beautiful."

But later, when she heard he had gone back to his wife, she decided to end the affair. So she visited him in a New York hotel.

Says Kathy: "We made love nonstop for two days and nights. As he had given me so much the first time we made love, this was to be my parting gift to him."

Instead, Engelbert gave her a parting gift 9 months later — baby Jennifer.

$5.5 million suit filed over wrong abortion

MONTGOMERY, Ala. (UPI) — A $5.5 million damage suit alleging an abortion was performed on the wrong patient was filed this week against a Montgomery clinic.

The suit alleges that the woman was not pregnant and never thought she was pregnant. Another patient with the same first name as her sat next to her in the waiting room, the suit says, and their charts were reversed.

The 18-year-old who went to the clinic for a pelvic exam suffered "great pain and suffering, infection of the vagina, medical expenses, vaginitis, great mental anguish, embarrassment and humiliation and future mental anguish," the suit says.

Palsy victim gets $11M

PONTIAC, Mich. (AP) — A 2¹/₂-year-old cerebral palsy victim and her parents have won a $11.1-million settlement in a lawsuit charging a hospital with negligence during the girl's birth.

Oakland County Circuit Judge Steven Andrews ruled in a consent agreement Wednesday that JoAnn and Michael Taylor should receive $1.3 million from Crittenton Hospital in nearby Rochester. The judge also approved monthly payments, totalling $9.8 million, to their daughter, Nicole, said Stanley Schwartz, the family's lawyer.

The suit claimed that hospital physicians failed to notice a fetal heart monitor, attached to Taylor during her nine hours of labor Sept. 5, 1978, showed the unborn infant was not receiving an adequate oxygen supply to the brain.

$5 million award in Toyota deaths

FORT LAUDERDALE, Fla. (UPI) — Toyota Motor Co. must pay a family $5 million for the deaths of three sisters in a fiery crash two years ago, a circuit court jury says.

The decision came after a six-week trial. The six-member jury found the world's third largest automaker negligent in the deaths of Wendy, Denise and Pamela Moll of Broward County.

The girls' parents, Betty and Wayne Moll, had sought $165 million from Toyota for the deaths July 16, 1979, when their 1973 Toyota Corona was rammed from the rear. The gas tank exploded; burning the three sisters to death.

Diet victim's family wins $230,000

MILLVILLE, N.J. (UPI) — The family of a woman who lost 100 pounds on a liquid protein diet and then suddenly died, has received $230,000 in an out-of-court settlement.

Gladys Wyckoff of Millville died in September 1977, seven months after being placed on the diet by a doctor at the Vineland Obstetrical and Gynecological Professional Association.

Mrs. Wyckoff's weight reportedly dropped from about 239 pounds to 139 pounds.

The tax-free settlement will go to Richard Wyckoff Sr., 39, the woman's husband, and the couple's son, Richard Jr., 13.

The settlement, announced this week, was reached between the family's attorney, Carl Valore, and the association's insurance carrier, Medical Inter Insurance Exchange of Mount Laurel.

Mrs. Wyckoff had been named by the U.S. Food and Drug Administration as one of 15 women in the country who died from the effects of a liquid protein diet.

Valore had charged Vineland Obstetrical with failure to conduct proper tests on Mrs. Wyckoff. He said she died of cardiac arrythmia caused by a loss of potassium.

Ex-lover sues Telly Savalas for $5 million

LOS ANGELES (UPI) — Actor Telly Savalas has been sued for $5 million in alimony and child support by the woman he once lived with. Sally Salavas, who never married the actor, is demanding support for her daughter Nicolette, 17, who was fathered by another man.

Fans sued the Bruins to save reputations

NEW YORK (UPI) — Four hockey fans who were involved in a brawl with the Boston Bruins last December said yesterday they had filed suit against the team because their reputations were ruined by the bad publicity.

The men, all New Jersey residents, said at a news conference that they have filed a $7 million suit against the Bruins and other defendants because they want the world to know "we're not a bunch of animals."

Emanuel Kaptain of Clark, N.J., his sons John and James, and Jack Gutteplan of Ocean, N.J., said they have lost credibility with their friends and associates since the incident.

Several Bruins players went into the stands Dec. 23 to fight with fans after a game with New York Rangers at Madison Square Garden.

Bruins, who had scored a come-from-behind victory minutes before, were arguing with the Rangers players on the ice when one of the Bruins claimed a teammate had been injured by a fan hurling a glass.

The suit, filed Tuesday in U.S. District Court in Manhattan, charges nine Bruins players with rushing into the stands and starting an unprovoked attack against the men. The National Hockey League, Madison Square Garden and the City of New York are also named as defendants.

Actor James Daly leaves tangled tale in will tug-of-war

Hell Hath No Fury . . . department Under California law a mistress can sue for the same financial rights given a wife.

And that's the law cited by male model **Randal Jones** in his claim to half of late actor **James Daly**'s $1.5 million estate.

Jones, 30, says Daly, 59, the co-star of TV's Medical Center, was his lover. Says Jones' lawyer: "It was an open and notorious relationship. This was no closet affair."

Roy Orbison and wife sue manager

NASHVILLE, Tenn. (AP) — Pop singer Roy Orbison and his wife, Barbara, filed a $50-million lawsuit yesterday against Orbison's manager and publisher and 13 businesses affiliated with Acuff-Rose Publications Inc.

They claim manager-publisher Wesley Rose, who owns Acuff-Rose publishing company with country singer Roy Acuff, "abused their trust" during a 24-year relationship.

Arab-style divorce is rich stuff

LOS ANGELES (AP) — They met in Paris. He was a young Saudi Arabian businessman ready to take a wife. She was a teenage British beauty touring with her mother.

"In 1961, I met and was attracted to Sandra Jarvis-Daley," Adnan Khashoggi would recall years later. "After a period of courtship, we decided to get married."

Sandra changed her name to Soraya, became a Moslem, took the veil and had five children. Adnan built a multi-billion-dollar business empire which took them to far corners of the world.

Now, 18 years after meeting, Adnan and Soraya Khashoggi are locked in a bitter court battle involving billions of dollars, their children and the details of a storybook marriage that failed.

It is no ordinary divorce case because Adnan Khashoggi is no ordinary man. An international arms dealer with a shadowy reputation, Khashoggi is considered one of the world's richest men.

Soraya's lawsuit, filed by lawyer Marvin Mitchelson, is the largest divorce action on record, seeking $2.5 billion, which she estimates as half of Khaghoggi's staggering wealth.

The case has international political implications as well.

"Government agencies will be watching this civil case," says Mitchelson.

Mitchelson said former president Richard Nixon was subpoenaed last week to give a deposition about his contacts with Khashoggi.

Coming weeks will tell whether the case of Khashoggi vs. Khashoggi will unearth enough data to threaten Adnan Khashoggi's power as middleman in the arms market.

The first step, getting Adnan to testify in a legal proceeding, is scheduled for Dec. 12, when he will make deposition either in Paris or in New York city at his $2-million townhouse on Manhattan's Fifth Ave., Mitchelson said.

One question is why an Arab and his British wife should have their divorce litigated in California.

Soraya, living in Los Angeles, seeks to take advantage of California's liberal community property laws.

Khashoggi said in a sworn affidavit his only business contacts are two banks he owns in Walnut Creek, Calif.

Mitchelson conceded that the request for a $2.5-billion settlement raised eyebrows, but he insists it's not outrageous.

"You have to look at it relatively," he said with a smile.

"We're talking about a man who has a $44-million yacht, 13 homes, three planes and who is reputed to have bought his Italian girlfriend a $20-million yacht.

"We're talking about a man with a great deal of money."

Prize-less complaint

Wendy Potasnik of Carmel, Ind., holds the lawsuit she filed against the Crack Jack Division of Borden Inc. because a package of the snack was missing the advertised "free prize in every box." The 9-year-old says in the suit that she wrote the company but received no reply. "I'm not buying any more until this is settled," she vowed.

Chrysler sued for $3.2 billion

WEST ALLENHURST, N.J. (UPI) — Neal Cowe bought what he thought was a new Dodge van in 1978. Now he's suing Chrysler Corp. for $3.2 billion, claiming the vehicle actually was used and reconditioned.

Cowe bought the van for $7,310.10, but he is asking high damages because that's the amount Chrysler originally sought in loan guarantees from the federal government.

The clue to his having bought a lemon came when he was issued a traffic summons and police found the vehicle number in their records did not match the number on his registration.

His suit charges that Chrysler sold a damaged and repaired vehicle as new.

Chapter 3

Police, Politics & Justice

An arresting encounter

LOS ANGELES (Reuter) — A prostitute tried to arrest her customer yesterday . . . and he tried to do the same to her.

Both of them were undercover police officers in Hollywood.

Neither was arrested but the "customer" is being investigated for using illegal entrapment techniques on the "prostitute." She was wired for sound.

"There were allegedly things said that weren't exactly proper," said Lt. Dan Cooke. "The male officer may have overstepped his bounds."

Police kill Good Samaritan

WEST HOLLYWOOD, Calif. (UPI) — Steve Conger could have ignored the elderly man he saw lying unconscious in a pool of blood.

But Conger, 28, ran to help the man, first carrying him up a flight of stairs to his room at the Fairfax Motel and then running back downstairs to phone police.

Moments later he was shot and killed by a startled sheriff's deputy who mistook him for the alleged assailant, another motel resident who apparently went beserk.

"He was a Good Samaritan," said Jack Gonor, 63, who wept when he was told of his rescuer's death.

"Give that young man credit. He could have stayed in his own yard, and he would be alive today and I could have bled to death.

"He laid down his life to save mine."

Floyd Taylor, 36, accused of attacking Gonor and the other two victims, was arrested later.

Black, white police fire at each other

FLINT, Mich. (AP)—A black policewoman was in custody in hospital yesterday after policemen shot at each other during an argument.

The incident started with a dispute on Saturday when a white policeman would not let the policewoman drive the patrol car they were to have shared for the day.

Police said the woman fired at the policeman first and he and some other officers returned fire.

Although officials said race and sex did not appear to be factors, the shooting was followed by a meeting between Chief Herbert Adams and the Flint Society of Afro-American Police.

Madeline Fletcher, 20, was in hospital with a single gunshot wound in the chest. Also, in hospital was Walter Kalberer, 34, an eight-year member of the force and her partner for the day, with a bullet wound in the left thigh.

Adams said charges may be brought against Fletcher.

Police said the two officers were not regular partners but were assigned to share the patrol car. Miss Fletcher got behind the wheel of the car and Kalberer tried to remove her.

Miss Fletcher swung her nightstick at Kalberer and he knocked the stick away with his nightstick. She then started to walk away, but spun around, pulled her .38 calibre revolver and fired two or three times, hitting Kalberer in the leg.

Kalberer fired four times at Miss Fletcher as two of three other officers nearby also shot at her.

He didn't believe in cell-ibacy

CARSON CITY, Nev. — (AP) — Stan Wilson, a convicted killer who married and fathered a son while in prison, achieved another goal when he was granted parole.

Wilson, 32, has been a prison leader, has not had any recent disciplinary problems and has been working outside the prison under minimal security for some time now, the state parole board said in granting him freedom.

Earlier in Wilson's almost 11 years in prison, he had a string of disciplinary violations including a 1974 violation of "visiting room etiquette" when he slipped into a bathroom with his new wife and consummated their marriage.

He met his wife, Rose, while taking a college course at the prison. She was working with the instructor on a book about black culture. They were married in a rare prison wedding in 1973.

Wilson said he experienced "a tremendous sense of relief" when granted parole, and was "looking forward to just being able to walk with my wife and kid, maybe kick a rock . . . nothing extravagant. I've developed an appreciation for the simple things."

Wilson was jailed for the slaying of a fellow pimp in a Las Vegas supper club during a fight over a prostitute.

Victim billed after robbery-rape

MILWAUKEE (AP) — Her car was stolen and wrecked and her daughter was raped. But for a Milwaukee woman, the troubles were only beginning.

First she got a $1,600 bill for the medical expenses of one of the men charged with the rape, for injuries he suffered when the car was wrecked.

Then the state told her she had to post a $2,300 security deposit because of the crash or lose her license to drive. The state later rescinded its request, but the city asked $1,260 for damages to a police car involved in the accident.

"They raped my daughter, tore up my car and I'm stuck with their bills," the woman said. "I don't believe it."

The trouble began in June when the woman's daughter, 18, was sitting in a car waiting for a friend. Two men stole the car with her in it, then raped her and let her go, police said.

Police spotted the car and began a chase which ended when the car went through a roadblock and crashed into two vehicles, one of them a squad car.

Then in August, the victim's mother said she received the $1,600 hospital bill for treatment of injuries suffered by one of the two men.

In Circuit Court last Friday, Arthur Williams, 18, was sentenced to 10 years on convictions for false imprisonment and second-degree sexual assault. Sentencing is scheduled Dec. 19 for the other man convicted on similar charges, Michael Scott, also 18.

Millionaire smugglers draw dime-store fines

Here are some examples of justice in Key West:

☐ Item: Following a tip, officers from four agencies interrupt a marijuana-offloading operation, nabbing 398 bales of pot and arresting 12 men after a chase.

The men were charged with possession of more than 100 pounds of marijuana, importation of a controlled substance and conspiracy to distribute.

Result: Only one of the defendants is sentenced — to one year in the county jail.

☐ Item: Sgt. Robert Brack is patrolling on Card Sound Road and notices a lock is missing from a private gate. His headlights pick up some frantic activity on a dock.

"Police officer!" he shouts, and is answered with gunfire.

Within hours, police seize two shrimp boats, a lobster boat, a van, three trucks, a car, two pistols, a semi-automatic rifle and 919 bales of marijuana — 20.8 tons. They also have 11 suspects, arrested in a nearby mangrove swamp.

Result: After two days of defence motions, all charges against the men are dropped.

Explained assistant state attorney Andrew Tobin: "We had a weak case."

Won't prosecute

☐ Item: After staking out a suspected marijuana hideaway, police arrest three men in three different cars. One car contains nine bales, another seven, the third has six bales. More than 150 bales were found at the hideaway.

Charges: Possession of more than 100 pounds of marijuana.

Result: Charges against one of the men are dropped. The day after the other two go to trial, before any testimony is heard, assistant state attorney William Kuypers announces a negotiated plea — guilty of possession of less than 5 grams, a misdemeanor.

The two men each paid a fine of $1,062.

☐ Item: Mark Walker of the Florida marine patrol stops a trimaran two miles off shore and discovers 74 bales of Jamaican marijuana. He arrests the two men aboard.

They are charged with possession of more than 100 pounds of grass, importation of marijuana and operating an unregistered motor boat.

Result: Assistant state attorney Kuypers declines to prosecute the two men on the importation charge. Later, the two defendants said they would plead guilty to the felony possession charge and pay a $3,000 fine in exchange for five years' probation. The judge rejects the deal as being too lenient.

'Solid case'

Five months later, Kuypers drops all felony charges against the men and files misdemeanor charges of marijuana possession.

Agreeing to forfeit the boat, the pair plead guilty to five misdemeanor counts of possession of less than 5 grams of marijuana. One of the men is fined $3,000 and put on probation for five years; the other gets probation.

☐ Item: Highway patrol officer Victor Pandolfi stops a Winnebago because its license plates are out of date. Noticing that the driver is covered with green and brown stems, the officer asks to search the vehicle and discovers 2,940 pounds of marijuana.

The driver is charged with possession of more than 100 pounds, and failure to carry proper vehicle registration.

Result: The Monroe County state attorney's office drops all charges because, according to court records, it is "unable to prove" them.

"Actually," says Pandolfi, "I thought it was a pretty solid case, myself."

☐ Robert Crespo, a father of five with no previous criminal record, is arrested for selling a small "baggie" of marijuana on a Key West fishing dock.

He gets eight months in jail.

Guilty, innocent and even police lay complaints

CHICAGO — What kinds of beefs do the people of Chicago make against their police? Here's a sampling of complaints lodged with the Office of Professional Standards, the police complaint bureau, last Saturday:

☐ A woman said a police officer hit her son with a gun.

☐ A man complained that a police officer — his wife — had threatened to arrest him.

☐ A driver, involved in a traffic accident, said he poked the driver who side-swiped his car and ran. Police chased him instead of the offending driver.

☐ A man claimed a police officer had dragged him into a police station and told him he'd "kick my butt." Citizen not arrested.

☐ A man said he was on his way to his car when three officers, for no reason, pointed a gun at him, searched him and shoved him against a wall. He was not arrested.

Called names

☐ A man complained that a police officer had called him an SOB.

☐ A man said a police officer had failed to respond when asked to help deal with obnoxious teenagers.

☐ A policeman complained that a fellow officer whose son had been detained after a fight with another youth threatened him, saying "If any of my children are arrested again, I'll get you."

☐ A nun complained that police didn't respond fast enough when she called them to eject a man from her school.

☐ A man said he'd been kicked by police while he was in lock-up — last June.

☐ A man claimed a $300 camera was missing after police searched his van.

Asked for aid

☐ A man claimed he had flagged down police for aid and they beat him up.

☐ An anonymous caller said he had heard a police officer ask for a bribe.

'Innocent' verdict -- three minutes too late ★★★

RICHMOND, Va. (UPI-AP) — A man charged with murdering an insurance agent switched his plea to guilty only three minutes before a jury found him innocent.

Harry Seigler's plea overruled the jury's decision, and he faces 40 years behind bars.

While the jury was deliberating for 4½ hours Wednesday, Seigler, his lawyers and prosecutors worked out a plea bargain agreement that included Seigler pleading guilty to a lesser charge of the first-degree murder of insurance agent Douglas Mitchell, who was found Dec. 2 with his throat slashed. Seigler could have received the death penalty if convicted of capital murder.

The jury began deliberating about 3 p.m., and plea bargaining started about 6.30 p.m.

At 7.25, Seigler was brought into the courtroom. Circuit Judge William Spain asked whether the defendant was satisfied and whether he was pleading guilty because he was guilty. Seigler answered, "Yes, sir."

At 7.28 p.m., the jury's verdict was ready. Speigler was taken from the courtroom.

When the jurors were told about the guilty plea, one slumped in a chair and another bolted upright. Later examination of the jury's verdict forms showed it found Seigler not guilty.

"Holy mackerel," prosecutor Warren Von Schuch said.

"Well, that's the risk you take," defence lawyer John Dodson said.

Seigler "had some fears" about what the jury might do because it deliberated for so long, but the plea bargain was his decision, the lawyer said.

During the trial, two convicted felons linked Seigler to the slaying but no physical evidence was presented to show he committed the crime.

★★

BOY'S LOST PUPPY UNDER ARREST

OLD ORCHARD BEACH, Maine (Special-UPI) — Police found 8-year-old Michael Fitzgerald's missing puppy — but they won't give it back.

The 3½-month-old collie had been in police custody more than 10 days and the law says after 10 days "you can dispose of the dog as you see fit," a spokesman said.

However, the real reason is that a female police dispatcher has taken a fancy to the dog, named Cotton, and doesn't want to give it up.

"The police have been very cruel to my son," said Michael's mother. "He's been in tears all day long, got his hopes up and then they wouldn't give Cotton to us."

Michael and several friends staged a protest over the weekend in front of police headquarters — to no avail.

'WISH YOU WERE HERE'

JACKSONVILLE, Fla. (UPI) — Judge R. Hudson Olliff, who sentenced Gary W. Sayers to 448 years in prison for burglary, sexual battery, kidnapping and robbery, got a Christmas card from the convict.

The inscription on the card, which arrived Friday, read: "Wishing you the inner peace that is the gift of Christmas."

Inside, Sayers wrote: "Having a wonderful time. Wish you were here."

Man deported for theft in 1943

NEW YORK (Reuter-UPI) — Michele Chiaramonte was 19 when he stole 60 pounds of olives and some firewood for his starving family in war-torn Sicily in World War II.

But he will be deported from the United States for these two crimes of "moral turpitude" 37 years ago, the U.S. Court of Appeals decided yesterday.

Chiaramonte, now 56, an illegal alien, has been trying to get permanent resident status in the United States for more than 10 years. He was refused an immigrant visa in 1970 and came to the U.S. on a visitor's visa the following year and stayed on after it expired.

During that time, the court ruled, he complicated his case by bringing his wife and two sons illegally from Canada to the United States.

Chiaramonte had urged the court to rule that his theft of olives to feed his family in such harsh times "does not evidence a lack of good character."

But the three-judge court ruled that such a crime would have been excusable if his family "had been going hungry amidst a sea of plenty, but it is different when . . . scarcity prevails."

The judges said that the theft might have deprived others of their fair share of necessities. "Thievery in this environment is as morally repugnant as any common larceny," the judges said.

UPI PHOTO

Telling photo: A story and photograph of Curtis Petty, 24, and his 83-year-old bride Mary raised a lot of interest — especially among probation authorities looking for Petty.

Lovebird now jailbird

CARLETON, Mich. (UPI) — Just a few days ago, Curtis Petty was basking in the limelight with his new bride — a woman 59 years his senior. Now the lovebird is a jailbird.

Petty, 24, and his bride Mary, 83, were photographed in the Detroit Free Press Tuesday, pictured hugging and cuddling in Mrs. Petty's home in Carleton.

The story gained a lot of attention. Monroe County authorities were especially interested.

They identified Petty as an accused walkaway from a halfway house in nearby Monroe where he was serving a 2- to 15-year sentence for breaking and entering a neighbor's house.

One of the witnesses who had testified against Petty at his 1980 trial was none other than the woman he married less than three weeks ago.

Hooked -- by a hoker ★ ★

HEMPSTEAD, N.Y. (UPI) — An undercover policeman dressed in a 38-B bra, tight sweater and snug jeans was alluring enough to bag 10 "johns" who thought he was a she.

Police said the patrolman wore a blonde-streaked wig and red lipstick and wiggled his way up and down Main St., netting prospective patrons, who ranged from a delicatessen owner to a real estate salesman.

The men were arrested on charges of soliciting for prostitution. Two alleged prostitutes also were arrested in the first day of the operation.

"We have to get the johns (men seeking prostitutes) to think that they're going to get in trouble if they come here," a police spokesman said, "This way, they don't know who's who. No johns, no hookers."

The decoy — whose name was not revealed by the police — took the men to a car parked around then indicated that it was business first, pleasure later.

By the time the john reached for his wallet, he was surrounded by policemen in uniform.

As the blond wig slid off to reveal the officer's short crop of dark hair, the client was shocked to learn he wasn't dealing with a hooker but had, instead, been hooked.

POLICEMAN SAVED BY AN EARLY GIFT

BETTENDORF, Iowa (Special)—A salesgirl's faith in human nature means that a policeman is alive to celebrate this Christmas.

Terri Schafter wanted to buy her husband, David, 29, a bulletproof vest for Christmas but didn't have the $127 cash. She offered sales clerk Janie Dennhardt $20 a month on a layaway plan but the clerk said: "Take it with you. You never know what might happen . . ."

That was five months ago and Terri gave David the vest early.

Recently, Schafer was shot by a gunman at point blank range. He was knocked cold but he awoke with only a bad bruising.

★★★★★★★★★★★★★★★★★★★★★★

The brighter side

Four U.S. criminals have been rounded up — by mail. Rather than go through the long and expensive process of tracking down the criminals — all on the most wanted list — U.S. marshals, posing as tour operators, sent letters to their last known addresses, inviting them to join a free trip to Atlantic City. They'd get $15 for the slot machines, free drinks and, said the letters, a "free surprise" — which turned out to be a marshal waiting with a warrant.

Blue lights stolen from police cruiser

When Lexington police officer Steve Lawson returned to work yesterday, he found something missing from his police cruiser.

Someone had entered the car, which was parked at the police station, and removed its blue portable lights by pulling back the floor mat and cutting wires.

Bald Eagle killer gets 10 years

SEATTLE (AP) — A man who admitted strangling a wounded bald eagle at the Woodland Park Zoo has been sentenced to up to 10 years in prison.

John Paul Mariano, 25, had claimed he wanted the feathers for Indian ritualistic purposes.

"Regardless of your philosophy, you knew that you were doing something that was beyond your right to do," said Judge Nancy Ann Holman.

Mariano had pleaded guilty to a second-degree burglary charge after breaking into a cage containing two eagles after the zoo had closed for the day. Only one eagle was harmed.

Warden, inmate go too far -- to Florida

MORGAN, Ga. (UPI) — John Stewart was doing time — you might call it "good time" — in jail here but he and the warden finally went too far. They went to Florida.

Stewart was serving seven years for drug-running, but for a small consideration of $1,000 Warden W. R. Royal allowed him to:

☐ Bring his mobile home into the prison and live in it.

☐ Have his girl friend in, or, if he preferred, be chauffeured into town to see her.

☐ Have his own, unlisted, telephone.

☐ Have a color television set, complete with recorder and pornographic tapes.

That went on for a year, but it all collapsed when the warden took Stewart to the Gulf Coast on a fishing trip.

Authorities caught up with them on the marina, and although Royal's lawyer claimed at his trial Monday that it was "just a fishing trip," the state saw Stewart as a fugitive from prison and the warden as his abettor in escape.

Judge Wallace Cato sentenced Royal, 58, to five years in prison, plus five years on probation, with a $10,000 fine. Stewart was given another five years and a $10,000 fine.

The judge told the pair they could split the court costs.

Candy bar theft brought 34 years

SCRANTON, Pa. (UPI) — In 1941, Lawrence Steubig broke into a railroad car and stole half a dozen candy bars.

He and his partner in the crime were arrested and charged with burglary and receiving stolen goods. The other man was convicted and served 9 months in jail, but the Steubig case was never heard.

Instead, the Quarter Sessions Court in Philadelphia declared Steubig mentally incompetent to stand trial. Records showing the reason for that decision were not immediately available. He was committed to a state hospital where he spent the next 34 years of his life.

Now, the 77-year-old Steubig is suing Farview State Hospital and current and former administrators for illegally holding him at the facility.

Steubig might still be at Fairview except that in 1975 a woman named Elizabeth Walsh remembered him as a friend of her husband and set out to find him after her spouse died. She located him at Farview and in a few months he was released to her custody.

In testimony Friday, Dr. Wolfgang Reiger, an associate professor at Pennsylvania State University who interned at Farview, said Steubig should have been held no more than a year before being released.

"People can commit rapes and murders and be let out of jail in 10 or 15 years," said Beasely. "Here's a guy who steals six candy bars and he spends 35 years imprisoned."

Gunman kills wounded policeman

NEW YORK (UPI) — A police officer having a drink in a bar after work was killed by a masked robber who shot him in the head as he lay wounded and helpless on the floor.

Officer Robert Walsh, 35, a father of three, tried to stop three men wearing ski masks who tried to rob the bar.

Toy gun guard shot to death

LOS ANGELES (UPI) — A security guard carrying a toy gun in his holster was shot to death outside a supermarket by two men who then robbed the store and fled with money.

"They could have just stuck a gun in his back and marched him inside the market," a police spokesman said, "but they shot him, apparently to make way for an easy robbery."

Hero dad faces fine

CAPE MAY, N.J. (UPI) — Bob Wernik may get a $130 fine for commandeering an ambulance to save his 4-year-old son's life.

Wernik, a security guard at the Cape May County Airport, has been ordered to appear in municipal court Monday on charges he took over an ambulance to drive his son Kevin, who was in convulsions, to a hospital April 5.

Terrorized judge goes for his gun

FORT LAUDERDALE, Fla. (UPI) — When the 6-foot-6 defendant hurled his 326 pounds at the bench the judge reacted swiftly — he ran to his chambers and got a gun.

"I saw him stand up and I said, 'Jesus Christ, the size of that man.' He was the biggest man I ever saw in my life," said Judge Thomas Coker. "He could have squashed me like a grape."

As Coker brandished his .357 magnum yesterday, 14 deputies subdued Joshua Thomas, 30, of Miami, and clapped him in handcuffs and leg irons.

Thomas, arrested after allegedly trying to take a gold necklace from a man, went into a frenzy as he was summoned to the judge's bench.

Thomas lunged, ripped Coker's nameplate off the bench and threatened to hit the judge with it.

The incident, as well as the pistol, stayed with Coker the rest of the day.

He said he had intended to order a stun gun to keep beside him in the courtroom, just in case, but added, "It would have taken a cannon for this dude."

A big 'welcome back' for woman policeman

(When she left the force she was a man)

By Bogdan Kipling
Toronto Star special

WASHINGTON — Bonnie Nora Davenport returns today to the Washington police force she left nearly a year ago as Ormus W. Davenport III, a man, widower and father of three.

She is a beneficiary of Washington's bylaw banning discrimination against transsexuals.

An eight-year veteran of the force, Ormus was top-notch. An undercover agent, member of Washington's famous "Sting" and "Gotcha Again" squads, Ormus helped put dozens of local crooks, fences and break-in artists behind bars.

But Ormus hated his life as a man and decided to become a woman.

As far as the District of Columbia police department was concerned, that's a strictly personal matter.

When Bonnie emerged from a hospital in Colorado last November, he had become a she in all respects but one. She can't bear children.

Bonnie's kids, two boys and a girl, 11, 12 and 13, now live with their grandparents.

Bonnie, 35, is publicity-shy. Requests for interviews from newspapers and TV networks from around the world have to be submitted through the Washington police department.

Even though photographs of Washington police officers are public, police officials have decided to honor Bonnie's request for at least temporary anonymity.

Washington cops are proud their force is mature enough to let Ormus come back despite the sex-change.

The Washington police department has a long history of hiring female officers and blacks. Some 300 women serve in the 4,200 strong force which includes 2,100 blacks — a higher percentage of women and blacks than in any other major American city

3-week-old baby moves into mother's prison cell

LOWELL, Fla. (AP) — Three-week-old Marc Stephen Miller, bundled in a bright yellow blanket, has moved into the state prison here after a circuit court ruling that a baby's place is with his mother — even if she's behind bars.

Marc was reunited this week with a beaming Elizabeth Miller in the lobby of the Florida Correctional Institution for Women.

A prison guard immediately escorted mother and son to a makeshift nursery and cell at the prison hospital.

Prison superintendent Bill Booth said five other pregnant women are serving time at the facility.

Miss Miller, 31, who has refused to identify the child's father, was pregnant when she was sentenced in December to five years in prison for grand larceny. She will be eligible for parole in January, 1982. Marc was placed in temporary foster care after he was born May 22.

Glider scheme grounded

MONTEREY PARK, Calif. (UPI) — A crash landing grounded the nation's first police ultralight plane squadron.

A glider piloted by Officer Ruben Echeverria suffered an engine failure, encountered a gust of wind and crashed onto the roof of a school, missing a playground full of youngsters. The officer was the only casualty — he suffered a broken thumb.

Inmate's coat of many colors aids escape

STARKE, Fla. (UPI) — A convicted murderer escaped from prison by painting his clothes the color of a guard's uniform and walking out the front gate.

Police were looking yesterday for former death row inmate Myran Fleming, 43, who sawed through bars in a shower stall near the entrance to Florida State Prison, spokesman Vernon Bradford said.

"He had a coat and a hat, apparently, and had painted his prison pants and shirt to a brown," like a guard's clothing, Bradford said.

Criminologist would 'bug' convicts, then set them free

SAN JOSE, Calif. (UPI) — Convicts could be allowed to roam free if they were fitted with electronic devices to track their movements, a criminologist suggests.

"We're losing the war against crime," Robert M. Weigel, chief probation officer in Santa Clara County, said in an interview last week. "And when you're losing you ought to start looking for new weapons."

Weigel's suggests that nonviolent criminals be given the chance to stay out of prison if they wear electronic devices, either on their wrists or implanted in their bodies, which would allow authorities to monitor their movements.

Some might even have devices implanted in their brains to monitor and possibly control their actions.

If a parolee strays from a restricted area, police would know about it immediately and could send a patrol car to pick him up.

As the technology develops, a brain implant could signal that a drug addict is back on narcotics and even be used to release counteractive drugs.

"It's kind of scary, I know. It sounds like 1984," Weigel said. "But if we're truly at war with crime, then let's set down some conventions and start fighting to win. We haven't exactly been knocking 'em dead, you know."

Worthless Junk

JEFFERSON CITY, Mo. (AP) — A self-help manual called Defending Yourself — How to Assist your Attorney in a Criminal Prosecution is "worthless junk" according to Donald Wyrick. He's the warden at the local slammer. The booklet was written by one of the prisoners.

Policemen play cops'n'robbers

NEW YORK (Reuter) — Two New York city policemen who robbed a Brooklyn grocery store at gunpoint made two mistakes — they were on duty and they were wearing their uniforms.

The store's owners didn't report the robbery last week because the shop was being used as a front for selling marijuana, but another officer saw it take place, police say.

Brothel Dean, 35, and Henry Goodman, 44, were arrested yesterday after a department investigation and charged with stealing $400.

Dean holds the department's highest award, the Combat Cross.

An officer heard from an informant that a robbery by policemen was taking place and arrived at the store as the two other officers were leaving, a spokesman said.

Prison sex probe

NEW YORK (AP) — Jailed organized crime kingpins have been operating a "pay-for-play" operation that allows them to leave Attica and Green Haven state prisons for sexual trysts, a newspaper says. Top crime figures jailed for offences ranging from narcotics to murder have bought the power to walk out and get sex on demand whenever they please, the Daily News says it learned. An investigation is also focussing on allegations that some female correction officers engaged in "paid sex" with organized crime figures, the report says.

★ ★ ★ ★ ★

Judge moonlit as loan shark

ALBANY, N.Y. (UPI) — New York City Civil Court Judge Jerome Steinberg has been removed from the bench for running a loan shark operation in his court offices.

A court of appeal found Steinberg had several times arranged loans for acquaintances that carried interest rates ranging up to 27 per cent.

For his services, which included arranging the loan and visiting the borrower to collect the monthly payments, the judge took up to 50 per cent of the interest rate for himself.

Sandwich costs 5 years' jail

BISBEE, Ariz. (AP) — A young man who pleaded guilty to the theft of a sandwich has been sentenced to five years in prison.

Andrew Pennington, 19, said he took the sandwich from a Douglas home when he could not find any money.

The burglary occurred after Pennington had been released from custody on a criminal trespass charge, Superior Court Judge Lloyd Helm said.

Pennington, of Huachuca City, had a long criminal record preceding the burglary charge but the record was not disclosed.

Fearless cop leaps aboard and halts driverless 18-wheeler

NEW YORK (UPI-Special) — A police lieutenant, weaving through heavy holiday traffic, leaped aboard a runaway 18-wheel tractor-trailer on the George Washington Bridge and safely brought it to a screeching halt.

The driver had abandoned the truck on the bridge and leaped to his death into the Hudson River. His body has not been found.

"He had all sorts of fancy buttons in there," Lt. Charles Lekowski said after the incident. "I didn't know what they were for, so anything that was pushed in I pulled out and anything that was out I pushed in."

The sudden braking left 15-foot skid marks on the road.

Lekowski said a motorist told him he saw the truck rumble down the bridge without a driver behind the wheel and that several people saw the driver jump into the water.

Jumping into his patrol car and swerving through traffic in the lanes alongside the truck, Lekowski got about 20 feet in front of the rig, left his car and — as the truck passed at about 15 miles an hour — "I put my right foot on the door step and my left arm around the windshield and just held on" Lekowski said.

A spokesman for the Port Authority, which operates the bridge, said he didn't "want to think what could have happened if he didn't stop it."

'Did Ave Maria in the buff'

PHILADELPHIA (UPI) — A Philadelphia opera singer has charged city cops forced him to strip and sing Ave Maria at gunpoint at police headquarters.

Mario Rice, 39, said he was "told to sing Ave Maria or get busted" after officers claimed they found a capsule, 16 pills and "green leaves in a paper towel" on him March 30.

At police headquarters later, Rice — who has sung with the Philadelphia Lyric Opera Co., the Royal Opera Co. and at the Brooklyn Academy of Music — was stripped and forced to sing Ave Maria again, then Danny Boy for an officer who said he was Irish.

Officers shouted "Figaro, Figaro" while he sang, Rice said.

Police, who are investigating the incident, claim a strip is routine procedure for suspects believed to be carrying drugs. Rice was not arrested or charged.

Fame, fortune find Mattie

Money pours in for woman who had to steal to eat

SAN ANTONIO, Tex. (UPI) — With Mattie Schultz growing wealthier with every mail delivery, Mayor Lila Cockrell wants a full report on why the 91-year-old was jailed overnight for shoplifting — starting her on the road to becoming an international celebrity.

Mrs. Schultz, jailed 24 hours last week for shoplifting $15 worth of food has been receiving cheques and cash in the mail since reports of her arrest appeared in newspapers around the world.

Mrs. Schultz was so confused by the rapid change of events that she is suffering from exhaustion, but convalescing in hospital.

A local senior citizens' council reported that it was inundated with mail containing an estimated $6,500 to $7,500, for Mattie.

A spokeswoman said donations ranged from five dimes taped to a brief note to a $700 cheque from one person.

Lorraine Wernert, president of the senior citizens' council, said the donations came from persons who told of their sympathy for Mrs. Schultz and anger at the authorities who jailed her.

"It's going to help others (elderly persons), too, because it's created an awakening," Mrs. Wernert said.

Mrs. Schultz said she was forced to steal food because she had difficulty making ends meet with her $251-a-month income. She said she had no money for food after paying her rent and utility bills.

Mrs. Cockrell sent a memorandum to the city attorney asking for details of how Mrs. Schultz ended up in jail for the night.

Mrs. Schultz, a widow who has no children, was bilked out of all but $10 of her $4,900 life savings by confidence tricksters in 1973.

She told reporters she was "tired of living" after her arrest.

Mob attacks shot officer

NEW YORK (UPI) — While a New York city policeman lay bleeding on the ground from five bullet wounds yesterday, a crowd of people tried to rob him.

Police officials said a gunman opened fire on Constable Thomas Kennedy, 23, during a chase in Brooklyn after Kennedy and his partner, Constable Dominic Martino, saw a man run out of a smoke shop with a wad of cash.

Kennedy jumped from the patrol car and chased the suspect. The gunman fired at least six shots from an automatic pistol; Kennedy was hit twice in the left thigh, once in each foot, and once in the buttocks. Another bullet was deflected by his bullet-proof vest.

As the crowd tried to rob Kennedy, Martino pulled up in the patrol car and they fled.

Kennedy was reported in serious condition in hospital.

Texas sheriff strip-searched tortured 'hippies' and blacks

HOUSTON (Reuter-UPI) — For six years a county sheriff tortured suspects, stopped innocent motorists who were black, long-haired, or rock music fans, and sometimes strip-searched men and women on a highway.

This week James "Humpy" Parker pleaded guilty to civil rights violations charges and struck a plea bargain allowing him to spend three years in prison and pay a $15,000 fine.

Parker, 48, was accused of using an illegal speed trap to stop blacks, "hippies", and cars carrying the bumper sticker of a Houston rock station or Louisiana license plates containing the letter "G."

Those license plates are issued to residents of northwestern Louisiana.

Lupe Salinas, chief of the U.S. attorney's civil rights division, said the sheriff had been under investigation for some time for operating an illegal speed trap between 1976 and 1982.

The occupants of the cars, both male and female, were strip-searched on the side of the highway and driven to the county jail at speeds above 160 kilometres (100 miles) an hour so the officers "could expeditiously return" to make more arrests, the prosecution alleged.

The prosecution also accused Parker and unnamed co-conspirators of subjecting prisoners to "a suffocating water torture ordeal in order to coerce confessions."

This generally included placing a towel over a prisoner's nose and mouth, and pouring water onto the towel until he began to show signs of suffocating or drowning, the prosecution said.

Rookie policeman held in tickets heist

NEW YORK (Reuter) — A young policeman accused of flashing his revolver to coerce a man into handing over two tickets to a sold-out Rolling Stones concert has been charged with robbery and suspended without pay, police say. Probationary police officer Scott Vogel, 23, a recent graduate of the police academy, approached the man outside the rock group's concert at Madison Square Garden, showed him a badge and gun and forced him to hand over two tickets. Police said the officer was off-duty

33 caught by police sting

HAWTHORNE, N.Y. (UPI) — Undercover police have arrested 33 people in a bizarre "sting" fencing operation that attracted offers of everything from a stable of prostitutes to an electric organ demonstrated by singing and dancing thieves.

Westchester police, who set up a storefront in Pelham, N.Y., and posed as gangsters during Operation Yellow Jacket, spent 14 months videotaping "career criminals" selling the police $1.2 million worth of stolen goods.

The items included 86 stolen cars, including two tractor-trailer truckloads of new cars, two computer terminals, television sets, jewelry, stolen credit cards, cheques, appliances and guns.

A prosperous pimp seeking early retirement to Florida offered the undercover cops his 11 prostitutes, an offer the cops declined, police said.

The solid gold speed trap

SALEM, Ore. (AP) — The police chief of Jordan Valley (population 210), made more than $70,000 last year from the $102,117 he collected in traffic fines.

Under his contract with the city, Paul Arritola, 38, gets the revenue from traffic fines less the state's share and the amount he spends to run the two-man police department. He pays his assistant $800 a month.

Arritola has been indicted for tampering with public records. Many people have accused him of running a speed trap in the community on the main highway between Boise, Idaho, and Reno, Nevada.

JUDGE DISMISSES HIS BOSS

SANTA CRUZ, Calif. (UPI) — Superior Court Judge Harry F. Brauer dismissed the prospective juror with a little lecture:

"You don't pay any attention to anything I say at home, and there is no reason to believe you would listen to anything I say here."

She was his wife, Georgia.

Going home for Christmas

MINNEAPOLIS (AP) — This Christmas will be a lot happier than the last one for Donna Mae Hollis, bank robber.

Last Christmas, the 40-year-old Minneapolis mother had only $6 and no presents for her three children. So she robbed a Minneapolis bank of $1,400, which she used to buy presents.

But she was caught. Last August she was sentenced to four years in the prison.

Now Mrs. Hollis is going home. This week, a judge signed an order reducing her sentence to time served.

"I think the order was appropriate," said her lawyer, Scott Tilsen. "It was a non-violent robbery. She was in trying circumstances when she did it, and she co-operated with the FBI. She was a first-time offender."

Get thee to a nunnery, madam told

SAN FRANCISCO (UPI) — A woman convicted of running a bawdy house in an elegant San Francisco neighborhood has been sentenced to 90 days in a nunnery.

Judge Daniel Hanlon meted out the punishment yesterday to 39-year-old Marlene "Brandy" Baldwin, whom he noted was a well-mannered and friendly woman-about-town.

Sister Mary Jane of the Sisters of the Convent of the Good Shepherd, who sat next to Ms Baldwin in court, said the convent was willing to take in the woman.

Defence attorney Art Groza said the sentence was right out of Shakespeare. "It's not unlike what Hamlet said to Ophelia: 'Get thee to a nunnery, go.'"

He didn't say that Shakespeare's nunnery was diametrically opposed to contemporary convents and, in fact, was just the sort of place Ms Baldwin was accused of running.

Sex offender jailed one year

TAMPA, Fla. (UPI) — John F. "Jack" Gregorio former president of Taxpaying Parents Against Kiddie Smut, was sentenced to one year in county jail and 10 years probation for sexually molesting two children. Gregorio, 46, had pleaded no contest Oct. 12 to charges of lewd and lascivious behavior with an 8-year-old girl and sexual battery of a 17-year-old boy.

CAHOKIA, Ill. (AP) — An elderly man drove through the wall of a Dairy Queen ice cream shop, climbed out of his car and calmly ordered an ice cream cone and a Coke. "The people were so taken aback that they served the guy," said police Lieut. Guy Westbrook. The 67-year-old driver finished the cone at the police station, where he was given a ticket for driving without a license. "There's nothing in the statutes for failure to yield to an ice cream store," Westbrook said.

Policeman's bark stops suspect

PITTSFIELD, Mass. (UPI) — Three years ago the Pittsfield police department eliminated its one-day K-9 unit. Now its officers do the barking.

The case of the dogged policemen started when patrolman Robert D'Ascanio and his partner Jim Bolan began losing a suspect in a footchase.

In desperation Bolan began barking.

"Okay, let the dog loose," d'Ascanio shouted.

The youth stopped in his tracks and was arrested.

D'Ascanio described the chase at the arraignment of Rodney Lewis, 17, on unarmed robbery charges.

Lewis allegedly snatched the purse of a 65-year-old woman late Saturday night.

Rookie policewoman fired for shooting innocent men

NASHVILLE, Tenn. (UPI) — A rookie policewoman who shot three innocent men fleeing from a store robbery has been kicked off the force.

She was fired yesterday — not for the man she killed, but for the two she wounded.

Police Chief Joe Casey said he was dismissing officer Joyce Faye Allen, 23, because she violated department regulations in shooting two customers who fled from Johnny's Sak-Ful Drive In Market Aug. 1.

District Attorney-General Thomas Shriver said his office won't pursue criminal charges against Allen.

Casey said he had concluded that the fatal shooting by the policewoman of Harry Walden, 37, the market's night manager "was within the shooting policy and rules and regulations of this department."

Allen, on the force only three months, methodically shot Walden, David Hayes, 27, and Anthony Seagraves, 21, when they bolted out the door of the market.

Investigators said all were running away from escaped convict Billy Guy Anderson, 30, who was robbing the market with a sawed-off shotgun.

Casey said Miss Allen, who had been on the force only three months, had reason to believe Walden was the robber because he ran out the door first and resembled Anderson.

But he said she could not be "reasonably certain" that David Hayes, 27, and Anthony Seagraves, 21, were involved in the robbery and should not have fired at them.

Casey said Walden ran from the market in a crouched position, did not have his hands in the air and resembled the robber.

He said in an armed robbery it can be "reasonably expected" that the first person to flee is the robber and not the victim or witnesses.

Casey said officers are told to use deadly force when there is no other way to stop a suspected felon from fleeing, or if the life of an officer or someone else is in danger.

Walden burst out of the market and was shot in the head at almost point blank range by Allen, who told investigators she thought Walden was the man she observed with the shotgun inside the market.

Hayes, 27, ran out the door next. He was shot in the side by Allen and stumbled over the body of Walden. Hayes was followed by Seagraves, who darted from the door with 12-year-old Michael Cates holding onto his pants leg.

Seagraves was shot in the arm, but the youngster was not injured.

Why is it that when you really need a cop . . .

 In 1972 the mayor of Newark, New Jersey, complained that municipal policemen were "lying down on the job," because a crack-down on graft and corruption "has seriously cut their income."

BRIDGEPORT, Conn. (UPI) — A policeman who underwent a sex change operation plans to return to duty in about two weeks as a woman.

Chester Collins, a 13-year-veteran of the force, has assumed the name Mary Collins and will be assigned to a clerical job in the central records division.

"I have to expect some flak," Collins said. "This is a medical problem. I am not ashamed of what I have done."

The 37-year-old Viet Nam veteran had an overwhelming desire to be a woman for several years, and decided to change his gender after four years of psychological evaluation and therapy.

He attributed his feelings to an inborn hormone imbalance.

"I know how I felt, but I went along and lived with it for years," the officer said.

The father of two children, Collins was divorced by his wife several months ago and now lives with his parents in Bridgeport.

★★★★★★★★★★★★

Dummy cop puts the brakes on speeders

PERRY, Ohio (UPI) — This village of 960 has a new policeman. And he's a real dummy.

Perry has only one full-time officer so the police chief Lee Lydic has fitted a dummy in an official shirt, tie, a badge and a regular hat. The phony is placed in a patrol car and parked at a different spot each day.

"It works very well in slowing down traffic," Lydic said.

Gambler bribed warden for jail favors

NEW YORK (UPI) — Reputed gambling kingpin James Napoli has been convicted of paying a warden $500 to receive special favors while in prison.

Napoli, 67, and co-defendant James Tuseo, 54, a wine merchant, were found guilty of the bribery charge, but innocent of paying deputy warden Ralph Grano $100 on another occasion.

The two face up to four years in jail at their sentencing Nov. 4. Napoli was returned to prison, where he is serving a sentence for racketeering. Tuseo was released on bail.

Entrapped pair

The prosecution had charged that in 1975, the two paid Grano, a deputy warden at the Manhattan House of Detention, a total of $600 on two occasions.

Napoli was serving a six-month jail term for failing to answer the questions of a grand jury investigating fixed boxing matches in Madison Square Garden.

The prosecution said that on Jan. 27, 1975, at a meeting in Grano's office, Napoli motioned to Tuseo, who responded by placing $500 in the deputy warden's pocket.

According to trial testimony, Grano went to the city's investigations department, became an undercover agent and wore a tape recording device during conversations with the two defendants.

'I love you,' mayor tells cop shot in bar

CHICAGO (UPI) — James Riordan, Chicago's first deputy police superintendent, was shot to death doing the work of a street cop. Just before he died, Mayor Jane Byrne told him, "I love you, Jim."

Riordan, 57, a "policeman's policeman" who once turned down the mayor's offer for the department's top job, was shot late Saturday in a posh downtown restaurant trying to stop a man who was "hassling a woman at the bar" with a switchblade. He was off duty at the time.

Told of the shooting, Byrne arrived at the hospital as Riordan, still conscious, was being taken to sur-

gery. The mayor told him, ' "I love you, Jim,' " a spokesman said.

Riordan, a 34-year police veteran, died shortly before midnight following 1 ½ hours of surgery.

Murder charges have been filed against Leon Washington, an ex-policeman in his mid-30s who now runs an employment agency. Washington was scheduled to appear in court today.

Witnesses said Riordan was shot three times at close range by the man who threatening the woman at the bar.

Riordan walked up to the man and said, ' "Hey, let's talk about it,' " a

witness said.

As he escorted the man out the door, the man stopped for his coat, pulled a pistol and shot Riordan.

Riordan, married and the father of four, including a son who is a police officer, was offered the superintendent's job by Byrne but turned it down for personal reasons. A streetwise cop who rose through the ranks, he was considered indispensable to Brzeczek, a lawyer with only limited street experience.

Said Captain William Lacy, "You don't think about higher-up officials being involved in this kind of thing . . . he was a hell of a guy."

Stripped of dignity

By The Associated Press

A woman arrested for drunken driving in Arlington, Va. was taken to the county jail, stripped naked and searched. So was a woman arrested for playing her stereo too loudly. And one who ate a turkey sandwich on a subway.

In Fremont, Calif., it happened to a woman who went to the police station to explain she didn't need a new dog license because her dog had run away.

Despite new laws and policies limiting strip-searches, many U.S. police departments still force people suspected of minor offences to undress and submit to searches.

These searches, according to the American Civil Liberties Union and the U.S. justice department, may include anal and vaginal inspections.

"The practice is rampant," says Harriet Kurlander, a civil liberties spokesman in New York.

Such strip searches are rare in Metro, according to Staff Inspector Forbes Ewing of the

Metro police morality squad, and are conducted mostly on prisoners held on drug charges.

Ewing said body searches for weapons can be done — always by police of the same sex as the prisoner — without judicial permission, but internal searches for drugs must be done by a doctor empowered as a justice of the peace.

Metro police use a doctor assigned by the RCMP in such cases, Ewing said.

Officials of the American Civil Liberties Union say they have no quarrel with the police practice of strip-searching people accused of serious crimes, but maintain too many police departments subject those accused of minor offences to the treatment.

"It seems to be strange that we require a warrant to search a home or office, but someone can put a finger into your body cavity without a warrant," says James Joy, a Colorado civil liberties official.

Police say strip-searches help keep drugs and weapons out of

the jails and protect officers and inmates.

U.S. court rulings have generally upheld the authorities' right to conduct such searches, but the U.S. Supreme Court has ruled that people who are illegally strip-searched can sue for damages.

Sex discrimination was the basis of the first major strip-search case in the U.S., decided a year ago when Chicago police were named in a civil liberties lawsuit alleging women were strip-searched more often than men.

The American Civil Liberties Union says the largest settlement is the $25,000 Suffolk County, N.Y. authorities agreed to pay legal secretary Diane Sala last March. She was subjected to a body-cavity search after failing to respond to a summons she never received.

"I'm happy with the settlement, yet . . . I will never in my life be able to forget the search," Sala said. "It was horrible. It will stay with me forever."

Sex-in-court judge convicted

AKRON, Ohio (UPI) — County Court Judge James Barbuto has been found guilty of gross sexual imposition and intimidation in his sex-bribery trial.

But he has been cleared on 10 other sex-related charges — seven counts of sexual bribery, attempted rape and two counts of complicity to obstruct justice.

Barbuto, 58, who is a powerful political figure here, admitted yesterday he had sex in his chambers.

But he said he was innocent of all 12 sexual bribery charges against him.

Barbuto earlier testified he kept sex devices in his chamber, including a dildo. Asked yesterday if he still had sex devices in his chambers, he said: "Yes I still have them." But he said he got them for his anti-obscenity lectures.

Asked if since 1971 he had sex in his chambers, other than with his wife, Barbuto paused, put his hand on his forehead and said "Yes." But he did not identify the person.

Seven women, including five prostitutes, testified against the judge.

The women testified the judge showed them pornographic pictures in his chamber.

Barbuto also faces trial on six additional charges relating to the alleged mishandling of weapons confiscated for trial evidence. Those charges include two counts of theft in office; two of dereliction of duty, and two of receiving stolen property.

Philadelphia cops must face brutality suit

The City of Brotherly Love? Bah, humbug, says the U.S. Justice Department which last week filed suits against Philadelphia Mayor and ex-policeman Frank Rizzo, 58, and 19 other city officials.

The Justice Department charges widespread police brutality and abuse of police powers in Philadelphia, which, with 8,085 policemen is the nation's fourth largest force.

Specifically the suit alleged Police routinely stop pedestrians and motorists without evidence of a crime and beat them if they protest; police commissioner Joseph O'Neill watched a videotape of an officer beating a handcuffed prisoner yet took no action; six detectives convicted of beating a confession out of an innocent arson suspect were promoted although they still face jail sentences and internal police investigators routinely accept "implausible" explanations by police officers for acts of brutality.

Death penalty is restored in New Jersey

Associated Press

TRENTON, N.J. — Calling it "a terrible, serious step," Gov. Thomas H. Kean yesterday made New Jersey the 37th state to restore the death penalty, and he recommended lethal injections as an execution method.

"People will know that from this date that if they go out and take a life, their life can be forfeited in exchange," Kean said.

Only those convicted of first-degree murder and people who hire killers would be subject to the death penalty under the new law.

"I'm relieved it's signed, and now we'll go through life hoping and praying we did the right thing," said the law's sponsor, state Sen. John Russo, a Democrat. His father was slain in 1970.

Kean said the death penalty would be a deterrent to violent criminals "but not to all people who commit crime or to all people who commit murder."

The governor said he would recommend that injections of a lethal drug be used for the executions. The Legislature must specify a method of execution in a separate measure.

The state used electrocution from 1907 to 1972, when the U.S. Supreme Court ruled all state death penalty laws were unconstitutional because haphazard administration violated protections against cruel and unusual punishment.

The last prisoner to be executed in New Jersey was Ralph Hudson, who was electrocuted in 1963 for the stabbing death of his estranged wife. The sentences of 22 state prisoners on Death Row in 1972 were commuted to life in prison.

The only bill pending in the Legislature to specify a means of execution would reinstate electrocution. Kean said he favors execution by lethal injection "because it seems to me that is the most humane."

New Jersey's law calls for a two trials and automatic review of death sentences by the state Supreme Court before a prisoner could be executed.

WOMAN TROOPER DROPS OUT

MIAMI (UPI) — Sandra Jones, the third woman ever admitted to the Florida Highway Patrol Academy, has quit, claiming she was knocked down nine times by the boxing instructor and forced to run until her feet bled.

Mrs. Jones, whose husband, Jimmy, is a highway patrolman, had tried for a year to get into the academy in Tallahassee but left this week after only eight days.

"I guess I'm never going to be a Highway Patrol trooper now," she said. "I wanted to be a law enforcement officer, not a gymnast."

Men ordered to write essays on soliciting

LANSING, Mich. (AP) — Sixteen men who pleaded guilty to soliciting a Lansing undercover policewoman for sex must write essays about the consequences of the crime on their home and work.

District Judge Charles Filice said he wanted the men to "pay a lot more than (they) ever thought possible."

Filice intends to make the essays public, although they won't have the men's names on them.

Most of the men were also ordered to pay $200 to $250 in fines or spend 30 to 60 days in jail.

Garbage man nailed for theft -- from dump

CHERAW, S.C. (AP) — The clothes and shoes were cast-offs. But that didn't matter to Raymond Sandsberry, who earns $112 a week driving a garbage truck.

He took them home from the dump to give as Christmas presents to his wife and seven pre-teen children.

Now he faces a jail term or a fine.

Sandsberry, 33, was arrested for trespassing for picking up several items of discarded clothing and shoes at the Chesterfield County landfill.

Police radar clocks tree ★ at 86 mph! ★

MIAMI (AP) — A tree has been clocked by police radar travelling at 86 miles per hour and a house apparently was doing a steady 28 m.p.h.

Impossible, of course, but these were part of filmed evidence of the inaccuracy of radar clockings shown yesterday at a court hearing on the use of radar speed traps.

Police radar units can clock the wrong targets and have even produced readings of up to 80 m.p.h. (128 kmh) by mistakenly measuring a car's air conditioning fan, a scientist testified.

"In many cases that reading on the 'gun' doesn't mean a thing," said physicist William Stern, a New York electronics consultant.

Public defenders and private lawyer's representing 27 motorists accused of speeding began their assault on one of the most cherished tools of law enforcement in the hearing convened by Dade County Judge Alfred Nesbitt.

The lawyers have asked Nesbitt to invalidate the Florida law allowing radar readings as evidence.

Although any decision by Nesbitt would cover only Dade County, the case seems certain to be appealed and take on broader ramifications both for the United States and Canada.

The courtroom was lined by expert witnesses, ranging from radar manufacturers and electronics experts to a former police officer who wrote a self-help guide for people who get traffic tickets.

Standing before a table laden with blunt-nosed radar guns, public defender Michael Lederberg declared of such equipment: "They are inherently unreliable and subject to error. They are inherently inaccurate."

Shoe thief tracked 7 years, 3,200 km

KENT, Ohio (UPI) — Barbara Christoper stole an $8.99 pair of shoes seven years ago — and the sheriff's office has been relentless in tracking her down.

Two deputies travelled 3,200 kilometres (2,000 miles) to Texad at the weekend to bring her back to Ohio. Now she's in jail here on $10,000 bond.

Christopher, 41, pleaded guilty in 1977 to stealing the shoes from a discount store in Streetsboro, Ohio, the Portage County sheriff's office said.

She later failed to show up for a probation hearing and was traced to Lubbock, Texas.

Last year, she was charged with failing to appear in court — which carries a maximum sentence of five years in prison and a $5,000 fine.

So the sheriff's office went after her. County officals wouldn't say how much the extradition cost.

"It looks to me like the simple thing for them to have done would have been to give her probation out here," said her Texas lawyer, Bill Wischkaemper. "It would have saved the Ohio county a lot of money."

He said his client is a kleptomaniac — a compulsive thief — and "was starting to get her life straightened out."

Patrol dogs for subway?

NEW YORK (UPI) — Attack dogs may be assigned to patrol the subways with police to combat crime on the 230-mile (370 kilometre) rail system, city officials said.

After a report on the successful use of the highly-trained animals by the Philadelphia police department, the city is giving serious consideration to new proposals calling for their use.

★★★★★★★★★★★★★

WHO STOLE CHIEF'S CAR?

ST. LOUIS (UPI) — Police are looking for their chief's stolen car — and his fireworks.

Police Chief Eugene J. Camp's car was taken from a parking space on the city's South Side. The 1973 gold-and-black Ford Mustang contined some tools, personal papers and fireworks, police said.

★★★★★★★★★★★★★

Police got to bottom of affair

AUSTIN, Texas (UPI) — A man needing a place to sleep for the night dropped his pants in the lobby of a police station in an effort to get arrested, but is likely to enjoy the hospitality of jail longer than he expected.

Thomas Thompson, 22, of Houston, was stranded Monday night and asked Sgt. Glenn Koons if there was any place he could stay in Austin. Koons suggested the Salvation Army, but Thompson said he didn't have the identification necessary to get a bed there.

Chapter 4

Crime, Violence & Guns

I didn't say, "Stick'em up."
I thought you said, "Stick'em up."

Anatomy of a mugging

Nolan Williams, a 67-year-old drifter, is beaten and robbed by two men outside a bar in downtown Dallas, Texas. First they knocked him down (left), then one man grabbed him by the hair and took $31 from him (centre). They left him groaning in agony on the ground. Williams had been with the men in the bar earlier and had been buying them drinks. Dallas Times Herald photographer Mike Smith came on the scene and took these pictures without being spotted by the muggers. Police were today studying Smith's pictures in a bid to identify the muggers.

'Normal' boy killed a 5-year-old

HAYWARD, Calif. (AP) — A boy who stuffed rocks in the pockets of a 5-year-old to drown him is "sort of a normal 11-year-old who just did something bad," his defence lawyer says.

"If you believe his story, it was an accident, or maybe gross negligence," said defence lawyer Robert Beles after the boy was convicted of second-degree murder. He said he will appeal.

Judge Hugh Koford said he has no doubt the boy intended to kill Frizzell Jones.

A witness at the trial said the defendant scuffled with the Jones boy, then made up. The following day he lured the younger boy to the water, weighed him down with pebbles, then tossed him into an inlet.

NY homicides up

NEW YORK (AP) — For the second year in a row, New York city has had a record number of homicides, with latest unofficial figures showing 1,739 violent deaths, six more than in all of last year. Chief-of-Detectives James Sullivan said he is "quite alarmed" at having two consecutive record-breaking years for homicide. He noted that in 1928, the year he was born, there were 228 homicides in the city with a population of 6,017,500. The city's population now is estimated at more than seven million.

1980's a riot for Reno revellers

NEW YORK (UPI-AP) — New Year was a riot for Americans in two cities when celebrators turned to fighting, looting, stoning and arson to see in the 1980s.

About 4,000 revellers streamed out of downtown casinos in Reno, Nev., and ran amok for three hours, stoning policemen, smashing store windows and looting several businesses.

Police used tear gas to disperse the mob and arrested 100 people.

One man was seriously injured as the mob rampaged through several blocks around the downtown's glittering casinos.

"They just went crazy," said Dennis Mack, manager of a pawn shop that was looted of $20,000 worth of goods. "They were acting like animals."

Sealed off

Police Lieut. Charles Nearpass said about 10,000 people had gone into the streets for the traditional New Year's celebration when the trouble broke out. About 4,000 took part in the violence.

"We were overwhelmed," said Capt. Charles Williams, one of several policemen hit by rocks.

About 300 policemen were called in and sealed off entrances to the big casinos to keep vandals away. Windows of many cars, including police cruisers and paddy wagons, were smashed.

Nearpass said rioters threw "rocks, bottles, anything they could get their hands on."

He said the initial trouble was caused by "booze" and "a spontaneous-combustion type of thing."

45 teenagers murdered California sheriff fears

LOS ANGELES (Reuter) — Two men in jail are suspected of raping, torturing and strangling five teenage girls — and there may be up to 45 victims, police say.

County sheriff Peter Pitchess refused to speculate on a final number, but police said they have listed as missing 45 young girls who lived in the areas where three of the bodies of the five girls were found.

"This case is complicated, complex and grizzly in its details and we may be just scratching the surface regarding crimes these suspects may have committed," Pitchess told reporters. "All five girls were subjected to sadistic and barbaric abuse.

"I'd have to speculate based on the information we have received there are additional bodies," he added.

The two men, Roy Norris, 32, and Lawrence Bittaker, 39, have been in jail since Nov. 20 when they were arrested in connection with an unrelated kidnapping and rape case. Pitchess said he would seek further charges against the men.

The kidnapping and rape charges have been dropped and replaced by assault charges because

the alleged victim, who said she had tear gas sprayed in her face, could not positively identify them.

Pitchess said the two men have been linked to a recording of a girl screaming and begging for mercy as she was being raped and tortured.

He said the suspects took more than 500 photographs of girls. "They are girls in their 'teens and were considered by them to be potential victims," he said. "We don't know which of the 500 may turn out to be victims."

He said the five alleged victims, aged 13 to 16, disappeared between last June and October.

Two of the girls are still missing, Pitchess did not say how he knew these two girls were dead, but he added Norris had co-operated with the police.

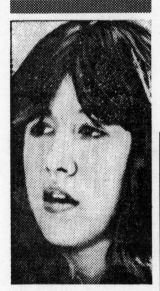

The trial of merchant seaman Lawrence Singleton, charged with raping and attempting to murder 16-year-old Mary Vincent (above) and hacking off both her arms with an axe has gone to the jury in San Diego, Calif. Singleton, 51, faces a possible life sentence.

Axeman splits bus rider's skull

PHILADELPHIA (UPI) — "There's trouble on the bus. There's a guy in there with a hatchet in his head," a man yelled in horror at two patrolling police officers.

The police dashed to the bus and found a man in the aisle, his clothes stained crimson, standing over his victim slumped in a seat with his head split open.

Police said Ronald Logan, 22, charged with murder and weapons violations, shouted "I'm crazy! I'm crazy!" as he was handcuffed.

The victim, Roosevelt Tilson, 26, died moments after the attack, police said.

Passengers told police Logan stood up from his seat, raised the hatchet and struck Tilson.

A police spokesman said "nobody really knows what provoked it."

In addition to the hatchet, police said they also took a mallet and a hammer from Logan. Asked why he was carrying the tools, Logan said: "I carry this stuff 'cause I want to be a boxer. I swing it to strengthen my arms."

Now New Yorkers are biting each other

NEW YORK (AP) — While dogs are biting fewer people, more people are biting each other, New York city's health department reports.

"The potential for humor in such happenstance is apparent," the department said in a news statement. "But this humor must be tempered with the stark understanding that human bites are causing amputations and deformities."

The number of human beings who bit other human beings in 1980 rose by 24 per cent, with 1,207 bites reported, the department said. By contrast, the number of human beings bitten by dogs dropped by 16.7 per cent to 13,177, still far ahead of human beings in total bites.

The department said 687 men and 520 females suffered bites from fellow human beings, but the statistics did not break down the biters by sex.

Mother killed babies to save souls, court told

SEATTLE (UPI) — Tanya Adams, on trial for allegedly murdering her two sons by dropping them from a bridge last winter, first tried to freeze them to death in snow outside her house, a defence attorney said yesterday.

Mrs. Adams, 25, wept as the attorney outlined the final hours of her sons, Ryan, 2, and Christopher, 1, who died Feb. 5 because their mother, a devout Mormon, wanted them to go to heaven before they grew older and became sinful.

"She first had decided to freeze them in the snow, outside (their home), but one of the boys started crying" and she could not bear to cause them pain, he said.

She then put them in her car and drove aimlessly around for hours, stopping at one point for gas and food.

Finally she drove to a bridge over the Columbia River and dropped her sons over the railing into the frigid water because she believed it would be a painless way for them to die and go to heaven, he said.

★ ★ ★

Fright may have killed man chased by N.Y. mob

NEW YORK (UPI) — A "good, clean kid" who was stripped naked and chased onto subway tracks by a jeering mob may have literally died of fright and not electrocution.

Medical officials reportedly found that 26-year-old Gerald Coury may have died from "heart stoppage" brought on by the terror of the predawn chase last Saturday.

New York police said Coury died instantly after he leaped onto the subway tracks, touched one hand to the electrified third rail and screamed, then put both hands on the rail and cried out again.

But pathologists told the dead honor student's brother, Charles, that an autopsy did not conclude Gerald was electrocuted because

there were no burn marks on the body. He said the autopsy did show a slight blockage in an artery leading to the heart.

Gerald telephoned his mother, Mary Coury in Torrington, Connecticut from New York's Grand Central station about 8 p.m. Friday.

He said he had been mugged and robbed of everything but the pants he was wearing and asked her to wire money. But the local Western Union office was closed.

"He was really, really upset," Mrs. Coury said. "He said, 'Get me out of here, Ma,'"

About eight hours later, police said, he was stripped of his pants and chased naked into Times Square.

Wife cremated husband after bizarre sex

GRANTS PASS, Ore. (UPI) — A woman who says her husband subjected her to bizarre sex acts because he was impotent pleaded no contest to killing him and cremating his dismembered body in their backyard barbeque pit.

District Attorney Bob Burrows said he reduced the murder charge to manslaughter because Tuanita Davenport had been "under the influence of extreme emotional disturbances."

Burrows said an investigation showed Mrs. Davenport's 59-year-old husband, Roland, "was impotent and subjected his wife to a variety of sexual activity including paraphernalia, a dog, threesomes and her own stepfather.

"She was dominated by her husband, and on March 24 burned all the paraphernalia," he said. "When her husband came home, an argument ensued and she fired a .25-calibre pistol."

Burrows said Mrs. Davenport told investigators her husband had wished to be cremated "so she dismembered the body and put the hand and feet into a pressure cooker and eventually burned all the body parts in the barbeque pit, located in the yard."

Mrs. Davenport will be sentenced Jan. 12.

Baby pulled from trash crusher

CHICAGO (UPI) — A baby boy was found in the trash compactor of a housing project building yesterday by a janitor who heard the infant's muffled cries just seconds before he was going to start the machine.

The baby, only four or five days old, was apparently thrown down the chute from one of the six floors of

the building, police said. He was in good condition in hospital.

Janitor James Bowman told police he was about to push the button when he heard muffled cries. Expecting to find a kitten, Bowman said he saw the "exceptionally pretty child" in diapers lying on top of the garbage heap.

Mother chose murder over street- life for Judy

BURLINGTON, Vt. (UPI) — Marilyn Dietl still can't believe that she murdered her 18-year-old daughter, Judy.

With tears in her eyes, Mrs. Dietl, 41, told a judge she took Judy for a drive in the family car one day last May and shot her dead to keep her from running away to become a prostitute.

"I must have gone crazy, because I couldn't let her go," she told Judge Ernest Gibson.

Mrs. Dietl had pleaded innocent by reason of insanity to a first-degree murder indictment. She changed the plea to guilty after authorities agreed to reduce the charge to second-degree murder.

Mrs. Dietl told Gibson it all began in 1977 when Judy went away to college in Boston. She said she soon learned her daughter moved out of the YWCA to become a prostitute.

"Judy got involved with a black pimp in Boston," she told the judge. "When I found out . . . I brought her home. I did everything I could to keep her home."

Finally, Mrs. Dietl said, she told Judy she would have to stay home and cut all ties with Boston or "leave the house and never come back."

When Judy decided to leave, Mrs. Dietl said she awoke the morning of May 5 and thought: "Today is the day she dies."

"It was as if she was already dead," Mrs. Dietl said. "I felt so relieved she was safe."

Mrs. Dietl said she found her husband's two guns, a .38-caliber revolver and a .22 derringer, in a closet.

She told her daughter they were going for a drive.

Mrs. Dietl asked her daughter to get out of the car. Then, she said, she began shooting Judy with the revolver.

"No mama!" Mrs. Dietl said her daughter cried. "No mama!"

"Judy, I can't let you go," Mrs. Dietl said she answered.

Breaking into tears in the courtroom, Mrs. Dietl testified she could not hear the sound of the shots.

"I kept hoping somebody would come out of the house (next door) and stop me," she said.

No one came. When police arrived, Mrs. Dietl said: "I just killed my daughter."

Retarded girl abandoned

PHILADELPHIA (UPI) — Kimberly Bowie, a severely retarded 12-year-old girl found naked and emaciated in her unheated home, is recovering from malnutrition at a hospital.

Denise Bowie, 27, her mother, has been charged with attempted homicide, reckless endangerment and endangering the welfare of a child. She faces a hearing Jan. 9.

Police said they discovered the girl in an empty, unheated and roach-infested house, using two trash bags to shield her naked 39-pound body from the cold.

Guns still too easy to buy, group says

WASHINGTON, (UPI) — Nineteen years and nearly 500,000 shooting deaths after the assassination of President John F. Kennedy, it is just as easy as ever to buy guns in the United States, a gun control group says.

"The assassins of John F. Kennedy, Martin Luther King and Robert Kennedy could just as easily now as then obtain the guns that fired those shots," said the National Council for a Responsible Firearms Policy, in a report marking the 19th anniversary of the Nov.22, 1963 John Kennedy assassination.

"Easy acquisition of the gun used in the attempted assassination of President Ronald Reagan in 1981 . . . further documents this shameful record of national negligence."

Since John Kennedy's death, more than 200,000 Americans have been murdered with guns, council executive director David Steinberg said. Another 190,000 have committed suicide with guns, and 50,000 more have been killed accidentally with guns, he said.

Over the same time period, 1.7 million people have been wounded with guns and another 2.7 million robbed at gunpoint. Half of all U.S. households have guns, Steinberg said, and "there may be nearly as many as there are people."

Bag is a shoplifter's dream — it slips past electronic eyes

CHICAGO (AP) — A U.S. inventor has come up with a shoplifter's dream. It's a "magic" shopping bag that can fool electronic eye alarm boxes. And it's selling like hot cakes. So far, 25,000 have been snapped up.

The bag's creator, Earlest Carter, says he never intended to help criminals with his invention.

But then again, the 34-year-old electronics whiz asks, why spend $450 for a leather coat when this $110 device can help shoppers — or shoplifters — slip undetected past the electronic alarm devices department stores have installed to catch thieves?

Carter has promised in one newspaper ad that buyers would "never be mistaken for a shoplifter again."

Carter allegedly approached a number of companies offering to show them the secrets of his device for financial considerations.

Carter has named the device Circe — for the enchantress in mythology who turned men into swine. The shopping bags are lined with a low-yield radioactive material that detectors can't pick.

James Finnelly, a spokesman for Pirie Scott, which has paid out $1 million on detection gear for 25 of its stores, said Carter has been into his office with an attorney.

"His whole thrust," Finnelly said, "was that he had something that defeated Sensormatic (a detection device) and that if the manufacturers were willing to pay him, he wouldn't market the product. Those were his exact words."

Carter denies trying to blackmail anyone.

"It's simply business," he said. "If you want to take it off the market, buy it. All I'm doing is selling advice."

Chicago police have warned merchants about the bag.

Meanwhile, Carter says he wants to move on to other projects, including a "cloak" that makes an entire person "invisible" to burglar alarms

9-year-old 'Billy the kid' surrenders after bank heist

NEW YORK (UPI) — A 9-year-old boy, nicknamed "Billy the Kid" and suspected of holding up a bank at Rockefeller Centre for $118, has handed himself over to the FBI.

The 4-foot-5, 90-pound youth, too small to be photographed by bank cameras and barely able to see over the counter, was accused of holding up a teller at the New York Bank for Savings with a chrome-plated revolver.

"This is a holdup. Don't say a silent word," he told her.

The boy, whose name was with held, surrendered with his attorney, Mel A. Sachs. He was later turned over to state juvenile authorities.

FBI spokesmen said the boy was possibly the youngest bank robbery suspect in city history. Sachs said he arranged the surrender after the child's parents contacted him.

"I want to make it clear that my client is surrendering voluntarily," Sachs said with a grin as the boy — dressed in blue jeans, a tan-colored ski jacket, plaid shirt with black tie and a gray wool watch cap pulled down over his brown hair — stared up at him wide-eyed.

"We're hoping he'll be released. "He's not going any place. He's going to be around New York and available," Sachs said without apparent irony.

The boy and Sachs went to the FBI office where a flustered receptionist summoned four burly agents who took the suspect and his lawyer into an inner office, leaving other agents and secretaries gaping after them.

Young mob heads for last round-up

NEW WESTMINSTER (CP) — The days of the Taxisquad Gang are numbered.

The gang, so called because its members, aged 10 to 13, took cabs to and from their crimes, spent their afterschool hours breaking into at least 75 homes, said police. And they netted about $20,000.

Now, police said, the mini-mob is being rounded up.

Most of the break-ins occurred at about 3.30. At least 26 homes were broken into in the past month, police said.

Stolen goods including cash, liquor, jewelry and gold have been found "stashed in empty garages, behind bushes, in walls, under rocks, everywhere, as they (the children) waited to fence it," police said.

About 20 charges have been laid in the past two weeks and police are expecting to arrest more.

A vacation tragedy: Couple shot by mistake

By Dale Brazao Toronto Star

The screams drowned out the echo of the gunshots . . . "Please mister, don't shoot! Don't shoot!" Folke Johansson begged as his fiancee lay bleeding on the sidewalk beside him.

But the sniper on the apartment balcony in Baton Rouge, La., ignored the pleas of the 24-year-old man and opened fire again with an automatic rifle.

Johansson was hit three times as he huddled over his 19-year-old fiancee, Lynn Palmer of Boiestown, N.B., trying to protect her. The couple were on a three-day visit to Baton Rouge.

"I got hit in the chest, in the shoulder and in the leg but my only concern was for Lynn," Johansson said in an interview in Toronto yesterday.

"She couldn't move. I tried to get her behind a parked car but she couldn't move."

Lynn couldn't move because the first of 12 bullets fired by the sniper as the couple strolled through a residential area, on the evening of March 9, had left her paralyzed from the waist down.

The paralyzing bullet had entered her shoulder, grazed her lungs and lodged between her shoulder blades. Another bullet grazed her mouth.

When the gunman stopped firing, Johansson dragged himself to a nearby home and asked for help. When he returned to his fiancee on the sidewalk, police had already arrested a suspect, who had descended to the street with his rifle.

"The Baton Rouge police believe it was a case of mistaken identity," Lynn's father Berne Palmer said yesterday after the family arrived at St. Michael's Hospital, where Lynn will undergo extensive rehabilitation.

Sniper kills 4 neighbors

CORAOPOLIS, Pa. (UPI) — The son of a city councilman, firing a high-powered rifle from his father's hillside home, killed four neighbors and wounded a fifth man then calmly drove the 10 miles (16 km.) to state police headquarters and surrendered.

Friends described Victor Belmonte, 23, as a quiet bachelor. A neighbor said Belmonte even had volunteered to drive elderly people to their doctor's appointments today.

But yesterday, two men and two women lay dead across the street from Belmonte's home in the sweltering Pittsburgh suburb of Coraopolis, after he began firing, apparently at random, with a high-powered rifle and a pistol from a second-floor window.

Police said Belmonte, firing with "deadly accuracy," took his toll within a five- to 10-minute period. At first, in the confusion, police said the shooting went on for an hour.

He then stopped shooting and calmly drove to the state police barracks in Carnegie to surrender.

Moviegoer steps on toe and is slain

MIAMI, Fla. (AP) — Alvin Arline stepped on a stranger's toe as he groped for a seat yesterday in a darkened downtown theatre showing a martial arts movie, A Force Of One.

Arline said, "Excuse me," but the offended man leaped up and plunged a knife into Arline with such force that it broke off in his heart, police reported.

$60 bought hit-man to kill dad who wouldn't let kids smoke pot

CLEVELAND (AP) — John White, a strict father who made his two teenagers observe a 9 p.m. curfew, walked into his living-room after work and came face-to-face with a killer hired by his children for $60, police say.

"He wouldn't let us do anything we wanted, like smoke pot," police quoted the children as saying.

They said the children — a 17-year-old boy and a 14-year-old girl — described how they hid the body of White, 41, in a back room after the slaying on Feb. 9, then cashed his $230 paycheque and used his credit cards to go on a 10-day spending spree.

They spent $2,000 on televisions, video games and other amusements, as well as food and entertainment, police said.

The teenagers were arrested Monday when they returned to their home in a working class neighborhood in southwest Cleveland. They are being held in a detention home.

No charges have been filed against the children, both juveniles, "because the investigation is still going on," a detective said.

Police said each blamed the other for hatching the plot.

An arrest warrant for aggravated murder has been issued for Jerome Watkins, 19, of Cleveland, who police said was a friend of the White children. Police raided two homes yesterday in a search for Watkins.

White's body was discovered Sunday when relatives called police after they were unable to contact him.

U.S. crime rate leaps by 9 per cent

WASHINGTON (UPI) — The U.S. crime rate jumped 9 per cent last year with a murder, rape, robbery or aggravated assault committed every 24 seconds, the FBI has reported.

The FBI's annual crime index of reported serious crimes for 1980 showed that 13-million offences were reported by more than 15,000 law enforcement agencies nationwide in 1980.

The murder rate nationwide rose by 7 per cent to 23,044 cases — one every 24 minutes, the index said. Firearms were the principal weapons used in committing the crimes.

The Southern states, the nation's most populous region, accounted for 31 per cent of offences in 1980 while the North-Central and Western states recorded 24 per cent each and the Northeastern states 21 per cent.

The violent crimes of murder, forcible rape, robbery and aggravated assault increased 11 per cent during 1980, and worked out to one such offense every 24 seconds. The property crimes of burglary, larceny-theft and motor vehicle theft rose by nine per cent.

Devil worship linked to mutilation killings

CHICAGO (UPI) — Another woman has been found slain as police said a series of sexual mutilations, rapes and slayings of women in the Chicago area may be linked to a devil worship cult.

The naked body of a woman in her early 20s, whose hands were tied, was found along the Chicago River and police were checking a possible connection with the other killings. Police said she had been stabbed to death.

Authorities earlier said they found material on devil worship at the apartment of Andy Kokoraleis, 19, one of four suspects in custody.

Police said they plan to distribute a special police bulletin on the four men nationwide in an effort to determine whether similiar crimes in other parts of the country could be linked.

Some of the victims' breasts were severed with a knife or piano wire. Some victims were forced to mutilate themselves.

One of the suspects, Robin Gecht, known to police as "Robin the Ripper" is charged in two mutilation attacks on women.

Kokoraleis and Edward Spreitzer, 21, have been charged with the murder and rape of Rose Beck Davis, 30, while Kokoraleis' brother, Tommy, 22, was charged Friday with the stabbing death of 21-year-old Lorraine Borowski.

Man pitchforked to death after bitter argument over Columbus

HARTFORD, Conn. (AP) — A city maintenance worker was stabbed to death with a pitchfork during an argument with a co-worker over who discovered America, police said.

John Plaza, 30, died in hospital about an hour and a half after being stabbed repeatedly in the chest and face by Charles Brown, 32, of Hartford, who had worked with Plaza for several years. He was charged with murder.

Police told The Hartford Courant the stabbing was triggered by an argument over whether Christopher Columbus discovered America.

Plaza and Brown were arguing as the city-owned truck they were in pulled into the parking lot of a golf course.

Croughwell said Plaza staggered to a nearby maintenance shed where another city employee who witnessed the attack called for an ambulance.

Sex, then murder, in grisly spree ★

Toronto Star special

LOS ANGELES — A chilling account of calculated rape, sodomy and murder is detailed in the Los Angeles County district attorney's complaint against Kenneth A. Bianchi with his cousin Angelo A. Buono Jr., in the Hillside Strangler case.

The 25-count complaint alleges that Bianchi and Buono planned and executed the strangling deaths of 10 young Los Angeles area women between Oct. 17, 1977, and Feb. 17, 1978.

Each of the 10 murders, the complaint says, was first discussed by Bianchi and Buono at Buono's home.

The two bedroom home, an unassuming structure from the outside, had a plush interior and was well stocked with stereo equipment, said a woman who had dated Bianchi and who had been inside Buono's house.

It was in this house, police say, that at least nine of the 10 women were strangled.

Five of the victims were abducted, the others entered the house voluntarily, although there was evidence of some subterfuge.

All of the victims were raped, and at least two of them were the victims of sodomy, or an unnatural sex act, according to the complaint.

Death house

Before starting on their grisly murder path, the complaint says, the two men discussed at Buono's house the prospects of establishing a prostitution ring.

The following month, Bianchi and Buono asked a woman "to recruit girls in Phoenix, Ariz., for prostitution in California."

During that summer, the two are then described as offering the services of two women to a telephone prostitution service in the North Hollywood area of Los Angeles, and that they participated in the proceeds from the women's income.

Additionally, the accused instructed one of the young women, not quite 16, "on how to extort money."

Here is the complaint's account of the murder spree:

In Sept. 1977, Bianchi and Buono, both handsome, ruggedly built men, met at Buono's home and "had one or more conversations about having sex with a girl and then killing her."

Their first victim was Yolanda Washington, a 19-year-old waitress, who was known to be a part of the Hollywood scene.

Miss Washington was picked up off the street voluntarily and subsequently handcuffed and raped.

Each of the succeeding victims, according to the complaint, was murdered in Buono's house with Buono and Bianchi carrying out the crimes. They were:

Judith Ann Miller, 15, strangled on Oct. 31, 1977. Her body was found on high in the La Crescenta foothills north of Los Angeles.

— Lissa Teresa Kastin, 21, strangled on Nov. 5, 1977. She worked as a waitress in a Hollywood health food store, but harbored an ambition to enter show business. Her body was found in a hilly area of Glendale near a fashionable country club.

— Jane Evelyn King, 28, murdered on Nov. 9, 1977. Buono and Bianchi "persuaded" the victim to get into a car with them in Hollywood the complaint says. The body of Miss King, an aspiring actress and model, was found near a freeway offramp not far from downtown Los Angeles.

— Dolores Cepeda, 12, and Sonja Johnson, 14, murdered Nov. 13, 1977. The girls were abducted in the Highland Park area of Los Angeles. Their bodies were found discarded near the Mount Washington area near the city's downtown.

— Kristina Weckler, 20, strangled Nov. 19, 1977. Miss Weckler was an art student in suburban Pasadena, Calif. The complaint says she was persuaded by Bianchi, who lived in the same Glendale apartment complex, "to accompany him to a party." Her nude body was found in Highland Park.

— Lauren Rae Wagner, 18, murdered Nov. 28, 1977. Miss Wagner, a business college student, was abducted near her home. Her nude and strangled body was dumped in a residential area.

— Kimberly Diane Martin, 17, murdered Dec. 13, 1977. Miss Martin was abducted from an apartment in Hollywood where Bianchi had lived. Her body was found strangled and nude on a hillside near downtown Los Angeles.

— Cindy Lee Hudspeth, 20, murdered Feb. 17, 1978. Miss Hudspeth, a Glendale cocktail waitress, accompanied Buono and Bianchi to the upholstery shop and then to the adjacent house where she was murdered.

The cousins will be arraigned in Los Angeles tomorrow.

LOS ANGELES TIMES

'Mean' mom beats up divorcee

TRACY CITY, Tenn. (UPI) — A mother irate over a Valentine's Day message to her son beat up the manager of the newspaper that published it and then pounded the author's head on the pavement, police say.

"I just wanted to show him I missed him on Valentine's Day," said Gail Bray, 28, a divorcee who suffered a concussion and internal injuries in the attack last week. "I reckon she thought I wasn't good enough for her son," she said as she left the hospital Thursday.

Bray said she has been dating Roger Phipps, 20, for the past five years on the sly and paid for publication of an anonymous Valentine's Day message in the Grundy County Herald.

The message read, "Roses are red, violets are blue. Thought I'd let you know, I'm missing you. Missing you on Valentine's Day. I love you honey and love me."

Phipps mother, Shirley Phipps, 39, promptly went to the newspaper's office last Thursday and demanded to know who paid for the message. She grabbed the paper's general manager, Dawn Brothers, by the hair, threw her to the floor and began hitting her until she got the information, authorities said.

Phipps was charged with two assaults and released from jail under $3,250 bond. She faces a preliminary hearing.

Jobless man's ulcers hurt — so he stole an operation

HOUSTON (AP) — An unemployed man suffering from bleeding ulcers used stolen insurance papers to obtain a $3,203.60 operation.

Convincing officials at Hermann Hospital that he was Robert Prater, whose medical insurance documents he had stolen, 25-year-old Daniel Rudolph underwent successful surgery Jan. 2.

But a chaplain-intern who was a friend of Prater's dropped in to visit him — and saw a stranger in his bed.

Yesterday, Rudolph was sentenced to five years in prison for theft of services — stealing the operation.

Rudolph pleaded guilty on Monday. He probably would have been put on probation, but he was on probation at the time for an earlier theft conviction, assistant district attorney Jack Millin said.

Millin said the scheme was novel, but nonetheless illegal. "It's just more sophisticated than going out and robbing a supermarket," he said.

Rudolph's lawyer, Mary Moore, said "it's just terrible" he was sentenced to prison.

"It isn't like he stole $3,000 and had a good time out there spending up a storm. He was in there suffering with bleeding ulcers."

She said it probably never occurred to Rudolph to go to a county hospital, where he could have had the operation performed free.

Upset flier's plane rams girlfriend's home

NEPTUNE TOWNSHIP, N.J. (AP) — A pilot upset over a broken romance sent his twin-engined airplane crashing into the house where his girlfriend was staying, authorities said.

William Fischer, 31, a former flight attendant for Eastern Airlines, was killed on impact in what police said may have been a murder-suicide attempt. The three occupants of the house, including a 3-year-old boy, escaped without serious injury, police said.

Fischer, buzzed the home at least seven times before the plane banked to the left, dived through electrical and telephone lines and rammed into the garage, police said. Both the house and plane erupted in flames.

Mugger knocks the crutches from under Christmas shopper

RIVERSIDE, Calif. (UPI) — A young woman whose rare illness has forced her to undergo 22 operations in the past 14 years was mugged while Christmas shopping by a man who kicked her crutches away and dragged her across a parking lot.

Susan Campbell, 25, was listed yesterday in good condition with a dislocated shoulder, and should be released from hospital in time for Christmas, doctors said.

Campbell, who suffers a rare disease that weakens ligaments, muscles, bones and the tissues that holds them together, was attacked while shopping for a gift for her husband Saturday night.

She hit her assailant with a crutch, apparently angering him. He knocked her down, grabbed her crutches and threw them aside, and dragged her across the lot until the purse broke.

Con tricksters drove sisters to suicide

By Richard Friedman
Toronto Star special

NEW YORK — Two elderly sisters — life-long companions — plunged to their deaths from a sixth-floor fire-escape yesterday in the bizarre aftermath of a confidence trick that failed.

Lee Young, 68, and Martha Young, 72, died in the courtyard of their Bronx apartment building two weeks after a confidence team tried to swindle them out of their life's savings by the found-money trick.

According to neighbors and police, no money changed hands, but the paranoia resulting from the con-artists' harassment apparently drove the elderly sisters to suicide.

"They broke down and poured their hearts out to us last Saturday night," Sally Elliot, a long time friend and their down-stairs neighbor, told The Star.

The "con" used on the sisters is one of the most common perpetrated on elderly people. Lee was approached by a well-dressed woman, about 25, who divulged a "secret."

"She told Lee she had found a briefcase that had fallen off a truck — filled with $50 and $100 bills — and that she'd like to share it with Lee," said Mrs. Elliot.

First, though, Miss Young would have to put up her own money as a gesture of "good faith."

She withdrew $17,000 from her bank account — believing that she would receive $25,000 in return from the con men.

So many elderly people have been victimized by such schemes the police have set up a unit, which is contacted by bank officials when an old person withdraws a large sum of money.

"We spoke to the sisters, and the money was transferred to a different account," Detective Ralph Friedman said.

Although no money changed hands, the sisters imagined everyone, from their neighbors to the meter-reader, was in on the scheme and they talked of suicide, said neighbors.

Despite the help of the police, bank officials and neighbors, the Young sisters grew increasingly confused under pressure from the con artists. It is likely that they went to their deaths thinking that their money was indeed gone.

Yesterday the sisters turned on the gas jets of their stove. Not willing to wait for the gas to take effect they climbed the fire-escape from their fourth-floor apartment to the sixth floor. First Lee and then Martha jumped, as neighbors looked on in horror.

2 held for beheading woman

PHILADELPHIA (UPI) — Two Philadelphia men are being held without bail for a hearing on charges they beheaded a Philadelphia woman with two swords and a machete.

Melvin White, 24, the father of the dead woman's son, and Gregory Tarkenton, 19, were charged with the murder.

White was standing naked on his front porch holding the head of Lynn Smith, 22, in his hand when police arrived there Saturday afternoon, homicide detectives said.

White refused to surrender, police said. He dropped the head on the porch and ran inside. Police entering the house found Ms Smith's headless body, the left arm partially severed, and the weapons.

Police said White and Tarkenton were arrested without resistence inside the house.

Ms Smith had gone to the house to retrieve Duane, 2, after a visit with his father. When she walked inside, according to police, Tarkenton allegedly hit her several times with the machete, then used the two swords to sever her head.

Police said the child was not hurt, and they knew no motive for the killing. A sister of the dead woman, Stephanie Smith, said the woman and White had not argued when they met earlier at the Smith home.

Bloody holiday in New York

NEW YORK (UPI) — Even for New York it was a bloody holiday weekend with at least 22 people slain in lovers' quarrels, subway muggings and a confrontation between two women over a cigarette.

The Christmas carnage also left two people, including a policeman, seriously wounded.

"It's been bad," a police spokesman said.

The worst violence occurred on Christmas Day when 10 people were slain. Nine more were killed on Saturday and three yesterday. The city's average murder rate is about five a day.

The latest victim was a man who was shot three times by a man-and-woman burglary team while his wife listened to him plead with them not to kill him.

Ronnie Wuerch, 27, was in serious condition last night with three bullet wounds in his chest. He was shot when he investigated noises coming from his father-in-law's apartment. Moments after he entered the apartment his wife, Tula, heard him pleading, "Please don't kill me."

In the cigarette incident, the 20-year-old victim took a cigarette from Carmen Velez without asking and an argument ensued. Velez, 24, then left the social club with her common-law husband, William Morales, 24, and returned with Morales carrying a sawed-off shotgun.

The victim, still unidentified, was shot in the neck as she left the club.

6 WATCH SUBWAY ATTACK AS MOTHER SHOOTS MAN

CHICAGO (UPI) — Annette Walker, 22, boarded a subway train with her 3-year-old son and a neighbor's 18-month-old child after seeing a movie—and quickly became aware of the man.

She told police the man was talking loudly and abusively to other passengers. Two uniformed policemen ignored him and got off the train.

Then, Mrs. Walker said, the man began calling her names. He slapped her. He grabbed her by the collar and dragged her up and down the aisle.

Police said five other passengers and the conductor watched but did not interfere.

Mrs. Walker endured the abuse for 15 minutes, then pulled a pistol from her purse and shot the man, identified as James St. Clair, 34, in the shoulder. He was charged with assault. She was not charged.

Wife uses car to slam husband to death in U.S.

LOS ANGELES (UPI) — Mrs. Ismael Alcaraz, angry at her husband, drove her car backwards with him clinging to the open door until he was hit by a fire hydrant and killed, police reported.

They said Alcaraz, 30, and his wife, driving separate cars, got into a quarrel in a supermarket parking lot yesterday. She broke the windows of his car, police said. He struck her and she got into her auto and tried to run him down.

When Mrs. Alcaraz smashed her husband into the hydrant the impact threw her from the car and she was taken to hospital with injuries.

Advice sought in skillet death, witness says

MELBOURNE, Fla. (AP) — A woman charged with beating her husband to death with a skillet telephoned her mother during the act and asked her advice because she was having trouble killing him, a witness has told police.

The mother told the daughter to continue beating her husband until he died, then to call police and an ambulance, the witness said in a sworn statement filed in court during the weekend.

The victim was Dr. John Bradford, 53, an optometrist found dead in his home last March 28.

Dr. Bradford's wife, mother-in-law and two women employees at his office were arrested last Thursday and charged with first-degree murder.

Police refused to discuss the statement or to identify the witness. But they said previously that when they arrived at the house after the slaying, the only ones present were the two employees, Mrs. Bradford and Eden, her 14-year-old daughter by an earlier marriage.

Police said Mrs. Bradford told them she was "fighting for my life" when she struck her husband. She said he had beaten her many times during their 3½-year marriage.

Man shot dead in car parking tiff

LOS ANGELES (UPI) — A 70-year-old Hollywood widow is under arrest for allegedly shooting and killing a 22-year-old man because his car was blocking her driveway.

It was not that she wanted to drive out herself. She doesn't even own an automobile, police said.

Kay Marion Beach was arrested sitting on a bus bench about seven hours after the shooting.

David Scott Bell, 22, who had moved here for Florida less than a year ago with hopes of becoming an actor, had parked his late-model Toyota in front of her North Hollywood home.

She asked him to move it, claiming it was partially blocking her driveway. Bell refused.

He walked to a nearby restaurant where he worked, punched in and told other employees he had to run out and move his car.

When he returned, he found animal excrement smeared over his windshield and roof, police said.

He went into Beach's front yard to get a hose to wash his windshield. He was shot once in the head.

Police believe the woman had come out of the house and shot Bell with a small-calibre handgun.

Police first thought she had barricaded herself in the house and called in special police units.

But when the officers entered the home, she was gone.

A telephone tip led to her arrest several hours later. She had just walked away after the scene, police said.

How you walk could get you mugged: Study

From the Washington Post

NEW YORK — Are you an easy mark? When you're out on the street alone at night, can the muggers tell by just one look that you're a natural victim?

It could be the way you walk.

Crime experts have long argued that many victims of mugging give off subtle signals that ask for trouble. "It's like they're surrounded," says one policeman, "by an aura of muggability."

But until now, they haven't been able to pinpoint what makes a person look "muggable". They'll talk about "a sixth sense I have" or "vibes I get".

That wasn't enough for Betty Grayson, a communications professor at Hofstra University in New York who was teaching a behavioral science course to a group of policemen when she became interested in the problem.

Grayson assembled the tapes of those selected as "most assaultable" and had a trained dance analyst evaluate each person's use of 26 different movements that are the basis of Laban analysis — a dance notation technique used to define and record movement.

"Five movement characteristics were common to all the victims," Grayson notes.

"First was the way they lifted their feet. Instead of walking from heel to toe they picked up their whole foot and put it down — like a Spanish dancer.

"They all used exaggerated strides — either too long or too short. And they moved laterally. Instead of swinging their right arm with their left leg, they moved the same arm as leg.

"Then there was the way the top of their body moved in conjunction with the bottom of their body. It was like their torsos moved at cross-purposes, with the right shoulder moving in conjunction with their left hip.

Football 'sissy' stabs boy, 8

NEWARK, N.J. (UPI) — A 10-year-old boy has been charged with stabbing an 8-year-old playmate to death with a steak knife because the younger boy called him a "sissy" for refusing to play touch football.

Robert Kratic, the victim, was playing touch football in a vacant lot, and apparently began taunting the 10-year-old and called him a "sissy" for not joining in the game.

The boy went home and returned to the lot with the knife, warning Kratic to leave him alone, Kratic, described as big for his age, moved toward the suspect and was stabbed in the back.

ALBANY, N.Y. (UPI) — Committing a robbery with a toothbrush is not the same thing as using a gun, and jurors must be told the difference, the state Court of Appeals has ruled here. It overturned a first-degree robbery conviction against Randolph Lockwood, ruling the trial judge should have explained the difference to the jury. Lockwood was charged with robbing a gas station attendant by holding an object to the back of his neck and threatening to shoot. After a police chase, Lockwood was arrested, but no gun was found — only a white toothbrush.

Gun-toting granny gets her man

PHOENIX, Ariz. (UPI) — A 77-year-old grandmother, a cool hand on a hot .38-calibre revolver, shot at a would-be burglar and then kept him at bay as she sat calmly in a rocking chair sipping bourbon and waiting for police to show up.

Gladys Kastensmith was awakened by a man trying to crawl through a doggie door in her home. She fired three shots to drive him away, but he managed to get in through another door.

Kastensmith was waiting for him.

"She had him down on all fours and told him if he moved she'd shoot him," a police spokesman said. But as she was calling police, he moved. "Just a minute, honey," she calmly told police and fired at least one shot at the man to keep him still.

When police arrived, they found David Snead, 28, still on all fours, with Kastensmith guarding him.

"She was sitting there in her rocking chair, drinking a glass of bourbon," the police spokesman said.

Police kill wrong man by mistake

NEW ORLEANS (AP) — A 25-year-old plumber working under a house near a suburban bank was shot and killed yesterday when police mistook him for the man who had killed a bank guard moments before.

"I understand he was shot by one of our men, said Sergeant A.J. Valente of the Jefferson Parish Sheriff's Department.

A resident of the neighborhood said he heard seven or eight shots in rapid succession and then heard someone say: "I think we shot the wrong man."

The lone gunman who tried to rob the Metairie Bank and Trust Co. got away.

The plumber, identified as Donald Herkes of New Orleans, was shot as he crawled from under a house, a wrench in his hand. He died en route to hospital.

Moments before Herkes was shot, a bearded man about 25 years old walked into the Metairie Bank just a few blocks away and killed Jefferson Parish Deputy Robert Cochran, 32. Valente said.

Valente said a department investigation has begun into the shooting.

You risk your life

By Joe Hall Toronto Star

NEW YORK — It's 2 a.m. in the world's biggest sewer.

All around me are two-legged rats, lice and leeches. The stench of fear spreads through this nightmare subterranean world crowded with a subhuman species of muggers, junkies and crazies.

I am on the New York city subway system where they've had four times as many slayings in the first three months of this year as the Toronto Transit Commission has had in the 25 years since its first subway line opened.

There are more crimes committed in an average two-week period here than the TTC suffers in a year.

Riders set ablaze

And it is a different kind of crime.

Latest thrill for the clockwork-orange-type kids on this subway is "torching" people — setting ablaze subway riders. Two dozing derelicts — among the scores who live in this underground hell clutching plastic bags with all their worldly possessions — were torched in one night earlier this month.

One man, Reilly Ford, 45, died. The other recovered from his burns and fright after newspapers were stuffed in his pockets and set alight.

Another trick of the sick thrill-seekers who cruise the 230-mile system, populated by some Son-of-Sam type psychopaths, is to push or throw innocent passengers from platforms into the path of trains. One man has been killed in just such an unprovoked attack this year. Others have survived.

Mayor Edward Koch last week ordered an all-out war to try to end the terror on the subway. In a plan which will cost the city $10 million, he authorized the recruitment of another 58 officers to the 3,000-strong Transit Police Force, cops to ride "shotgun" on all trains between 6 p.m. and 2 a.m. and police on every station platform at night.

Since the crackdown started last Monday

there have been fewer than 80 crimes reported — compared to an average of more than 40 daily before. The TTC subway, which carries 700,000 passengers a day, compared to New York's 3.5 million, had 837 crimes reported last year — less than three a day. And the type of crime in the two cities' subways is hardly comparable.

Toronto has had two slayings in its subway since the first section of the Yonge St. line was opened 25 years ago. New York has had nine already this year.

While New York is trying to end the slaughter on its subway, a TTC spokesman told The Star one of the major concerns of the Metro police, who are mainly responsible for law and order on the TTC, is halting the growing number of indecent assaults which happen chiefly in the summer months when women passengers are wearing fewer clothes.

Last week I spent 48 hours cruising the 75-year-old New York subway system through the Bronx and Harlem, Queens, Manhattan and Brooklyn. Even with the extra patrols of uniformed transit police, it was a journey through hell for someone used to the boring safety of the Yonge, Bloor and Spadina lines.

On my journeys I visited the 10 most dangerous stations in the subway where the most violent crimes take place in dimly-lit passageways and alcoves.

Staying sober and alert, I moved quickly through the battle zones — skirting dangerous situations as rapidly as possible. Even so, I felt my skin tingle and the knot in my stomach tighten several times:

☐ Riding the Independent line through Brooklyn near midnight, a young man with blank eyes climbed into my subway car. There were only the two of us in the car but he walked half its length and sat next to me. I moved to the seat opposite. He moved next to me again and appeared to fall asleep. As his body slumped against mine, I decided to stand.

At that moment, the lights in the car went out. With only the dull, eery emergency light on, I edged away down the car. Those five seconds the lights were out seemed like five minutes. The perspiration stood out on my brow.

As the lights came back on, the young man with the cod's eyes was half-standing, facing me, his hand groping inside his coat. I remembered the warning I had been given by an eminently respectable professional man who regularly travels the New York subway to "carry some metal" (a knife or a gun for my own protection).

Suddenly there was a loud bang behind me.

I wheeled round to the happiest sight — a transit cop, with a .38 in his holster and a two-foot-long night stick in his hand, had just walked through the connecting door from the next car.

★ ★

'Possessed' tot dies

NEW YORK (UPI) — A 4-year-old girl, tossed from a fourth-floor window by her mother apparently because the mother thought the child was "possessed with the devil," died yesterday in a Brooklyn hospital.

The mother, Adele Scott, 23, was in police custody on charges of attempted homicide.

Miss Scott's grandfather, Cephus Scott, told police 4-year-old Latasha came out of the bedroom shortly after 2 a.m. after an argument with her mother and told him her mother had said she was "possessed with the devil" and threatened to throw her out the window.

The grandfather told her to go back to bed, and a few minutes later the mother tossed the child out the window, police said.

Bikers' girls in sex slavery

Bought, sold, raped, beaten by every gang member,

WASHINGTON (UPI) — "White slavery," sexual assaults, beatings and being traded for cycles are all in store for girls who mix with motorcycle gangs, says one woman who knows.

For 12 years, Mary was the "old lady" of a member of the Banditos, one of the biggest U.S. motorcycle gangs. She has a message for young girls tempted to take a ride with a tough-looking biker:

Don't go.

"In a crowd of young teenage girls, there is always at least one who will want to go for a ride on a motorcycle," Mary told a hearing by House Republicans yesterday on the criminal activities of motorcycle gangs.

"This is the first mistake. When she does that, she becomes involved in a white slavery market. Often that first ride with a biker will take the girl to a club meeting where she will be sexually abused by each club member."

Mary didn't give her last name or show her face to the cameras. She's 28, from Houston, and has been under police protection since she escaped from her husband in February.

Her tale was sordid: Sexual favors bought and sold by gang members, brutal sexual assaults on women, severe beatings and forced involvement in prostitution and drug dealings.

At the time of her escape, Mary said, she was being beaten daily by her husband because she had refused to participate in wife-swapping with another Bandito couple.

"I was bound with tape around my wrists, elbows, knees and ankles and then my wrists and ankles were bound for five days. Each day I was beaten when my husband woke up. I was kicked until my entire body was swollen," she said.

"I was told I would not see the sun come up the next day. He was going to kill me," she said.

Once a young woman joins a gang, she has the responsibility of bringing in living expense money, Mary said. Most often, the women work as topless dancers or waitresses in bars, being paid in cash to avoid taxes.

When more money is needed, they are forced to become prostitutes or sell the drugs Mary says bring in millions of dollars to motorcycle gangs each year.

★ ★ ★ ★ ★ ★ ★ ★ ★

A new hazard on highways -- getting shot or beaten up

By WILLIAM ENDICOTT
Special to The Star

SAN FRANCISCO — During a fight prompted by a highway lane change, a passenger in a pickup truck grabbed a rifle and gunned down the driver of the other vehicle.

After a minor sideswiping incident on another highway, a passenger in one car was shot and killed by a driver of the other.

Whether born of impatience, frustration, rudeness or meanness, an increasing number of arguments between motorists in California are erupting into violence, and veteran traffic officers say they have never seen anything like it.

"I was a motorcycle patrolman for 11 years, 1948 to 1959, in Los Angeles," said A. A. Cooper, deputy commissioner of the California Highway Patrol, "and I can't ever remember the incidents of discourtesy, let alone violence, like we have now."

MAN, 83 SLAIN FOR A SEAT

MIAMI BEACH. Fla. (AP) — An 83-year-old man was fatally beaten and stamped because he refused to give up his chair when a younger man demanded it for his girlfriend, police say.

Billy Lyons, 36, is charged with second-degree murder in the death of Sam Kronenberg.

Police said Lyons and a young woman approached Kronenberg as he sat in front of a hotel where he was visiting friends. Lyons told the old man to get up and "give my girlfriend your chair," witnesses told police. Kronenberg refused, police said.

"He beat him, knocked him down and stamped him," police Sgt. Frank Tootle said. "There was no reason to hit an old man like that."

Kronenberg died Nov. 12 at a nursing home nearly three months after the Aug. 15 attack.

★ ★ ★ ★ ★ ★ ★ ★ ★ ★ ★ ★ ★ ★ ★

Scoutmaster charged after boys branded

MOBERLY, Mo. (AP) — A scoutmaster and his assistant have been charged with six counts of second-degree assault after six Boy Scouts were branded with a metal clothes hanger during a camping trip last weekend.

J. D. Gatzmeyer, 37, and his assistant, Kenneth Willard, 19, were charged after six of the seven boys agreed to drop their pants and get branded on the right buttock with a clothes hanger heated in a bonfire. One of the boys also was branded on both arms.

One scout refused to be branded, police said.

The scouts' parents had complained that their sons submitted to the brandings because they were threatened with physical harm.

The alleged assaults took place last weekend in a wooded camping area in north-central Missouri. The brandings were reported to the sheriff Sunday after the boys returned home, police said.

The branded scouts were examined by doctors, and none appeared to be seriously hurt.

Murderer put girl victim's body on show

MILPITAS, Calif. (UPI) — At least one of the 13 teenagers who were shown the body of a girl murdered by a classmate and kept it a secret has been taken away from his high school in handcuffs.

With camera crews swarming around Milpitas High School and the principal angry over charges of callousness from the unreported crime, police arrived yesterday to make the first arrest from among at least 12 boys and one girl implicated by their silence.

The discovery of 14-year-old Marsha Conrad's partially clad body on Nov. 5 and the arrest of her ex-boyfriend, Anthony Broussard, 16, led to the disclosure that Broussard had allegedly bragged of the crime then took his disbelieving classmates to view the body.

Police spokesman Don Zies said one of the youths picked up a rock and dropped it on the body — dumped down a hill in a remote area and partially covered with debris — to see if there was life in it or to

test if it was real.

All of the young witnesses kept the murder and corpse location a secret, some to protect the killer, police said. They viewed the corpse on Nov. 4, a day after the murder, and again the next day "just to see the dead body."

Investigators said Broussard led his classmates to the body because they doubted his claim that he raped and strangled her.

Thief strands family in N.Y.

By Kelly McParland Toronto Star

A Scottish family whose tourist trip to the Big Apple turned rotten is back in Metro, shaken but forgiving of the thief who left them stranded.

Bill and Isabella Paterson, and son Michael, 17, went to New York in hopes of seeing the Statue of Liberty and a few skyscrapers when they left a relative's Toronto home on a sidetrip on their month-long Canadian vacation.

Instead, the Aberdeen family was stranded in Brooklyn Friday when a hitchhiker they had picked up stole their car and all their belongings stored in it.

"I trusted the chap. He seemed like a nice kid," said Bill, 50, of the young man wearing jeans and a T-shirt whom they picked up on the American side of Niagara Falls.

"He didn't talk much. He just said he was going to visit a sick friend. It's natural to pick someone up back home."

The man gave his name as Hebert Nekow and said he was from Oklahoma. He seemed to know his way around, so the Patersons let him drive, and even share their motel room overnight Thursday.

Early Friday they drove into Brooklyn and stopped for coffee. The hitchhiker borrowed the keys, to get a map from the car. It was the last they saw of him.

The car contained their clothes, five cameras, airline tickets, travellers' cheques, gifts and Bill's hearing aid. Luckily, they had about $300 in cash and their passports with them.

In all, they estimate the loss at about $3,700, plus the 1975 Cordoba they had borrowed from Bill's brother, Doug Paterson, of Chelsea Ave., Toronto.

Pistol-packing town up in arms -- by law

Toronto Star special

KENNESAW, Ga. — The people of Kennesaw are up in arms. At least, they'd better be by March 24.

The council of this city of 10,000 on the edge of Atlanta has ordered every household to be equipped with a gun by that date.

Mayor Darvin Purdy said the ordinance was passed Monday as a warning to thieves to stay away from the city, where the Civil War's Battle of Kennesaw was fought.

But resident Ted Colton, a veteran of two wars, called it "pretty irresponsible" and fellow citizen Richard Butler said it will make Kennesaw a "laughing stock."

Purdy estimated about 85 per cent of Kennesaw residents already own guns, and those interviewed by The Star last night agreed.

"If I were a criminal, I wouldn't come to Kennesaw for fear of being gunned down," police chief Robert Ruble said. While acknowledging the city has a low crime rate, he said robberies were up last year.

Albert Armstrong, a 40-year-old commercial painter, said he owns a shotgun and wouldn't hesitate to use it if he was confronted by a burglar.

But "I don't think it should be the law" that a person have a gun, he said. "That should be up to each individual."

Colton, who doesn't own a weapon, said, "I don't think that's necessary. Using guns hasn't worked before."

However, "Wild Man" Myers, who owns what he calls a Civil War surplus store, said he loves the new law.

Innocent plea in grader killing

CHICAGO (UPI) — A man who allegedly smashed into dozens on cars, killing one man, with a road grader during snow removal last month, yesterday pleaded innocent to four charges.

Thomas Blair, 46, of Cedar Lake, Ind., reportedly told police when he was arrested: "I hate my job. I want to go home."

Blair had been working 12-hour shifts for more than a week in Chicago's attempt to clear record snowfall. He worked for a contractor hired by the city.

Blair pleaded innocent in Cook County Circuit Court to charges of reckless homicide, negligent driving, driving while intoxicated and leaving the scene of a personal injury accident.

He allegedly rammed the grader into 34 parked and moving cars on the city's South Side on the night of Jan. 24.

Playmates ignore pleas -- boy drowns in dunking

MIAMI (AP) — Eight-year-old Ricardo Anderson told his playmates he couldn't swim and begged them not to throw him in the water. He managed to get out of the murky canal twice after being pushed in, but the third push drowned him.

A 9-year-old classmate has been arrested and charged with manslaughter.

Henry and Lena Anderson, Ricardo's parents, who have lived along the canal in Northwest Miami for four years, said that Ricardo had been warned never to play in the back yard.

Anderson said he believes the other five boys persuaded his son to play near the canal. "The boys came here and killed him. It tears me up inside."

Detective Rafaei Nazario said Rick pleaded with the 9-year-old boy, "I can't swim. Don't throw me in," but the boy didn't listen.

And "when Rick didn't come up after the third try, the young boy threw rocks at him hoping to get him up."

Dog drags home macabre find

BALTIMORE, Md. (UPI) — Authorities searched a park here for a woman's body after a dog dragged home an 11-inch, ripped-off portion of a leg.

"There's got to be something out there. This leg is no more than two or three weeks old," Capt. Robert Lecain, of the Baltimore County police homicide squad said yesterday.

Lecain said a woman called police on the weekend to tell them that either her dog or another dog in the neighborhood had dragged an 11-inch portion of a leg, plus an ankle and foot, to her house, apparently from nearby Leakin Park.

Earlier in the week, a dog brought a pair of women's shoes to the same address, Lecain said.

Police quickly took the leg portion to the state medical examiner's office, who identified the leg as that of a woman who had died two to three weeks ago, Lecain said.

Assistant Medical Examiner Dr. Virginia Delan told police a "big dog" could have ripped off the portion of the leg.

The two shoes were light blue with low heels, Lecain said, leading police to think the leg belonged to a woman.

About 25 police began searching the park yesterday afternoon for a woman, Leakin said. "It's a place where we find a lot of bodies," he said.

A Baltimore magazine last year named the park the "Worst Place to Hide a Body" because of the large number of bodies found in the park.

Three cemeteries are located near Leakin Park, a sprawling area, Lecain said. "But we don't think it came from the cemetery. We think it's a woman who died recently. That dog has found something out there."

U.S. home violent place study finds

WASHINGTON (UPI) — Only a battlefield or a riot are more violent than the American home, according to a national survey of household violence presented to a House of Representatives Subcommittee yesterday.

Child abuse, wife and husband beating, sexual assault and sibling violence — all within the "haven of love and mutual support" of the family — were described by three witnesses at the opening of three days of hearings on family violence.

"Violence occurs between family members more often than it occurs in any other setting except with armies in war and police during riots," testified Murray Straus of the University of New Hampshire, who directed what he said was the only national study of violence in American families.

Two sisters try to burn their parents

SLIDELL, La. (UPI) — Two sisters upset that their mother refused to give them another piece of bread for dinner tried to kill their parents by setting fire to the family trailer.

The sisters — aged 9 and 13 — were charged with attempted murder after sheriff's deputies discovered they originally had discussed shooting their parents to death before deciding to set fire to the three-room trailer.

"This is one of the most bizarre things I've ever seen," Sgt. Emily Holden, a juvenile investigator, said yesterday. "You very seldom find children that young with no compassion."

The two juveniles, whose names were not released, used a lighter early Saturday to set fire to drapes and clothes in the house trailer, which was gutted in the blaze.

The parents, Truett and Glenda Simpson, were taken to hospital yesterday with second- and third-degree burns over most of their bodies.

The mother was more seriously burned because she returned to the trailer in an attempt to save her daughters, but the girls had packed their bags and fled as soon as they ignited the drapes.

The 13-year-old, who has been treated for mental illness and returned to her parents in December after spending three years in a children's home, drove her sister in the family station wagon to the institution in New Orleans, cross the 24-mile (40-kilometre) Lake Pontchartrain Causeway, early Saturday.

Husband wielded sword of vengeance

SAN ANTONIO, Texas (UPI) — A man wielding a 3-foot samurai sword captured a teenager who allegedly raped the man's wife earlier in the week.

Officers said the teenager broke into the man's house and raped his wife — while threatening her with a knife — after her husband left for work. He said he would return the next night.

When he did, the husband met him at the door armed with the sword and held him until police arrived. Danny Cortez, 19, was charged with aggravated rape.

Lie test allowed in axe killing case

McKINNEY, Texas (UPI) — Candace Montgomery testified she had to defend herself from a 3-foot axe first thrust at her by the wife of her former lover. When the struggle was over, school teacher Betty Gore had been hacked to death by 41 axe blows.

A jury is scheduled to begin deciding the guilt or innocence of Mrs. Montgomery today.

Eight days of testimony in the standing-room-only trial ended yesterday.

Judge Tom Ryan said defence and prosecution attorneys would each receive an hour to give final arguments and jurors would then retire to begin deliberations.

Ryan allowed testimony from a lie detector expert who said Mrs. Montgomery was truthful in saying she was not the aggressor in the axe attack.

The defence rested its case after Don McElroy, who administered the test to Mrs. Montgomery, supported the claim that she killed Mrs. Gore in self-defence.

McElroy testified Mrs. Montgomery did not lie when she said she did not go to the Gores' Wylie, Texas, home with the intention of harming Mrs. Gore, a school teacher.

Mrs. Montgomery said she went to get a bathing suit for Mrs. Gore's daughter, who was babysitting.

Doctor led double life – as burglar

COLUMBIA, S.C. — Dr. Ian Gale is a psychiatrist earning $100,000 a year. He is also a trained locksmith and police say he used this talent to burgle expensive homes and pile up $500,000 worth of stolen goods.

"He's a modern-day Jekyll and Hyde, a reserved man who practiced medicine by day and was a cat burglar by night," says Sheriff Frank Powell.

Today Gale, 41, was being held without bail here on eight charges of housebreaking and he is being investigated in connection with a total of 150 burglaries over the past five years.

Police who opened a sealed room in Gale's house yesterday found a half-million-dollar cache in gold, silver and rare coins and antiques, as well as the number of a secret Swiss bank account.

They also found an arsenal of rifles, shotguns, pistols and hand-grenades that he'd stockpiled "to protect himself against Communists," authorities said.

Raped girl, 7 hurled off roof N.Y. boys held

NEW YORK (Reuter) — Three boys, aged 10, 11 and 12, were arrested here yesterday for allegedly raping two girld, aged 7 and 9, and throwing the younger girl to her death from a tenement rooftop.

The boys stopped the girls on a ghetto street in the Bronx yesterday afternoon, forced them at knifepoint onto the roof where they attacked them, police said.

The younger girl fell about 60 feet to her death. The older girl escaped and was treated in hospital.

"It's unusual, but it happens now and again," a detective said.

Boy bandit hired limo for robberies

LOS ANGELES (UPI) — A teenager who held up banks in chauffeur-driven limousines because he was too young to get a driver's license has been sentenced to nine years in a state juvenile prison.

William Swanson III, identified by his teachers as a mentally gifted minor, was arrested May 29 following a string of 11 holdups that netted the ninth grade dropout over $8,500.

Swanson, 15, admitted to five robberies last month and told investigators he rented $35-per-hour limousines because he was too young to get a driver's license.

Between holdups, detectives said Swanson lived in some of the city's swankiest hotels and enjoyed vacations in Hawaii and Las Vegas.

Police caught Swanson, described by county detectives as one of the most precocious bank robbers they had ever encountered, when a booby-trap hidden in some stolen currency exploded, covering him with tear gas and red dye.

Swanson's holdup career started in Omaha, Neb., where he was visiting his father, authorities said. The youth then returned to his home state and robbed banks throughout Southern California.

Victim's boyfriend crushes rapist

NEW YORK — A Brooklyn man who was told to strip naked, shot in the ankle and forced to watch his girlfriend raped and sodomized ran down the rapist with his car and killed him.

"It was a case of justifiable homicide," a police spokesman told The Star last night.

Andrew Brown, 25, of Brooklyn, burst in on George Wood, 33, and a 25-year-old woman whom police refused to identify while the couple sat in Wood's car on a dark Brooklyn street, police said.

Brandsishing a pistol, robber Brown forced Wood to strip naked and lay down in the back seat of the car.

Brown took away the couple's jewelry, then raped and sodomized the woman.

A fight broke out in the car and Brown fled, with Wood chasing him on foot.

Brown fired several shots, hitting Wood in the ankle.

Wood was then picked up by his girlfriend who had started the car and followed.

Wood took over the wheel and continued

the chase through the Flatlands section of Brooklyn untilhe caught up with Brown who had stopped to reload his gun.

Wood rammed him with the car, "pinned up against a wall", severing both his legs.

Girl's 'surprise' is bullet for mom

YOUNGSTOWN, Ohio (UPI) — Laura Ellen Coleman, who told her mother to "close your eyes, I have a surprise" and then fatally shot her April 14, pleaded guilty yesterday to a delinquent murder charge.

Laura, 15, was immediately sentenced by Judge Martin Joyce to an Ohio Youth Commission facility where she will remain until she turns 21 or is rehabilitated.

Joyce ruled that the girl's father, Rev. Bobby Ray Coleman, will not be allowed to visit or communicate with his daughter without the permission of the Youth Commission.

'Eye for an eye'

The judge said he felt Coleman's "eye-for-an-eye" philosophy contributed to Laura's murder of Donna Lee, 37.

In a hearing before Joyce last Friday, Coleman admitted he taught his daughter to defend herself when she is attacked and told her, "An empty gun is a useless gun."

Coleman also told his daughter, "if somebody steps on your rights you handle it."

He said different lifestyles of his wife and daughter led to continual arguments between the two.

Mrs. Coleman was shot in the living-room of the family's home after Rev. Coleman had gone to work.

Taken drugs

Police said Laura told them that she had earlier hidden a gun in the couch and when she arose from the couch to go to her bedroom, she told her mother, "I love you. Close your eyes, I have a surprise for you." She then opened fire.

A psychologist told the court last week that Laura was a "gifted" girl who had taken drugs since she was 11, had a history of running away with older men and had been drinking the night of the shooting.

'This is war' gunman kills 4 in church

DAINGERFIELD, Texas (UPI-AP) — A man dressed in combat gear and armed with four guns burst into a church service, announced "this is war" and began blasting away at worshippers.

The gunman had tried but failed to get several parishioners to testify for him at his incest trial, which was to begin today, sources said.

Four people were killed and 11 wounded before Alvin Lee King III turned a pistol on himself. He is in stable condition in hospital with a head wound.

King, 45, burst into the auditorium of First Baptist Church yesterday morning as the choir was midway through More About Jesus and opened fire with an army assault rifle, police said.

A 78-year-old woman and a 7-year-old girl were killed before King could be wrestled out of the building.

Once on the front lawn, King pulled a .22-calibre pistol and killed two men who had tried to subdue him, officers said.

He then went across the street to a fire station and shot himself in the head.

Nurse used antifreeze to spike husband's booze, police say

ST. CHARLES, Mo. (AP) — A nurse charged with killing her fourth husband by spiking his beer and wine with antifreeze may have killed a previous husband and may have tried to kill a third, a prosecutor says.

Authorities said the woman, Shirley Allen, had taken out a $25,000 life insurance policy on her husband. She told neighbors he was suffering from an inoperable brain tumor as he became steadily sicker from the antifreeze over a period of months.

"We think there are suspicious circumstances surrounding the death of one of the woman's previous husbands," said prosecutor Bill Hannah.

Mrs. Allen, 40, was being held in lieu of $500,000 bond in the St. Charles County Jail after her arraignment Monday. She was charged with capital murder in the death of 40-year-old Lloyd Allen, her fourth husband.

Toxicology tests showed Allen's body tissues were saturated with ethylene glycol, the main ingredient in antifreeze.

The woman's 17-year-old daughter, Norma, told authorities, "Mom was poisoning Dad," Sheriff Edward Uebinger said.

Hannah said the investigation into the death of an earlier husband and the alleged attempt to poison another began when the daughter told police Mrs. Allen had tried to kill her second husband with rat poison. The prosecutor said the second husband was still alive and apparently suffered no ill effects.

A medical examiner said yesterday there is a "good likelihood" authorities will exhume the body of one of Allen's former husbands, Daniel D. Null who died in 1978 apparently from a heart disease and acute alcoholism.

'Gentle' guest holds up hotel

NEW YORK (UPI) — A man who checked into the plush Mayfair Regent Hotel checked out with $200,000 in cash and jewels from the hotel's safe deposit boxes.

During the 50-minute stick-up yesterday, the gentlemanly robber — with four accomplices — loosened handcuffs on request, answered the hotel's door and let an employee break news of the hold-up to an elderly telephone operator.

Among the guests at the time was former health, education and welfare secretary Joseph Califano, in town for his parents' 50th anniversary. "I didn't have any valuables, so we're safe," Califano said as he packed his bags.

In a heist reminiscent of the $3.5 million Pierre Hotel robbery in 1972, the robbers, gentlemen all, looted 10 of the 15 safe deposit boxes. Two carried guns.

Pistol-packin' preachers held

Toronto Star Special

WINDSOR — Twelve pistol-packing American Baptist ministers, armed with everything from .22-calibre revolvers to a .357 magnum, were arrested and jailed by Windsor police as they crossed over the border from Detroit.

"They're real fine gentlemen, each one of 'em, and we hated to arrest them but our gun laws are different than in the States," a spokesman for Windsor police said today.

The 12 preachers, all from the deep South and ranging in age from 34 to 75, were attending a religious convention in Detroit and were going to Windsor to do some shopping when they were arrested yesterday, the spokesman said.

He said they were released after $500 bonds were posted for each one. If convicted, they face fines of up to $350.

"Packing guns is a way of life in the U.S.," the spokesman said. "The guns are registered there but not here. We had no choice. We had to arrest them.

"We're always stopping Americans at the border and taking away their guns. Most of them ordinary people — nurses, truckers even housewives — but all packing hardware," he said.

Fast-draw police chief shot to kill

PINEDALE, Wyo. (UPI) — A fast-draw expert testifying in a Wyoming murder trial showed the jury how it's done — he drew and fired a blank at a deputy before the man could pull the trigger of his already-cocked and drawn weapon.

Bill Jordan, a former Border Patrol officer appeared as a defence witness in the trial of Ed Cantrell, a former police chief who shot his own undercover narcotics agent in 1978.

Cantrell admits shooting Michael Rosa.

For the fast-draw exhibition, defence attorney Gerald Spence called a courthouse security guard, who took a cocked gun loaded with blanks and pointed it at Jordan.

Cabby delivers slain gunman

NEW YORK (UPI) — A cab driver fired five shots into a gunman who robbed him, then delivered the dead body to a police station.

The driver, Albert Lew, 41, was promptly arrested yesterday and charged with homicide and possession of an unlicensed gun, police say.

Lew had picked up Bao Yeuh Lee, 38, who pulled a .38-calibre revolver and robbed Lew of $225 as they were driving.

When the bandit left the cab, the driver produced his own gun — an unlicensed .25-calibre automatic — and shot Lee three times in the head and twice in the chest.

Lew then drove the body to a nearby stationhouse and turned himself in, police said.

Six charged in abduction

SCOTCH PLAINS, N.J. (AP) — Five boys and one girl, ranging in age from 12 to 17, have been charged with kidnapping in the abduction of a 10-year-old boy who was held for $12,000 ransom.

The arrests came after the parents of Thomas Beattie paid the ransom and were reunited with the boy, who was unharmed.

Brady takes aim at gun ★ makers

WASHINGTON (UPI) — Presidential press secretary James Brady has filed a $100 million damage suit against the firms that made and assembled the gun used to wound him in the attack on President Ronald Reagan, Brady's lawyer, Jacob Stein, said yesterday.

She lived in fear -- in a VW

BOSTON (UPI) — A terrified Boston woman lived for eight months in a red Volkswagen "bug" after her brother was fatally beaten by robbers in their East Boston home.

Valerie Goetz, 52, has finally decided it is no place to spend the winter.

Miss Goetz, who had rejected several offers of help, moved in with her sister this week.

She began living in her 1969 "bug" last spring. Robbers had broken into her home and fatally injured her brother. She and her brother had moved to the city because vandals had burned down their home in suburban Medford.

"She became terrified," said Paul De-Natali the Maschusetts Bay Transportation Authority which owns the lot where Miss Goetz parked her car.

Many people volunteered to take her into their homes after a Boston newspaper ran a story about her plight recently.

But she refused all help until Tuesday night when temperatures dipped below freezing. After that, Miss Goetz said she would move in with her sister, Sophie Szynczak, 64, in Malden, just north of Boston.

DeNatali said Miss Goetz earned about $100 a week as a seamstress with a Boston clothing manufacturer.

"It wasn't that she could not afford to live in a home it was that she was afraid," he said.

After her brother's death, she suffered several heart attacks.

While iving in her car, DeNatali said Miss Goetz would leave every day for work and eat most of her meals downtown. "She was very elusive and we felt bad for her," he said.

The woman paid $4 each week to park in the lot and sleep.

"Our major concern was for her safety," DeNatali said. "But now the situation is resolved."

As for the Volkswagen, Miss Goetz is keeping it in sight, parked right outside her new home.

Beaten, stabbed Eddie King finally slew woman he loved

By Paul Dean
Los Angeles Times

LOS ANGELES — Eddie King doesn't want to talk about it. He has told his lawyer he just wants to forget that he shot and killed his wife in self-defence.

His lawyer, Florida state public defender Pat McGuiness, says in this King is typical. "Being a battered husband is as much a stigma for a man as rape is for a woman."

King, a 47-year-old roofer and trucker from Jacksonville, Fla., shot his wife, Betty, during an argument on the porch of a friend's house when she reached into her purse. He was charged with assault, then second-degree murder when his wife died last July 4.

An investigation showed that in four years of marriage, Betty King had beaten, slashed, stabbed, thrown dry acid on and shot at her husband.

Last month, Florida dropped its charges, freed King and the media pounced on the classic man-bites-dog story.

McGuiness remains a little surprised at the attention. In the past two years, he says, he has successfully defended five male victims who had retaliated.

"There was a battered lover last year where the woman was every bit as mean as this one (Betty King)," he continues. "He wound up beating her up but was found not guilty in about six minutes.

Not uncommon

"There was another case this year in some other part of Florida (Melbourne) where four women, including the wife and mother-in-law, are alleged to have spent two hours beating an optometrist to death with a skillet.

"These cases are obviously extremes, but the question of violence on the part of women is not that uncommon."

How common is it?

□ Jean Matusinka, a deputy district attorney in charge of Los Angeles County's Child Abuse and Domestic Violence Unit, estimates that last year husbands were the victims of wives in 15 per cent of spousal assaults involving her unit.

□ Dr. Susan Saxe, staff psychologist for the Los Angeles Police Department who has counselled male officers battered by their wives, estimates the incidents of wife-initiated violence were 2 per cent of husband-wife disputes where blows fell. She thinks it may be time for society to establish services and maybe even shelters for abused husbands.

□ Of the 3,500 cases prosecuted or investigated annually by the Los Angeles city attorney's Domestic Violence Unit, says supervisor-lawyer Susan Kaplan, an estimated 10 per cent of the spousal attacks were against husbands.

Hit with phone

In the main, she says, the victims are husbands married to younger women, men outweighed by their wives, or the infirm — such as the disabled veteran who required hospital treatment after his wife hit him over the head with a telephone.

A 1980 study authored by sociologists Murray Straus, Richard Gelles and Suzanne Steinmetz said more than 2 million husbands annually are assaulted by their wives — compared to 1.8 million wives beaten by their husbands.

Wives generally are beaten more severely, but the wife-husband homicide rate is close to 50-50. And the breakdown of methods of assault is equally surprising.

The number of wives who throw ashtrays at their husbands is almost double the number of husbands who pitch mugs at their wives. More women, says the survey, kick or use objects to thump their spouses. On the other hand, more men push, slap, beat up or actually use a knife or gun on their wives.

The battered-husband phenomenon is a final arc in a full circle of domestic violence that, over the past two decades, has been subject to statistical scrutiny.

Horrific histories

Some case histories are horrific. A doctor is severely beaten by his attorney wife and regularly uses cosmetics to cover his bruises and face bites.

A multiple amputee says his wife kicks him "just for being so useless, I guess."

A trucker, a college administrator and a minister were attacked by their wives with fists, beer bottles, broom handles and a full arsenal of identifiable flying objects.

California university and government workers report boiling water poured on a husband's genitals, hot fat thrown from a skillet and many attacks by wives waving broken bottles.

Yet these cases are the extremes.

Chuck is more typical of the quiet majority of battered husbands who have taken it on the chin, chest, shins and groin without calling police.

"Beth's anger was really vicious from the standpoint that there were no escalations in any argument with her," he said in a no-last-name interview.

Children tortured by babysitter

MILWAUKEE (UPI) — Two teenage youths have been charged with torturing three young children while on a babysitting job.

The 16- and 17-year-old youths were accused in delinquency petitions this week of burning and cutting the hair of the children, aged 1 to 4, and branding each child on the hands with a red hot screwdriver. The children's mother discovered they had been hurt after returning from a weekend trip last month.

Wheelchair wife killed husband

ST. LOUIS (UPI) — A 76-year-old woman, who is confined to a nursing home and appeared in court in a wheelchair, has been placed on five years' probation for manslaughter in the shooting death of her 84-year-old husband.

Josephine Naccarato shot her husband, Sam, twice in the back and once in the head and shoulder during a quarrel two years ago.

Mrs. Naccarato told authorities she shot her husband in self-defence after he tried to kill her three times.

Furor rages over rapist's release

TRENTON, N.J. (UPI) — The controversial case of Joseph "Jo Jo" Giorgianni, a 500-pound asthmatic rapist set free after serving a week of his 15-year sentence will be appealed this week.

The appeal came after nationwide protests from people enraged by a judge's decision to release Giorgianni because the stress of prison and the lack of air conditioning threatened the obese man's life.

Judge Richard Barlow set aside Giorgianni's sentence Aug. 6 and ordered him to serve three years probation and pay a $2,000 fine after hearing testimony from a doctor who said Giorgianni might die in jail.

Dr. Albert Valenzuela, who said Giorgianni requires air conditioning and a ready supply of oxygen because of a breathing problem, told Barlow the stress of being in jail was "life threatening" to Giorgianni.

Six rape victims as well as the mother of the 14-year-old girl Giorgianni was convicted of raping were among the hundreds of angry citizens who swamped the prosecutor's office with protests when the decision was made public.

Giorgianni and a second man were found guilty in 1980 of raping the 14-year-old girl behind Jo-Jo's Steak House, a Trenton restaurant owned by Giorgianni.

The second man convicted with Giorgianni, Clarence Sindora, 26, began serving a 15-year sentence for the crime two weeks ago.

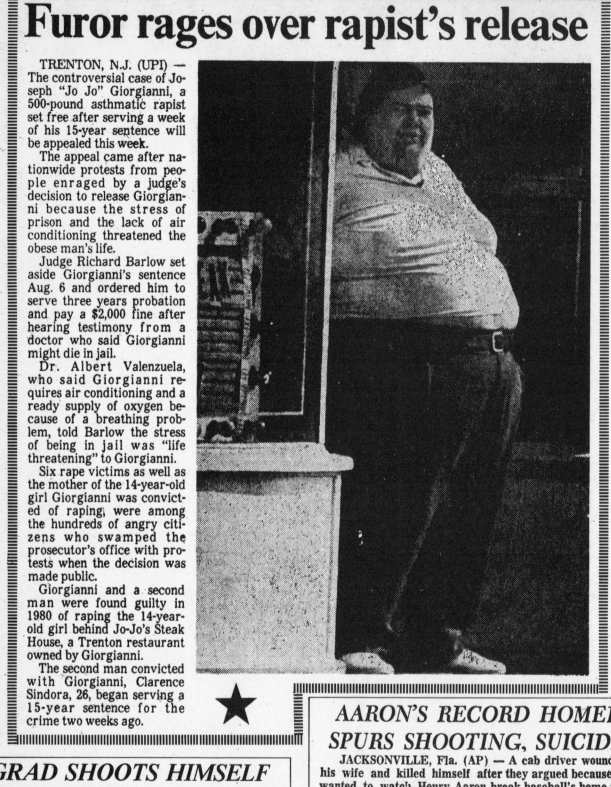

GRAD SHOOTS HIMSELF

WEYMOUTH, Mass. (AP) — Karim Thompson stepped to the microphone at his high school graduation, said, "This is the American way" and shot himself.

Thompson, 17, was listed in fair condition in hospital today. A bullet was removed from his left side.

Police and school officials said they knew of no reason for the shooting Saturday.

AARON'S RECORD HOMER SPURS SHOOTING, SUICIDE

JACKSONVILLE, Fla. (AP) — A cab driver wounded his wife and killed himself after they argued because he wanted to watch Henry Aaron break baseball's home-run record instead of working, police said yesterday.

Detectives said Clarence Weatherspoon, 57, took time off from work to see if the Braves' slugger would hit his 715th homer.

He was watching the game on television when his wife, Annie, 33, insisted that he get back to work. The argument became heated and Weatherspoon pulled out a pistol and shot his wife in the hand and ear.

Violence claimed all four lives

PEORIA, Ill. (UPI) — Donald Shreeves is mourning the last of his four daughters. Like her three sisters, Candace, 33, died a violent death.

She was murdered. So was Beverly, in Chicago in 1977 when she was 27 and Denise in Chicago in 1978 at 26.

Debbie was killed in a fiery auto crash on Easter Sunday, 1972 when she was 20.

Last Thursday, as Shreeves buried Candace, her husband Robert Lang was being charged with her murder in the couple's home near Pekin.

"They're all gone now," said Shreeves, 55, a retired Corps of Engineers employee. "It just couldn't happen. No way it could happen."

But it did.

Shreeves, who lives with his wife, Bea, in Princeton, Mo., painfully recalled some of the circumstances.

"The first three died on holidays," he said. "That's why my wife begged me to stay home on Feb. 22 (George Washington's birthday) when I told her I was going to drive to Peoria to check on a house we had up for sale.

As Shreeves drove, he heard on a radio newscast of a murder in Schaeferville, a small town near Pekin. The victim was Candace.

Beverly and Denise had not adjusted well to city life in Chicago and had become involved with its seedy elements.

Beverly was murdered in her apartment on Labor Day 1977 and Denise, whose body was "injected with enough drugs to kill a horse," was found Dec. 11, 1978, in an apartment building near the one Beverly had occupied.

That was her father's birthday.

Feminist faces murder charge

LOS ANGELES (AP) — A leading California women's rights activist has been arrested on a charge of beating a man to death with a tire iron.

Police Cmdr. William Booth said Ginny Eleanor Foat, 42, the state president of the National Organization for Women, was arrested early yesterday on a warrant charging her with murdering a man in Louisiana 18 years ago.

A woman who answered the telephone at NOW's office in West Los Angeles confirmed that Foat was the organization's state president. The woman refused to give her name.

Foat is accused in the robbery-slaying of Moises Chayo, 62, a Buenos Aires man who was visiting a sick son at a New Orleans hospital, Sheriff Harry Lee said in Gretna, La.

Booth said Jefferson Parish authorities contacted Los Angeles police to say they had learned Foat was in the Los Angeles area.

"She is being held on the murder warrant until they (Louisiana police) can pick her up," Booth said.

Teenagers held in shooting

BOSTON (UPI) — Three white teenagers were arrested yesterday for firing a "random shot" that critically injured a 16-year-old black high school football player as he huddled with teammates on a football field. The boy is paralyzed from the neck down.

Rabbit attacks hunter

BLACKFOOT, Idaho (UPI) — Two hunters told the Bingham County Sherrif's Department they were attacked by a vicious rabbit in the Arco desert.

One described the attacker as "a fairly large rabbit." They said the animal squared off and then charged.

As one hunter attempted to knock the rabbit away with his gun, he shot himself in the foot.

"He was dead serious about the incident," Sherrif's Dispatcher Lynn Woods said yesterday. "He even brought his buddy in to verify what had happened. He sure wasn't smiling."

Deputies speculated the rabbit could have been rabid or may have been protecting newly born bunnies.

Man haunted by memories

Wife, 7 children murdered but he built a new life

PROSPECT, Conn. (AP) — Even now, five years later, the thought of it is sickening and staggering.

On July 22, 1977, Fred Beaudoin's wife, all seven of their children and a playmate sleeping over were bludgeoned to death with a tire iron, their bodies sprayed with gasoline and the home set afire while he was at work on the night shift.

His foster brother, Lorne Acquin, 32, was convicted of the murders and is serving a 105-year prison sentence. A clear-cut motive was never established, says Acquin's lawyer, John Williams, who is appealing the verdict.

In the intervening years, Beaudoin, 38, has built a new life and new home. He has survived the pain with prayer and the help of a woman friend he married two years ago. He has started a second family with his new wife, Jeanine, 25, and their year-old daughter, Jolene.

After taking a lot of time off from his job at an aircraft engine plant following the tragedy, Beaudoin has returned to work but now is on the day shift.

While agreeing to an interview in his home, Beaudoin declined to be photographed, citing his need for privacy.

He says he likes to be alone with his new family and keeps busy with his job and his hobby of woodworking.

"We've got a few friends. We go out together. But my main wish was just to be left alone so I could be quiet and tranquil.

"I have a new life now. That's the way I look at it. I'm really happy with the life I have now. I have a good wife, a fantastic little daughter. I'm a lucky person. Not many people get a chance to pick themselves back up and stay there."

Killer of 6 in Texas 'tired of being pushed around'

GRAND PRAIRIE, Tex. (AP)—A heavily armed trucker who killed his boss and five other people in a half-hour rampage before being shot to death was "tired of being pushed around" at work, his brother says.

"If you kick a dog too many times, he's going to turn on you," Murphy Parish, brother of gunman John Parish, told the Dallas Morning News. According to police and friends, John Parish had been upset about his pay.

"The man obviously had an agenda," said Police Chief David Kunkle, at the end of Parish's half-hour spree Monday at four locations in this suburb west of Dallas.

Three people were wounded and three others were injured in the chase before Parish was killed.

THE VIOLENCE ended after Parish, 46, smashed a stolen 18-wheel truck into a police car and shot it out with police.

"It was like a Wild West show," said Wayne Standefer, who owns Wayne's Custom Automotive across the street from where Parish was killed. "They were shooting in every direction in the world."

Parish, of Dallas, had been employed for two years at the WTS Enterprises trucking company.

According to police and witnesses, Parish showed up at about 8 a.m. at the operations warehouse of a WTS subsidiary, Western Transportation Systems, and shot and killed three men, including his boss, Eddie Eugene Ulrich.

Parish was armed with a shortened .30-caliber carbine rifle, a .25-caliber automatic pistol, and a .38-caliber revolver, Kunkle said.

PARISH NEXT stole a truck and drove to WTS headquarters in the same industrial park, where he killed an executive secretary and wounded a receptionist and an operations manager, police said.

Parish then drove to another industrial park about 4 miles away and killed two supervisors and wounded another at the Jewel-T Discount Grocery Distribution Center, Kunkle said.

Jewel-T had used Parish as a driver but told WTS he was a troublemaker and asked that he no longer be assigned Jewel-T jobs, Kunkle said.

After the Jewel-T shootings, Parish went to the parking lot and commandeered a truck from a driver who suffered a broken foot while fleeing.

FIRING AT HIS pursuers, Parish led police on a 1½-mile chase to a trucking terminal where he drove the stolen 18-wheeler head-on into a parked police car, knocking down a stop sign and a utility pole as the truck overturned and slid, smashing a hole in the terminal building.

Officer Alan Patton, shooting at Parish from behind his patrol car, was knocked 50 to 100 feet and his car was thrown 20 feet, Kunkle said.

Parish crawled from the cab of the wrecked truck and into the terminal, firing at police until he was struck seven or eight times by return fire, ending the violence at 8:27 a.m., authorities said.

★★★★★★★★★★★★★★★★★★

6 teens set youth on fire

ROCHESTER, N.Y. (AP) —Six teenagers, four of them girls, have been charged with beating, whipping, stabbing and stripping a 17-year-old youth, and then setting him afire with lighter fluid, police say.

Michael Mader was listed in satisfactory condition in St. Mary's Hospital yesterday with bruises, burns, kidney damage, stab wounds, smashed teeth and parts of his scalp knocked off.

"He was hit over the head repeatedly with a broom handle and I don't think he knew what was happening through most of it," one policeman said. Two of the girls were 14, police said.

Boy, 10, charged with killing sitter

BUFFALO (AP) — A 10-year-old boy who admitted shooting his baby sitter to death with a 12-gauge shotgun has been charged with second-degree murder.

The boy admitted aiming the gun at the babysitter and pulling the trigger, police said.

The boy told them he took the gun from a closet and put a shell in the chamber, but didn't think it would fire because he had not attached a magazine loading mechanism, they said.

Frances Drozdzak, 16, was found dead in the apartment Thursday night with a single gunshot wound in her back.

N.Y. policeman shot

NEW YORK (UPI) — A man who tried to enter the subway without paying the 50-cent fare scuffled with a transit police officer who tried to stop him and then killed the officer with his own gun, police said today. Lawrence Harris, 27, was arrested a block away.

★ ★ ★ ★

Mom guns down teenager who molested her son, 9

NEW YORK (UPI) — A mother calmly shot and killed a teenager who had sexually assaulted her 9-year-old son more than a year ago.

Denise Spencer, 29, of the Bronx was grabbed by police several blocks from where she shot 15-year-old Leonard Mosby over the weekend.

She was charged with murder, possession of a weapon and possession of marijuana.

Spencer walked up to Mosby in Queens where he was standing with a few friends. She pulled out a .38-calibre revolver and shot him four times.

"She fired twice while he was standing, and twice while he was lying on the ground. After she shot him she said, 'You little bastard,' " detective Horace Balmer said, adding, "She was very calm, very mild" when arrested.

Witnesses to the shooting followed Spencer and pointed her out to police.

She told police she shot Mosby in retaliation for sexually assaulting her son in May last year.

Driver guns down rescuers

Horrified mom watches as car falls back on boy

HARTFORD, Conn. (AP-Special) — Neighbors screamed in horror as they watched 12-year-old Todd Joiner and his bicycle being dragged beneath a car as it sped through a stop sign.

But when they tried to lift the car to free the pinned youngster, the driver began blasting away at them with a .22-calibre rifle. Seven people were wounded.

Witnesses said the boy was dragged about 65 feet when the car struck him in an intersection in a low-income housing development.

The driver jumped from the car after it stopped and ran off but returned a moment later, said Hector Martinez, 20.

The driver said nothing but acted "like he was mad" when about a dozen people, including the boy's mother and his brother, gathered to help free the youth.

Martinez asked the driver if he had a jack and the man went to his trunk as the gathering crowd tried to lift the car.

"Next thing I knew," said Elaine Joiner, the boy's mother, "he started shooting and people started falling."

Martinez said the crowd had lifted one side of the car about three feet off the ground when the shooting started. They scattered, dropping it back on the injured youngster. The driver then fled.

Martinez was hit in the ankle. He and five others were treated at hospital for leg wounds and released.

Todd was listed in stable condition in hospital today with injuries to his head and other parts of his body after three uninjured men managed to roll the car on its side to release the unconscious youngster.

Police are hunting for Alonzo Davis, 21, on seven counts of first-degree assault and one count of first-degree reckless endangerment.

Girl, upset over pet's death, sets herself afire

WASHINGTON (UPI) — A 15-year-old high school sophomore, apparently depressed by bad grades, the death of the family dog and a leg injury that prevented her from trying out for the school's diving team, has doused herself with turpentine and set herself afire.

The girl, identified only as a student at Annandale High School in suburban Fairfax County, Va., is in critical condition in hospital with third-degree burns over 80 per cent of her body.

She was found after her sister and a neighbor heard her screams coming from the bathroom of the family house.

"I would never in a million years imagine she could do something like this to herself," a shocked neighbor said.

"She had a lot of friends . . . nobody can believe she would do something like this," one friend said.

Others said the girl was despondent following the death of her pet, a 14-year-old mongrel dog.

Burst balloon cost his life

CHICAGO (UPI) — A balloon vendor shot and killed a man who refused to pay for a balloon the victim had burst with a lit cigarette.

Clinton Williams, 30, has been charged with the murder of Robert Johnson, 22, of Valparaiso, Indiana.

Driver pulls gun riders move back

PHILADELPHIA (AP) — A bus driver who thought passengers were moving too slowly to the back of the bus pulled out a .357-calibre Magnum to speed them up, police say.

The driver was arrested after several upset passengers got off and notified police.

Trivia test killer gets 99 years

FORT WORTH, Texas (UPI) — A 28-year-old man has drawn a 99-year prison sentence for shooting to death a buddy with whom he had argued over a football trivia question.

Jurors took more than five hours to convict Ruben Lee Dobbins in the slaying of Kenneth Sauls.

Dobbins was convicted of shooting Sauls with a high-powered rifle after an argument over whether the Tampa Bay Buccaneers had reached the playoffs in the National Football League in 1979.

Classmates rape girl, 7, police say

SYRACUSE, N.Y. (UPI) — A 7-year-old girl was raped by three of her schoolmates, once on the floor of a moving school bus and again in the hallway of a housing project, police said.

Her alleged assailants were boys, 6, 7 and 8 years old, and because of their ages, the names of the girl and the accused boys were not released, they said.

The boys allegedly raped the girl on the floor of a school bus headed home from Bellevue School this week.

The bus driver told police he didn't notice anything because of the usual noise and none of the children reported anything amiss.

When the bus stopped the girl got off and the boys accompanied her. They are accused of subsequently forcing her into a hallway at the housing project and raping her again.

The girl's mother took her daughter to the hospital for an examination and treatment.

Police said the boys would be petitioned into Family Court as juvenile delinquents. Their ages preclude any other penalty.

Baby slain for refusing apple sauce

SYRACUSE, N.Y. (UPI) — A judge sentenced a young woman to 25 years to life in prison for beating her 2-year-old daughter to death in a restaurant for not eating her applesauce.

Precious Bedell Murray, 26, was convicted of second-degree murder Oct. 31 for severely beating her daughter, Lashonda Bedell, in the restroom of a restaurant Nov. 7, 1979.

The child died four days later in a hospital. Doctors said her skull was fractured in at least eight places.

Onondaga County Judge Ormand Gale said he imposed the stiffest possible sentence because a probation report indicated she was "a threat to the well-being of this community."

Trial testimony showed the woman struck Lashonda several times while in the restaurant's dining room because the girl smeared applesauce on her face and refused to eat any more.

Mrs. Murray then took the girl into the restroom and beat her, testimony showed. She told the court the girl was injured when she fell and struck her head on a radiator.

Jury frees man in killing of snowball-throwing teen

From Washington Post

TOWSON, Md. — A mostly middle-aged Baltimore County jury today acquitted 68-year-old Roman G. Welzant of charges he willfully killed one teenager and seriously wounded another after his suburban townhouse had been pelted with snowballs.

The verdict came after more than 10 hours of deliberation in a murder case that made Welzant, in some people's eyes, a symbol of the indignities inflicted upon the old by the young.

The shootings, which he said were in self-defence, culminated a dozen years during which he and his wife had been harassed by teenagers in their suburban neighborhood of Eastwood.

About 60 persons were in the courtroom for the verdict, more than half of them media. Judge Austin Brizendine admonished those in the court, "there'll be no demonstration on the rendition of the jury's verdict." But he could not stifle the audible sighs of relief and outcries of despair.

Russell J. White, Welzant's attorney, emerged from the courthouse to face a mob of camera crews, still photographers and reporters. He said he was surprised at the length of the deliberation.

The prosecutors, meanwhile, congratulated the jury on the job they had done. Prosecutor Thomas Basham said he was sure they had considered the years of harassment suffered by the Welzants since "it was in evidence."

Fans commit suicide after news of slaying

NEW YORK (UPI-AP) — Despondent over the murder of John Lennon, a 16-year-old Florida girl and a 30-year-old Utah man have killed themselves.

One died of an overdose of pills, the other by placing a pistol in his mouth and pulling the trigger.

Colleen Costello of Brooksville, Fla. was found dead on the floor of her bedroom with an overdose of unspecified pills. In a suicide note, she said she was "depressed about the killing of John Lennon up in New York."

Her mother, who found the body when she came home for lunch, said Colleen — who idolized Lennon — had cried yesterday morning when told of Lennon's murder.

Colleen's father had committed suicide last February, and "Lennon's death was the last straw that broke the camel's back," her mother, Jean Costello, said.

In Salt Lake City, Michael Craig was so upset after learning Lennon had been shot to death, he announced: "I think I'll end it all."

He then took a pistol from his pocket, placed it in his mouth and fired one shot.

Wife survives magnum force bullet

MOUNT AIRY, Md. (AP) — Bill McCall bought a .357 magnum pistol in 1979, brought it home and tried it out on a cinder block. The bullet pierced the front of the block and "blew the back away." He figured the gun would do just fine to protect his wife, Judy.

But this week, the gun, in the hands of their three-year-old son, Joe, put a bullet through Mrs. McCall. As McCall reconstructs it, the boy pointed the pistol at his mother and, just before firing, asked her, "Is this what I pull?"

Mrs. McCall was taken by state police helicopter to the University of Maryland's Shock-Trauma Centre in Baltimore in critical condition, but doctors yesterday said her chances of recovery are good.

"I don't know what you want to call it — God or what — but it didn't bust," he said, speaking of the explosive, soft-tipped bullet fired at his wife at point-blank range.

Robbed twice right down to his pants

MEMPHIS, Tenn. (UPI) — Frederick Jackson was robbed twice in less than five minutes and when it was all over, he had nothing left but his pants — and the second set of holdup men wanted them as well.

They took his shirt and shoes, but finally drew the line on his humiliation.

"They tried to go for my pants, but I said they couldn't have them," he said.

First shot kills robber

DALLAS, Tex. (AP) — Forty-year-old cashier Kathy Carter says God guided her hand when she whispered a prayer, then shot and killed a pistol-weilding bandit who was robbing the workers.

foodstore where she worked.

The 23-year-old robber was shot once in the head after he burst into the store and threatened to kill the manager and the workers.

'Dying will be easy'

ATMORE, Ala. (UPI) — Alabama death row inmate John Louis Evans III said yesterday dying will be easy — it's the waiting for it that is hard.

In an interview on Holman Prison's death row 10 days before his scheduled execution, Evans accused the media of "making a circus" of the event.

"A lot of kids out there are associating with this thing and they think a life of crime is great," said Evans, who has chosen not to fight his death sentence. "This is wrong and they need to be told that right now. I'm fixing to die because I was stupid enough to take a chance on losing my freedom."

Evans, 29, was convicted in 1977 of shooting a Mobile pawnbroker in the back after robbing him. He had been on parole from an Indiana prison. His execution in an electric chair would be the first in Alabama since 1965.

The Beaumont, Texas, native said he has been deluged with letters from young people, especially teen-agers, who see him as a hero.

"I want them to know that there are laws in society and there always will be," he said. "If they think they can beat the system, they're wrong. This is the only place they can end up."

He said the wrong message is getting across. "Everybody is worried about making a buck off me going to the electric chair. They have made it into a glorious affair and turned it into a circus."

"The easy part of the whole thing is dying," he said. "The wait is the hard part. I just want to get it all over with."

Evans said he invited several of his friends to witness his death. "It will be up to them if they show up, but I don't really expect them to be here to see anything so gross."

He said he did not invite his family and did not want them present.

Prison officials have agreed to provide a last meal of steak, baked potato and a six pack@of beer.

Wife slain -- for $1

TOMS RIVER, N.J. (UPI) — Vito Poliseno and his young girlfriend arranged to have his 53-year-old wife killed so they could collect her $50,000 estate. What they didn't know was that Mrs. Poliseno was leaving her husband $1, police say.

Josephine Poliseno, a cleaning woman, was beaten to death last Saturday. Apparently aware of her husband's years of infidelity, she had changed her will last October, leaving him only $1. Vito Poliseno did not learn of the change until after her death.

Poliseno, 53, and his 20-year-old girlfriend, Barbara Gill, have been charged with the killing along with her twin brother, William, and her older brother George, 21.

Except for the $1 inheritance, she willed the rest of her $50,000 estate to her son and four grandsons.

★ Sorry, wrong back ★

HOUSTON (UPI) — Clarence Ramsey, 17, was standing on a street corner yesterday when a man stabbed him in the back.

Ramsey turned around and saw someone he did not know. The man had a pocketknife ready and was about to stab him again. Then he looked Ramsey in the eye. "Sorry, I thought you were someone else," the man said, and walked away.

Man beaten to death in soup kitchen line

MIAMI (UPI) — A 65-year-old man waiting in line for food outside a soup kitchen was beaten to death with a pipe while more than 300 people watched, police said.

Earl Smith, 41, was charged with second-degree murder in the death of Ivory Scott.

Police said yesterday the incident occurred Monday when Smith and Scott began arguing while waiting for Camillus House, a Catholic charity, to open. Smith left his place in line, got a pipe and began beating Scott on the head as 300 to 400 people watched, police said.

Brother Paul Johnson, director of Camillus House, said he heard the fight and rushed outside to stop it, shouting at Smith, but Smith ignored him.

"He (Smith) kept hitting and didn't stop. No one in the line moved," Johnson said.

BUFFALO (AP) — A man was shot to death by a fellow factory worker yesterday in a dispute over who earned the bigger pay cheque.

Russian roulette kills boy

DETROIT (UPI) — A lunch-hour game of Russian roulette killed a 12-year-old boy who might have been acting out a scene from the movie The Deer hunter.

Danny Turowski shot himself in the head with a revolver at Our Lady Queen of Angels School, Wednesday and died in hospital yesterday.

Classmates said Danny liked to imitate television and movie actors, and may have been portraying a scene he saw recently in the Viet Nam War movie.

The Deer hunter has several scenes of soldiers forced to play Russian roulette.

Classmates saw Danny place a small-calibre, five-shot revolver to his forehead and pull the trigger twice.

When the gun didn't fire, he said "Oh shucks." He pulled the trigger again and slumped to the floor with a head wound.

"I'm sure it was an accident," the boy's teacher said. "There's not a single kid in my class who would even contemplate suicide.

"Danny's a happy-go-lucky kid. He gets along well with other kids and with his family. He would not do something like this on purpose," said Donna Pnjewski, 23.

Dogs scare officer into shooting himself

CHICAGO (Reuter) — Constable Carl Brader, caught unaware yesterday by two large barking dogs in a car on which he was placing a parking ticket, pulled out his revolver and opened fire. He shot himself in the right leg.

There's no work shortage in the mugging business

They say someone is mugged in New York city every five minutes — and one victim Carlos Mazzini. Mazzini, according to New York police, was waiting for a train at the Times Square subway station when two men attacked him, beat him up, and robbed him of his money and valuables.

Mazzini, dazed by the attack, went looking for help. He was approached by another stranger, who demanded his wallet. When the would-be mugger heard Mazzini's explanation, he walked away in disgust.

VALENTINE LEADS TO STABBING

CHICAGO (UPI) — A man screaming "I am not your father" slashed his 6-year-old stepdaughter with a sickle yesterday after she presented him with a Valentine's Day card addressed "To Daddy," police said.

Dorothy Cory was in fair condition at Roseland Community Hospital with a wound to her chest and facial cuts. Police said a heavy coat she was wearing may have saved her from more serious injury.

Thieves sting beekeeper

FERTILE, Minn. (UPI) — Beekeeper Ivo Leiting is one of the latest to be stung by rustlers.

A sheriff said someone loaded up 35 colonies — "bees, hives, honey and the whole works."

The theft brought the bee-rustling toll in the state to about 5 million bees and 13 tons of hives, worth about $20,000, since last spring.

★★★★★★★★★★★★★
Stripped of his dignity

LIMON, Colo. (UPI) — John Smith wasn't hurt by the four robbers he said stopped to give him a ride...but he admits his pride was damaged a little at having to walk naked 16 kilometres to notify police.

Police are searching for two men and two women, all in their early 20s, who picked up Smith, 27, while he was hitchhiking, drove him to a creek bed south of town, forced him to strip and stole his clothes, a suitcase, $43 in cash and a turquoise ring.

Police said the Dallas man suffered no injury "except to his dignity."
★★★★★★★★★★★★★

Daughter held in decapitation

FLEMINGTON, N.J. (AP-Special) — A 48-year-old woman was under guard at a psychiatric hospital today after crashing her car up the state house steps, wishing a trooper "Merry Christmas" and tossing her mother's severed head at him.

Police said she then tried in vain to slash her throat before being subdued.

A prosecutor said a variety of charges are being prepared against Jean Zelinsky in connection with the strangling and decapitation of her mother, Julia, 78.

The incident occurred as state workers left for the holiday weekend. Witnesses said Miss Zelinsky swerved in front of the state house and drove up the steps until her car was halted by a marble pillar.

New York's gold-snatchers a brazen bunch

Toronto Star special

NEW YORK — If you're thinking of taking a business or pleasure trip down to New York soon, leave your gold jewelry at home.

Gold-snatching by gangs of young thieves — some as young as 13 — is the latest crime wave to hit the Big Apple.

Armed with brass knuckles and knives, the gold-snatchers prowl the subways and shopping districts. With sneakers on their feet and their eyes open for gold of any kind, the gangs grab gold watches, bracelets and rings. But their main target is women wearing gold necklaces.

The thugs can make up to $500 a week stealing the jewelry and then selling it to eager fences, police say. In July and August alone, 1,300 necklaces were stolen in street grabs.

Two deaths

The new criminal fad has resulted in two deaths, and has forced the city to assign a special force of 150 plainclothes police officers to stalk the thieves.

Police Inspector Edward Cappello says some of the chain snatchers have become so brazen they rip off necklaces even as police are in pursuit.

Cappello told how a numble chain snatcher reached into the window of a 42nd Street crosstown bus, stalled in traffic, and swiped a passenger's $1,600 necklace.

"We apprehended that one," said Cappello. "Usually, it's a fast yank and they're gone."

Dragged two blocks

Dora Papapanagiatou, 32, was walking home when she was called over to a car to give directions. One of the two passengers grabbed Mrs. Papapanagiatou's heavy, gold chain. It did not break, so the car sped off, dragging her two blocks before she died.

The average age of the gold-snatcher is 16, although Cappello has talked to suspects as young as 13.

With gold selling for nearly $700 an ounce, the thieves have no trouble disposing of the stolen property.

Pizza parlors, groceries and even auto repair shops throughout the city have acquired jeweler's scales. Secondhand jewellers post signs that read, "No questions asked."

For $100 or $200 they can buy a gold chain from the chain snatchers still sweating from their dash from the subway station.

LSD in french toast

SAN DIEGO (UPI) — A woman who plotted bizarre ways to kill her husband — ranging from LSD-spiked french toast to tarantula pie — before finally bashing his skull in with a hunk of steel has been sentenced to life in prison.

"The actual killing was about the most brutal one could imagine," Superior Court Judge William Low said before sentencing Carol Louise Hargis, 36.

During the trial, co-defendant Natha Mary Depew described a series of plots she and Mrs. Hargis developed to get rid of Marine Sgt. David Hargis for his $'0,000 insurance policy. Miss Depew pleaded guilty to a murder charge before the Hargis trial.

Stabbing in line-up for gasoline

NEW YORK (UPI) — Police are seeking a motorist who stabbed another driver to death in a fight over a place in a gasoline line at a Brooklyn service station. It was the second gasoline-line slaying in the city in 10 days.

Girl slain waiting for police

MIAMI (UPI) — Rena Pollard, 13, told the emergency police dispatcher in a calm voice, "There's someone trying to break into my house right now."

Dispatcher Glenn Metzler asked her address and how to spell her name. Calmly, she answered. He classified her phone call as routine.

When a patrol car finally arrived 40 minutes later, Rena Pollard was dead — raped and stabbed.

Officials said yesterday that they are investigating the handling of the girl's emergency call last Friday afternoon.

"I'm not at all pleased with the way this call was handled," said Clyde Burdick, supervisor at the Dade Emergency Communications Centre. "We are investigating it."

★ ★ ★ ★ ★ ★ ★ ★ ★

N.Y. CROWD LOOKS ON AS MAN IS STABBED

NEW YORK (AP) — A 20-year-old man was stabbed to death in Times Square as a crowd of more than 100 stood and watched, police said.

"I had to push my way through the crowd to see what was happening," said officer James Nestor.

Nestor said that when he and his partner reached the centre of the crowd, they found "the suspect was bent over his victim plunging the knife into his body — his hands were covered with blood."

Officers said 23-year-old Pedro Reys Rodriguez of Manhattan was charged with murder and taken to hospital with a knife wound on his right leg.

Nestor said some in the crowd cheered when he and his partner arrived but that others shouted: "Mind your own business!"

Police were unable to identify the dead man.

★ ★ ★ ★ ★ ★ ★ ★

Man ordered to kill son trial told

LOS ANGELES (UPI) — Orlando Catelli says reputed underworld chieftain Angelo Marino ordered him to kill his son with a knife after he had been forced at gunpoint to watch the youth being kicked and beaten.

Marino, 55, head of the California Cheese Co. who has been identified as a ranking underworld figure in San José, is charged with murder in the October 1977 shooting of Catelli's son, Peter, 24, and the attempted murder of Catelli.

Schoolboy bandits

NEW YORK (UPI) — Two 13-year-old boys with fully loaded pistols robbed a 10-year-old schoolboy of his bus pass. Plainclothes police chased the teen bandits and caught them in Central Park. One boy was carrying a fully loaded .38-calibre pistol and the other had a .22-calibre pistol, also fully loaded. They will be charged with juvenile deliquency, robbery and possession of deadly weapons.

Woman loses 3 sons to bullets

DETROIT (UPI) — Mary Moore has watched as her three sons were shot to death — one by one — on city streets. No charges have been filed in any of the slayings.

"I don't have any boys left now," Moore said. Her third son, Darnell, 22, was shot to death Friday on the porch of her home on Detroit's West Side.

The killings began in July, 1975, when Donnie, 14, was shot in the back. His body was found in a field. In January 1981, her oldest son, Sidney, 32, was shot in the chest by a man who raced off in a van.

None of the slayings were ever solved.

"There is no justice in Detroit," Moore said. "They're all gone.

"I'm just crying and carrying on," she told reporters as she held her 6-year-old grandson, Edward, Sidney's son. "I don't think I'll be over this ever."

On Friday, a tenant, Tommie Bradley, 35, went to Moore's two-family apartment to remove his belongings because he was behind in the rent. He began quarreling with Darnell.

"He (Darnell) said he didn't want nobody messing with me," Moore said.

Darnell had a handgun, Bradley a shotgun. In an ensuing shootout, Darnell suffered fatal head and chest wounds. Bradley was in fair condition at Henry Ford Hospital with a gunshot wound in the leg.

Police said Bradley wouldn't be charged in the case.

Callers swamp bank that offered free handguns to 6-year investors

By Vincent Schodolski
Special to The Star

FINDLAY, Ill. — A Southern Illinois bank is being deluged with calls from people across the United States who are willing to make a 6-year deposit of $2,500 to get two free, custom-made Colt handguns.

"It is a good investment," said Greg Bohlen, spokesman for the Bank of Findlay. "It sure beats 6 per cent. In the last six years, guns like these have doubled in price. That is sure better than a toaster."

The smaller bank first made the offer through advertisements in local newspapers two months ago. But after a New York article about the offer Sunday, the phone hasn't stopped ringing.

"My phone has not stopped since Sunday," Bohlen said yesterday.

"We have had 15 to 20 calls already this morning," Bohlen said two hours after the start of business. He said the calls had resulted in 12 or 13 firm deposits from all over the country.

"We have had calls from California, New York and Chicago," he said. "Some people want five or six sets."

The weapons are worth about $1,100, Bohlen estimated, adding that the offer is designed for both collectors and people "simply looking for a good investment."

The pistols, a .357-calibre Python and a .22-calibre Diamondback, are in place of interest on the deposit. They come in a custom-made walnut case made by a local craftsman.

The pistols are made only on special request and are ordered after a deposit is made.

William Cannon, president of the bank, said the pistol offer is a gamble for a bank with only 1,200 checking accounts — Findlay's population is estimated at 800 — and deposits of $7.1 million.

But now, encouraged by the response following the New York story, the bank is going ahead with plans for a national advertising campaign to attract customers.

CHICAGO TRIBUNE

Crowd laughs as train kills man

CHICAGO (AP) — Dozens of bystanders laughed and jeered as a man with one arm in a sling clawed at a platform, trying to climb out of the way of a subway train roaring into the station.

But no one went to the aid of Stanley Simmons, 32, an unemployed cement mason and father of two children. He was crushed between the platform and the train in a State St. station in downtown Chicago.

Subway traffic was tied up for 25 minutes while firemen freed Simmons with a hydraulic jack that tilted the train away from the platform.

Simmons died three hours later in hospital.

Fireman John Victor said he was told at the scene that the crowd was "laughing and jeering" as Simmons tried to climb back to the platform, hindered by an injured arm he had in a sling.

"People don't like to get involved with people who seem down and out," Victor said.

Police said Simmons may have been intoxicated and was carrying a bottle.

Connie Ray, 22, a college student, was among the bystanders.

About 60 or 70 people watched him grabbing for the platform without helping, he said.

"When he heard the train, he tried to get up, but he couldn't," Ray said.

"His arm was in a sling. Everybody saw him. They didn't help. He didn't ask for any. But they should have anyway, I guess."

Pregnant mom robs bank

SWAINSBORO, Ga. (UPI) — A pregnant 27-year-old woman walked into a bank with a gun, forced employees to fill a diaper bag with money and fled in a black Cadillac with two of her children in the back seat.

Emanuel County Sheriff James Mason said Phyllis Kirkland has been charged with armed robbery.

1 in 5 kids make TV full-time job: Study

ANN ARBOR, Mich. (AP) — One of five children watch so much television that their viewing hours are the equivalent of a full-time job, a researcher at the University of Michigan says.

John Murray, a visiting professor with the university's child development program, said that by the time young viewers reach the age of 12 they will have logged more than 12,000 hours watching television.

Although television has often been viewed as a means to better educate children, Murray said hundreds of studies have produced more evidence highlighting the negative aspects of TV.

"When children spend up to five or six hours a day watching television the first thing you wonder is what activities are they missing," Murray said.

Some studies have shown TV causes a sharp reduction in the time a child devotes to radio, movies, comic books and playing outdoors, but book reading, hobbies and organized activities remain about the same.

The most serious concern about TV and children, Murray said, involves the impact of violence. According to one study, 8-year-olds who preferred violent programs show aggressive behavior by age 18, he said.

APARTMENT OWNER HELD AFTER BOY IN POOL SHOT

MIAMI (AP) — A 13-year-old boy swimming with four friends was shot and killed yesterday by a woman who ordered them away from the private pool at her apartment building and then fired at them, police said.

Johnnie Perez was shot once in the head but managed to run across the street before he collapsed on the grass and died, police said.

About three hours later Maria Otero, 56, the owner of the apartment building, surrendered to police.

Catnapped Cry Baby gets day in U.S. court

HARKERS ISLAND, N.C. (AP) — The case of two women charged with trying to extort $18,000 from two brothers by kidnapping their pet white and yellow tomcat has gone before a grand jury.

The owners said they were prepared to pay the ransom for the safe return of the cat, which they said is like a member of the family.

The victim, Cry Baby, is identified on arrest warrants as "one domesticated male cat, white in color with yellow tail."

"It's kind of a humorous crime, but we're taking it seriously — as seriously as if they'd broken in your house and stolen $18,000," deputy sheriff Frank Galizia, said.

Ava Willis, 21, and Sherri Styron, 19, both of Harkers Island, N.C., were charged June 25 with extortion, breaking and entering and larceny. Testimony before the grand jury was completed yesterday.

The cat was taken June 24 from the residence of Frank and Charles Guthrie in Harkers Island, a seaside community of about 2,500, Galizia said. The animal was recovered the next day after police arrested Willis and Styron.

"We got him back, safe and sound," Guthrie said. "That's all we were worried about. It shook us up and I still can't help feeling bad about it."

Tiny thief trained by mom

SEATTLE, Wash. (AP) — City police say they caught a mother teaching her 2-year-old son a trade — shoplifting.

A department store security guard saw the tyke strolling through the budget department, helping himself to a matching set of children's underwear priced at $4.99. The toddler stuffed it into a shopping bag before meeting his mother.

In the handbag department, with his mother at his side, the youngster reached under a counter and filched a shopping bag.

The guard told police the mother repacked the stolen goods and let the child carry them out to the street. Washington state's department of social services will decide what to do with the child.

Pepper mom goes on trial

BUENA VISTA, Va. (UPI) — A woman accused of killing her 3-year-old daughter by cramming black pepper down her throat is to stand trial on a charge of murder today.

Defence attorney William Roberts and Buena Vista Commonwealth's Attorney W.T. Robey said yesterday Diane Michels Pugh, 30, intended to enter a plea before Circuit Judge Rudolph Baumgardner rather than defend herself.

The woman was indicted Jan. 26 on a charge of murder in the death of her daughter, Mary Elizabeth Pugh, July 16.

An autopsy by Dr. David Oxley, deputy chief medical examiner for Western Virginia, showed the girl suffocated on a large amount of pepper that filled her stomach, throat and lungs. She also had bruises, old and new, on her face, chest, back, buttocks and lower extremities.

The girl weighed only 17 pounds when she was pronounced dead at Stonewall Jackson Hospital.

Robey said, Pugh, who is separated, emptied a large container of pepper into her daughter's mouth to try to stop her from crying.

Axeman slays 'rival' deacon

NEW YORK (UPI) — A deacon was decapitated with an axe outside his church by a man who apparently believed the deacon had seduced his former wife.

Parishioners chased the suspect, Woodrow Webb, 36, for several blocks before he was captured.

Driver waved girl to death

NEW ORLEANS (UPI) — Police are searching for a motorist who motioned a 4-year-old girl to cross an intersection as a traffic light changed, then fled after she was hit by a truck.

The child died on her way to hospital.

Police said a driver waved at the child, indicating it was safe to cross the street, but a traffic signal changed and she walked into the path of a truck.

No charges were filed against the truck driver.

WOMAN SHOOTS, KILLS TEENAGE FLASHER

WAUCHULA, Fla. (UPI) — A 55-year-old woman shot and killed a teenage boy yesterday. She said he had been exposing himself outside her house for more than a year.

Deputies said the woman, who lived alone, fired a .38-calibre revolver and killed Max Lee Stinson Jr., 17.

The sheriff's office said they had received several calls from the woman, whom they did not name, reporting that a man was exposing himself. The first call was made April 18, 1977.

No charges have yet been filed.

Vandalism curb: Let students bash dummy principal

By David Vienneau Toronto Star

DALLAS — One of the best ways to cut down on student vandalism is to hang up a tackling dummy with the school principal's name on it in the boys' washroom, a Pennsylvania school superintendent says.

Robert Muldin of Harbor Creek says students will then take out the frustrations on the dummy-principal rather than by defacing walls, clogging toilets, and ripping sinks off the walls.

"We did it in one of our schools, and vandalism fell right off," he said yesterday at the annual meeting of the National School Boards Association, which has attracted more than 15,000 American and Canadian educators.

Student violence and vandalism is a serious problem in the U.S., Muldin said. Last year it cost taxpayers more than $170 million and costs are going up annually.

"Those are dollars that have to be reallocated from our school district budgets," said Muldin, who was participating in a workshop on student violence and vandalism. "We're not teaching anyone with that money."

Violent crime committed by American youth is also increasing. The latest figures from 1977 show that 28.2 million teenagers between 11 and 17 committed 35.2 per cent of the country's armed robberies, 17 per cent of the rapes, 9 per cent of the murders and 51 per cent of the burglaries.

Earlier this week, a 14-year-old Dallas pupil took a loaded rifle to school and threatened to kill a vice-principal but gave up his weapon to another teacher before anyone was injured.

Robert Morgenstern, a criminologist at Eastern Washington University, said school-age youths are more violent today than ever before.

To control the crime boom, he suggested school boards require their teachers to know the basics of criminology, abnormal psychology and drug abuse control. He also said schools should make the police welcome in their buildings.

"Finally, I think we should exclude those students who will not or can not behave in an acceptable manner," he said.

MAN SHOOTS NEIGHBORS AFTER ROW OVER LEAVES

CHICAGO (UPI) — A man shot and killed two of his neighbors yesterday in an apparent dispute over raking leaves.

Harry Curtis, 35, broke off an argument with Clyde Steele, 30, and his wife, Ruth, 27, in front of their home, ran into his house, came back with a gun and shot each of the Steeles once in the face, police said.

After the shootings, Curtis barricaded himself in his home, but later surrendered to police without a shot being fired.

Police said they were told that Curtis and the Steeles had been quarrelling for several months over the raking of leaves.

'Samaritan' shot in head

NEW YORK (UPI) — A good Samaritan helping a bartender put a drunken patron aboard a subway train was shot in the head and critically wounded at a Times Square station.

Police said the man is in critical condition at Bellevue Hospital. A transit authority spokesman said the man, who was said to be in his fifties, was helping the bartender take the man down the stairs to the station when they encountered four youths going upstairs.

The youths asked if the men wanted a hand and when the victim turned toward them, he was shot in the head "for no reason," the spokesman said.

The youths escaped.

★ ★ ★ ★ ★

High-stakes poker was deadly game

ODESSA, Texas (AP) — A roomful of card players "jumped up and pulled their guns" at a poker game, and when the shooting was over the floor was littered with money and three men were dead, police say.

Two people were wounded in the shootout early Sunday. Police found $5,000, three pistols, scattered playing cards and pools of blood in the apartment where the shootout began.

"Right now it doesn't make much sense except that we got three people dead over a poker game," police spokesman Rusty Baker said. "Sometimes it doesn't take much to cause a shooting."

Baker said, "From what it sounds like, the guilty ones are already dead. They more or less shot each other."

★ ★ ★ ★ ★

Gun found in trash wounds boy in class

NEW YORK (UPI) — A 9-year-old boy found a loaded .32-calibre pistol in a trash can on his way to school yesterday. As he examined it in his classroom it went off, critically wounding a classmate.

Killer sniper

Tears streaming down her cheeks, Brenda Spencer, 17, pleaded guilty to killing two people and wounding nine in a sniper attack at a San Diego elementary school. Deputies lead her to jail where she will await a sentence of from 25 years to life in jail after the incident she claimed happened because "I hate Mondays. I wanted to liven up the day."

Frightened Americans armed

By Val Sears *Toronto Star*

MIAMI — The mayor of Golden Beach stands by the sentry post blocking off the only road into town and says: "We're circling the wagons in case of attack . . . we've had enough, we've got to fight back."

In south Miami, a young couple, lovers, hover over the store's glass case. She points to an item, fingers its smooth contours, its sleek design.

"My boyfriend wants me to have it," she says, shyly. "He's worried about me."

He pays and pops the snub-nosed Smith and Wesson Bodyguard pistol into her purse.

Way up north, in Morton Grove, Ill., a skinny blonde girl, clutches a miniature American flag at a town meeting and shrieks: "You think you're gonna control guns? No way. No way. I'm gonna be home one night alone and somebody's gonna break in and they're gonna try to rape me and if I don't have anything to protect me, I'm gonna be one pregnant lady, Right?

"No way . . . I'm gonna have a gun and shoot that sucker dead."

Crime.

It's exploding in America. There were 23,000 people dead at the hands of murderers last year, up from 9,000 two decades ago. There were 82,000 women raped, half a million people robbed, a car stolen every 28 seconds.

Men and women are buying handguns in unprecedented numbers; over 5,000 a month are being bought in Miami's Dade County alone. And the violence, property loss and fear are driving more and more Americans in the direction of tougher laws, more cops, the gas chamber, an eye for an eye.

Waiting there to receive the frightened, the hurt and the angry is the New Right.

Principally, they are single-issue groups such as the National Rifle Association with its two million members and $30 million budget to lobby against any form of gun control.

But it also includes conservative politicians anxious to capitalize on the swellign public demand that government "do something" about murderers, rapists, thieves, con men and bent cops.

Further off to the right, are a raggle-taggle bunch of tough guys — the Ku Klux Klan, the John Birch Society, the slack-jawed fans of gun magazines, the wild-eyed survivalists and The Citizens Committee for the Right to Keep and Bear Arms.

Says New Right historian Alan Crawford: "While often unprofessionally organized, ad hoc, and confined to local controversies, they nevertheless make up an important part of the New Right constituency."

The focus of the conservative thrust toward law and order is President Ronald Reagan, a gunner's victim himself.

"There has been a breakdown in the criminal justice system in America," Reagan told the International Association of Chiefs of Police. "It just plain isn't working. All too often. repeat offenders are getting away with murder.

"The people are sickened and outraged. They demand we put a stop to it."

Nowhere in America is the outrage deeper than in Miami, the most crime-ridden city in the country. In fact, of the nine cities reporting the highest per capita rate of violent crime, three are in Florida — Miami, West Palm Beach and Orlando, the home of Disney World.

Police find human remains stored in man's refrigerator

NEW ORLEANS (AP) — A man who told police he ate dogs to survive has been held for murder after investigators found human remains in his refrigerator and learned that his roommate was missing.

Lawrence John Crowley, 25, of Chicago was charged with killing Earl Nolan, 37, the tenant of an apartment from which police evicted Crowley after the landlord complained he was living there illegally.

Crowley originally was charged with cruelty to animals after police found a dog carcass in the bathroom and about 22 kilograms (10 pounds) of dressed, foil-wrapped meat in the refrigerator.

Investigators said the carcass of a small dog or cat was found in the refrigerator, along with other pieces of flesh.

Coroner Frank Minyard said human remains included pieces of a shoulder blade with muscles attached, a larynx covered with white skin that appeared to have been shaved, and a rib cage bearing traces of a stab wound.

Lawrence John Crowley: Told police he ate dogs.

Beer diet kills baby

CHICAGO (Reuter) — An admitted alcoholic has been convicted of murdering her 4-month-old infant daughter by feeding her daily doses of beer and water. The woman, Diane Kent, 19, told police that she fed her daughter a mixture of beer and water twice a day "to calm her down" from the time she was three weeks old until her death last June. The baby died from "acute alcohol intoxication." She had a fatty liver, indicative of chronic alcoholism, an autopsy showed. Kent faces a minimum prison term of 20 years.

Boy, 3, kills himself with mother's gun

LOS ANGELES (UPI) — A 3-year-old boy playing with his mother's .38-calibre handgun shot and killed himself as she slept beside him, police say.

A police spokesman said the fully loaded gun was kept near the headboard of the mother's bed.

He's the ultimate victim

Think you've got troubles?

Well, you're probably better off than 56-year-old **Mike Maryn** of Passiac, N.J., who in the past five years has:

☐ Been involved in 17 car accidents;

☐ Had his house broken into nine times, with the burglars beating him up four times,

☐ Had his luggage stolen 13 times;

☐ Been swindled twice on real estate deals.

So after all that, it's no surprise that Mike is now resting in hospital — after being mugged for the seventh time.

NEW YORK (UPI) — A French free-lance photographer taking pictures for a magazine article on how safe New York City parks are for children was stabbed by a man trying to steal his camera in Central Park. "The irony of it was a little weird," said Norma Rothenberg, of McCall's Working Mother magazine.

She loved him to death

SANTA ANA, Calif. (UPI) — Harry Weisen, whose girl friend trusted him with her life in a game of Russian roulette, has been convicted of involuntary manslaughter for taking it.

According to trial testimony, Weisen, 32, asked Diane Thorn, 22, how much she trusted him.

"With my life," she replied.

To test her faith, Weisen placed a .38-calibre revolver, with four of the six chambers loaded, to her head and pulled the trigger. The pistol fired, killing her instantly.

'Demented nude' puts the bite on

PHILADELPHIA, Pa. (AP) — A 65-year-man and a police officer are recuperating from bites suffered in an encounter with what police described as a "demented, nude male."

Officer James Farmbry, responding to a call, found John Garrison, 65, being attacked and bitten by a man identified as Herman Gunther, 19. Garrison's wife told police the attack began when her husband answered the door.

Farmbry lost the tip of his thumb when the man turned on him in the weekend incident, police said. The thumbtip was sewn back but doctors are not certain it would stay, police said.

"He was also bitten on the cheek," the spokesman said, "and the guy just stayed with it — hung on. It took a second officer to get the guy off him."

Witch scalds man to death

CHICAGO (UPI) — A self-proclaimed witch scalded, beat and starved her male roommate because he "twisted the little paws" of her four pet cats, her murder trail has been told.

And having scalded him, she didn't call for an ambulance for six days.

Yvonne Kleinfelder, 45, has been charged with the murder of John Comer, 46, found naked on the foor of her apartment May 1, critically burned over 50 per cent of his body.

A key witness, Hermia Ruby Brewer has testified that Kleinfelder had allowed cats to climb all over the dying man for six days.

Brewer told court the woman had told her: "I scalded him and beat him with belts. I was sick of his mouth, and he twisted the little paws of my cats."

The victim, Comer, himself had told police when he was being put in an ambulance: "Yvonne boiled me." He died in a hospital the next day.

★ ★ ★ ★ ★ ★ ★ ★ ★ ★ ★ ★ ★ ★ ★ ★ ★ ★

NEW YORK (UPI) — A man who was hit over the head with a teacup in an argument with another man fell down a flight of stairs and died, police said. The second man has been charged with homicide.

★ ★ ★ ★ ★ ★ ★ ★ ★ ★ ★ ★ ★ ★ ★ ★ ★ ★

Elderly afraid of teens: Study

UNIVERSITY PARK, Pa. (UPI) — Elderly people living in American cities are so afraid of teenagers many of them remain indoors after 3 p.m., a new study reports.

The study by Geoffrey C. Godbey, Pennsylvania State University professor of recreation and parks, also found that fear of crime keeps many of the elderly away from senior-citizen centres, parks and other places where they would normally go.

Godbey found that 66 per cent of about 2,000 people in his study said fear of crime affected the use of such facilities.

"Everyone knows that many older

people are afraid to leave home after dark, but we were surprised to find that 3 p.m. is a cut-off hour, too," Godbey said. "About one-fifth of the elderly in our study wanted to be home by the time school let out."

The fear of teenagers is so great, the study found, that 88 per cent of those surveyed said many times they cross the street or change directions to avoid them.

The study, funded by the Andrus Foundation of the American Association of Retired Persons, was conducted in several U.S. cities including Pittsburgh, Philadelphia, Boston, Baltimore, and Newark, N.J.

Nine per cent of the elderly in the study had been crime victims within the 12 months before the survey. Most had been robbed or had their homes burglarized.

"There is a tendency to think old people are unreasonable in their fear, that they curtail activities when there is no need to do so," Godbey said. "But we found a high correlation between fear and victimization."

A total of 33 robberies, 22 assaults and 5 other crimes had been committed against the elderly en route to senior citizen centres in a 12-month period, the researcher was told.

'David did it,' dying mom tells daughter as son, 14 held in shotgun slaying

DALLAS (UPI) — "I just shot both my parents with a shotgun."

With those words, police say, 14-year-old David Keeler turned himself in following the brutal slayings Sunday of Texas oil executive William A. Keeler and his wife, Anita.

The couple were found in their north Dallas home by their daughter, Barbara, 27. Keeler, 53-year-old president of ARCO Oil and Gas Co., was unconscious. Mrs. Keeler was barely alive.

"David did it," Barbara said her mother told her just before she died.

Yesterday, an attorney asked that psychological tests be conducted on the youth, who is being held on two counts of delinquent conduct. Because of his age, he cannot stand trial as an adult and will not serve more than four years if convicted, the Dallas County district attorney's office said.

The shootings took place shortly after Keeler and his parents returned from church on Sunday.

Investigators found a 12-gauge semi-automatic shotgun and seven spent cartridges at the scene.

Doug Mulder, an attorney hired to defend Keeler, asked in a hearing yesterday that psychiatric and psychological tests be conducted on the youth.

"A juvenile judge cannot sentence Keeler to a term beyond his 18th birthday (in the juvenile detention centre)," said Dee Miller, assistant district attorney. Under Texas law, a

David Keeler: Will not serve more than four years if convicted of shooting deaths of his parents.

youth must be 15 to be certified as an adult or stand trial in criminal court, said assistant District Attorney Hal Gaither.

"Everything from misdemeanor to capital felony is considered delinquent conduct," he said. "We simply cannot charge a 14-year-old with murder. He's not considered a criminal in the eyes of the law."

★★★★★★★★★★★★★★★★★★

Party host shot dead

NEW HAVEN, Conn. (UPI) — The host of a New Year's Eve party was shot dead early yesterday during an argument with a guest over when the house party should end, police said.

Calixto Rodriguez was arrested in his car on the Connecticut Turnpike 30 minutes later and charged in the slaying of William Pujols, 30, of New Haven. Police said party guests said the shooting followed an argument between the two men.

★★★★★★★★★★★★★★★★★★

Boy, 13, tries to rob bank — with knife

AUSTIN, Tex. (Reuter) — A 13-year-old boy armed with a hunting knife tried to rob a savings bank so that he could get some money to go and live near the Canadian border, police said yesterday.

The boy, whose identity was withheld because of his age, walked into a North Austin bank, pulled out the knife and told a receptionist he was robbing the bank, a police spokesman said.

Boy bandit threatens to kill waitress

DALLAS, Tex. (AP) — In the second hold-up this week by a boy bandit, a tough-talking robber between 10 and 12 years old, threatened to kill a fast-food restaurant waitress if she resisted.

The boy, along with a companion who police say was about 20, robbed two restaurants in 25 minutes and made off with $600, police said yesterday.

At the second restaurant, the boy, backed by his gun-toting companion, told the waitress "if I resisted he would blow me away," said Sharon Bautisti.

A 9-year-old unidentified New York boy dubbed "Billy the Kid" by reporters, surrendered to the FBI Friday for robbing a bank of $118.

In the Texas case, a female restaurant employee told police the pair walked up to the counter and handed her a note saying: "This is a hold-up. Don't be scared." The bandits took $400.

Woman watched son killed for bad spelling gets 8 years' prison

INDIANAPOLIS — A woman who did nothing to save her 4-year-old son from a fatal beating has been given eight years in prison.

A jury ruled LaHanna Smith, 21, was guilty of involuntary manslaughter and neglect of a dependent by not going to the aid of her son, Eric, while he was being beaten by her boyfriend for failing to spell "butterfly." The boyfriend has been convicted of murder and sentenced to 60 years in prison.

Spanked boy stabs grandma

CHARLOTTE, N.C. (CP) — A 12-year-old boy, angry over a spanking, has been charged with stabbing his grandmother to death with a butcher knife, police say.

Police said yesterday O'Nellie Chambers, 71, of Monroe, was stabbed several times as she lay in bed.

Britons beaten up in Florida

MIAMI (AP) — A British family has decided not to look for a home in Florida after being terrorized and robbed of $4,500 in cash and traveller's cheques by a dozen assailants who surrounded their car after a minor accident.

"They (police) said I never should have stopped," Joseph Miller said yesterday. "But in our country you don't have a accident, no matter how small, and not stop."

Miller, his wife, Lillie, their two children and two nieces were driving from the airport to their motel when they got lost and had a collision in an area of Miami where several people were pulled from cars and fatally beaten during riots last May.

Miller got out to talk to the other driver and was surrounded by about a dozen people, who demanded money and beat up Miller and his 32-year-old wife, police said.

Flight bag

The assailants escaped with Miller's wallet and flight bag, containing passports, airline tickets, $2,000 in cash, $2,500 in traveller's cheques, credit cards and jewelry.

"We stayed there," said Miller, who suffered minor injuries. "We didn't know what to do."

Miller, runs a heating and plumbing business in St. Mellion, England and considered looking for a second home in Florida, said the incident "changed our minds."

Bank Robbery Prevention Foiled

NEW YORK (UPI) — While Police Commissioner Robert McGuire was telling reporters of his plan to halt New York city's bank robbery spree, two more banks were held up. And two more. Then there was a $2-million armored car heist.

Today, authorites were still trying to figure out how much money was taken in 11 robberies yesterday — 10 banks and the Brink's armored car were hit.

And while police and bank officials argued over whether bank security was as tight as it should be, the armored car robbery brought this wry comment from one cop: "They're cheating on us now. They aren't even letting them get the loot into the bank before they swipe it."

Soaring robberies

This is how bad things have gotten in the nation's largest city:

☐ In July, a record 125 banks were held up in the city. The old record was 84 in a single month. In the first 21 days in August, there have been 119 bank robberies.

☐ So far this year, police said, there have been "more than 570" bank robberies, compared with a total of 677 for all of last year.

☐ Last Friday, a police officer was killed after a bank robbery near Grand Central Station; Monday, a bank teller was killed when a gunman robbed a European-American bank branch; last month, a plainclothes officer was seriously wounded in a shootout near Times Square after another hold-up.

McGuire has responded to the bank holdups by criticizing the banks for "giving in" to criminals. And he announced yesterday he was creating special squads to deal with the recent rash of thefts.

It was as McGuire was detailing his plan to reporters that two banks were held up. Shortly after he finished speaking, another pair were hit.

McGuire said he will talk with bank officials about what he said was a "sense" among detectives that banks have reduced their attempts to stop the robberies.

"There is a sense now there is no viable security in banks," he said. "The suggestion people are safer by giving in to lawlessness is not borne out by experience."

The recent fatalities, McGuire said, proved it was not productive to "do away with all security, allow people to rob your institution, and hope you're not injured in the process."

A trade-off

Citibank acknowledged there was "always a trade-off" between security and providing a pleasant environment for customers to do business.

But Richard Kovacenich, senior vice-president for Citibank's New York banking division, said Citibank has not found armed guards or bullet-proof glass to be particularly effective in stopping robberies. "We have robberies in branches where there are bullet-proof barriers and armed guards," he said.

McGuire said the FBI and city police were preparing a joint team of investigators to handle the robberies.

But he said it is unarmed "note-passing" robberies that are escalating the fastest. In those heists, a robber simply hands a cashier a note demanding money and walks out with the cash.

Note jobs

Seven of yesterday's holdups were "note jobs" in which a robber simply walked into a branch, passed a note demanding money, and walked out with cash.

In the Wall Street area, two gunmen forced their way into a Brink's armored car carrying $2,193,000 in 38 bags. The FBI said 34 of the bags were taken by the robbers, who drove off in a fish truck with a guard and a bystander as hostages. The thieves later parked the truck and fled with the loot. The captives freed themselves.

The FBI said it was not until the two hostages reported what had happened that the police realized the armored car had been robbed because the other two guards were still collecting money inside the building.

Brinks officials offered a $100,000 reward.

It was the third multi-million-dollar holdup in New York City in eight months. Gunmen took $5 million in cash and $850,000 in jewelry Dec. 11 from a cargo terminal at Kennedy Airport — the biggest cash heist in U.S. history. Robbers took more than $2 million from a Wells Fargo armored car on Staten Island Dec. 20.

In January, the FBI told the city it would no longer investigate unarmed "note-passing" heists because it did not have enough agents to cover all the cases.

Teen shot dead

LEVELLAND, Tex. (AP) — A 71-year-old man has shot dead a teenage driver of a stolen pickup after the vehicle crashed through the living room wall of the man's home. Police said the pickup ran a stop sign at an intersection, then jumped a curb and slammed into the house. The youth got out of the pickup and began hitting the man's wife. He then attacked the man who fired once.

Nun kills mom with crucifix

SAN FRANCISCO (AP-UPI) — A nun charged with beating her 75-year-old mother to death with a crucifix in a seven-hour exorcism ritual has been found not guilty of manslaughter by reason of insanity.

Even as the mother, Rose, lay dying, Anna Sangiacomo, 45, was making plans to take her on a vacation in Europe, Judge Claude Perasso said.

She continued to beat her mother with the crucifix and a slipper even after the old woman had died, he said.

Teenage Jews learn to shoot

By Mark A. Stein
Los Angeles Times

LOS ANGELES — Gingerly, the thin, frail-looking 13-year-old girl lifts a heavy, .38-calibre revolver at arm's length and takes aim down its thick, blue-steel barrel.

Cooly, Dina Mizrahi, squeezes off three deafening rounds . . . boom! and her determined grimace melts into a wide satisfied grin.

A short while later, 16-year-old John, who refuses to give his last name, helps his baby-faced younger brother Eric to shoulder a powerful semi-automatic BK91 — the civilian version of the West German army's G3 assault rifle.

With John helping him absorb the weapon's sharp recoil, Eric begins eagerly blasting away at a neat row of human silhouettes printed on paper targets and embellished with bright white swastikas.

Dina, John and Eric are three of perhaps hundreds of people here — ranging from pre-teenagers to post-retirees — who've been trained at various locations in the nearby Santa Clarita Valley in the last decade. The training is organized by the militant Jewish Defence League to counter increasingly active neo-Nazi groups and the resurgent Ku Klux Klan.

"We don't believe a race war or another Holocause is imminent," says Barry Krugel, self-described chief of operations for the league here, "But the potential for violence against Jews is real.

"We want to prepare our people for any eventuality . . . We have to be ready to defend ourselves."

Defence for the Defence League comes in two stages — the "familiarization" class for beginners, such as the one at which the three teenagers practiced, and an advanced class for people who Krugel says "show promise."

Krugel, Jewish Defence League leader Irv Rubin, and David, a weapons expert who also declined to give his last name, estimate that from 400 to 900 people have taken the basic course since it was first offered in 1971.

The quasi-military operation — "We're not a paramilitary organization," says one leader, "because we don't want the police causing us trouble" — is not unique.

Neo-Facist groups such as the Ku Klux Klan have recently unveiled similar training camps for their followers. The KKK and the Hare Krishna religious sect, are under surveillance by the FBI because of their potentially illegal weapons caches. But the Defence League is not.

The exact size and composition of the league's arsenal is unknown.

Among other things, Krugel says, it contains:

☐ "Several" Ruger Mini-14s, an easy-to-conceal version of the M-14 rifle, the standard weapon of U.S. forces in the first years of the Viet Nam War;

☐ "Several M-1 carbines also used in the past by U.S. armed forces; and

☐ A number of .22-calibre rifles.

Even the youngest of the trainees express a fatalistic acceptance of the need to be armed.

"To tell the truth, firing a weapon is not all that fun," says 13-year-old Dina Mizrahi, who was born in Egypt but now lives here, "It's kind of scary. But I tell you, it's a lot scarier to be around a gun if a Klansman is pointing it at you."

Group's founder held in rattlesnake attack

LOS ANGELES (UPI) — Charles Dederich, Founder of the Synanon drug rehabilitation movement, was arrested in Arizona yesterday on a California warrant charging suspicion of conspiracy to commit murder in a rattlesnake attack on a Los Angeles lawyer.

Dederich was wanted in connection with the attack on Paul Morantz, who was bitten on the hand Oct. 10 by a rattlesnake — with its warning rattle removed — that had been placed in the mailbox of his Pacific Palisades home. Morantz had won a $300,000 judgment against Synanon.

Two die for parking space

HARTFORD, Conn. (UPI) — A man was charged today with beating his brother and sister-in-law to death in a dispute over a parking space in the back yard of the home they shared.

Oscar Martinez DeJesus, 41, of Hartford, was holding a metal pipe and standing next to the two badly beaten bodies when police arrived at the home where all three lived, an official said.

Woman shoots self on TV

SARASOTA, Fla. (AP) — A local television personality shot herself in the head today while h e r morning program w a s on the air. The woman, Chris Chubbuck, was reported in critical condition in hospital.

Officials of WXLT-TV said Miss Chubbuck, 3 0, suddenly announced on the air: "In keeping with Channel 40's policy of having the news first you are going to s e e another first—an attempted suicide." Then she put the gun to her head and pulled the trigger.

Pair's pistol practice backfires

MIAMI (UPI) — Bert Koota, 65, and his wife, Shirley, 62, went to a pistol range to learn how to use their new 22-calibre automatic. It didn't work out very well.

In the midst of the lesson, Mrs. Koota squeezed off a round and the hot cartridge flew from the chamber of the pistol down the front of her dress. It startled her so badly she whirled around and shot her husband in the leg. Koota was taken to a local hospital. Police said his condition was not serious.

'Death's Angel' nurses bet

LAS VEGAS, Nev. (UPI-AP) — A nurse nicknamed "Death's Angel" decided which patients would die and her co-workers in a hospital near Vegas' famous gambling strip made bets on who would die each day.

The midnight supervisor of the hospital's 10-bed life support unit disconnected the life-lines of critically ill patients with the help of a boy friend, an informed source said yesterday.

Her co-workers at Sunrise Hospital knew what was going on and made bets on the life-and-death game, said a law enforcement source.

The bets were placed on the time a patient would die and money was put in an envelope until the winner was determined.

Police began a probe last week but refused to disclose details.

"It makes me as sick as anything I can think of," said David Brandsness, administrator of the hospital.

He confirmed that "more than two" hospital employees were suspended yesterday.

The Las Vegas Review-Journal said one patient's oxygen supply had been tampered with and that there were other cases in which life-sustaining measures had been impaired.

How many patients might have died in this way is unknown. Because the nurse worked at the 666-bed hospital for three years, investigators are poring over coroner's reports and medical records of patients who died in the special unit during that time.

The investigation began when a nurse went to police after overhearing a conversation about the death of a woman March 1, followed by the death of a man a day later.

She heard two hospital staff members discussing the woman's death, and a remark that life support equipment had to be switched on and off several times before the patient expired.

Mistook mom-in-law? So he axed her

VIRGINIA BEACH, Va. (UPI) — Disne Lloyd, 30, confessed she killed her mother but her husband, Orval Wyatt Lloyd of Dallas, Texas, who told police he mistook his 270-pound mother-in-law for a raccoon, has been convicted of second-degree murder for slaying Margaret Wise, 49, with a hatchet.

A Virginia Beach circuit court jury deliberated four hours Friday before finding Lloyd, 33, guilty and sentenced him to five years in prison for unpremeditated murder of Wise on the garage floor of her Virginia Beach home. She had been hit more than 18 times with a hatchet.

Man took muggers' 'toy' gun, shot friend

SANTA MONICA, Calif. (AP) — A man who took home a pistol he had wrested from muggers accidentally shot his room-mate to death.

Then, when three other room-mates went to get help, all three were robbed and one was wounded by a gunman, Santa Monica police say.

Mauricio Garcia, 44, was walking home early yesterday when he was beaten and robbed by two men, but he managed to grab a pistol from one of them before they fled.

Thinking the gun was a toy, he took it home and showed it to his room-mates. He playfully pulled the trigger twice, hitting one in the abdomen. Garcia was booked for investigation of murder.

30 days for shooting thumb off

ECKVILLE, Alta. (CP) — An 18-year-old area youth who shot his girlfriend's thumb off with a .303-calibre rifle has been sentenced to 30 days in jail.

David Duncan pleaded guilty to the dangerous use of a fire-arm after an Oct. 1 domestic dispute at a home in this community about 35 kilometres northwest of Red Deer.

Court was told the girl's thumb was shot off after she tried to take the rifle away from Duncan. She placed her thumb over the end of the rifle and did not remove it when Duncan threatened to shoot.

"I can't take anything but a serious view on this," said Judge John MacKenzie in passing sentence.

She sure wasn't clowning around

MINEOLA, N.Y. (UPI) — A woman who dressed as a clown and burst into the apartment of her husband's girlfriend, intending to kill her with chemicals, was convicted yesterday on a charge of forcible entry.

Sonnie Bonom, 40, of Wantagh, was acquitted of five other charges, including attempted murder.

Police testified they found Bonom — dressed in a clown costume and clutching a handful of helium-filled balloons — in her rival's apartment.

Blasted tattoo just had to go

OMAHA, Neb. (UPI-Special) — Someone should tell an 18-year-old here there are easier ways of removing tattoos.

Police said yesterday the unidentified youth, upset because his girlfriend refused to go steady with him, tried to "erase" her tattooed initials from his arm with a 12-gauge shotgun.

He was listed in good condition in hospital. Doctors say fortunately his muscles and tendons weren't damaged by the blast.

Burning bodies found in U.S.

DEARBORN HEIGHTS, Mich. (AP) — The burning bodies of two teenagers were found last night in this Detroit suburb.

Police said the bodies were found in a wooded area.

They said the victims had been tied with nylon cord and set afire.

Police said both teenagers were black, a boy about 18 and a girl several years younger. They were burned beyond recognition.

'Hardened criminal' in N.Y.

NEW YORK (CP) — The age of the hardened criminal in New York city, say the police, seems to be dropping each year. Right now it's down to age 7.

"We're seeing a lot more 7 year olds now than we used to," said Capt. Francis Daly, executive officer of the police deaprtment's youth aid division. "They seem to be getting younger and younger every year."

Under New York state law, he explained, children under 7 cannot be charged with a crime since they are considered to be "legally incapable" of committing a crime.

Daly, veteran of 20 years in the juvenile field, said the number of serious crimes committed by children between the ages of 7 and 16 went up 650 per cent between 1964 and 1972.

As a sampler, here are recent headlines from the city's juvenile crime front:

—Two 13 year olds mugged and raped a 9-year-old girl and then threw her to her death from the top of a 20-storey Bronx building.

—A gang of six boys, aged 11 to 13, stabbed a 14 year old to death in a Brooklyn subway station when he refused to give them a nickel.

ATTLEBORO, Mass. (UPI) — A masked bandit entered Nap's Package Store, slapped an eight-inch kitchen knife on the counter and said, "Give me the money." Clerk Robert Sirros replied by rapping a metal pipe on the counter. Police said the robber then lowered his sights: "Just give me $20." The clerk didn't budge. "Can I take a bag of chips?" the robber finally pleaded. "No," said the clerk, and the hapless bandit ran out the door.

Baby tossed 6 storeys dad guilty

NEW YORK (UPI) — An all-male jury has convicted a man of second-degree murder for tossing his infant daughter out a sixth-floor window because he had wanted a son.

After a night and morning of deliberation yesterday, the jury found Bernard Yarusevich, a 27-year-old short-order cook, guilty of murder for dropping his six-month-old daughter from the window of a lower east side apartment. He faces a sentence of 15 years-to-life in prison.

His 25-year-old wife Gail told the court her husband, who "really wanted a boy," had "put the baby out the window and dropped it."

Yarusevich testified he took his daughter, Barbara Ann, from her crib and was playing with her when she fell out the window.

Mom blames it on demons

WICHITA FALLS, Texas (UPI) — The case of an unwed mother who believed she was taunted by demons and instructed to carve out her daughter's heart is to go to the jury tomorrow.

Psychiatrist Enrique Macher, testifying for the defence in the trial of Patricia Ann Frazier, 25, said Miss Frazier's mind saw the demons.

Miss Frazier has entered a plea of not guilty by reason of insanity

Bedroom boo - boo

HOUSTON — (UPI) — Leslie Wayne Robinson was practising his fast draw when his wife walked into the bedroom, naked, slipped up behind him and said, "boo." Robinson, 30, whirled from his crouched position and shot his wife, Frances, 27, in the chest.

She is in fair condition in Ben Taub Hospital. No charges would be filed. "It was an accidental fast draw shooting," a detective said.

Thieves got more than $10 million police say

NEW YORK (UPI) — Estimates of the take in the United States' biggest cash robbery topped $10 million as officials reported some good leads in the hunt for the bandits who looted an armored car depot.

The size of the take could not be revealed for "investigative reasons," although a review of Sentry Armored Car-Courier records was completed, a Federal Bureau of Investigation spokesman said yesterday.

But city detectives, who asked not to be identified, said the inventory disclosed "in excess" of $10 million was taken by the bandits who cut their way through the roof of the Sentry building and handcuffed the only guard on duty Sunday night.

Joseph Valiquette of the FBI said 40 FBI agents and New York city detectives were pursuing "several good leads" in the case, but he refused to elaborate.

Investigators believe the robbers might have been helped by current or former Sentry employees because the gang appeared to have a detailed knowledge of the building's layout and alarm system.

HEY, DON'T YOU KNOW IT'S CHRISTMAS?

DETROIT (AP) — "Hey, man. Don't you know it's Christmas?"

Those were the last words spoken by a Grand Rapids teacht Tuesday night before he was shot to death by a hold-up man on a Detroit street.

Fred Hoffert, 26, and his father-in-law, Harry Vogelaar, were just leaving a neighborhood tavern when a hold-up man approached the pair and told them to throw their wallets on the ground.

When Hoffert reminded the man it was Christmas, he answered with a single shot that left Hoffert dead at the scene.

★★★

Now it's gas at gunpoint in U.S.

LOS ANGELES (AP-UPI-Special) — A man pulled his car in front of a line-up of 50 cars and began pumping gasoline. When angry motorists turned on him he pulled a pistol and held them at bay.

He was still pumping gas when police arrived to arrest him for carrying a concealed weapon . . .

About 20 people tried to mug a tow truck driver when he delivered six gallons of gasoline to a driver whose car had run dry while waiting in line.

A young couple were burned on the face, hands and arms while trying to siphon gasoline from their powerboat to their car with a vacuum cleaner. A spark from the vacuum apparently touched off the explosion and fire that destroyed the couple's garage and 18-foot cruiser . . .

A young man showed up at a gas station with a sink with a drain hole plugged and asked to have it filled up. He was turned down. Sinks are not approved gasoline containers in California . . .

It was all part of the mad scramble for gasoline over the weekend here as block-long lines of motorists waited for hours — sometimes even overnight — for gas stations to open. But few were open yesterday.

California was perhaps the worst hit as gas stations closed across the U.S. and others were ringed by lines of anxious motorists yesterday. Many stations, however, did receive new May fuel shipments.

California hopes to ease the crunch through an odd-even gasoline distribution system pinned to car license plate numbers.

Across the continent, the mood was carnival-like at two Boston gas stations where gas went for 25 cents a gallon for two hours. The bonanza was part of a promotion by two radio stations. They estimated they sold about 7,500 gallons at a cost of more than $4,000.

Meanwhile, President Jimmy Carter's gasoline rationing plan, deemed critical in the event of severe shortages, could die in Congress this week.

The U.S. Senate and House of Representatives have reluctantly agreed to bring up the plan this week and the White House has been frantically trying to round up enough support before Friday's deadline.

The government already has enough coupons — about 4.8 billion of them — to get gas rationing off to a good start. But the bureaucracy to run it will probably take about eight months to set up even under a "crash program."

Arthur Harriman, program analyst with the Energy Department, says it will take six months until the program is at a "readiness state" and another 45 to 60 days to get "off and running."

★★★

It's murder in St. Louis

ST. LOUIS, Mo. (AP) — Street violence — most of it in the blighted black neighborhoods on the north side — has made St. Louis the murder capital of the United States.

Police recorded 230 murders in the midwestern river port in 1978, 46 for every 100,000 residents — highest ratio in the country and more than double the rate in New York city.

Last year, killings increased by 24 per cent to 57 per 100,000. So far this year, 46 persons have been killed — down from 68 murders last year at this time.

"A stick-up in St. Louis used to be 'Your money or your life,' " said a cab driver. "Now it's 'Your money *and* your life.' "

‖‖‖‖‖‖‖‖‖‖‖‖‖‖‖‖‖‖‖‖‖‖‖‖‖‖‖‖‖‖‖‖

And now 'ear this . . .

CHICAGO (UPI) — A quarrel between a jealous wife and her husband's girlfriend that interrupted Easter Sunday mass ended with the wife ripping off her adversary's earlobe.

Estela Avalos, 31, confronted her husband's girlfriend at St. Francis of Xavier church and the two exchanged harsh words, said police.

Mrs. Avalos became incensed during the exchange and, in a moment of rage, tore one of Guadelupe Cuellar's earlobes off in full view of the nuns and other parishioners.

Ms Cuellar was taken to the hospital, where a spokesman said she would undergo surgery to rejoin her earlobe to her ear. Mrs. Avalos was arrested.

‖‖‖‖‖‖‖‖‖‖‖‖‖‖‖‖‖‖‖‖‖‖‖‖‖‖‖‖‖‖‖‖

Pupils paid to turn in drug users

LEWISVILLE, Texas (UPI) — Officials say paying high school informants up to $100 to turn in classmates who use drugs is not fostering a class of "Hitler youth-type" spies, but civil liberty groups blasted the nationally publicized program as unconstitutional.

Educators across the U.S. said they were looking to north Texas and studying the Lewisville High School system of using paid informants to help fight the epidemic of youth drug

abuse. Fourteen students have been expelled so far, and all face criminal charges.

"Lewisville is doing what works in Lewisville," said Jim Parcell, PTA coordinator for the Texas War On Drugs, a campaign founded and largely funded by Dallas computer magnate H. Ross Perot.

"There are 2,200 kids in school in Lewisville," he said. "Their right to go to school in a drug-free environment must be protected. In this case, the

principal has been courageous and concerned. It seems like a good program for the situation in that city. A lot of educators are looking at it."

Said Doug Killough, principal at Lewisville who founded the program: "Somebody has to do something and this is working.

"I have no patience for people who call our system un-American," he said. "This is not a snitch campaign."

Yet it is the use of informant money that inflames critics.

Policeman thought toy gun was real — so boy, 5, died

STANTON, Calif. (AP) — All Officer Anthony Sperl saw when he kicked in the door of the darkened apartment was a menacing figure and a "very realistic" pistol.

He fired and 5-year-old Patrick Mason fell dead, still clutching his toy gun.

Yesterday, in an attempt to calm public outrage over the shooting, police released photographs of the toy pistol.

'Very realistic'

The black plastic toy gun is "quite comparable to an actual .38-calibre, 2-inch barrel" gun, Sgt. Robert Ohlemann said yesterday, adding that it was "very realistic looking."

Sperl shot Mason when the child was alone in his mother's apartment last Thursday. Sperl, entering the darkened room, saw a gun pointed at him and a figure he couldn't make out, so he fired, police say.

The figure turned out to be the 1.2-metre (four-foot) boy.

Police had between 80 and 100 calls over the weekend, said Stanton police Capt. James Brown. "It's about 50 (per cent saying) that we're cold blooded killers and 50 (per cent) that the officer had no other choice."

Officer suspended

An organization called the John Brown Anti-Klan Committee planned a demonstration Monday afternoon at the Los Angeles Civic Centre to protest the shooting. The child was black and the officer is white.

Sperl, 24, was suspended from the police force as a routine matter while authorities investigate the shooting.

Sperl had gone to the apartment after a neighbor called police to say she had not seen the boy's mother, 29-year-old Patricia Ridge, in two weeks. Ridge was at work and Patrick was home alone when the shooting occurred, Brown said.

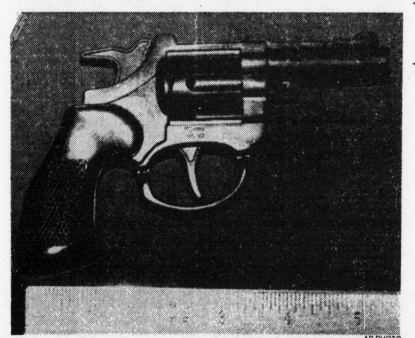

AP PHOTO

Fatal toy: Police say this toy pistol is the one pointed at a policeman by 5-year-old Patrick Mason. Officer Anthony Sperl fatally shot the boy in Stanton, Calif.

Bungling burglar shoots friend

NEW YORK (UPI) — A pistol tossed away by a burglary suspect during a bungled holdup hit an air conditioner and went off, killing his accomplice, police said yesterday.

The suspect, identified as Wayne Pack, 18, was arrested. The dead man, said to be in his late teens, was not immediately identified.

Two policemen spotted the two suspects inside a drug store. One of the suspects, standing near the door, allegedly threw away a loaded .38-calibre pistol, which struck the air conditioner and fired.

Shot man 'died of a cold'

NEWARK, N.J. — An autopsy on the exhumed body of a man whose cause of death was officially listed as a bad cold has revealed he had been shot four times in the head.

As a result, at least three more bodies linked to murder probes will be exhumed because they, too, did not undergo autopsies, Prosecutor George Schneider said.

Shooting rampage

NEW YORK (UPI) — A minister's son who police said hated homosexuals was charged today with killing one man and wounding seven others in a shooting rampage in Greenwich Village. Ronald Crumpley, 38, of Manhattan, told police that, armed with a submachine-gun and three pistols, he drove a Cadillac stolen from his father to Greenwich Village, where he opened fire on groups of men at a homosexual bar.

"It is irrational, inexcusable neglect to confuse pneumonia with four slugs in the head," he said of the medical examiner's office.

Rape of movie star with barrel of a gun tests new U.S. law

LOS ANGELES — A new law that expands the definition of rape faced its first test today in the case of actress Carrie Snodgress, who claims she was raped with a gun barrel.

The case is one of the first filed under the new statute, which carries a maximum term of five years in jail.

Other cases involve the gang-rape of a girl on a beach in which sand was forced into her vagina and a sexual assault with a wine bottle.

The new law is an outgrowth of the so-called "Born Innocent" case in which a 9-year-old San Francisco girl was raped with a beer bottle in 1974 by four juveniles after a similar sexual assault was portrayed in a television movie.

Jack Nitzsche, a 42-year-old Hollywood musician, composer and record producer, pleaded not guilty to raping Miss Snodgress.

Miss Snodgress says she and her son, Zeke, were asleep in their bedrooms when Nitzsche came in and began pistol-whipping Miss Snodgress, dragging her around the bedroom by her hair.

She suffered a fractured cheekbone, bruises, abrasion and a cut thumb that required 18 stitches.

After he threatened her son, Miss Snodgress testified, Nitzsche forced her into a bathroom, where he raped her with the barrel of the revolver.

Miss Snodgress, who refused to be interviewed, told the prosecutor she managed to escape when Nitzsche put the gun down momentarily and she wrestled him off balance until he fell to the floor.

She ran out of the room and hid in some bushes by the swimming pool until he left.

Nitzsche, a talented and versatile musician, worked with Toronto-born singer Neil Young, leader of a rock group called Crazy Horse, during the six years that Young lived with Miss Snodgress.

The creator of numerous hit records with Phil Spector and Sonny Bono during the 1960s, Nitzsche also worked with the Rolling Stones and wrote the score for the movie One Flew Over The Cuckoo's Nest.

Miss Snodgress, 33, was nominated for an Academy Award for her part in Diary of a M d Housewife.

'Thieves' had plenty of help

NEW YORK (UPI) — Nearly all of the 8,000 New Yorkers who watched "thieves" break into automobiles for a study, either ignored or did not see the "crimes." Some offered to help for part of the loot.

Harold Takooshien, a social psychologist at Fordham University, staged about 250 broad-daylight car break-ins in Manhattan with the help of student volunteers to test the reaction of New Yorkers to street crime.

The vast majority, about 7,000 people, simply didn't notice what was going on while only about a dozen actually intervened or attempted to stop the crime, the study reported.

A larger group of about 40 passers-by offered to help the student "thieves," but five of them demanded part of the loot.

Los Angeles detectives are checking the strange story of two city bus drivers, one male and the other female, who said they were robbed by two kinky gunmen who then stripped the woman, tied her up and plastered tartar sauce on her body. "I can safely say it is one of the more bizarre robberies I have ever heard of," said police Lt. Duane Gansemer, chief of detectives in the Southwest Division.

Gang war movie sparks stabbing

SEEKONK, Mass. (UPI) — Two young men have been held on $100,000 bail each on charges of stabbing three other youths after the Christmas Day showing of a gang warfare movie Quadrophenia, featuring the British rock group The Who.

Wife's digging reveals murder

WICHITA, Kan. (UPI) — A man became so upset at his wife's efforts to plant rosebushes in their backyard he confessed he murdered his first wife 14 years ago and buried her there.

Denver Permenter, 55, was arrested after police found the skeletal remains of his first wife, Florence.

Permenter reported her missing in 1966. He divorced her two years later, when she was already dead, police said.

"Apparently his present wife was wanting to plant some roses," said Police Capt. Richard Granger. "He got upset because she was digging around the area where the body was in.

"His conscience got to him and he told her about it."

BUMPED OFF!

NEW YORK (UPI) — A motorist shot another driver to death yesterday over a rush-hour traffic accident in which their cars bumped fenders.

Police said George Smurra, 43, was involved in a minor fender-bender with Luther McGill, 42, and was so angry that he fired four shots at McGill, killing him.

Three passing off-duty prison guards chased Smurra through a car wash before they could catch him. Smurra was charged with second-degree murder.

Ex-driver of church bus accused of sodomizing boys

From Staff, Wire Reports

BOWLING GREEN — A 54-year-old Bowling Green man pleaded innocent yesterday to charges that he used his position as a church bus driver to lure boys into homosexual activities.

Warren Circuit Judge J. David Francis scheduled trial Oct. 13 for Robert Norman, who remained in the Warren County Jail in lieu of $100,000 cash bond.

Norman, who worked for the Tennessee Valley Authority here until he recently took early retirement, had been a deacon until five years ago at the Glendale Baptist Church in Bowling Green and until recently had driven a bus for the church. He is married and has three grown children.

He was indicted by the Warren County grand jury Monday on charges that he engaged in illicit sexual activities with seven boys between the ages of 10 and 15.

The indictment included 35 sodomy counts, 26 sexual abuse counts and one count of attempted sexual abuse.

Donnie Hines, a detective with the Warren County Commonwealth's Attorney's office, said yesterday that Norman often carried children on the church bus and that police believe he used the job to make initial contacts with the boys involved.

The charges followed an investigation by the Bowling Green police juvenile division into incidents dating back to 1979, Hines said.

According to Hines, the investigation began on July 16 after a sister of one of the boys called police.

"The juvenile had been complaining to his mother, but she had chosen not to believe him and apparently thought the story was fabricated," Hines said.

"Later on, he told the story to his sister and she immediately called the police."

He said parents of most of the children cooperated in the investigation, although some parents refused to allow authorities to talk with their youngsters.

"In a couple of instances the police know of boys who were believed to have been involved, but whose parents will not allow them to be interviewed," Hines said.

"Some of them seem to be trying to protect their children or they simply don't want to believe their children were involved.

"A few people have been very reluctant to cooperate," he added. Hines said the investigation showed sexual contacts occurred at Norman's home and at the Tennessee Valley Authority building where he was employed.

In addition, Hines said police believe some contacts occurred at the church, on the bus and in a van that Norman also drives.

The Rev. Richard Oldham, pastor of Glendale Baptist Church, called the charges "repugnant to us. We absolutely guarantee such a thing will never happen again."

He said he recalled Norman as being "interested in helping all people."

"I don't feel the church was in any way responsible, and I am hurt," Oldham said.

Norman has no criminal record, according to authorities.

Bloody day in Dallas

DALLAS (Special) — It was the bloodiest day of the bloodiest year in Dallas police history. By the time it was over, five people had been killed.

A 32-year-old truck driver was shot to death in a bar and his father was arrested.

A birthday celebration for a young wife in her South Dallas apartment ended with her beaten to death, her husband was taken into custody.

A man was stabbed with a butcher knife as he tracked down the woman with whom he lived; a 72-year-old man was shot to death in his brick home and his wife of more than 40 years was arrested; the bullet-ridden body of a 23-year-old man was found in a vacant lot.

The latest slew of homicides this week was the most in one day this year.

Mother-in-law slays groom on wedding day

COLORADO SPRINGS, Colo. (AP) — A bridegroom was accidentally shot to death during an argument between his in-laws at a wedding reception, investigators say. His mother-in-law was arrested.

Marvin Simmons, 24, a soldier at nearby Fort Carson, was shot in the head with a small-calibre rifle at his in-laws' home.

Police said the bride's parents Lonnie and Shirley Harris, had been arguing in a bedroom during the reception Sunday night when Mrs. Harris chased her husband out into a family room with a rifle.

Victim's feet set afire

DETROIT (UPI) — A man is in fair condition after being robbed of $100, pistol-whipped, then dumped into a trash can after four bandits set his feet on fire with lighter fluid.

Cops say they have no suspects in the attack on Tony Watkins, 24, who is suffering from burns and lacerations.

Watkins said the bandits "laughed and giggled" when they threw him into the trash can.

Auto thief, 8 trips up

FORT LAUDERDALE, Fla. (UPI) — An 8-year-old boy has been found driving a stolen car — for the second time in two days.

The youngster and a 16-year-old companion were caught by two police officers after they crashed a 1971 sedan into a fence and then careened into a parked car.

The child was driving because the 16-year-old didn't know how, said police.

The 8-year-old told officials he wrecked the car Tuesday because his legs weren't long enough to reach the brake pedal.

Woman jailed for killing lover's wife

MILWAUKEE (AP) — Janet Goodall, 35, charged with second-degree murder in the 1976 shooting death of a minister's wife who discovered her in bed with the pastor, has been sentenced to 10 years in prison.

Mrs. Goodall testified that Vanice Tabor had discovered her and Rev. William Tabor in bed. She said she was holding a .pistol when Tabor grabbed her arm and the weapon went off, and that Tabor then fired two more shots. Tabor was not charged.

Gun-toting judges?

SPRINGFIELD, Ill. (UPI) — State Senator John D'Arco wants judges to be allowed to carry guns. He said four judges had told him they fear for their lives.

BOY, 8, ARRESTED FOR MURDER

TUCSON, Ariz. (Reuter) — An 8-year-old boy has been charged with second-degree murder here in the shooting death of a truck driver.

The boy was arrested in his Grade 3 classroom yesterday and taken to a juvenile detention centre.

He allegedly fired his father's single-shot rifle several times in his front garden last week and one shot hit 41-year-old George Wood as he was working on his car.

Three shot after man fails exam

PHILADELPHIA — (UPI) — A quiet mathematician, apparently angered by his failure to earn a doctorate, wounded two professors in a burst of gunfire inside a University of Pennsylvania lecture hall yesterday and then fatally shot himself in the mouth.

Police said Robert H. Cantor, 33, of Philadelphia, an instructor at Temple University and a former Penn graduate student, acted out of a grudge when he stormed into a mathematics colloquium and started shooting a .45 calibre automatic.

He fired five shots at his former adviser, Dr. Walter Koppelman, 40, and the former mathematics department chairman, Dr. Oscar Goldman, 45.

Bullet can't kill true love

OKLAHOMA CITY (UPI) — Harry Ray Miller says he still loves his wife, although she shot him when he mumbled another woman's name in his sleep.

Miller's wife told police her husband called her by another woman's name, "Christina," so she shot him.

Miller told police from hospital that he won't press charges against his wife because he loves her.

★

★

★

Girl, 13, arrested in stabbing attack

AYER, Mass. (UPI) — A 13-year-old girl who allegedly stabbed and critically wounded another girl was to be arraigned here yesterday on juvenile charges of assault with intent to kill and assault with a dangerous weapon. The victim, also 13, was found stabbed repeatedly with a "carpenter's file or an ice pick" on a wooded path near her home, police said. She was in critical condition but police said she was expected to recover.

Elderly gardener beheads wife, 73

VICKSBURG, Mich. (UPI) — An elderly man who took meticulous care of his garden and loved to pass out cookies to neighborhood children has been charged with beheading his wife with an axe.

★ ★ ★ ★

MAN SLAIN FOR TRYING TO SAVE DOG

DETROIT (UPI) — A 64-year-old man was stabbed to death Monday night because he tried to save a dog's life.

Police said Joseph Peoples tried to stop an unidentified man from slashing a dog's throat.

The man killed the dog, according to witnesses, and then told Peoples to "shut up, old man, or I'll kill you too."

The assailant left the scene, police said, but returned later with four friends and repeatedly stabbed Peoples in the chest.

★ ★ ★

A child's revenge

ASHTON, Mich. (AP) — A couple and three children aged from 5 months to 3 years died in a house fire near here yesterday — and police say the blaze was started by one of the four surviving children. The survivors were in school when fire engulfed the frame house but one admitted having set a dresser alight before leaving. The children told police they had been victims of child abuse and had at other times in the past fought back by starting fires.

U.S. city fined for refusing gun permits

Special to The Star

GARY, Ind. — The city of Gary, its mayor, and two top police officials have been ordered to pay $880,000 in damages for denying handgun-permit applications to city residents.

Gary's mayor, Richard Hatcher, imposed the ban in January, 1980, as a crime-stopping move.

A jury ordered the payment after lawyers for people who were denied applications said that the applicants' civil rights had been violated and that Indiana handgun laws were ignored in the ban.

"There is no basis for these damages," said Hamilton Carmouche, attorney for the city and the public officials. He said he will appeal.

"It's wonderful, it's exhilarating," said Terry Gray, attorney for the gun applicants.

Hatcher was ordered to pay $612,800 in punitive and compensatory damages. Virgil Motley, deputy chief of police, was ordered to pay $68,800 in punitive and compensatory damages. Frederick Kowsky was ordered to pay $12,000, and the city was ordered to pay $186,400.

The class-action suit named 2,000 plaintiffs who will split the damages if the verdict is upheld.

The jury found no fault with a fifth defendant, John Shettle, superintendent of the Indiana State Police.

During closing arguments in the case Tuesday, Gray said Hatcher acted like a dictator when he denied handgun-permit applications.

Hatcher's order was issued on Jan. 3, 1980. On Feb. 5, 1980, it was overturned in Superior Court.

CHICAGO TRIBUNE

Luck Ran Out

LOS ANGELES (Reuter) — A masked gunman took $180 from a shop cash register here — and then his luck ran out. As he fled, the bag into which he had stuffed the money burst and the money sprayed over the ground; his shotgun fell apart and he left the butt behind; his mask slipped off before he could get into the getaway car; 90 minutes later, the robber and his driver returned to the scene of the crime but a police lieutenant recognized the robber from a description and gave chase. Victor Cross, 21, and Herbert Taylor, 26, were held in custody today on suspicion of robbery.

Burglars Give Up

ARLINGTON HEIGHTS, Ill. (UPI) — Burglars who spent weeks attempting to break into the vault of the Bank & Trust Co. of Arlington Heights were forced to give up when their drill bits broke. The burglars finally abandoned efforts to break through a 20-inch-thick concrete wall in the bank last weekend but left the message, "Win some, lose some" scrawled across a painting in the bank lobby to indicate they weren't crushed by their defeat.

Mayor 'had to pull gun' on council

SEAT PLEASANT, Md. (UPI) — Mayor Henry Arrington said yesterday he was forced to draw a gun on angry town council members and citizens to protect his life during a stormy meeting at town hall in this Washington suburb.

Arrington, who has been bickering with council members for weeks over his control of the purse strings and their refusal to let him drive the town's pick-up truck, said the trouble began when he adjourned an executive ses-

sion Thursday night after three citizens crashed the meeting.

Following adjournment, a mob of citizens and council members gathered outside

the town hall, shouting obscenities and threatening "we're going to kill you," Arrington said. He said he was struck on the forehead by a rock.

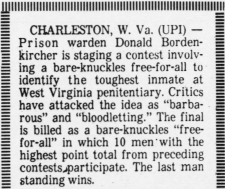

CHARLESTON, W. Va. (UPI) — Prison warden Donald Bordenkircher is staging a contest involving a bare-knuckles free-for-all to identify the toughest inmate at West Virginia penitentiary. Critics have attacked the idea as "barbarous" and "bloodletting." The final is billed as a bare-knuckles "free-for-all" in which 10 men with the highest point total from preceding contests participate. The last man standing wins.

SPOKANE, Wash. (UPI) — Charles Cavendar blew his main chance at being a master criminal. He hit the Washington Trust Bank in Spokane for nearly $3,600 earlier this month, walking out free and clear with his booty after handing the teller a hold-up note. Trouble is, he wrote the note on the back of a personalized cheque blank. It listed his name, address and phone number. He has been sentenced to seven years in jail.

Rootin' tootin' Roy Rogers shoots down gun control

Over my dead body, Roy Rogers says.

The California Legislature has proposed new gun control laws — but rootin' tootin cowboy Roy says *no one's* going to control his handgun.

"They'll have to shoot me first to take my gun," Rogers said yesterday. "I've always been against gun control."

With quick-firing rhetoric such as this, it's understandable why Rogers has been recruited by the National Rifle Association to shoot a number of TV spots protesting gun control. The 69-year-old former movie, TV and radio star likens gun restrictions to tactics used by Nazis during World War II.

"I wouldn't feel safe if I didn't have a gun in the house," says Roy, who operates a western museum with wife Dale Evans in Apple Valley, Calif. "With all the robberies and rapes, I think it's necessary."

Keep those guns ablazin', Roy, and Happy Entrails To You.

CHICAGO (UPI) — A pistol-packing "frail, little old lady" fired at police from her barricaded apartment, holding officers at bay for five hours before they rushed in and grabbed her from behind, said police.

Louise Gordon, 70, bit one officer and slightly injured another.

The door was open, and officers found Ms. Gordon in her bedroom with a .38 calibre revolver. She fired about four shots at the officers, who dived for cover. Then she broke a window in her apartment and fired randomly out the window, a police spokesman said. While she was at the window, with her back to the officers, they rushed in and grabbed her.

Tragedy of 'perfect American family'

By John Barnes
Special to The Star

LOS ANGELES — Palos Verdes estate near here is a quiet, exclusive neighborhood with immaculate lawns and magnificent clifftop views of the Pacific. Behind the dazzling white walls of the Miller home lived the "perfect American family."

"They didn't drink, they didn't smoke, they went to church. They were like all of us — very, very straight, moral people," neighbor and friend Judy McFarland said.

But Roy and Marguerita Miller had something the other neighbors didn't have — easy access to the president of the United States. Roy Miller is Ronald Reagan's personal attorney.

But tragedy has befallen the Miller household. Michael Miller, 20, is now in the Los Angeles jail under a round-the-clock suicide watch, accused of raping his mother and then battering her to death with a wooden club.

Her nude body was found by police after Roy Miller phoned them from a neighbor's house.

'Bloody towel'

He had just returned from work, he said. "Something's terribly wrong. I saw a bloody towel and broken glasses with blood on them."

A few days later, in nearby Long Beach, 17-year-old Eric Washington was arrested by police and charged with beating and strangling to death **his** mother. As they carried him manacled hand and foot from the house, he was screaming, "I didn't do it," then "I

Special report

didn't mean to do it," and finally, "God, what have I done?"

The incidents were among several violent episodes involving children on America's West Coast.

In the middle-class Gernada Hills suburb of Los Angeles, Thomas Tabor, 18, has been charged with shooting his mother and sister to death. A few miles away, in Sun Valley, another 18-year-old allegedly did the same to his father and step-mother. Farther north, in Washington state, Jimmie Mathis, 12, gunned down his mother after a spanking.

'Perfect family'

The Miller case is the most extraordinary. Michael graduated from Palos Verdes High School in 1980. One of his teachers, Donald Brough, remembers him as a "warm, sensitive young man — part of the perfect American family."

Shortly after Michael entered college in northern California, however, his elder brother, Jeffrey, killed himself with an overdose of Aspirin in a Los Angeles psychiatric clinic.

Michael dropped out of college, went to New York to take up acting, but soon returned home unemployed. Then he began to receive psychiatric treatment.

Preliminary psychiatric tests after the murder of his mother describe him as a psychotic, schizophrenic and possibly not competent to stand trial.

LONDON SUNDAY TIMES

Woman forced to cut head off slain bartender

NEW YORK (Reuter) — A man on a drinking and drugs spree killed a bartender, then raped one woman in the bar and forced another to cut off the dead man's head, police said yesterday.

The killer later went on a wild drive through the city with the victim's head, wrapped in newspaper, next to him in a hatbox.

Police called the crime one of the most gruesome they have encountered.

Charles Dingle was drinking heavily at a bar when he got into an argument with owner Herbert Cummings, 51.

Police said Dingle, 24, shot Cummings dead in front of three women, tied them up and raped one.

When a fourth woman entered the bar, Dingle found out that she was a professional mortician and at gunpoint made her cut Cummings' head off with two kitchen knives. He forced everyone in the bar, including Cummings' tied-up wife, to watch.

Police said Dingle apparently wanted the head severed so he could get the bullet back. After letting two of the women go early yesterday, Dingle decided to flee the bar with the other two women.

He took them to his parked van and put the head in the back, but couldn't get the vehicle started.

Police said Dingle then went back to the bar and called a cab. when the cab arrived, Dingle tied the driver up, robbed him of his car keys and cash and forced the two remaining women into the cab.

The three then went on a wild drive through the city until Dingle realized he had left the severed head in his van, police said.

He sped back to get the head and then drove off with the two terrorized women still in his stolen cab.

When he reached Manhattan, the drugs and alcohol he had been taking all night finally caught up with him and he passed out at the wheel, police said.

The two women fled and called police.

Police said Dingle was found in the car with Cummings' head wrapped in newspaper in a box next to him.

Stabber nabbed?

LOS ANGELES (Reuter) — The Skid-Road Stabber has been caught, police believe.

Bobby Joe Maxwell was arrested yesterday in connection with 10 skid road murders in a run-down area of central Los Angeles late last year.

Police Chief Daryl Gates said the 29-year-old suspect is known to frequent the skid road area, a sanctuary for tramps and drunks.

The 10 murders took place between Oct. 23 and Nov. 23 and all the victims were stabbed in the upper parts of their bodies. Police believe the murderer killed for pleasure.

Tycoon's ex-wife shoots herself

FORT WORTH, Texas (UPI) — Priscilla Davis, ex-wife of millionaire Cullen Davis, shot herself in the hand yesterday trying to unload a pistol.

Mrs. Davis was in her chauffeured limousine, riding with Tarrant County prosecutor Jack Strickland and his girlfriend and unloading the pistol when it discharged. The bullet passed through the webbing between her index finger and thumb and shattered the car's side window. No one else was injured.

Strickland unsuccessfully helped prosecute Davis in vo murder solicitation trials and a murder trial.

Five killed in Bronx slaughter

NEW YORK (UPI) — A woman and four preschoolers for whom she was babysitting were killed yesterday in a bloody "slaughter" in a low-income housing project in the Bronx.

The body of Delores Harris, 55, and the children, two believed to be 3 years old and two 4 years old, were found at 3 p.m. when the woman's daughter walked into the apartment in the three-building, complex.

Police said there were unconfirmed reports the attacker used a baseball bat and scissors in the attack. A spokesman said the killer used "more than one weapon," and committed the crimes "within an hour."

Chicago's 'Ripper' held

CHICAGO (UPI) — Three men, including a man police described as Robin the Ripper, are under investigation in the slayings of up to 16 women and one man and the slashings of prostitutes.

Robin Gecht, 28, an unemployed carpenter and father of three, was held yesterday on $1-million bond after being indicted for two nonfatal slashings of two prostitutes. When he was arrested, police described him as "Robin the Ripper."

Three shot dead as bikers clash

DETROIT (UPI) — Two motorcycle clubs have clashed in a fierce gunbattle that has left three people dead and six wounded.

The shootout erupted during an early morning party yesterday celebrating the opening of a new headquarters for the U.S.S. Enterprise Motorcycle Club.

Bikers held in rape-torture

GOSHEN, Ind. (UPI) — Three members of a motorcycle gang known as the Death Nomads are being held on $300,000 bond each and lawmen are hunting three others in the rape-torture of a 16-year-old girl.

Held in Elkhart County jail are Franklin King, 24, Billy Woolverton, 24, and Jack Eberly, 35.

They were charged with rape while armed with a deadly weapon, criminal confinement and battery. They are scheduled for another court appearance tomorrow.

Investigators said the victim was held about 30 hours at an Elkhart house last week where she was allegedly beaten with steel bars, chains and belts and raped repeatedly.

Police, looking for runaways, found the girl in the basement of the home where the alleged attacks occurred. She was taken to hospital with a fractured nose and other injuries.

Murder try called communication gap —or 'pure hatred'

ALLENTOWN Pa. (AP) — Police say Anthony Toto's wife tried to kill him out of "pure hatred."

Toto says it was simply a "big lack of communication."

So the pizza maker paid $50,000 to bail her out of jail and returned to work. Now the couple serve customers in the pizzeria — together.

But, according to police, Toto's 38-year-old wife Frances was prepared to give her man the works — she and several others allegedly plotted to kill him.

Toto, who still has a bullet lodged in his head, was shot once in the head Jan. 26.

He survived.

Then he was drugged with barbiturates and shot again on the left side of his chest Jan. 28.

Still he did not die.

Two days later police rescued him from his home, where he lay wounded, and charged his wife and two men with attempted murder. Another man was charged with criminal conspiracy.

Two of Toto's children, a 17-year-old girl and a 13-year-old boy, have been charged in the case but police would not divulge details. They would only say the motive appeared to have risen from "pure hatred."

Asked why he thought people might want to kill him, Toto said: "In my opinion it was a lack of communication — a big lack of communication. Lots of people have a problem. I had a big problem . . . me and my family."

Dad's gun kills daughter

NORTH HAVERHILL, N.H. (UPI) — Erika Weeks, 5, died from a bullet in the face in the bedroom where her father kept five loaded handguns as well as rifles and air guns.

Jeffrey Cecil Weeks taught his daughter to shoot an air gun when she was only two, but she died from a bullet from Weeks' .357 magnum pistol.

A Grafton County Superior court jury convicted Weeks, 40, of negligent homicide in his daughter's death Aug. 4, 1977. He will be sentenced tomorrow and could receive up to seven years in prison.

Weeks believes the loaded gun was knocked off a rack by a cat the child was chasing.

Bang! Bang! IT'S dead . . .

CHARLESTON, S.C. (UPI) — It was not your average bank heist.

A man handed a note demanding money to an automatic teller machine at a Bankers Trust branch in the wee hours of the morning.

Getting no response, he whipped out a .38-calibre pistol and pumped two bullets into the machine, then hopped into his car and drove off.

But a police officer saw the aborted stick-up and gave chase.

Police arrested Harold Thomas and seized a pistol, a ski mask and a note.

They said he had been drinking.

Lived for days before beheading

HOLLYWOOD, Fla. (UPI) — A 6-year-old boy, abducted from a department store toy section July 27, apparently lived for three or four days before he was decapitated, authorities say.

Broward Medical Examiner Dr. Ronald Wright said several more days of tests will be necessary to determine — if possible — how Adam Walsh was killed and dismembered.

Only the boy's head has been found and Wright said it showed Adam had lived "three, maybe four" days after disappearing from a Hollywood shopping mall.

Two fishermen found the head Monday in a murky canal along Florida's Turnpike west of Vero Beach.

Baby pushed to her death

LOS ANGELES (UPI) — A 33-year-old woman allegedly pushed her 18-month-old daughter from an overpass onto a busy freeway yesterday, killing the child.

Police questioned Virginia Relanzia, then booked her on murder charges at Sybil Brand county jail.

Lt. Charles Long said the woman told investigating officers she was distraught over problems with the man who was living with her.

"I saw the woman standing at the bridge rail," one witness told investigating officers, "The little girl was seated on the railing. She pushed the baby off. It was awful."

The child, Valinda, landed in the fast lane of the southbound Hollywood Freeway. Police said she was run over by at least one car.

Beheaded in Detroit

DETROIT (UPI) — Police have arrested one suspect and are seeking four more in the beheadings of two men and a woman last year in a territorial dispute between drug dealers. The suspects are believed responsible for at least a dozen other Detroit slayings during the past two years. Police said the three victims were shot in the head and decapitated. The killers also cut off the men's hands and one of the woman's hands.

Parents face charges for abandoning boy, 9

COLUMBIA, S.C. (AP) — Police say they will seek prosecution of a couple who threw their nine-year-old son out of their home on Christmas Eve, saying they no longer wanted him around.

"We're not going to forget this," Sgt. Bob Connell of the Columbia Police Department said yesterday. "We're going as far as we can with it."

The unidentified boy was being kept at a youth shelter operated by the state social services department. Officers said the case will be turned over to the department when it reopens Monday with a request for an investigation.

The cold, wet and hungry boy was found by a passer-by walking on a highway at 1:30 a.m. on Christmas Eve, officers said.

The boy told officers his parents "just didn't want him any more and if they didn't want him, he didn't want them."

Before taking him to the shelter, officers gave the boy gifts during their annual Christmas Eve party at the station. They presented him with gifts of a small football, wrist watch and about $25 in cash.

"He was well-mannered and we just felt sorry for him," said Sgt. R. G. Knox. "We don't know a thing about his family except that they didn't want him."

Connell added: "He is a likable little guy they threw out at the wrong time."

Connell quoted the boy as saying his parents were "after him all the time and blamed him for everything." The boy was considering running away when his parents ordered him out, the officer continued.

Connell said a patrol car was sent to the parents' home with a message to call police headquarters. When no one called, Connell said he and another officer drove the boy to the parents' home.

"They absolutely refused to take him back," Connell said.

Teen kills grandmother

COMPTON, Calif. — A 53-year-old grandmother is dead after shooting it out with a teenage gunman who tried to hold her up as she walked out of a store she managed.

Ernestine Mays, whose son-in-law is a Compton police officer, was shot in the head as she and another employee, Johnny Washington, 55, left Bill's Food Mart.

Mays, also taken to hospital, died two hours later.

Teacher's aide third arrested in California sado-sex probe

SACRAMENTO, Calif. (UPI) — A teacher's aide, who worked with handicapped children by day, changed into skimpy black leather outfits at night and used whips, chains and electric shock devices in sex acts with naked men, police say.

Pamela Gitthens, 40, has been arrested in the case of a football coach and his wife who allegedly operated a sado-masochistic brothel in Sacramento, Calif.

Gitthens turned herself in after authorities allegedly identified her as the woman in a photograph who was dressed in skimpy black clothes, engaged in sex acts with naked clients.

She was charged with operating a house of prostitution along with Bill Benton, 41, head football coach of Elk Grove High School, and his wife, Cheri, 38, an assistant to a junior high school principal in Elk Grove.

The Bentons were due in court Monday for arraignment, but the hearing was delayed pending further investigation.

The Bentons have been placed on administrative leave by their school district and Gitthens has been suspended from the substitute teaching list.

Inside a condominium owned by Benton, detectives last week found photos of two women engaging in sex acts with naked men, using whips, chains, a torture rack, electric shock devices and other sado-masochistic equipment.

Mrs. Benton, who allegedly advertised sado-masochistic services in an underground newspaper, was arrested April 3 after reportedly offering to perform sadistic sexual acts for $80 an hour with an undercover police officer.

BABYSITTER KILLED BY OWN GUN

JACKSONVILLE, Fla. (AP) — An 8-year-old Jacksonville boy has been charged with murdering his 79-year-old babysitter, police said yesterday. The babysitter was shot on June 27 after trying to discipline the child, who became angry, found the babysitter's revolver, and fired three shots at him.

104-year-old chased rapist from her house, court told

GRAND RAPIDS, Mich. (AP) — A 104-year-old woman chased a 39-year-old man out of her house with a metal chair leg after he raped her, a court has been told.

"He said he was going to kill her," prosecutor Don Zerial said yesterday. "She said, 'You're going to have to and we'll both go to hell together.'

"She is a spry old woman. She's tough."

J. C. Coney, 39, pleaded no contest after the rape charge was reduced to third-degree criminal sexual conduct to spare the elderly victim the rigors of a trial, Zerial said.

At his preliminary hearing, Coney said he was under the influence of alcohol and drugs when he was arrested near the woman's house.

The woman said she discovered Coney sitting in her living room and smoking a cigarette. She ordered him to put out the cigarette and leave, but instead he attacked her, police reported.

Coney also pleaded guilty to a felony theft charge, and could get up to 22½ years in prison on the two charges, Zerial said.

STOCKTON, Calif. (AP) — A man who called a taxi after he robbed a Wells Fargo Bank here wishes he had taken the bus. Police Lieut. Robert Lund said the man handed a teller a note reading: "I have a gun. Give me $3,000, or I'll kill you." The teller gave him the money, then tripped the silent alarm. The robber called a taxi and sat in the bank lobby to await its arrival — but the police came first, with guns. The robber didn't have one.

Prison escaper **Clarence Lee** is, apparently, a firm believer in comparative shopping. Knowing that the law would finally catch up with him following his July 30 escape from an Atlanta, Ga., jail, Lee began checking through his buddies on the conditions at various prisons. Then he surrendered to officials in Dania, Fla, after being told their place was the best.

RICHMOND, Va. — Hijackers have pulled off a big heist that netted them 150,000 clams — not as in dollars, clams as in seafood.

The bandits forced the drivers of a tractor trailer to transfer their load of chowder bivalves — worth $18,000 — into another truck and then sped off.

Smashing good trade

NEW YORK (Reuter) — Business boomed for David Merkatz's auto window repair firm for three months.

About 1,000 cars had had their windows broken by shots from a pellet gun.

The spree ended yesterday when police spotted a man shooting out windows and arrested Merkatz.

GRETNA, La. (UPI) — Randy Ward's Labor Day apparently did not go as planned. Ward was identified as the armed robber who held up a gas station and escaped — briefly — with a fistful of cash. During his getaway he tripped on a sidewalk curb, fell and shot himself. He was in satisfactory condition in a local hospital.

WASHINGTON — Again.

The bloody list just seems to go on . . . again and again and again.

Somewhere, deep in the American psyche, there's a fixed idea among a television-bred, macho-raised, gun-loving people that there is a simple solution to problems, real or perceived: Kill the president or the messenger or the symbol.

Pump a bunch of bullets into him, and the pain in the head stops or the left wins over the right, or blacks stop being so goddam uppity . . . or something.

But why America? Why is the list of American assassinations so long? Four presidents: Abraham Lincoln, James Garfield, William McKinley, John Kennedy. Why were bullets the way to deal with Robert Kennedy and George Wallace and Martin Luther King and, yes, John Lennon?

Part of the reason is fear: Guns. There are 50 million handguns loose in America and there were almost 10,000 handgun killings last year, about half the total number of slayings.

In a nation where kids can stay up and become obsessed — along with their parents — about who shot J.R. in the TV series Dallas, there were more murders by children under 10 than the total number of killings in Britain by people of any age.

This is frontier country — where Nancy Reagan once kept a little, itsy-bitsy gun under her pillow; where her husband, the cowboy, thinks a constitutional right to bear arms is okay and extends it to the Saturday Night Special; where, as Stokely Carmichael says, violence is as American as apple pie.

The real thing that obsesses Americans about assassinations, sadly, is not why it was done or even who did it but, Lord save us, be sure it's not a conspiracy.

CHICAGO (UPI) — A diet doctor, who fired 30 machine-gun shots at police while he was clad in a German helmet and bullet-proof vest over his pajamas, posted bond and was released from jail here but tasted less than a moment of freedom. Almost as soon as he was freed, Dr. Sinisa Princevac, 40, charged with attempted murder, punched a TV cameraman filming the release. Princevac was then charged with battery and returned to the men's lockup. "I think the doctor needs a doctor," a narcotics Lt. Lawrence Forberg said.

Thieves put the bite on clams

RICHMOND, Va. — Hijackers have pulled off a big heist that netted them 150,000 clams — not clams as in dollars, clams as in seafood.

The bandits forced the drivers of a tractor trailer to transfer their loan of chowder bivalves — worth $18,000 — into another truck and then sped off.

Chapter 5

Sex — sort of

Credit card brothel faces U.S. charges

LAS VEGAS, Nev. (UPI) — Four men arrested for setting a brothel on fire were charged with a U.S. federal offence — destruction of property used in interstate commerce — because the brothel accepted credit cards.

A U.S. attorney said because the brothel's customers used credit cards, the establishment was engaged in interstate commerce.

During a grand jury's investigation, the owner of the brothel, produced receipts showing 80 per cent of his customers were from out of state.

Man breast-fed child for months -- doctor

NEW YORK (UPI) — A physician claims that he enabled a transvestite father to nurse his infant daughter seven years ago by treating the man with acupuncture and a drug commonly used to induce labor in women.

Dr. Leo Wollman, an endocrinologist-psychiatrist associated with Maimonides and Coney Island hospitals in Brooklyn, said that following the treatment, the unidentified man and his wife alternated suckling their daughter for six to eight months.

Wollman said he combined acupuncture with use of the drug Pitocin to treat the 41-year-old man after the patient told him he wanted to share equally with his wife the experience of rearing their infant.

"If she's nursing, I should be too," the doctor quoted his patient as saying.

"This was a bizarre request; however he was a very forceful individual," Wollman said in a telephone interview.

The physician said he placed three needles under the man's breast and one on his sternum "which may have helped stimulate lactation."

Pitocin is a pituitary hormone that can be produced synthetically. It induces labor by causing the uterus to contract.

When the infant stopped nursing, the father stopped lactating, even though he contined taking the hormone, Wollman said.

The child, now 7, is unaware of the special nurturing she received as an infant, Wollman said.

He added that she is above average in size for her age, possibly because of the special care she received.

Medical authorities, asked to comment, said males, given enough female hormones, may produce small amounts of breast secretions, which normally are not enough to meet complete nutritional needs of an infant.

Wollman said of his treatment, "This is not a miracle but simply the idea that a man wants his equality too."

Jailed 16 years for raping wife

POMONA, Calif. (UPI) — A man convicted under California's new spousal rape law has been sentenced to 16 years in prison for forcing his teenage wife to have sex in a stolen recreational vehicle.

Frank Martinez was sentenced on 13 counts including rape, kidnapping, forcible oral copulation, auto theft and four counts of spousal rape.

It was one of the first convictions under the state's new marital rape statute.

Martinez was arrested last Jan. 7 on charges of raping his 18-year-old estranged wife and a 19-year-old saleswoman for a recreational vehicle dealership.

The saleswoman testified that Martinez asked to be shown a van, commandeered the vehicle and took her on a 10-hour ride, during which he raped her four times. The next day he went to the home of his estranged wife and forced her into the van and raped her.

★★★★★★★★★★★★★★★★★★

New policy sought for teenage moms

NEW YORK (AP) — One in five of today's 14-year-old girls in the United States can expect to become pregnant before completing high school, says a new report on teenage pregnancy.

The year-long study asked the government to stimulate a countrywide effort dealing with adolescent pregnancy.

The study was conducted by Family Impact Seminar, a policy research program of the Institute for Educational Leadership at George Washington University, D.C.

The report said current policies focus too narrowly on pregnant teenage girls as individuals and not enough on the full-scale impact of the problem of the family as a whole.

"We are still taking the Band-Aid approach to the problems" the report said.

The issue of parental consent for abortions is only one of many family issues involved, said the report.

Teenage pregnancy costs $8.3 billion in medical and welfare costs a year on local, state and federal levels.

Playgirl to put privates on parade

SANTA MONICA, Calif. (AP) — Playgirl magazine is looking for a few good men, attractive, muscular types — preferably out of uniform.

And the fracas over military women posing in the altogether for Playboy is not going to stop the presses at the magazine specializing in male centrefolds.

Officials at the Santa Monica-based Playgirl, Inc. say they are recruiting raw talent now for a summer photo layout saluting men in power, including military men.

"We've never covered — right, uncovered — men in uniform before," vice-president Rand Richardson says.

Men in Power, a four-page spread for the July issue, will feature not only military men but also policemen, pilots and other uniformed males.

"We're looking for hunky guys, but not macho city," said art editor Alison Morley, who is co-ordinating the talent search. "They have to be good-looking, relatively articulate and have good personalities."

Playgirl, with a circulation of 4 million, will stand behind any men who find themselves in compromising positions with their commanding officers, Richardson says.

Military women posing nude or seminude for Playboy magazine have been running into trouble with the brass. One woman marine who posed for the upcoming issue has been discharged, and in San Diego the U.S. Navy has reprimanded a 22-year-old sailor for being out of uniform and disobeying orders against outside employment that would "tend to discredit the Navy."

Therapy by mail for sex problems

LA JOLLA, Calif. (UPI) — For $59.95 — including postage — Hal Rogers hopes to start a new sexual revolution.

The California sexologist is opening a mail-order business selling sex therapy.

For $59.95, Rogers sends a one-hour cassette tape recording with sexual advice and relaxation techniques "custom tailored" to each patient's needs.

He claims his idea could revolutionize sexual therapy, making it more accessible and affordable to those otherwise inhibited by a visit to a therapist.

"Some areas, such as small rural centres, might not have a qualified sexologist," Rogers said. "And the cost generally restrict it to the upper middle class, who can afford $2,000 for three weeks of therapy.

"By offering therapy through the mail, a person can work in the privacy of their home or office where they can review the material at their own pace in an atmosphere where they're comfortable.

"The anonymity is a big plus, since many people may be afraid to admit their sexual problems or be too embarrassed to go for help, in case a friend saw them or found out."

Rogers, who holds a doctorate from the San Francisco Institue for Advanced Study of Human Sexuality, said he can diagnose a patient's problem by reviewing an explicit, 300-question personal sexual history that his clients fill out.

"Then I'll work out a therapeutic program with very specific suggestions and homework for them to do," he said.

'Artificial' dad wins full paternity rights
Mother of boy inseminated herself

VINELAND, N.J. (AP) — A man whose semen was used by an unmarried woman to artificially inseminate herself has won the right to have the baby bear his name, to visit the boy and make support payments.

The man, who also is unmarried, is identified in court records only as C. M. The mother was identified only as C. C.

Her lawyer, Philip Lipman of Vineland, said she inseminated herself. The child, a boy, was born in 1976.

The case was decided in October by Judge Steven Kleiner of Cumberland County superior court in a closed family court session.

> ## Grandma 'pimp' depraved, judge says
>
> PROVIDENCE, R.I. (UPI) — Calling Martha Lee Saunders "despicable", a judge has awarded the state custody of her two granddaughters after she allegedly used the girls, aged 10 and 13, for prostitution.
>
> "You, Martha Saunders, are despicable and depraved," Judge Thomas Fay said.

Lawyers for the man and woman refused this week to identify their clients. Lawyers said both were in their 20s and lived in Vineland when conception occurred.

Kleiner rendered his decision Oct. 2 and submitted it to legal journals for publication. On Oct. 29, a Supreme Court committee approved the judge's report for publication.

Lawyers said the man and woman were friends in 1976 when the woman decided she wanted to have a baby. C. M. agreed to provide the semen to the woman free.

A baby boy was born, the records showed, and the father sought to visit his son. When the mother refused, he claimed visitation rights as the father and won in a closed session.

In return, he agreed to make support payments and provide a medical insurance policy for the boy. The records said the father found he could not obtain the insurance policy because the child's birth certificate listed teh father as unknown.

The father went back into court asking the birth certificate be amended listing him as the father and that the child be given his last name. The mother refused to consent to the changes.

In his opinion, Kleiner called the father's motivation "laudable and is clearly in the child's present and future best interest."

Lipman said each parent remains single. He said he did not think they were still friends.

Women curious about brothel so madam throws a party

BATTLE MOUNTAIN, Nev. (UPI) — Madam Julie Hickman said the ladies of the community always ask her about life in a brothel, so she threw a big party to let them see for themselves.

Hickman, operator of the Calico Club, invited about 300 women from Battle Mountain and neighboring towns. Men were not on the invitation list.

The women sipped champagne, tried on the latest styles at a fashion show and talked with the six prostitutes employed at the place.

"I wanted to do it for the ladies because they always ask me what it's like in here," said M. Hickman, a member of Business and Professional Women's Club, Chamber of Commerce and the Humane Society in this northern Nevada community.

Most of the women said they attended out of curiosity.

"I just wanted to peek around a bit," one said.

One of the prostitutes handed out tickets for door prizes.

Bisexual marriage comes out of closet

By Frank Rasky Toronto Star

When you first meet the Kohns you feel they belong on the cover of Ladies' Home Journal.

Barry, 37, strikingly handsome with curly brown hair, cleft chin, dazzling smile, is a Philadelphia lawyer who until recently served as Pennsylvania's deputy attorney-general in charge of investigating discrimination cases against minority groups.

Alice, 35, equally attractive, with golden blonde hair and a keen intelligence, is a psychiatric social worker who holds a master's degree and has practised as a family therapist.

They have a 7-year-old son, Danny, and live on a tree-lined street in Philadelphia.

But their's is a marriage with a difference.

It is no longer based on traditional notions of monogamy, fidelity and heterosexuality. Both partners are bisexual.

Kinsey study

They each have sexual relationships with lovers of both sexes within their open marriage.

The couple — in town recently to promote their new book, Barry And Alice: Portrait Of A Bisexual Marriage (Prentice-Hall, $13.95) — maintained their bisexuality is not all that abnormal.

They said Dr. Alfred Kinsey, in his North American sexual study 30 years ago, found about half the population had at least fantasized about relationships with the same sex. Surveys since 1950, say the Kohns, indicate that more than 15 per cent of adults have had sexual experiences with both sexes.

Most bisexual married couples are secretive; "they're terrified of being found out," said Alice Kohn. "You're guilt-ridden. You feel so terribly alone, with nobody to talk to."

Her husband said that's one reason they wrote the book.

"We felt so isolated in our dilemma," he said. "There was no literature we could consult, no models for what we were facing. But since coming out with our book and exposing

our private lives in media interviews, married couples keep telling us, 'You've told our story'."

Their story is what Alice Kohn called the "love story of a boy and girl who grew up in the '60s and lost their innocence yet found sexual liberation in the '70s."

She recalled the night eight years ago when Barry confessed his bisexuality, opening up a Pandora's Box of repressed emotions for both of them.

Alice was then three months pregnant with Danny. Because their marriage of six years had grown stale, she'd been having a love affair with another man.

Barry, in turn, blurted out that he'd been having an affair with another man.

He further admitted he had briefly experimented with homosexuality as a 12-year-old boy at summer camp. But he had long since renounced it, and now he was confused by his seeming ambisexuality. He still felt deeply in love with Alice.

Alice was stunned and responded with a mixture of emotions ranging from fury to sadness to fear.

She remembered thinking, "How could he risk losing me, the relationship we'd built together, the life style we'd come to value? What kind of strange need did he have within him? And what would people say?

"All the repressed anger I'd ever had toward homosexuals came exploding to the surface," she said. "I was angry that I had to deal with the question at all. Why me?"

Sense of sorrow

Mixed with the shock and repugnance was a sense of profound sorrow. "It was as though someone I once knew very well, someone close to me, had died," she said. "I was mourning the loss of a way of life."

They wept together and then agreed to consult a psychoanalyst. Barry vowed he'd try to "cure" himself of his sexual deviation.

But after four years of therapy and of providing legal counsel for the gay rights movement, he came to accept the dual nature of his sex-

uality as something to be cherished rather than repudiated.

Alice adapted more slowly to the bisexual marriage. She says she at first was repelled by the thought of erotic attraction to other women.

"My stereotype of female homosexuality was that it was a weird aberration," she says. "Lesbians were masculine. They didn't wear makeup and couldn't be pretty. Like most women in my generation, I was taught it was improper to touch another woman affectionately."

Strengthen love

She now has had romances with men and with women, but, she said recently, "I make it clear from the beginning that my marriage is my primary relationship, that I'm committed to my life with Barry, and I intend to keep it that way."

Both Alice and Barry claimed their "expanded marriage" has strengthened their love for each other.

But how has their open bisexuality affected their son?

Danny, according to the Kohns, has thus far not been teased by playmates at either the Hebrew school or the progressive private school he attends.

Alice says she has found as a family therapist that it's the lies, never the truths, that undermine family stability. Consequently, she and Barry have adopted a policy of not hiding the facts from Danny.

"He has never seen us having sex with each other or with anyone else; we do not intend for that to happen," Barry said. "Neither does he understand as yet what bisexuality means. When the time comes for him to ask us, we'll tell him the truth."

By their notoriety, are they not imposing unfair pressures on their child?

"He'd suffer the same form of problems if his parents were well-known actors," said Alice. "He may have some painful times ahead of him because of our publicized lives. But you can't protect children from the reactions of others all their lives."

Pair pleads guilty to incest

Brother, sis met as adults

SALEM, Mass. (AP) — After pleading guilty to incest, brother and sister David Goddu and Victoria Pittorino drove off together without comment for an undisclosed location. And they may still be living together — legally, said a lawyer for the woman's adoptive parents.

"A brother and sister can legally together, and who is to know what else goes on?" said lawyer Margaret Mahoney. "Who is to know if they have sex."

Pittorino, 24 and Goddu, 22, who were raised in different adoptive families and were separated for 20 years, yesterday pleaded guilty to incest. Superior Court Justice Francis Lappin fined the couple $100, placed Pittorino on probation for one year and Goddu on probation for two years and ordered them to have counselling.

"I'm not surprised they pleaded guilty," Mahoney said. "It was a very smart legal manoeuvre. They can live together, and the law can't hassle them. They're brother and sister and eyebrows can't be raised."

The lawyer added: "She (Pittorino) will have to have the psychiatric counselling and I have to hope it will cause her to view David as a brother and not as a husband, as something other than a lover.

"We just hope they'll get sick of each other."

Pittorino's adoptive parents originally brought the incest charge in an effort to force their daughter into counselling.

Pittorino found her brother last April. In May they married, but the ceremony was deemed illegal under a state law prohibiting incest.

In Massachusetts, an incest conviction carries a maximum penalty of 20 years in prison.

Sex gadgets sold in homes

COLUMBIA, Md. (AP) — A former high school English teacher has found that a lot of things can be sold at in-home parties, including sex paraphernalia.

Helen Wermuth says selling sex gadgets at home is "an intelligent alternative to the sex shops or mail-order catalogues."

Cuba exiles homosexuals in thousands

From the Washington Post

WASHINGTON — Thousands of homosexual Cubans came to the United States in the Cuba-to-Key West sealift, and as many as 20,000 of them are still in refugee camps awaiting resettlement, federal officials say.

U.S. and private agency sources said the federal government is working with national homosexual-rights organizations to find sponsors for the Cubans. Figures obtained from such organizations as the Metropolitan Community Church and government refugee agencies indicate homosexuals account for up to 50 per cent of the 40,000 Cuban refugees still in camps throughout the country.

How and why so many homosexuals found their way to the United States in the Cuban refugee flow remains a matter of conjecture.

"We've had this conversation many times with our staff people here, and we still haven't come up with any solid answers," said Bill Traugh, director of Federal Emergency Management Agency refugee operations at Ft. Chaffee, Ark.

The most common speculation is that Cuban President Fidel Castro wanted to insult the United States by sending this country as many "undesirables," including homosexuals, among the refugees as possible.

Though homosexuality is not illegal in Cuba, it is considered shameful. The U.S. does not bar entry to homosexuals.

Acknowledged homosexuals at the camp have "self-segregated themselves" into two barracks, each holding up to 125 persons, Traught said. Similar forms of self-segregation have occurred at the remaining three Cuban refugee camps around the country, according to federal and private sources.

Frequent sex fights cancer study shows

CHICAGO (AP) — Too little sex might contribute to prostate cancer.

A connection exists between a build-up of male hormones and cancer of the male prostate gland, says Dr. I. D. Rotkin of the department of preventive medicine at the University of Illinois.

Rotkin and his colleagues found a pattern of lifelong sexual repression in a study of 430 prostate cancer victims who were compared with an equal number of men without cancer.

The researchers found that while the cancer victims had a greater than normal sexual urge, they actually engaged in less activity than the men who didn't have cancer.

Rotkin's theory is supported by the work of Dr. Richard Ablin of Cook County Hospital's Hektoen Institute.

He says semen reduces the prostate's natural ability to fight disease by 16 to 80 per cent.

Ah, there's the rub

CHARLOTTE, N.C. (AP) — When is a masseuse not a woman? Apparently when she used to be a man.

Charlotte has a law against people of one sex massaging those of the opposite. But a masseuse who had a male-to-female oper-ation escaped charges twice recently because court officials couldn't figure out whether the defendant was a man or a woman.

So they couldn't say just what the opposite sex would be.

The district attorney's office thinks the problem will work itself out.

"If the word gets out that people giving massages have had sex change operations," a spokesman said, "the average male won't show up."

'SHE LIKES BEING PREGNANT'

Rent-a-mom gives birth to first baby

By DICK CHAPMAN
Staff Writer

It may be the dawn of Womb-for-Rent medicine.

But Dr. Richard Levin, the Lousiville, Ky., surgeon who masterminds a babies-for-sale surrogate plan, says nobody minds.

"Only the press has called it '1984' or made any criticism," Levin, 35, told the *Sunday Sun.*

Levin's first surrogate mother, an unidentified Illinois woman a.k.a. "Elizabeth Kane," 38, has been paid "less than $10,000" for producing a child for a Louisville couple.

It's the first of 100 babies Levin says will be born in the next year under his Surrogate Parenting Associates, Inc. plan. Since March, more than 12 Louisville women have become surrogates.

Strict requirements of the childless couples — who provide sperm for the surrogate — narrow the field to potential moms of "the highest quality."

Black surrogates have applied but so far no black couples. "Blacks view infertility in a different light than white people," says Levin.

Levin's first surrogate birth, an 8-pound, 10-ounce boy, arrived last Sunday. Mrs. Kane was "allowed" to visit him in hospital but Wednesday, under terms of a contract illegal in many other states, the adoptive parents took possession.

By Friday, Kane, who'd answered a newspaper ad a year ago, drove back to her husband and three other kids. Legal moves had terminated Mrs. Kane's parental rights.

The program has received wide publicity. Levin's heard from childless couples in Canada, France, the U.K., Germany, Mexico, Greece and Italy.

Levin refused to tell a news conference yesterday exactly what Kane was paid and said he got nothing. But future kids-for-cash packages will cost childless couples over $20,000 for legal and medical fees, Dr. Levin said.

None of his stable of surrogates will get more than $12,000 for the nine months' work, he said.

"Many of them want to do it for nothing," said Levin, who says he's happily married with four of his own daughters.

Homosexuals invited to party with Fonda

SANTA BARBARA, Calif (UPI) — Actress Jane Fonda has asked 40 homosexual men to her 200-acre Laurel Springs Ranch for a "Gay Western Weekend," a two-night, three-day fund-raising fling starting Friday.

The event, a benefit for the so-called Campaign For Economic Democracy, "is restricted to 40 gay males," said a press release. "Price per person is $50, which includes all meals, lodging and fun and games."

Lodging will be "bunkhouse-style."

Planned activities include a hoedown featuring country and disco music Friday and Saturday nights, chuckwagon barbecue, softball games, swimming and hiking. Stables are also available for those wishing to bring horses.

Levin says he's doing it "for love, not money. The government already takes 60 cents of every dollar I make. It would be stupid to make more."

Levin says new laws are needed to avoid the nightmare that awaits if a surrogate mother changes her mind about surrendering a baby.

Because of the fee, "there is no precedent. This is different. We'd have two mothers and two fathers. Each side has one biological parent."

Levin told reporters Kane felt the experience was "tremendously fulfilling."

Earlier, he told the *Sunday Sun* she'd done it for three reasons: Because she wanted to "do something nice" for somebody; because she empathized with her own sterile relatives—and "she just likes being pregnant."

Brothel knows its tax tricks

WASHINGTON (AP) — The U.S. Internal Revenue Service says a Nevada brothel owner owes more than $7 million in taxes but concedes that he can deduct prostitutes' salaries as a business expense.

Joe Conforte, challenging the assessment in the U.S. tax court here, said the IRS should also let him deduct rebates to cab drivers plus his brothel's legal fees and linen costs.

Prostitution is legal in Nevada's Storey County, where Conforte owns Mustang Ranch, the state's largest brothel. The IRS makes little distinction about the legality of a business when it assesses taxes or allows deductions.

116

Washington police put transsexual and homosexual officers in the same squad car

By David Miller Toronto Star

Bonnie Davenport and Bobby Almstead are not your usual police officers.

She's the first transsexual in the history of the Washington police force and he's the force's first acknowledged homosexual. And, for the last three months, the two have been working in partnership in a patrol car in the city's affluent northeast section.

"No, this is not a policy change for the force," says Lieut. Hiram Brewton, who trained Davenport. "Bonnie was a he before she became a she and worked nine years on the force. Then he went away and had a sex change operation at John Hopkins in Baltimore and returned a she.

"Because he was a veteran, he, or I guess I should say she, qualified for the force. She was retrained and passed with flying colors. Hell, she's six-foot-one, 175 pounds and has bigger feet than me."

Almstead, Brewton acknowledged, may have been a test from homosexual rights groups, but "there was no reason to reject him."

"He took the course, passed the exams and was investigated extensively. Just because he acknowledged up front he was a homosexual was no reason to reject him."

Almstead, 30, joined the force almost 18 months ago and Davenport, 39, came back six months ago. Both worked in various areas before they were finally assigned together.

Supervisor Frank Weinsheimer says they were put together because they were an effective team, but other police spokesman say they are together because male officers refuse to work with them.

Brewton says there was "no idea to put them together because they were different."

"When a precinct gets a rookie, we always have him or her ride with a senior officer."

Odd couple on patrol in D.C.

Brewton said the pairing has produced "varying" opinions from other officers, but there's no doubt that Davenport is "totally female."

She has shoulder-length blonde hair, a steady boyfriend and three teen-aged children from her first marriage when she was a he.

"Bobby is a lot shorter than Bonnie, but he doesn't flaunt his homosexuality. There are other homosexuals on the force, but none as open as he. Simply, he applied for the job and got it because he was qualified."

Davenport and Almstead, meanwhile, work a straight midnight shift by choice as crime patrol officers on the 3,880-member force. The job allows them freedom to roam the whole district and specialize in family-dispute and disorderly conduct calls.

Because of the spate of publicity last month when their assignments were first revealed, both now refuse to talk to the press.

However, in an interview with the Washington Post, Davenport said she had the sex change operation because she was tormented by a desire to become a woman.

"Police work gets into your blood," she said. "I came back because I had to decide if I would be better off returning to some of the old parts of my life. When I came back, I felt as though I had never left."

Almstead says he is comfortable with his homosexuality and told police recruiters and his classmates at the academy that he was gay.

Genetic risk from sperm donors?

DENVER (UPI) — Some generous sperm donors are fathering so many children that their children "may someday meet and marry" without knowing they're related.

Dr. Paul Wexler, chief of obstetrics at Rose Medical Centre, said individual donors may be siring as many as 15 children over a given three-year period. He is worried about the consequences such generosity may have on society in the form of genetic disorders.

"If we have a donor who has been working three to five years for more than one physician, there is a risk that his children may someday meet and marry," he said, adding that the donor's offspring would be about the same age and would likely be in the same social and economic group.

Girl gets $6,250 for porn shock

COLUMBUS, Ga. (AP) — A 12-year-old girl who was "shocked and mortified" when she accidentally purchased an adult magazine has received a $6,250 out-of-court settlement, lawyers say.

The girl's mother, Ann Cox, filed suit asking for $1.2 million in damages after her daughter mistook a now-defunct magazine, Slam, for a children's publication. Slam was distributed by a company owned by Larry Flynt, also owner of Hustler magazine, court records said.

"I was shocked by the magazine being sold to my child," Mrs. Cox said. "I myself was shocked and humiliated by seeing the magazine. I was ashamed for myself and other adults responsible for this trash."

The cover of the magazine depicted a young boy in a baseball uniform playing with spiders, the suit said.

"The word, Slam is printed in children's letters and the magazine cover is intended to appeal to a child's mind," the suit stated.

Child 'sold' to sex offender found unharmed

Toronto Star special

HIGHLAND, Calif. — Five-year-old Mary Agnes Cahail, who police say was "sold" by her cousin to a registered sex offender for $230, has been found well and apparently unharmed by two policemen in a small town in northern California.

Police spotted a car owned by John William Dickey, 41, in a restaurant parking lot. They charged him with kidnapping.

Authorities believe Mary Agnes' 16-year-old cousin entered her home found the family asleep, awakened and dressed the child and took her from the house before 8 a.m.

They believe the cousin struck a bargain to sell Dickey a child — not necessarily Mary Agnes.

When the cousin was charged with kidnapping, he had only $6 of the $230 he received. Police say he "blew" the rest. His 14-year-old girlfriend also was charged with kidnapping.

Temporary care

Dickey, who buys and renovates rundown property, was declared by a judge to be a "mentally disordered sex offender" in 1976. He was confined to a mental hospital in 1976 and released in 1977.

The child was reunited briefly with her parents yesterday afternoon.

But Mary Agnes will not stay with her family at present, authorities said. She and her 3-year-old brother Darrell will be in the temporary care of Child Protective Services.

Less than an hour after they were reunited with their daughter, the parents left the courthouse, the mother weeping.

The Cahails, who are divorced, said they plan to remarry.

LOS ANGELES TIMES

Gay 'spouse' given survivor's benefits

SAN FRANCISCO (AP) — San Francisco has awarded survivor's benefits to the gay lover of slain supervisor Harvey Milk and proposed that unmarried city workers and their partners — gay or straight — get the same benefits as married couples.

The San Francisco Retirement Board, whose decisions must be approved by the state, ruled 3-1 Tuesday that Scott Smith — Mr. Milk's business partner and lover — was entitled to a $5,500 settlement.

Also Tuesday, a committee of the San Francisco Board of Supervisors unanimously urged giving the unmarried partners of all city employees — whatever their sexual preference — the same benefits as are granted spouses.

Mr. Milk was shot to death by Dan White, a former supervisor, on Nov. 27, 1978, after Mr. White had slain Mayor George Moscone. Mr. White was convicted of voluntary manslaughter and is serving a prison term

The usual estimate of San Francisco's homosexual population is more than 100,000 of the city's 674,000 residents.

Lesbian mother awarded custody of two children

FLEMINGTON, N.J. (UPI) — A lesbian mother who lives with her female companion has been awarded custody of her two children in a landmark decision by a New Jersey judge.

Superior Court Judge William Dannunzio made the ruling in the case of Rosemary Dempsey, 35, a Rutgers law student who has shared her Trenton home with her friend and their children since 1976.

Ms Dempsey's ex-husband, Edward Belmont, 34, of East Windsor, a Mercer County public defender, had asked the court to award him custody of his daughter, Christina, 10 and son, Eddie, 11, charging it was harmful to raise them in a lesbian household.

Ms Dempsey's companion, Margaret Wales, 42, is now involved in a legal battle with her former husband over the custody of their three children.

Taxes may pay for sex-change

MADISON, Wis. (UPI) — Once, he wanted to join the marines and be one of a few proud men. Now, he wants to be a woman, at taxpayers' expense.

If a lawsuit filed by the city fails, the 33-year-old welfare recipient will get his wish. City taxpayers will get the bill, which could total $25,000.

Taxpayers have complained loudly since the Welfare Appeals Committee voted to fund an operation for the man identified only as "Theresa."

Last week, Mayor Joel Skornicka and the city council rushed to court with a lawsuit to block the panel's action.

The panel cited compelling medical reasons for paying for the man's sex-change operation. The city contends the law prohibits using public funds for such an operation.

"Financially, we can't afford it," Skornicka said.

The case has been set before Judge William Eich, who faces a dilemma: If he denies the surgery, the man could carry out his threat to commit suicide. If he approves the surgery, the taxpayers could revolt.

The case is confidential, protected under state privacy law. The man's name and story was disclosed when a dissenting committee member quit in protest.

Groom found lacking — finally

MEMPHIS, Tenn. (UPI) — A 17-year-old bride who was married for four months before she discovered her 19-year-old "husband" was a woman has been granted an annulment.

Chancellor D.J. Alissandratos ordered the marriage annulled yesterday after reviewing a birth certificate of the young woman's spouse, showing the husband was born a female.

The young woman, who now works for a Memphis restaurant, was asked during the hearing only if she knew her spouse was a woman when they married in 1978.

"No, ma'am," she told attorney Audrey M. Scott.

Alissandratos granted the annulment based on a Tennessee law forbidding homosexual marriages.

The minister who married the couple in a large, formal ceremony said the discovery the bridegroom was a woman came as a complete shock.

'I'm a certified sex therapist,'' said the minister who asked that his name not be used. "I'm not that easily fooled."

LEG-WATCHERS RATED TOPS ON PERSONALITY

CHICAGO (UPI) — Men who like leggy women tend to have nicer personalities than those whose fascination with the female form centres on breasts or buttocks, a researcher has reported.

And women with certain physical characteristics, researcher Nancy Hirschberg said, usually have personalities similar to men who like those features.

About 100 men were shown 15 nude silhouettes of women with varied sizes of breasts, buttocks and legs and asked to select the silhouette they preferred. Later the men were given personality tests.

After the information was gathered from both of the men's tests, about 100 women with varied physical features were given personality tests.

Ms Hirschberg, psychology professor at the University of Illinois-Chicago Circle, has spent 10 years studying what kind of men are attracted to which physical features of women.

Men who like women with large breasts tend to be outgoing, showoffy, independent and don't care to help other people, Ms Hirschberg said, while women with large breasts are adventuresome, undependable and impulsive.

Males who preferred women with large buttocks are orderly, socially dependent, guilty and self-abasing, she said, while women with large buttocks also are guilty, self-abasing, introverted and socially inactive.

Leggy women are preferred by men who are socially active and willing to help others, while the women tend to be outgoing, feminine and concerned with making a good impression.

A 'father' serves time in women's jail

SAN JOSE, Calif. (AP) — A seemingly male office clerk with a moustache is serving time for vehicular manslaughter in a women's jail because doctors say he is a female from the waist down.

Paul Becerra, who began a 90-day sentence this week, looks like a man, talks like a man and acts like a man, but has functional female sex organs.

Bacerra, 41, had pleaded guilty to vehicular manslaughter after the car he was driving while drunk crashed into a truck last February, killing his 2-year-old daughter.

An investigation revealed that Becerra was born a female in San Francisco and underwent a sex change operation 10 years ago. But he ran out of money and was never able to complete the transformation.

He married and became a father when his wife was artificially inseminated. That child was the one killed in the accident.

Incest case the 'wildest ever'

OKLAHOMA CITY (UPI) — A 13-year-old girl and her baby daughter, both with the same father, are under guard in hospital in what one detective called the "wildest case of incest I have ever seen."

Authorities said an Alabama man's wife died 16 years ago and he soon began having sex with his four daughters.

One of the daughters had another daughter by the man, and when she grew up the man had sexual relations with her, producing another daughter.

The youngest girl and the middle girl were spirited away from Alabama by the older girl and the younger two now are being held in protective custody in Oklahoma while being treated for shock.

Free-lance male stripper wanted

VALPARAISO, Ind. (AP) — Police are seeking a man who knocked on the doors of two women and performed a strip-tease after saying he was from a company that provides male stripper for a fee.

Twice recently, a man in his 40s with thinning gray hair showed up on the doorsteps of local women, claiming to be from a Chicago company called Show and Telegram, authorities say.

A later check showed no one at Show and Telegram, had ever heard of the man.

I'd have skied down Everest in nude for Mormon lover

EPSON, England (UPI) — A disillusioned former beauty queen says she once loved Mormon missionary Kirk Anderson so much. "I would have skied Mount Everest in the nude with a carnation up my nose."

But three judges ruled yesterday that Joyce McKinney, 27, must stand trial at the Old Bailey (central criminal court) on charges of kidnapping the 21-year-old Mormon, tieing him to a bed and forcing him to have sexual intercourse with her.

"Now I don't want anything more to do with Kirk. He does not know what eternal love is," she said after the decision. "Let me pick up the pieces of my life."

She was released on $3,600 bail but was promptly re-arrested by police for illegal entry into Britain. Defence sources said she probably would be granted bail on that charge as well.

Fake revolvers

No date was set for the trial of Miss McKinney, of Asheville, N.C., and Joseph Keith May, 24, of Maywood, Calif., who face a joint charge of possessing chloroform and separate charges of having fake revolvers which the prosecution says were used in last September's kidnapping outside a Mormon church in Ewell, Surrey.

Miss McKinney sat placidly during the concluding arguments, wearing a loose-fitting pink dress with a white ribbon in her blond hair. May carried a Bible and occasionally put his arm around Miss McKinney.

Miss McKinney, a Miss Wyoming beauty queen in 1973, said during the three-day, pre-trial hearing that she took Anderson to a secluded cottage 185 miles southwest of London for three days in September.

Shackled to bed

Anderson of Provo, Utah, was shackled to a bed and admitted having intercourse with Miss McKinney, although he said he did not consent.

"I have been played up as a very wicked and perverted woman," Miss McKinney said. "It is not true."

Eearlier she told the court her relationship with Anderson began in 1975 and developed to the point where "We even had our children named. I asked if he could support me and he said, 'Honey, I would work five jobs to support you.'

"To a woman this means something," she said. "These are pretty heavy promises."

She told a packed courtroom Anderson was shackled to the bed because "sexual bondage turns Kirk on because he doesn't have to feel guilty. I like to do things the normal way. Who is the sexual pervert, me or him? I wanted to help him fulfil his fantasy."

Carnival sex romp draws crowd

SAN ANTONIO, Texas (UPI) — A pair of carnival workers provided an unscheduled side-show yesterday — sex atop a giant slide.

Workers at the courthouse next door cheered as the pair, apparently unaware of the onlookers, undressed and engaged in a passionate carnival of their own. The couple had spent the night sleeping on top of the giant slide, witnesses said.

The carnival was assembled in a parking lot next to the Bexar County Courthouse as part of the city's 10-day Fiesta celebration.

As word spread through the courthouse, employees scrambled for choice views from the windows, cheering and applauding the amorous pair.

The woman, after the sexual encounter, dressed and slid down the carnival slide to more cheers.

A Sheriff's department spokesman said authorities would check out the incident, but could not do anything unless a complaint was filed. Carnival officials said the pair would no longer be allowed to sleep on the side.

Judge sentences them to life term -- of marriage!

NEW ULM, Minn. (UPI) — A Minnesota judge is sentencing minor offenders to a life sentence — marriage.

For the past 20 years, Judge Noah Rosenbloom has made marriage a condition for probation. When the judge learns an individual seeking probation is living with a girlfriend or boyfriend, he gives the probationer three choices — get married, move out, or go to jail.

Rosenbloom, 58, sees three or four such cases each year. So far, no one has chosen jail, he said.

The judge says the first condition of probation is obeying all laws — and fornication is against the law in Minnesota.

But Public Defender Bill Kennedy says: "Sex is here to stay, whether or not the judge is aware of that."

Marrying: Charles "Tex" Watson, who called himself Charles Manson's "lieutenant for killing" plans to marry tomorrow in the California prison where he now preaches. His bride is 20-year-old Kristin Svege. Watson was found guilty in the seven grisly Tate-LaBianca slayings.

Anti-rape senator faces morals charges

By Douglas Thompson
Toronto Star special

LOS ANGELES — A California state senator who has long championed tough anti-rape laws appears in court this week on nine charges of having sex with two teenaged girls.

Allan Robbins will defend himself by dragging out the sexual backgrounds of his two accusers — even though he introduced a law in the Senate making it difficult to bring evidence regarding the sex history of rape victims.

Robbins, 38, is charged with having oral sex with 16-year-old Regina Cullimore in his state capitol office.

The other eight charges involve his having sex with Lori Terwil-liger, who was 16 when he seduced her on her school-organized trip to the capitol.

He has hired private investigators to probe the girls' sexual backgrounds.

The Democratic senator was involved with another teenager but those charges have been dropped.

If convicted, he faces a jail term and probably expulsion by the Senate.

But it is the evidence of Cullimore and Terwilliger that Robbins wants to attack.

Cullimore has told a grand jury that when she accepted an invitation to Robbins' office and went there, "he loosened his tie and unzipped his pants and took them down. Not to his knees. Just above his knees. I orally copulated him."

Sex slave at the firehall

KNOXVILLE, Tenn. (UPI) — Warrants were served yesterday on nine city firemen and a deputy sheriff charged in the gang rape of a woman in a city firehall last month.

The 25-year-old woman told authorities she was tied to a bed in the rear of the firehall and raped by 25 to 30 men over an 18-hour period. The 10 were identified by the victim in a police lineup.

The woman told police the deputy offered her a ride to her job at a convenience market. Instead of taking her to work, she said, she was taken to the firehall.

Two different shifts of firemen were on duty during the 18-hour period, a total of 24 men.

"This office has received a lot of calls from families of firemen wanting to get this thing resolved," Mayor Randy Tyree said.

Nude driver had truckers over-revved

ST. LOUIS (UPI) — A 44-year-old woman has told police she drove nude on Interstate 55 for 20 minutes because she got too hot in her car.

A St. Louis County police spokesman said the unidentified woman was seen driving north on the highway south of St. Louis Monday.

She drove about 20 miles before she pulled into a shopping centre parking lot and got dressed, authorities said.

The spokesman said the woman told officers she did not realize she could have caused an accident.

Police said the highway became jammed with truck drivers when the report of a woman driving nude was broadcast by a trucker over a Citizens Band radio.

The woman was no detained.

School buses like 'porno city'

SEATTLE (AP) — Drivers of some Seattle school district buses say their passengers are out of control.

One bus driver was shocked when a glance in the rearview mirror revealed that some junior high school girls had partially disrobed and were parading in the aisles.

"It was rather strange because in less than two minutes, the back of the bus looked like porno city," the driver reported to the school principal.

The district employs 158 supervisors for 500 buses and there isn't enough money to hire more. Biggest problem is marijuana smoking, but conduct on unsupervised buses includes student violence, vandalism, obscenity and rowdy behavior.

Drivers have reported fist fights in which noses were broken, knife cuts, rocks and eggs thrown, drivers or students being threatened at gunpoint, broken bus windows and even bus seats being ripped out and thrown from moving buses.

Mother-son love ends in jail

FREDERICKSBURG, Va. (UPI) — Christopher Lillie says he couldn't turn off the love he feels for his mother — and as a result mother and son will be jailed for five years for incest.

Lillie, 20, and his mother, Jean Marie, 42, were convicted of incest in January by Stafford County Circuit Judge J.M.H. Willis, Jr.

Willis gave the two a five-year sentence, but changed it to probation on condition the two never see, talk with or correspond with each other again as long as they live.

The pair admitted violating the probation two weeks after it was imposed and Willis sent them to prison.

Lillie said he made love with his mother "one or two times" since the probation order.

Angry women plan march over brutal barroom rape

NEW BEDFORD, Mass. (UPI) — Hundreds of angry women plan a candlelight march Monday to protest the brutal rape of a 21-year-old woman on a barroom pool table while 15 patrons cheered.

Police said the woman's clothes were ripped off while several men pinned her to the table and sexually assaulted her for 2½ hours before she escaped and flagged down a motorist.

The barroom scene in Big Dan's Tavern was described by one police officer as a cheering frenzy.

"She cried for help, she asked for help, she begged for help, but nobody helped her," police Sgt. Ronald Cabral said yesterday.

Police said the rape occurred Sunday night after the woman went into the bar to buy cigarettes and stayed to have a drink with a friend. When she tried to leave, a man grabbed her and dragged her to a pool table, where she was repeatedly raped for at least two hours.

Watching and cheering

"It is our information that at least some of the men were watching and cheering," Cabral said.

Cabral said the bartender, Carlo Machado, told police he gave a patron a dime to call the police, but the customer dialled a wrong number.

Asked why none of the patrons in the bar tried to help the woman, Cabral said: "They were scared. Everybody said they were afraid to do anything for fear they would get beaten up."

Rose Amado, a member of the Coalition Against Sexist Violence, who is organizing the march, said yesterday: "No human being — woman, man or child — should be violated and we want to have some say to make sure these people are prosecuted,"

Amado said yesterday that at least 300 people will march to New Bedford's city hall to hear the tavern's license formally revoked.

District Attorney Ronald Pina has been preparing a case for the grand jury against four men accused of raping the woman Sunday night.

"There are charges right now of rape, unnatural acts upon a human being, and there could be civil rights violations, assault and battery and accessory charges," Pina said.

A bartender said no one went to the woman's aid because one of the alleged attackers menacingly brandished a butter knife.

Four men have pleaded not guilty to rape-related acts. All are free on $1,000 cash bail.

Meanwhile, the tavern's liquor license was voluntarily relinquished and the bar permanently closed Wednesday, making Monday's hearing a formality, a spokesman for the district attorney said yesterday.

Yesterday, a sign on the door read "This place is closed," as workers cleaned out furniture, cut up the bar with a chainsaw, and removed tables, chairs and the pool table.

No sex please, U.S. is busy watching TV

NEW YORK (AP) — Sex lags far behind watching television as the most popular daily pastime in the United States.

A new study ranks sex 14th, but says the low rating is because only 11 per cent of those surveyed said they engaged in sexual activity every day, or almost every day.

The 179-page study entitled Where Does the Time Go? is the result of 1,000 telephone interviews conducted in May, June and July. Its margin of error is 3 per cent.

When polled, 72 per cent said they watched television every day or almost every day, 70 per cent said they read a newspaper that often and 46 per cent said they listen to records or music tapes.

Other favorite activities include hobbies, gardening and exercise.

The report was commissioned by United Media Enterprises, a Scripps-Howard company.

Mom-for-hire learns husband fathered baby

By Lynda Hurst Toronto Star

CHICAGO — Alexander, the potentially brain-damaged baby born to a surrogate mother, isn't the son of the man who paid her $10,000 to have his baby.

In a scene that rivalled a made-for-TV movie, lawyers for both parties announced on The Phil Donahue Show yesterday a new blood test proved that Alexander Malahoff of Queens, N.Y., isn't the father of the boy born Jan. 10 in Lansing, Mich. to Judy Stiver.

Malahoff looked at the ceiling in relief. Judy Stiver and her husband, Ray, stared stonily ahead. The audience gasped in sympathy — and outrage — when Donahue read the verdict, after calling the case as "as big a nightmare as there could be."

The birth of Alexander has focussed dramatic attention on what has been a slowly developing phenomenon in the past 10 years:

Surrogate motherhood — the artificial insemination of a woman by an unrelated man, usually one whose wife cannot conceive.

It has become a commercial venture with "brokers" or potential donors advertising for surrogates and surrogates advertising their availability.

But in the case of the Stivers, the rent-a-womb venture went wrong.

When the baby was born on Jan. 10, it apeared to be defective — and neither party wanted it.

But after blood tests provded conclusively that Stiver — and not Malahoff — was the father, the rent-a-womb mother, who admits she's formed no maternal bond with her son because she has "never held the baby," said the couple will file for its custody in Michigan probate court tomorrow.

Woman bares all and Mardi Gras stops being a drag

NEW ORLEANS (UPI) — The heterosexuals bested the homosexuals yesterday at the French Quarter corner of Bourbon and Dumaine Sts. The transvestites mounted a street platform for their annual drag queen contest to pick the "he" best dressed as a "she."

The narrow streets began clogging early with Mardi Gras voyeurs and other spectators. Men dressed as butterflies, bumblebees and swans began pirouetting about the stage and the tourists politely applauded.

Suddenly a great shout went up from two short blocks away at the corner of St. Peter and Bourbon Sts.

A young woman appeared on a wrought iron balny.

She all but stopped the drag show up the street.

Men below the balcony began chanting words never to be uttered in front of children.

The brunette hoisted her sweater. She was wearing nothing underneath.

Back at Dumaine and Bourbon, the butterflies were beginning to pout and two flower girls wilted.

The growing crowd under the balcony shouted for more.

The brunette leaned over and told the males they could see more if they showed her something.

On of the men promptly threw his trousers to the balcony.

She peeled off her brown jeans.

The crowd cheered. "This is the end!" shouted the young woman, and showed what she meant.

More than skirts lifted

GLENDALE, Calif. (UPI) — Five women who lifted their skirts to lift the wallets of two dozen unsuspecting elderly men face robbery charges. Police said one member of the female gang would expose herself to her elderly victim, fondle him and offer to perform a sex act — then pick the distracted fellow's pocket.

Sexual harassment rife in U.S. schools

CHICAGO (UPI) — A high-school swimming coach picked his female competitors on the basis of their breast sizes. A male teacher harassed and finally coerced several of his students into having sex with him.

Such sexual abuse of students by their teachers is reaching epidemic proportions in the United States and involves pupils from preschool to high school age, witnesses told the Illinois House Rape Study Committee earlier this week.

Susan Champagne, a former teacher at a Chicago high school, told the panel that fear of failing a class often makes students hesitant to report the incidents.

She said students told her a swimming coach selected his swimming team members "not on swimming ability, but on breast size or on the sexual favors that might be granted by the potential team member."

She said the coach was transferred to another school following complaints from three students, but kept his teaching job because "he tracked down and threatened" the pupils until they dropped their charges.

Ann Benedict, a Chicago ex-teacher, said a survey of college students who recently graduated from high school showed more than 25 per cent knew of or were victims of sexual abuse during high school.

Sex-change inmate moved

SPRINGFIELD, Ill. (UPI) — An inmate going through a sex change by operations and hormone treatment has been shifted from a men's prison to one for women.

The young inmate, a Chicagoan serving a 1-year sentence for theft who has completed about 75 per cent of the sex change, was assigned to an all-male jail.

Spare my blushes!

MIAMI (UPI) — An elderly Texas nun who lives in a San Antonio convent has asked a federal court to make the homosexual-oriented Blueboy magazine stop sending her photos of naked men. Blueboy publisher Don Embinder, asked for comment on the suit, responded: "We sent a mailing to a Catholic WHAT?"

Man helped 4 boys rape girl: Police

COLTON, Calif. (AP) — A retired U.S. Air Force master sergeant "got in line and participated" when he discovered four teenagers raping a 12-year-old girl in a shed in his backyard, police say.

Richard Bender, 40, heard noises in his shed on Friday and went out to investigate, police detective George Nunez said yesterday.

"He should have broken it up," Nunez said. "Instead, he apparently got in line and participated."

Bender was arrested along with one 14-year-old and three 13-year-old boys, for investigation of rape, oral copulation and sodomy.

The girl and the boys came from the schoolyard adjoining Bender's property, Nunez said.

"They took all her clothes off at one point and refused to give them back to her until she co-operated," he said.

Some students who heard rumors about what was happening informed teachers, Nunez said.

On Monday, Principal Dale Chilson of Colton Junior High School provided students with counselling sessions on rape.

"The kids were aware what had happened and there were just a lot of misconceptions that good girls don't get raped and girls just don't tell," Chilson said.

He said faculty members have talked to the students a lot to eliminate the gossip. "We want it to go away from their minds."

Women equal -- in bed: Survey

NEW YORK (UPI) — A survey of the sex habits and attitudes of 106,000 women readers of Cosmopolitan magazine suggests the so-called sexual revolution has brought women equality, at least, in bed.

For example, 54 per cent of the married women said they had had extramarital affairs.

Fifty-five per cent of all those answering the survey said they had made love on their lunch hour at least once.

Asked if they had slept with a man on the first date, 69.4 per cent said they had at least once, and 47.4 per cent said they had slept with more than one man in the same day.

Twenty per cent said they had made love with more than one person at the same time.

And 82 per cent said they had seduced a man at least once.

Of those surveyed, 45 per cent said they were married or living with a lover.

Sixty-nine per cent said their sex lives were satisfactory. Of these, 67 per cent were unmarried.

Thirty-six per cent said they had sex three to five times a week. Eight per cent said they had it at least once a day, and 33 per cent said they had it once or twice a week.

Of those under 18, about 62 per cent said they had sex with a man for the first time before age 16. Thirty-three per cent said they had their first sexual experience with a man between 16 and 18.

Almost 62 per cent said they preferred the traditional position for making love, and 87 per cent said they preferred making love with the lights dimmed.

About 48 per cent said they liked foreplay to last up to 30 minutes; about 36 per cent said 5-15 minutes.

In lovemaking, 94.5 per cent said they enjoy having the man undress them, and 20.8 per cent said they liked to pretend to fight with the man or try to get away.

Seventy-one per cent said they sometimes are the aggressors in lovemaking.

Only 27.6 per cent of those under 18 said they had fantasies during intercourse. About 41 per cent of those over 35 said they did. Almost none, however, said they fantasized about celebrities, just their own partners.

Almost 23 per cent said they use no birth control at all, and 24.9 per cent of those having sex at least once a day said they used nothing.

The Pill, however, is still the most popular form of birth control.

Breast surgery on rise

The Los Angeles Times

LOS ANGELES — At age 30, Sharon Hughes took a monumental gamble that she hopes will save her life.

She underwent a double mastectomy in hopes of virtually eliminating her chances of getting breast cancer. She didn't have any signs of the disease at the time.

"I know I couldn't handle breast cancer mentally," said Hughes. "And I didn't want to spend the next 10 to 15 years worrying about it. I haven't regretted it at all."

★★★★★★★★★★★★★★★★★★★★★★★★★

★ ANNAPOLIS, Md. (AP) — The X-rated gingerbread men and women sold at a shop here may be "disgusting" but they're not illegal, say prosecutors who refused to pursue a complaint about the cookies. The gingerbread people sold at the Gingerbread Man Store feature prominent sex organs and big smiles. "These are obscene cookies, and there's no way you can get around that," said James Wright, executive director of the Maryland Moral Majority. But, Frederick Paone, an assistant state's attorney, said he found the cookies "personally disgusting" but not illegal. ★

★★★★★★★★★★★★★★★★★★★★★★★★★

Striking wives cut off cuddles

SMITHFIELD, R.I. (UPI) — Fifteen angry housewives have stopped cleaning, cuddling and cooking services in a bid to force their husbands to recognize the work they do.

"Appreciation isn't too much to ask for a slave who is on call 24 hours a day," said Terry Waterman as she and some other young mothers picketed outside their homes, carrying signs saying "Have You Hugged Your Wife Today?"

'Honest' cop busts brothel

CHICAGO (Reuter) — An undercover cop sent to check on a clandestine brothel was surprised when he was confronted with a lie-detector test.

He was asked questions such as 'Are you involved with any law enforcement agencies?" and "Are you here to conduct an investigation?"

But he was even more surprised when he was told three days later he had passed the test and could avail himself of the establishment's services.

He went back and engaged the services of one of the prostitutes. As soon as she had disrobed, the police vice squad raided the place.

★ Ads lured high-school girls into high-price call-girl ring

DALLAS (UPI) — A real-estate agent is accused of recruiting high-school students as call girls through classified ads for baby sitters.

William Lathrop, 54, of the wealthy University Park section of Dallas, was charged with two counts of compelling prostitution.

Police says he ran ads in Dallas newspapers seeking "pretty, clean, active, nice" baby sitters and promised extensive travel and high-figure salaries. But a vice-squad officer said the girls were forced into prostitution.

"This is not an on-the-street type of deal at all," the vice officer said. "You're talking big money."

Police believe at least six girls were involved in the prostitution ring.

The newspaper ads promised trips to Acapulco, Rome, Paris, Colorado, California and Hawaii and salaries of $600 a week.

The ring was uncovered after a 15-year-old girl told a policeman stationed at her high school that she worked for Lathrop for several months as a prostitute and was paid several hundred dollars each time she had sex with his clients.

Most girls in U.S. have sex by age 19

By Spencer Rich
Toronto Star special

WASHINGTON — Two out of three U.S. females have sexual intercourse by age 19 — almost all of it premarital — according to a new study by three population experts.

The study, just published in the new issue of Family Planning Perspectives, is based on a sampling of 2,193 women in the year 1976.

It shows a sharp increase in the incidence of sexual intercourse among teenage girls since 1971, when the researchers from Johns Hopkins School of Hygiene and Public Health conducted their first pioneering study of teenage sexual activity.

The 1971 survey showed that about 55 per cent of American girls had sexual intercourse by age 19. The 1976 figures just released were up to 63.3 per cent.

The biggest increase is among white teenagers where the average jumped nearly 10 percentage points over the five-year period and reached 60 per cent in 1976. The figure for black girls was 82.8 per cent.

The researchers also said that "one in 10 U.S. women become pregnant before age 17, a quarter before they are 19, and eight in 10 of these pregnancies are premarital."

Richard Lincoln, editorial director of the magazine, said the rising incidence of sexual activity by teenagers — the figures show that one in five females have intercourse as early as age 16 — reflects "the greater sexual permissiveness that has been going on for a long time."

The increase in sexual activities began even before the "sexual revolution" of the 1960s and has been continuing, he said.

Although a quarter of the young women get pregnant at least once by age 19, not all these pregnancies result in live births because of miscarriages and abortion. Only three-quarters of those who get pregnant actually have the babies, the study showed.

Linda Lovelace nearly broke

MINEOLA, L.I. (UPI) — Deep Throat star Linda Lovelace, apparently nearly broke, has asked for a court-appointed manager to handle expected earnings from the sale of her autobiography.

Attorney Ira Block, named last summer as guardian of Lovelace and her three-year-old son, Dominic, submitted an affidavit in state Supreme Court saying she has "virtually no income at this moment."

He said Lovelace, 30, is "unable to deal with complex money problems, and this has left her in dire financial straits."

He said that she has signed a contract for the publishing of her as yet untitled memoirs by Lyle Stuart, a Manhattan firm.

Block charged that unidentified persons had swindled Lovelace, and that Lovelace was intermittently receiving welfare assistance.

Sex 'therapy' woman wins $200,000 award

SAN FRANCISCO (UPI) — A 26-year-old college student whose psychiatrist persuaded her to have sex with him has been awarded $200,000 in the biggest psychiatric malpractice settlement in history.

The psychiatrist, Dr. Jack D. Shonkwiler, 40, of Campbell, Calif., who admitted having sex with his female patients, was given a six-month jail term for fraudulently billing Medi-Cal for the therapy sessions.

The woman was being given therapy for "manic depression". Her attorney said.

Where no nudes is bad news for wives

FORT WALTON BEACH, Fla. (AP) — This town near Eglin Air Force Base is to ban nudity and X-rated movies at drinking establishments.

Over the pleas of women who said they support their families by working at local clubs, the council approved an ordinance prohibiting "persons from exposing private parts and female breasts, engaging in sexual conduct and causing depiction of nudity and sexual conduct" in bars.

Sex with patients 'useful' many U.S. doctors admit

NEW YORK (UPI) — One doctor in five surveyed in a university study feel "erotic contact" with female patients is useful to their patients and many admit pursuing it.

The poll, published yesterday in the June issue of Ladies Home Journal, said 13 per cent of doctors surveyed said they had such contact with female patients.

Erotic contact included everything from kissing to fondling and sexual intercourse.

Of the 460 physicians responding to the survey by University of California at Los Angeles professors Sheldon Kardener, MD, and Ivan N. Mensh, PhD, 19 per cent said they "actually felt this was useful to patients."

Mensh noted that figure compared closely to a study that showed 25 per cent of medical students believed it was all right "under the right circumstances" for such "erotic contact."

Over-counter sperm kits forseen by U.S. magazine

CHICAGO (UPI) — The rapid growth of commercial sperm banks eventually may lead to artificial insemination kits sold over-the-counter, the U.S. magazine Advertising Age reports this week.

The magazine said commercial sperm banks in several major U.S. cities have reported growing numbers of donors, particularly from men who choose to store their sperm before undergoing vasectomies.

The article said some specialists believe home insemination kits "could eventually become available."

Dr. Cappy Rothman, founder of the New York-based Cryobank, one of the largest and oldest commercial sperm banks, said the threat of nuclear accidents may also increase interest in storing semen as a safeguard against the possibility of "involuntary sterilization."

CLEVELAND, Ohio (UPI) — Beverly Irwin, 37, has filed for divorce from another woman, Carol Lupardus, 35, alleging extreme cruelty and gross neglect. They were "married" in a June, 1972, ceremony in which both exchanged vows and rings.

Hookers track hunters in search of big bucks

REED CITY, Mich. (UPI) — As deer hunters flock into northern woodlands, dozens of prostitutes hoping to catch some big game themselves are right on their heels.

The 15-day deer season, which officially began at daybreak yesterday, is expected to attract up to 700,000 hunters and more than 100 prostitutes.

A state police spokesman said the ladies of the evening arrived earlier this week from Grand Rapids, Toledo, Detroit and Chicago.

He said the women planned to set up camp in and around the town of Idlewild with others establishing an operations base at nearby Baldwin.

Last year, the women offered their services in hotels, motels, rustic cabins and client's camping vans, while others brought their own motor homes and trailers.

Hypnotist offers bigger breasts

PENNSAUKEN, N.J. (UPI) — Women can add up to four inches to their bustlines through hypnosis, says — who else — a hypnotist.

All they have to do is concentrate, it seems.

Frank Lodato, who claims to be a psychologist, says he developed the bustline treatment 14 years ago and has helped as many as 75 women between the ages of 17 and 60 become more buxom.

He charges $350 for the course, which includes an office visit and home study by cassettes.

"Maybe there's a large feminist movement but a lot of women are getting back to being feminine."

One woman, even gave the treatment to her daughter "as a graduation present," he says.

Lodato says the bust development hypnosis grew out of requests from clients who wanted to lose or put on weight in specific places. When a request for developing the breasts was made, he simply adjusted the weight-changing formula and told his clients to concentrate on adding pounds on top.

"Once the woman is given the hypnotic suggestion, we have control of the nervous system which allows the blood to flow into the breast freer and easier," Lodato explains.

"All have shown some type of increase, from one to as much as 4 inches. The average is 2 inches."

Some women have more trouble enlarging their busts because "they are embarrassed," Lodato says. "Either they were tom-boys when they were young or embarrassed by developing early."

The New Jersey Consumer Affairs Department reports that so far no complaints have been lodged against Lodato's clinic.

21-year-old adopts gay son, age 23

MILWAUKEE (UPI) — A 21-year-old homosexual has adopted a 23-year-old son, also a homosexual.

"It was an unusual petition but there was nothing to indicate they were homosexuals," said reserve Circuit Judge Elliot Walstead, who granted the petition. "And if there was something, I don't know if it would have been any of my business."

The adopted son agreed to talk to reporters if his name and that of the father were withheld.

He said the adoption was the best and most economical way to achieve their goal — making each other heirs without drafting a will. They also wanted to share each other's last name without hiring a lawyer.

"I suppose we could have flown to California and gotten married," he said, "but that would have been expensive. And this is better. Adoption is more permanent than marriage. Marriage can end in divorce or be annulled."

His natural parents, he said, know of the adoption.

"They understand I'm no longer their legal son, but they love me."

Biker too big for 'cuffs

MINEOLA, N.Y. (UPI) — A 450-pound biker knows as "Big Daddy," who was too big for handcuffs or the police paddy wagon, has been charged with luring young girls to his apartment and photographing them in sex acts.

John Adams, 35, lured more than two dozen teenagers to his apartment with offers of free or cheap drugs. The victims were "knocked out" with such drugs as laughing gas and photographed with a delayed-action camera, officers said.

Police were unable to handcuff him because his wrists were too large and he had to be taken to the county jail in a special car because he couldn't fit in the paddy wagon.

At Adams' house, police seized more than 500 photos, sexual devices and photographic equipment. At least 25 girls were depicted in the photos.

Want a baby? Try cough syrup: Doctor

PHILADELPHIA (AP) — A doctor has successfully used cough syrup to treat a kind of infertility that affects up to 20 per cent of all women who have problems becoming pregnant.

Dr. Jerome Check, an assistant professor of obstetrics at Jefferson Medical College, said in an interview yesterday that the treatment worked because of an ingredient contained in many cough medicines called guaifenesin.

The substance thins mucus in the nasal passages and makes it easier for a person to cough. But it also thins the mucus in the cervix, thus allowing sperm to penetrate more easily.

Of 40 women who took part in a study check conducted, 15 became pregnant after being treated with Robitussin cough syrup or simply guaifenesin in capsule form.

"A fair number of women are going to get pregnant on Robitussin alone," the obstetrician said. He said he chose that brand simply for convenience.

Experts in the field said the idea is promising, but stressed that more study is needed.

Dr. Robert Keenan, a spokesman for Robitussin's manufacturer, the A. H. Robins Co. of Richmond, Va., said the procedure was being tried in fertility clinics.

"It's a logical and fruitful avenue of research," said Dr. Marvin Yussman, a professor of obstetrics at the University of Louisville.

Check said a common cause of infertility in women is abnormally thick cervical mucus, which also contains chemicals that kill sperm. He said that in addition to making the cervical mucus less viscous, guaifenesin dilutes the chemicals that destroy sperm.

★★

'Wife wanted' ad leads to altar

YADKINVILLE, N.C. (UPI) — When Robert Evans advertised for a wife he went straight to the point. His ad called for "a nice woman, well-built . . . should be able to drive automatic car . . . be able to tend a large garden."

Evans, 71, said his ad succeeded and he plans to marry a woman whose husband died.

"I found her," Evans said. "I don't know if we'll get married before Christmas or after."

The bride-to-be, Beulah Hutchins Brewer, said:

"I live alone by myself and he's by himself, so we decided, 'why not get together?'"

Mrs. Brewer, 67, said she first heard of Evans' search on a radio station and came to his house last week.

You've ruined our lives, New York 'johns' lament

NEW YORK (Reuter) — A man in Chicago and several from New York and New Jersey woke up today convinced their lives have been ruined by New York Mayor Edward Koch.

Their names were among nine broadcast on a city-owned radio station in the debut yesterday of the John Hour, a program conceived by the mayor to publicize the names of men who solicit prostitutes.

A John is a slang term for a prostitute's customer. Under a unique city law, these men are liable to the same legal penalties as prostitutes.

Koch thinks holding them up to public ridicule will do something no New York mayor has been able to do since the Dutch founded the city in the 17th century — clear its streets of prostitutes.

But so far the John Hour has produced only anger, despair, threats to sue the city and claims of innocence — at least from its first batch of Johns.

"I am a married man. This is going to ruin my entire family life," said Walter Klein, 33, of Chicago, one of the men who achieved instant fame yesterday.

"This whole thing will put my future in jeopardy. My girl friend is very upset," said Chris Avery, 21, of New York, another name featured on the program.

Avery said that while he was arrested for soliciting, he was never convicted and now he thinks he might sue the city. He added that it was a friend of his who actually solicited a woman police decoy posing as a street prostitute.

Another John claimed that he was a victim of entrapment. He said he was approached by a police decoy and asked if he wanted a good time. When he said she was asking too much, he was arrested.

But Koch said he thought the John Hour would have a positive effect, making men think twice before they engage a prostitute in conversation on a city street.

The Johns have one consolation: Very few New Yorkers listen to the radio station that features the John Hour.

TOLL BOOTH SEX GETS GIRL FIRED

HARRISBURG, Pa. (UPI) — A female toll collector was fired for making love with a truck driver in a collection booth on the Pennsylvania Turnpike. Now she has been re-hired but she cannot get back pay for the time she was off work, according to a court ruling.

The woman, identified in court only as "Ms. X," was allegedly observed with the trucker at 4.30 one morning.

When she was reinstated her union sought the back salary but yesterday a court ruled there were not "compelling reasons" for awarding back pay.

10-Year-Old Girl Gives Birth to Twins

United Press International

INDIANAPOLIS — A 10-year-old girl who gave birth to twin daughters may have made medical history and almost certainly is the youngest mother of twins in U.S. history, medical experts said Friday.

Doctors who helped in the premature delivery at Indiana University Medical Center called the births "extremely unusual." The American Medical Association went one step further, saying it was an unheard of occurrence.

"I've never heard of anything like it before," said American Medical Association science and news editor Frank Chappell in Chicago.

"There have been births to girls so young, girls as young as 6 years old in some certain Indian tribes, so a 10-year-old girl giving birth is unusal but it has happened before — but twins!"

Citing privacy rights of the mother and her family, officials have refused to identify her or to say what will become of the twins. The identity of the father also was withheld.

The babies were born by induced labor last week. They were six weeks premature and weighed 3 pounds, 6 ounces each, a doctor said.

The mother was released from the hospital Monday but the twins will be kept a couple weeks longer.

"There still are people in this county who think you shouldn't give sex education to kids in junior high school that includes contraceptive information," said Helen McCalment, director of the Planned Parenthood Center of Indianapolis. "Maybe now critics of the courses will have second thoughts."

She faces trial for rape

MOBERLY, Mo. (UPI) — A 27-year-old woman has been charged with rape and sexual assault in incidents involving three juvenile boys under Missouri's new criminal code.

The suspect, Debra Lee Timmons, is apparently the first woman charged under the new code.

She was charged last week with one count of statutory rape involving sex with a 12-year-boy, and two counts of first-degree sexual assault involving two boys aged 14 and 15. Randolph Country authorities said additional charges may be filed.

Miss Timmons, held in the county jail on $45,000 bond, posted bond Monday. A preliminary hearing on the charges is scheduled for Oct. 30. The woman's attorney, Joseph Matteson, said she will not plead guilty.

The Missouri attorney general's office said Miss Timmons is apparently the first woman to be charged under the state's new criminal code, which went into effect Jan. 2. And she may be the first woman ever charged with rape in Missouri.

Prior to the new criminal code, the woman could have been charged with contributing to the delinquency of a minor. That offence carries a maximum six-month jail term. Under the new code, Miss Timmons, if convicted, faces a maximum sentence of 15 years in prison on the rape charge and seven years on each count of the sexual assault charges.

Police of this central Missouri town said the boys were willing participants but said the youths were underage. They said the new law classifies sexual intercourse as a crime in such instances.

Millionaire freed on molesting charge

SEATTLE (UPI) — An heir to the Thompson submachine gun fortune has been found innocent by reason of insanity on charges of molesting an 8-year-old girl, and an angry prosecutor responded by saying "watch out for your kids."

"I think I'm as sane as the average person," millionaire Russell Maguire said after he left the courtroom a free man. Under federal law he will not have to undergo psychiatric treatment. Maguire, 57, tensely wiped his brow and said a short prayer before the verdict was announced. He wept silently after learning he was free.

★★★★★★★★★★★★★★★★★★★★★★
★ Arthritic? Try sex ★
★ ★
★ CHICAGO (AP) — Sexual activity ★
★ can relieve the pain of arthritis, says ★
★ Dr. Jessie Potter, director of the Na- ★
★ tional Institute for Human Relation- ★
★ ships in Chicago. Sex stimulates the ★
★ adrenal glands to produce more corti- ★
★ sone "and this alone provides from four ★
★ to six hours of relief from arthritic ★
★ pain," she says. Doctors say three times ★
★ as many women as men suffer from ar- ★
★ thritis. ★
★ ★
★★★★★★★★★★★★★★★★★★★★★★

Boy has male date for prom

ALLENTOWN, N.J. (UPI) — A 17-year-old homosexual student at a high school here will not be barred from bringing a 30-year-old male date to the senior prom.

The unidentified student has bought prom tickets for himself and his date, a local man involved in the homosexual rights movement.

The school district's legal counsel determined "there are no laws or school regulations that would prohibit a male student from bringing another male to the prom."

Many students were upset and some had threatened the student if he shows up with his male date for the prom, scheduled for tomorrow, Superintendent Stephen Sokolow says.

In a similar case in Rhode Island, homosexual high school student Aaron Fricke appealed to a federal judge Tuesday after his principal banned him from attending the senior prom with a male companion.

Teachers moonlighted as sensual sadists

SACRAMENTO, Calif. (UPI) — In her suburban hometown, she was known as Cheri Benton, a former beauty queen and assistant to the principal of a Sacramento area junior high school.

In a San Francisco newspaper ad, she was "Ms Brandi," a sensual sadist offering sexual services to a "few select supplicant slaves."

Offered to resign

Her husband, Bill, was the coach admired by his high school football team and his colleagues.

At night, he was the protector in the sadomasochistic brothel where his wife, Cheri, and their friend, Pamela Gittens, plied their craft with chains, leather straps, whips and other implements of torture.

Last week, the Bentons and Gittens, a substitute teacher's aide working with handicapped children, pleaded no contest to a misdemeanor charge of operating a house of prostitution.

They lost their jobs and face a maximum penalty of six months in jail or a $500 fine.

"They volunteered to resign their positions and that's why we accepted the disposition," said Brian Myers, the prosecutor who handled the case.

The state Commission on Teacher Licensing will consider revoking their credentials once the trio is sentenced on June 10.

On Easter Sunday, Benton, 41, a head football coach, and his wife, 38, were arrested by undercover officers who were solicited at Benton's condominium.

A few days later, Gittens, 40, turned herself in when she was identified as the skimpily clad woman who posed with naked men in photographs found in the brothel.

'Horrible commentary'

Ralph Flynn, executive director of the California Teachers' Association, says he doubts the three ever will be hired again by any school district.

"The question is: As the father of four children, would I want my kids taught by someone engaged in sadistic and masochistic activities? The answer is no!"

But, Flynn said, "It's a horrible commentary on the economics of education that a teacher is reduced to that type of moonlighting."

A long-time spokesman for the American Civil Liberties Union said although he, too, felt teachers should be held to a higher moral code, he believed that "to have them pilloried is another thing."

"It seems to me they are going to be bearing the scars and the blackening of their names for a long time and that seems to be a damn shame," ACLU lawyer Brent Barnhart said.

Remodelled as dungeon

The Bentons' condominimum, drab on the outside, was remodelled to look like a dungeon. The trio ran it for at least four months, detectives said.

They found a client list with hundreds of names, including some men from out of state.

Authorities were tipped by an ad in a San Francisco newspaper that read: "Ms Brandi, sensual

sadist now granting permission to a few select supplicant slaves to enter her dungeon."

Before she married Benton in 1966, Cheri was third runner-up in the Miss Teenage American contest and Miss National Wool.

Benton, who led his football teams at Elk Grove High School to the playoffs for three of the last four years, also grew up in Bakersfield, a descendant of a pioneering California family.

"It just didn't fit anything I knew about him," said Will Sawyer, the principal at Elk Grove high school who worked with Benton for the past nine years.

'Family suffering'

"I talked to him just once since his arrest, and he was extremely apologetic."

Benton last month was named president of the newly formed Sacramento Football Coaches Association and told reporters after his arrest, "Our whole family is suffering. I just can't talk about it."

One of his students, Lyman Magee said, "I have a lot of respect for the coach, and nothing is going to change that."

Gittens spent much of her spare time with a church group and worked with mentally retarded children in schools, friends said.

Gittens denied being a prostitute, saying she only agreed to the plea bargain to stop the case going to trial.

"I've already been punished enough by having my name in the newspapers," she said.

"I'm not condeming women who would do that (prostitution), but it's not something I would engage in."

Study finds U.S. has 1.3 million prostitutes

WASHINGTON (UPI) — The publisher of a newsletter catering to the U.S. sex industry says there are 1.3 million prostitutes in the United States — double the number previously estimated.

Dennis Sobin said in TAB Report the figure includes large numbers of housewives and secretaries who pick up cash in their spare time.

Sobin said his staff came up with the estimate by first going through phone books and newspaper ads in the 300 largest cities to determine the number of massage parlors and escort services.

He then calculated the number of houses of prostitution, their employees, and the number of street walkers by talking to police officials in those cities.

"If anything we're on the conservative side," he said.

The 1.3 million estimate represents about 2 per cent of American women, Sobin said. Previous estimates had set the number of prostitutes in the country at 500,000 to 750,000, he said.

Sobin, who says he holds doctorate degree from New York University and once taught a sociology course for police, reported the existence of about "33,000 massage parlors, escort agencies and modelling services presently operating around the country where sexual services are routinely provided."

Lie-detectors get the massage

WASHINGTON (UPI) — Enterprising outcall "massage" and "escort" service owners are turning the tables on police and using voice-stress machines to screen telephone calls, a trade journal for adult businesses reports.

By using the voice-stress machines and other security devices, TAB Reports says, the firms can enhance employee security when the masseuses and escorts leave the office to answer client calls.

The most popular voice-stress machine — which claims to detect if an individual is lying — is connected to red and green lights, allowing those taking the calls to decide if a caller is legitimate or is a crank, prankster or policeman. The machines cost about $1,800.

Among the questions the escort service operator can ask, keeping an eye on the blinking lights, are: "Are you now or have you ever been a member of a police force?" along with "Are you an informer?"

X marks the spot of teen protest over erotic movies at only cinema

OXNARD, Calif. (UPI) — Protesters carrying placards and chanting slogans picketed the Marina Cinema because it was showing the X-rated movies Sweet Cakes and Hot Cookies.

An ad for the movies described them as a "collage of erotic fantasies" and said "The girls are yummy."

The protesters were neighborhood kids, all under 14 years old, who were fed up at not being able to go to the movies on their summer vacation be-

cause it hasn't shown any movies for children.

The picketing was the idea of Adam Bartlett, 12, and his sister, Lee-Anne, 13, of Oxnard, who explained that last summer the movie house showed G-rated movies and they could spend a day for $1.50 watching Disney and other such films and eating popcorn and candy.

"It isn't fair that they have their movies and we can't come and watch our own movies," Adam said.

★ ★ ★ ★ ★ ★ ★ ★ ★ ★ ★

Girl, 15, shot her stepfather to stop rapes, court told

KISSIMMEE, Fla. (UPI) — Attorneys for a 15-year-old girl who claims she shot her stepfather to stop repeated rapings says she is "not remorseful" and fear she will be dealt a harsh sentence.

Laura Ann McIntyre was to be sentenced today on a manslaughter conviction by Judge Russell Thacker. He can issue a judicial warning or commit the girl to a detention centre until she is 19.

She claims her 31-year-old stepfather began fondling her when she turned 13 and raped her five times.

At her trial, friends testified the girl boasted about her stepfather, who be-

came her mother's second husband when Laura was 2 years old.

She testified that one night, McIntyre grabbed her in his bedroom and ripped her blouse while her mother was at work. Laura said she ran from the room and grabbed a rifle.

She said she could hear McIntyre laughing when she poked the gun barrel through his bedroom doorway, closed her eyes and fired.

Assistant State Attorney Jon Morgan rejected her story, saying, "The victim was shot in the back from a distance of less than two feet with a .22-calibre rifle. There was never any proof of sexual assault. It was not self-defence."

McALESTER, Okla. (UPI) — Ardel (Brickyard Nell) Mesles, 84, is back in the Oklahoma State Penitentiary for the second time in five years for making improper overtures to female nursing home patients. Mesles, the state's oldest prison inmate, is confined to a wheelchair. He gained the nickname Brickyard Nell from working 16 years in a prison brickyard.

Soft porn upstages Bible show

COCOA, Fla. (UPI) — They tuned in for Oral Roberts but got soft core porn instead.

It all happened when a timer switch at a remote antenna in central Brevard County lost power.

So instead of Oral Roberts, and the familiar opening song, Something Good is Going to Happen to You, those who had been watching a religious service got women nude from the waist up frolicking on the screen.

Only one called in to complain.

Incest rate 10% for women poll says

NEW YORK (AP) — Ten per cent of the women who responded to a Cosmopolitan magazine questionnaire said they had engaged in incest, and 47 per cent of those said the incident involved a brother.

Thirty-one per cent of those who said they had committed incest said the partner had been their father, and 22 per cent said it had been an uncle.

106,000 answered

About 106,000 female readers took part in the survey by filling out and returning forms that appeared in the January issue of the magazine.

The results, to be printed in the September issue, were released this week.

Of those polled, 40 per cent said they were using the Pill, despite charges they are unsafe. Nearly half of those were in the 18-to-24 age group.

Abortion rate

Twenty per cent of the women said they were not using any type of birth control and 25 per cent said they had had an abortion. The largest group that reported having had abortions — nearly 34 per cent — were in the 25-to-29 age group.

Half the married women said they have had an extra-marital affair, with 42 per cent of those saying it had no effect on their marriage, 34 per cent saying it helped, and 25 per cent saying it was harmful.

Banker sued for wife's herpes

KANSAS CITY, Mo. (UPI-AP) — The wife of a bank president has filed a $6 million lawsuit saying her husband caused her "permanent and progressive injury," by giving her herpes.

In the four-count suit filed Monday, Joanne St. Clair said J. Wesley St. Clair, 46, "willfully, wantonly, maliciously, and with callous disregard for the rights of others, purposely subjected (Mrs. St. Clair) to herpes."

The suit says that when the couple married in 1979 "St. Clair did not warn his wife he had herpes until sores broke out on his hands. The failure to warn brought permanent and progressive injury."

St. Clair, who has been married twice, was chosen one of the 10 best-dressed men in America last year by the Men's Fashion Guild of America.

Judge awards stewardesses $52 million in sex bias suit

WASHINGTON (UPI) — A federal judge has ordered Northwest Airlines to pay $52.5 million in back pay and interest to more than 3,000 stewardesses who won a lawsuit nearly a decade ago charging they were paid less than male pursers.

U.S. District Judge Aubrey Robinson awarded the money to the 3,364 stewardesses in what their lawyers say is the largest amount ever won in an employment discrimination case.

Philip Lacovara, the airline's lawyer, said Robinson's action clears the way for the company to appeal the case. The stewardesses will not be able to collect their money — some as much as $50,000 — until the appeal is resolved.

Robinson ruled in 1973 that female flight attendants were paid less than male attendants performing the same work. Between 1967 and 1976, male flight attendants received up to $3,000 more a year than stewardesses.

Homosexual sues ex-lover

MOUNT CLEMENS, Mich. (UPI) — A Windsor, Ont., man hopes to prove homosexuals have legal obligations to one another with a property settlement lawsuit against his male ex-lover.

Daniel Strocken claims the man defrauded him of his rightful share of a home the two shared in Windsor from 1974 to 1978 when their relationship ended.

Strocken also is seeking unspecified damages for mental anxiety.

Chicago: 1 rape every ½ hour

CHICAGO (Reuter) — The 40-year-old widow was grateful when a passing jogger stopped to lend a helping hand after her car broke down on a busy city expressway.

But her faith in human kindness was soon shattered. The man in the track suit pulled a gun, jumped into the car and raped her in broad daylight as thousands of motorists sped by.

Two 13-year-old girls were abducted from school during their lunchbreak and raped at gunpoint.

Women afraid

Such horror stories are becoming increasingly common in Chicago newspapers. Rape is rampant in the city.

Women are afraid to walk the streets at night, wait at bus stops or answer doorbells in some neighborhoods.

Once every six hours, a woman reports she has been raped. But the situation is much worse than that because experts say only one rape victim in 10 goes to the police.

On that basis, a woman is raped in Chicago every half hour.

The number of reported rapes is running a disturbing 20 per cent ahead of last year — about 1,100 up to the end of August in this bustling city of three million people.

That's not as many as in either New York or Los Angeles. But what is disquieting is that the number is increasing almost twice as fast in Chicago as in the other two cities.

New York last year had 3,882 reported rapes, Los Angeles 2,467 and Chicago 1,341.

Mother, 12, accused of neglecting baby

KALAMAZOO, Mich. (UPI) — A 12-year-old rape victim who was unsuccessful in a court battle for an abortion has been accused of neglecting her 5-month-old daughter's emotional well-being and may lose her custody.

The baby was born in February but the mother was separated from the child in April through the actions of the Kalamazoo County Department of Social Services.

At a closed hearing this week, the department presented evidence of "emotional neglect" and a juvenile court referee found sufficient cause to hold a hearing. This must be held within 42 days to determine if the child has been neglected.

The young mother was raped by a family friend who was convicted and sentenced for criminal sexual conduct. She was put into a foster home last year as a victim of neglect herself.

'Permissive' girl, 5 lands man in jail for sexual contact

PRAIRIE DU CHIEN, Wis. (UPI) — A judge who sentenced a 24-year-old farm worker to a brief jail term for sexual contact with a child described the 5-year-old victim as an "unusually sexually permissive young lady."

Ralph Snodgrass was placed on probation for three years and sentenced to 90 days in jail for sexual contact with the youngster.

During the sentencing, Judge William Reinecke said, "I am satisfied we have an unusually sexually permissive young lady and he (Snodgrass) did not know enough to refuse. No way do I believe Mr. Snodgrass initiated sexual contact."

Testimony at Snodgrass' jury trial indicated the incident occurred when the girl climbed on top of him while he was sleeping in the nude. Snodgrass' attorney, Maureen Kinney of La Crosse, said she believed the child was merely curious.

The youngster, child of a woman friend of Snodgrass, told a school teacher about the incident and authorities were notified.

Tough times force brothel into bankruptcy

RENO, Nev. (UPI) — Hard times have caught up with the world's oldest profession. The Mustang Ranch, Nevada's largest brothel, has declared bankruptcy.

Attorney Stanley Brown said the owners of the legal brothel, Joe and Sally Conforte, acted to protect the business from the taxman's efforts to sell it.

Under federal bankruptcy laws, tax officials now can't seize the Mustang Ranch's assets and must give the brothel owners time to reorganize their finances.

The U.S. Bankruptcy Court petition shows the brothel has assets of $25 million, unsecured debts of $257,000 and secured debts of an unknown amount to the Internal Revenue Service.

Joe Conforte fled the country two years ago to avoid a sentence for tax evasion. Since then, there have been reports the IRS might seek to sell the brothel to collect money it claims the Confortes owe.

Various reports have placed the debt at around $10 million.

Pet sues over 'photo sex'

CHARLOTTE, N.C. (AP) — A 19-year-old Charlotte woman is suing Penthouse magazine, saying she was coerced into using cocaine and having "continuous" sex with a photographer during a Pet of the Month photo session.

The lawsuit claims Teresa Mackey was not paid for the photo session.

The suit accuses the magazine, its publisher Bob Guccione and art director Joe Brooks, a photographer, of fraud, and seeks more than $1.6 million in damages.

Brooks, the suit charges, lured Ms Mackey to Florida and promised her she would be Pet of the Year — a title worth $150,000, in order to have sex with her during a photography session in August in a hotel in Coconut Grove, near Miami.

In three days, Ms Mackey's suit says, Brooks took 1,728 pictures and forced her to have "continuous" sexual relations with him.

One-sex marriage ruled illegal

LOS ANGELES (AP) — A U.S. federal judge in a case where two men claim to be legally married has ruled same-sex marriages are invalid, saying the word spouse means a relationship between a man and a woman.

One of the men, Anthony Sullivan, said the ruling denies homosexuals due process and equal protection of the law. He said the decision by U.S. District Judge Irving Hill probably will be appealed.

Hill's ruling upheld an immigration and naturalization service denial of Sullivan's immigrant application as a spouse.

Sullivan, who is from Australia, and Richard Adams obtained a marriage license and were married in Boulder, Colo., in 1975. Sullivan later sought permanent immigrant status as the spouse of a citizen.

Sullivan and Adams moved to Hollywood and in late 1975 Sullivan received a letter from the immigration service denying him immigrant status.

"You have failed to establish a bona fide marital relationship can exist between faggots," the letter said.

Sex spa caters to married couples

DOWNERS GROVE, Ill. (AP) — Ken Knudson has transformed a quiet little motel into an erotic sex spa with a novel touch.

The Sybaris Inn, named after an ancient Greek pleasure city, caters for married couples.

"I'm a great believer in marriage — the concept of living through life with the girl of your choice is such a beautiful thing," says Knudson, 35.

"I believe in being in love with your wife and in rekindling the passion that was there when you got married, before the kids and the bills and all the rest."

Rekindled

Knudson said the average age of his patrons is 40 "and we have some in their 60s."

He added: "This is a rekindling place where they can get away from it all for a new sexual experience. We're pushing romantic marriage here — people doing things they just don't normally do."

For those things not normally done, each unit has a king-size waterbed with a remote control panel and white fur bedspreads and chocolate-colored sheets.

Mirrors

There are mirrors on the ceiling and walls, mood lighting, plush carpeting everywhere, a refrigerator for cooling wine, adult movies on closed-circuit TV, heat lamps, a fireplace, stereo, shower, bath and bidet.

"We get a lot of calls from swingers groups and the like but we try to discourage them," said Knudson.

Ads in suburban newspapers invite readers to "escape with your loved one for an anniversary, honeymoon, birthday or just to get away."

Want a penpal?

SALEM, Ore. (UPI) Oregon Penitentiary inmate Michael Archie Easton, 27, serving 15 years for robbery, has advertised for a bride, promising her no sex and a fee of $250.

He only wants her for three years — the period the Veterans Administration will pay him $59 a month extra (a total of $2,124) if he is married and taking college classes behind prison walls. He says he'll pay costs of an uncontested divorce at the end of the three years.

Oregon law does not prohibit prison marriages — but doesn't allow conjugal visits.

39 policemen disciplined over sex with divorcee

MEMPHIS, Tenn. (Reuter) — Thirty-nine Memphis policemen have been disciplined in a case in which police admitted having sexual relations with a 19-year-old divorcee from Paris, Ark.

Police director Jay Hubbard said 24 of the men had sexual relations with the woman and the other 15 were supervisors who "failed to exercise judgment and control."

Hubbard said police were able to prove that only two of the incidents took place while the men were on duty.

Rape victim says wrong man jailed

PHOENIX, Ariz. (AP) — A Tucson man has been convicted of rape, kidnap and armed robbery — despite the victim's testimony that he wasn't the one who attacked her.

James Fitch, 33, claimed mistaken identity in his defence during a two-week trial.

The victim, 40, told a Maricopa County Superior Court jury she was working as a grocery store clerk when a man raped her.

She interrupted the trial proceedings by saying that she had been closely observing Fitch and he was not the assailant.

But Deputy County Attorney Sherry Lancy had the woman concede that Fitch might have been the man and introduced letters Fitch wrote asking her to drop the charges.

Why she posed nude

NEW YORK (UPI) — A policewoman whose nude pictures appeared in sex magazines has told her departmental misconduct trial she feared she had cancer and was depressed about a pending operation

Officer Cibella Borges, 25, a member of the Public Morals Division, was suspended without pay in July when she admitted she was a model for Beaver magazine.

At the time, Borges had recently discovered she would have to undergo a second operation to remove cysts.

Borges later learned she did not have cancer, and she was declared medically fit.

Admission: One condom

WASHINGTON (UPI) — Planned Parenthood's use of U.S. federal funds for National Condom Week Rubber Disco dance — featuring a condom-blowing contest — was an "outrageously crude" waste of taxpayer money, says the health and human services secretary.

Richard Schweiker says he has asked his department to look into sponsorship of the Feb. 19 dance, which included a condom-blowing contest with a $35 prize. The disco was festooned with multi-colored condoms for the occasion.

Amy Fine, a spokesman for Planned Par-enthood of Metropolitan Washington, said the group spent about $1,000 in federal funds for the week's activities. She estimated 200 people attended the dance.

"Admission free with a condom," read the invitation by Planned Parenthood's Men's Centre. "Dress: Informal."

Marine assault on ex-nun

DENVER (UPI) — An ex-Marine, who said he was forced to use his Kung Fu training to resist the sexual advances of a former nun, has been convicted of first-degree sexual assault.

An 11-woman, one-man jury have returned the verdict against Leon E. Brouillette, 34, after several hours of deliberation.

The incident occurred, following a Christmas party at the woman's home.

Brouillette, who testified he had become sexually impotent in Viet Nam, said he was the last person at the party and was preparing to leave when the woman became passionate. He said he responded with a "nice hug."

As he was heading for the door, Brouillette said he heard "growling, screaming coming at me from behind" as the woman struck him. He said he instinctively turned and hit and kicked the woman repeatedly.

Brouillette said the fight lasted for several hours and that the woman becoming violent each time he rejected her. At one time, he had to "peel her off like a damn banana."

The former nun testified Brouillette choked her because she resisted his advances. Brouillette unsuccessfully attempted intercourse, but forced her to engage in oral sex several times, she said.

DES MOINES, Iowa (UPI) — Transsexual Audra Sommers has filed a sex discrimination suit against her former employer, who she claims fired her over her insistence on using the women's restroom while at work. Ms Sommers, formerly Timothy Cornish, still is undergoing sex change therapy. She said she was fired by Des Moines Budget Marketing Inc. after company officials said she could not use the women's restroom because she was not really a woman, nor could she use the men's restroom while dressed like a woman. "What did they expect me to do, go outside in a bush?" she asked.

Flight could be a bust

ATLANTA, Ga. (Special) — Inflation in the West is going sky-high, but we didn't know stewardesses might go bust.

Dr. Charles Fullett of Atlanta reports some startling findings in the American Medical Association Journal.

He says stewardesses who had silicone breast implants put in at sea-level might have them expand to twice normal size when flying at 18,000 feet. There's worse — at 30,000 feet the air in the implants would expand three-fold.

Fullett suggests stewardesses might find the skin-stretching painful, and suggests they check it out in a decompression chamber.

HAPPY DAYS AGAIN FOR 'SLICE OF LIFE' STUDENT

ATLANTA (AP-Special) — A university student who underwent a penis reattachment operation three months ago has been pronounced as having "full and satisfactory function" by the urologist who headed the team of surgeons attending him.

The student was attacked by a laborer in his dormitory room at Clemson University. The university authorities said the student had been dating the laborer's estranged wife.

Urologist Dr. David O'Brien said he used the microsurgical technique already employed successfully in other operations in the U.S. and Japan.

'He' or 'she' it's all the same

Lawyers involved in the trial of Michael R. Moyle in Denver, Colorado, are facing an unusual problem — they don't know whether to refer to Moyle, charged with advertising orgies and "quickie" sexual meetings and then failing to deliver on his promises — as a "he" or a "she."

Seems Moyle, 32, is a transvestite, a male who prefers to wear women's clothing. A courtroom compromise has been reached now, with the prosecutors referring to the defendant as "he," while the defence counsel will refer to his client as "she."

Sex ruling reversed

SANTE FE, N. M. (UPI) — A Court of Appeals ruling that sexual intercourse between a 23-year-old woman and a 15-year-old boy is permissible has been reversed by New Mexico's Supreme Court without comment. Appeals Judge Ramon Lopez had said the woman had been "contributing to the boy's education rather than his delinquency."

Breasts 'burst,' so she sues

BALTIMORE (UPI) — A New York city woman is suing the Dow Corning Corp. for negligence because prosthetic devices implanted in her breasts in 1965 burst three years ago.

Joy Klein said in her lawsuit she underwent surgery in 1965 in Maryland and had devices known as silastic round mammary prostheses placed in her breasts for cosmetic purposes.

The suit said Dow Corning was negligent in making the devices, which burst in her chest in 1978.

Her breasts became "horrendously disfigured" and the devices had to be surgically removed, causing "scarring, mutilation, mental distress, and cancer anxiety," the suit said.

They'd rather talk than do it!

By Val Sears Toronto Star

WASHINGTON — You wanna talk about sex?

Or would you rather just go ahead and do it and shut up?

In a study that a communications specialist said was "frightening," 84 per cent of a sample of university males said they'd rather hold a press conference about a night with a reigning sex queen — that never happened — than really spend a night with her and never be allowed to talk about it.

"It's the triumph of the image over the act," Gerald M. Phillips, a journal editor in the department of speech communication at Pennsylvania State University told a conference seminar here. "And it's an example of how sexually screwed up we are."

A seminar on intimacy, love and lust at the Fourth General Assembly of the World Future Society yesterday was jammed to hear Phillips, and especially sex researcher Shere Hite, author of the Hite Report on Female Sexuality.

The trouble with understanding female sexuality, she told the Communications and the Future Conference, was that it was defined by men.

Penetration myth

"If we didn't have an orgasm, there was something wrong with our heads. The men were supposed to be doing just the right thing with all that thrusting.

"Well, 82 per cent of women can bring themselves to orgasm and it has practically nothing to do with penetration.

"Even the terms we use are male. We talk about vaginal penetration. Why not penile enfolding?"

Hite argued that most of the women who answered her sex questionnaires said they didn't like one-night stands. They preferred to have some good feelings about a man before going to bed with him.

"But their feelings had very little to do with how much they enjoyed the performance. That was more likely tied to the time of the month."

21st century forecast: Three marriages each

BOSTON (UPI) — In the next century, American men will routinely marry three times, taking their first wife for romance, their second to bear children and the third for mature companionship, a professional forecaster says.

More women will initiate premarital sex and more will bear other people's children for a fee, "but the birth rate will fall as more emphasis is placed on self," says Marvin Cetron, president of Forecasting International Ltd. of Arlington, Va.

Cetron, who works mostly for industrial clients, said he used a computer analysis of current events and trends to depict what American life will be like in the 21st century.

He predicted Americans will live longer but also work longer, which will be necessary to keep up with inflation and finance a more active lifestyle.

Vast medical breakthroughs will be achieved, he said, including the discovery of medicines to cure addiction to drugs and alcohol.

Special Babies

By Edwin Chen Toronto Star special

SAN DIEGO, Calif. — Three babies will be born later this year into the world's most elite club — the products of an exclusive sperm bank made up only of winners of the Nobel prize in science.

Their mothers, all selected for their youth and exceptional intelligence and all with infertile husbands, have been impregnated from a sperm bank of the kind first advocated a quarter-century ago by controversial geneticist Hermann Muller.

The man behind the unique sperm repository is Robert Graham, a 74-year-old self-made business tycoon from California who, behind a veil of secrecy, has nurtured his deceased friend's dream to fruition.

The sperm bank's existence was disclosed in an article in the Mensa Bulletin. Mensa is a group of men and women whose IQs place them in the upper 2 per cent of the population. Graham is a member as are the women who have been inseminated.

Controversial Professor William Shockley — often branded a white racist — admits he's one of the sperm donors.

Woman charged in proxy rape

TIBURON, Calif. (AP) — A 56-year-old widow who had dated the city's lawyer became so jealous when he married another woman that she tried to hire an ex-convict to rape his new wife and kill her unborn baby, according to criminal charges filed here.

Marrian Peters Comstock, former administrative assistant for this waterfront suburb north of San Francisco, faces arraignment on charges that she solicited Hansel Smith, 30, a man known locally as "the bus stop rapist" to rape 29-year-old Sharon Conn.

"I'm not even sure I've heard about this in a soap opera," said District Attorney Jerry Herman.

Mrs. Conn was married last April to Robert Conn, 55, a close companion of Mrs. Comstock for several years before his wedding. Mrs. Comstock is free on $2,500 bail.

Smut fighter on sex rap

TAMPA, Fla. (UPI) — The president of an anti-smut group has been charged with sexual battery of a 17-year-old boy and lewd and lascivious behavior involving an 8-year-old girl.

Jack Gregorio, 46, was arrested earlier this week and police spokesman Johnny Barker said the alleged offences occurred between September and April. No other information was provided in an attempt to protect the identity of the children.

Gregorio is president of Taxpay-ing Parents Against Kiddie Smut, which has been campaigning to have sex education books removed from the public library.

As recently as last week, Gregorio was photographed at a City Hall protest carrying a sign reading "Save Our Kids From Smut," while walking between two children.

Last month, Gregorio was quoted as calling a disputed book "filth" and saying it should "be burned along with its author."

Rag doll gives birth to latest toy idea

TALLAHASSEE, Fla. (UPI) — Natalie, a $22 rag doll that gives birth has gone on sale to catch the U.S. Christmas trade.

"Kids that benefit most are children who are about to have a sister or brother," said Jan Alovus, 35, of her 22-inch fabric doll.

The idea for the doll came in 1977. "I had a young friend who was about to have a baby brother or sister delivered at home and I wanted to do something to help him deal with it," she said.

For him, she designed a pregnant monkey doll of socks and yarn with a baby monkey inside that could be delivered.

"I began to get inquiries about possibly making a human doll to help prepare a child for a sister or brother," she said. So she designed Natalie — the name came from natal — who is an adult doll with breasts and a three-inch baby in her stomach, attached by a detachable umbilical cord. The baby can be pulled through Natalie's vagina to simulate the birth process. It also can be nursed.

She also has a doll that can deliver by Caesarean section.

Ms. magazine recommended the dolls for Christmas toys.

"I don't expect to make a lot of money, and this is not my principal business," said Alovus, a freelance art consultant, art teacher and mother of boys aged 4 and 6.

"I'm not try to prove anything, but to make something available to people who want it and adults to take to groups who need it to help children deal with a subject that is often difficult for parents to explain and children to understand.

Man wins $196,500 for female boss' come-on

MADISON, Wis. (AP) — What's sauce for the gander is sauce for the goose when it comes to sexual harassment, a U.S. jury has ruled.

David Huebschen has been awarded $196,500 after he charged his refusal to give in to his female supervisor's advances cost him his job.

Huebschen's lawyer, Michael Fox, had argued that stress resulting from sexual harassment by 37-year-old Jacqueline Rader had caused his client to become "withdrawn, depressed, paranoid, to lose interest in hobbies and unable to feel continuing happiness when his wife was pregnant and his first child was born."

The jury ruled that Huebschen's realationship with Rader was a "motivating factor" in his demotion from a unit supervisor job at the state Bureau of Social Security Disability.

"I'm relieved that it's over — I hope that it's over and we can start getting back to the lives we had before," said Huebschen after the verdict, referring to himself and his wife, Arimanda.

Bernard Stumbras, who heads the division of economic assistance in the Department of Health and Social Services, was also assessed for compensatory and punitive damages.

Stumbras had been cited by the five women and one man on the jury for his "callous indifference" to Huebschen's complaint.

The verdict will be appealed.

Nun vows to keep massaging

ST. PAUL, Minn. (UPI) — Roman Catholic nun and masseuse Sister Rosalind Gefrey has taken a vow to reopen her massage parlor — the latest establishment closed by police — to keep in touch with her "healing ministry."

"I don't know why we have to go through all this rigamarole," she said after police closed down her Professional Massage Centre, which she opened this week without a city license. "But we will comply with the law."

Police closed the parlor Wednesday.

PITTSBURGH (AP) — Things are looking up for Jeff Holt, who came here from Houston for the chance to look a woman straight in the eye and kiss her without bending over from the waist.

Holt, at six-foot-four, is in the right place — the annual gathering of Tall Clubs International. There are 230 taller-than-average folks from the U.S. and Canada gathered for activities that include a beauty contest, a steamboat ride along Pittsburgh's three rivers, eating, drinking and dancing.

The women are all five-foot-10 and up, the men stand at least six-foot-two.

"It's very refreshing," said Holt. "I can hide in the middle of this group and blend in the background. It's nice when you're all the same size."

Terri Vogt of Pittsburgh agreed. "I can wear my spike heels tonight. I can't wear heels at work or I won't fit through the doorways." She's six-foot-five.

Prostitution decoys luring U.S. hunters

IDLEWILD, Mich. (UPI) — State police here are using women decoys to snare deer hunters on the browl for prostitutes.

The new strategy, which already has resulted in nine arrests, could substantially reduce the annual November influx of big-city hookers to this normally placid northern Michigan resort village, officers said.

But tavern owners say police are spending so much time trying to stifle the sex trade that other seasonal criminal activities such as break-ins, thefts and even barroom violence have been allowed to flourish.

"Just the other night, me and my partner had a fight in here with a guy who's been accused of breaking in trucks and cars to steal rifles," said one bar owner. "There were (undercover) police officers in the building who never lifted a hand to stop the fight or anything."

A state policeman said the strategy was developed at the end of the 1977 deer season when an estimated 100 hookers from around the Midwest invaded the area in mobile brothels.

Drugs and Food

Pryor victim of new drug fad

LOS ANGELES — The freak blaze that turned comedian Richard Pryor into a human torch was started when a chemical he was using to purify cocaine exploded in his face, doctors say.

Pryor, in hospital here with serious burns to 50 per cent of his body, has become the first celebrity victim of a new California drug craze.

Pryor, 39, who once said he used enough cocaine "to buy Peru" told a doctor he was using ether to purify the drug for smoking when it exploded, melting his polyester shirt onto his body and turning him into a human torch.

"The type of accident that apparently happened . . . is a very dramatic example of what has been going on in the closets of Los Angeles for several years now," said UCLA Medical Centre psychiatrist Dr. Ron Siegel, who says cocaine users can go through $2,000 to $12,000 worth of the drug a week.

"It's very hazardous. You have an open flame juxtaposed with a volatile solvent — the ether — and we are seeing a large number of accidents, people who have been burned when they come down from the euphoria or 'nod out.'

"When you come down from the high — which lasts only a few seconds — you crash very hard. Many users nod out into their food or into the torches."

"I screwed up man, I screwed up," a neighbor heard Pryor scream as he fled from his posh eight-acre San Fernando Valley home in a panic of pain last night.

Police officer Richard Zielinski and his partner found the comedian walking near his home but at first didn't recognize him. His upper body was so charred he appeared to be wearing theatrical make-up.

U.S. agents make $170 million drug bust

MIAMI (UPI) — U.S. federal agents yesterday seized nearly 700 pounds of cocaine valued at more than $170 million smuggled aboard a Panamanian freighter.

U.S. Customs spokesmen said 13 people were being held in a Dade County jail here, including 10 crew members, the ship's captain and two Cuban-Americans who live in the Miami area.

Agents made the arrests after watching crew members from the 200-foot Panamanian freighter Mar Azul unload two barrel-like containers into a car shortly before midnight. A customs spokesman said the vessel had sailed from Colombia.

The seizure of the cocaine is probably the second largest drug bust in Miami, Woods said.

The largest cocaine seizure occurred last March, when customs agents discovered 3,906 pounds of the drug hidden in a shipment of blue jeans at Miami International airport, he said.

'Grandma Mafia' charged in $25 million cocaine racket

SAN FRANCISCO (UPI) — Eighteen people, many of them "essentially straight" middle-aged women, have been indicted as alleged members of a drug ring dubbed the "Grandma Mafia," which is accused of laundering more than $25 million in cocaine profits.

The drug ring operated in California as well as outside the state, with most of the laundered $25 million, from at least two major drug operations, coming from San Francisco, the San Francisco Examiner reported.

"These were essentially straight women," one federal official said. "They just kind of slid into it. They liked the excitement as much as they did the money."

At least four of the 18 people indicted were fugitives, and the rest were awaiting trial.

Among the fugitives was Barbara Mouzin, 43, of Florida, according to court documents the self-described "chairman of the board" of the money laundering scheme, who handled as much as $1.8 million in cash at a time.

Mouzin and Lois "Rusty" Widdicombe, 51, were identified by agents as the two well-dressed businesswomen who delivered $1 million to federal agents posing as go-betweens in the laundering operation.

Widdicombe who has grown children, was identified by "Mafia" members as a courier of cash and cocaine between Los Angeles and San Francisco, court documents said.

Happy dad gone to pot

TAYLOR, Mich. (UPI) — Charles Kile, a former auto worker and onetime alcoholic, says his children have shown him a way to break his drinking by switching to smoking marijuana.

"My kids turned me on and it's changed my life," Kile said.

"I was a factory rat and a drunk," he said. "For 20 years I neglected my family because of booze. Now I smoke marijuana and it's totally different."

Kile, 39, and his wife, Betty, 39, have founded the United Marijuana Smokers of Michigan, campaigning for legalization of marijuana.

The Kiles are on probation for selling marijuana to an undercover police officer in November 1977.

Editor: Cooke returned Pulitzer Prize because this report is false.

At 8, Jimmy is hooked on heroin

Mom's live-in lover helps him to fire up

By Janet Cooke Washington Post

WASHINGTON — Jimmy is 8 years old and a third-generation heroin addict, a precocious little boy with sandy hair, velvety brown eyes and needle marks freckling the baby-smooth skin of his thin arms. He nestles in a large reclining chair in his comfortably furnished home in southeast Washington.

There is an almost cherubic expression on his small, round face as he talks about life — clothes, money, the Baltimore Orioles and heroin. He has been an addict since the age of 5.

His hands are clasped behind his head, fancy running shoes adorn his feet and a striped Izod T-shirt hangs over his thin frame. "Bad, ain't it," he boasts to a reporter visiting recently. "I got me six of these."

Part of life

Jimmy's is a world of hard drugs, fast money and the good life he believes both can bring. Every day, junkies casually buy heroin from Ron, his mother's live-in lover, in the dining room of Jimmy's home. They "cook" it in the kitchen and "fire up" in the bedrooms. And every day, Ron or someone else fires up Jimmy, plunging a needle into his bony arm, sending the fourth grader into a hypnotic nod.

Jimmy prefers this atmosphere to school, where only one subject seems relevant to fulfilling his dreams.

"I want to have me a bad car and dress good and also have me a good place to live," he says. "So, I pretty much pay attention in math because I know I got to keep up when I finally get me something to sell."

'Can I get off?'

Jimmy wants to sell drugs, maybe even on the District's meanest street, Condon Terrace, and some day deal heroin, he says, "just like my man Ron."

Ron, 27, and recently up from the South, was the one who first turned Jimmy on. "He'd be buggin' me all the time about what the shots were and what people was doin' and one day he said, "When can I get off?" Ron says, leaning against a wall in a narcotic haze, his eyes half closed, yet piercing.

"I say, 'Well, s- - -, you can have some now. I let him snort a little and, damn, the little dude really did get off.'"

Six months later, Jimmy was hooked. "I felt like I was part of what was goin' down," he says. "I can't really tell you how I feel.

"It be real different from herb (marijuana). That's baby s - - -. Don't nobody here hardly ever smoke no herb. You can't hardly get none right now, anyway."

Jimmy's mother Andrea accepts her son's habit as a fact of life, although she will not inject the child herself and does not like to see others do it.

Fast money

"I don't really like to see him fire up," she says. "But, you know, I think he would have got into it one day, anyway. Everybody does. If he wants to get away from it when he's older, then that's his thing. But right now, things are better for us than they've ever been . . . Drugs and black folk been together for a very long time."

On street corners and playgrounds across the city, youngsters often no older then 10 relate with uncanny accuracy the names of important dealers in their neighborhoods, and the going rate for their wares.

Ayatollah's revenge

The heroin problem in the district has grown to what some call epidemic proportions, with the daily influx of so-called "Golden Crescent" heroin from Iran, Pakistan and Afghanistan into the United States.

The "Golden Crescent" heroin — sometimes called "Ayatollah Khomeini's revenge" — is expected by the RCMP to ultimately find its way into Canada, too.

Medical experts, such as Dr. Alyce Gullatte, director of the Howard University Drug Abuse Institute, say that heroin is destroying the city.

Death has not yet been a visitor to the house where Jimmy lives.

A fat woman wearing a white uniform and blond wig with a needle jabbed in it like a hatpin, totters down the staircase announcing that she is "feeling fine." A teenage couple drift through the front door, the girl proudly pulling a syringe of the type used by diabetics from the hip pocket of her jeans.

Another fix

"Be cool." Ron admonishes him, walking out of the room.

Ron comes back into the living room, syringe in hand, and calls the little boy over to his chair: "Let me see your arm."

He grabs Jimmy's left arm just above the elbow, his massive hand tightly encircling the child's small limb. The needle slides into the boy's soft skin like a straw pushed into the centre of a freshly baked cake. Liquid ebbs out of the syringe, replaced by bright red blood. The blood is then reinjected into the child.

Jimmy has closed his eyes during the whole procedure, but now he opens them, looking quickly around the room. He climbs into a rocking chair and sits, his head dipping and snapping upright again, in what addicts call "the nod."

"Pretty soon, man," Ron says, "you got to learn how to do this for yourself."

U.S. wakes up to danger of sleeping pills

Toronto Star special

WASHINGTON — The U.S. government has launched Project Sleep — a bid to help millions of insomniacs who swallow sleeping pills for dangerously long periods of time.

More than 50 million Americans — one in five — have trouble sleeping, and nearly 2 million take sleeping pills on consecutive nights for more than two months at a time, a public health official said.

Charles Krauthammer of the science division of the Alcohol, Drug Abuse and Mental Health Administration, who is heading Project Sleep, said that there has been an explosion of knowledge about sleep disorders, and the effects of sleep-inducing drugs.

But he said many physicians have not been educated about the findings.

Pot third largest industry in U.S.

ATLANTA (UPI) — America's appetite for marijuana has grown to 12 tons a day and has made pot smuggling the nation's third biggest industry — behind only Exxon and General Motors, a former White House health adviser says.

Dr. Peter Bourne said Saturday that pot trafficking has become somewhat like Prohibition-era rum running — flourishing and difficult to stop.

He said the commerce department estimates that the marijuana business totals $48 billion a year.

"In Florida, it's the state's largest industry, exceeding even tourism," said Bourne, now a Washington consultant on health programs. He said foreign bank accounts in Miami totalled $25 million two years ago, but now are $250 million — "a substantial amount of it" financing marijuana.

Bourne said marijuana can be a health hazard, and that its popularity among the young is particularly dangerous because they lack the judgment older pot smokers have.

THIEF BAGS POT

COOS BAY, Ore. (AP) — Penalties for marijuana possession in Oregon have been lenient for several years, but state police nevertheless were surprised when a woman reported that her bag of pot had been stolen.

"When people have their marijuana taken, we're normally the last to know," said officer Robert Gale.

Gale said the woman reported that a burglar broke into her mobile home in Coos County on Saturday and stole a small bag of marijuana given to her for Christmas.

'Granny Grass' gave pot to kids

VENTURA, Calif. (UPI) — Lois Faulkner is known as "Grandma Grass" to the neighborhood children she attempted to cheer up with free baggies of pot.

Miss Faulkner, 68, and her 63-year-old brother, Joseph, were arrested last month for running a marijuana sales operation out of their Simi Valley apartment.

The couple, free on $1,000 bail, face a preliminary hearing today. Both are charged with felony possession of marijuana for sale, while Miss Faulkner also faces two additional felony counts of selling marijuana.

The elderly woman freely admits she sold and occasionally gave marijuana to children and adults during the past two years, despite police warnings to stop.

9-YEAR-OLD POT USERS ARRESTED

WILLMANTIC, Conn. (UPI) — Police say a 9-year-old, arrested yesterday in a marijuana crackdown, knew drug terminology so well they had to call in a narcotics expert to translate what the juvenile was talking about.

Police Chief John Hussey said of the 52 arrested at school and charged with use or possession of marijuana, 40 were juveniles from 9 to 15.

DeLorean's wife gives new wardrobe a trial run

Toronto Star special

NEW YORK — Cristina Ferrare, model wife of automaker John DeLorean, has ordered a new wardrobe to wear at her husband's trial.

DeLorean is charged in a $24-million cocaine-smuggling deal to save his sports-car company.

The DeLorean company in Northern Ireland, financed by the British government went into receivership in February and at that time Cristina hocked four sable coats at $15,000 each. Now it appears she is dressing for the court appearance.

To do so she is seeing Albert Caparo, designer for Betty Ford, Polly Bergen, Gina Lollobrigida and others. Caparo visited her in the $6-million apartment on Fifth Avenue she and DeLorean put up for security for his bail.

Fashion layout

Caparo has designed clothes for Cristina before, including those for a proposed fashion layout in a U.S. magazine before DeLorean's arrest in Los Angeles last month.

Yesterday the New York Times reported that Cristina says millions of dollars had been offered for film rights to her husband's story. DeLorean is free on $10 million bail and said Cristina, "This whole trial is going to cost us a lot. We will need the money."

The couple is considering selling the 20-room Fifth Avenue home to raise money for legal fees; the luxury apartment is expected to go on sale for $6 million.

Cristina, a former covergirl, married DeLorean in 1973, a month after he left General Motors to start his own car-making company.

The couple also owns a 25-room house in New Jersey on 25 acres. With cottages and stable it is reported to be worth $3.5 million.

Bogus drugs flooding U.S. dupe police

MIAMI (AP) — Drowsy truck drivers, overweight housewives and youngsters looking for kicks are being duped into buying millions of capsules that look just like uppers but aren't, U.S. federal drug agents say.

One police force bought $190,000 worth of the caffeine-filled capsules thinking they were buying illegal amphetamines. Police in Omaha, Atlanta, Jacksonville, Fla., and Tampa have been duped.

Drug agents say there's no way to stop the sales because the capsules contain only caffeine — a jolt equal to two cups of coffee — and other legal stimulants — nothing as potent as amphetamines. The fakes sell for $1 to $5 each on the street and cost three cents to make.

"If you get caught, you're not violating the law," said Earl Simmons of the U.S. Drug Enforcement Administration. "And if your buyer catches on, who's he going to complain to? Is he going to call the police and say, 'Hey, I bought some dope that wasn't real dope?' "

But Simmons fears the ruse could lead to a fatal overdose.

"A 14-year-old kid gets some of these and thinks he's taking biphetamines, so he takes four or six to make it until school gets out at three," Simmons said. "Then all of a sudden he buys the real ones, takes six and he's dead."

"They're legal because they contain no illegal substance," said George McWit, who distributes the 250-milligram capsules. "But they sell just as well as speed on the streets. You show people what they are and they'll buy them up."

He said truck drivers and overweight women are his best customers.

. . . You can never find one

In 1972 the New York police department admitted that 80 pounds of pure heroin, seized in the "French Connection" bust and worth $16 million on the street, had disappeared from the police property office. Later, in Gary, Ind., a policeman named Fred Spiker was charged with selling heroin from a black-and-white police cruiser on a downtown street corner.

In this U.S. family drugs are business

BROCKTON, Mass. (UPI) — Three generations of a Brockton family, including an 86-year-old grandfather, have been arraigned on drug trafficking charges.

Arthur Perry, his 63-year-old daughter Jean McDonald, and her son Peter McDonald, 18, appeared Tuesday in district court and were ordered back June 22.

Perry and McDonald were charged with possession of marijuana and cocaine with intent to distribute. The grandson was charged with possession of marijuana with intent to distribute.

Brockton police arrested Perry and the others on Jan. 16 following a raid on their home.

Police at the time said the family claimed they were selling cocaine and marijuana to supplement their Social Security income.

'Drug-buster' judge is busted

FORT PIERCE, Fla. (Reuter) — A pistol-packing judge with a reputatation for strict sentencing of drug dealers has been busted in Florida — for smuggling marijuana.

Judge Tom Coggin, 41, of Decatur, Ala., was arrested in his light airplane at Fort Pierce airport with 150 pounds of marijuana worth about $100,000.

Coggin, who had about $2,500 in one boot and a .38-calibre revolver in the other, was charged with drug trafficking and carrying a concealed weapon.

Last week he sentenced a drug dealer to 13 years in jail.

LOS ANGELES (Reuter) — Mickey Mouse is being used to boost the sale of the drug LSD to schoolchildren, police say. They said counterfeit drawings of Mickey Mouse and other Disney cartoon characters, including Goofy and Donald Duck, are appearing on stamps laced with the illegal drug, which causes hallucinations. Drug "pushers" are apparently trying to give the drug an aura of respectability among schoolchildren, police said. The stamps have the drug on the back in place of glue.

HEY DOPEY MAKE MINE VANILLA

BOSTON (AP) — Three ice cream vendors have been arrested here for allegedly selling heroin from their truck in addition to popsicles and ice cream cones.

Police said they seized a quantity of what they believed was heroin and a handgun after they stopped the truck.

Professor ran 'drug factory' U.S. court told

NEW YORK (UPI) — A prominent U.S. educator has been charged with using his students to make tens of thousands of dollars worth of illicit drugs at his human studies laboratory at New York University.

John Buettner-Janusch, a geneticist and chairman of the Anthropology Department at NYU, allegedly used university money to buy chemicals and equipment. He set up a dummy corporation to launder the proceeds from making quaaludes, LSD and other drugs, the indictment said.

Cocaine kills more in U.S.

ATLANTA (UPI) — Cocaine deaths have tripled in the past six years and many users who don't die suffer ugly side effects such as facial disfiguration and hallucinations that their skin is crawling with insects.

The National Centres for Disease Control, citing statistics from the National Institute of Drug Abuse, said almost 10 million Americans are now snorting, injecting or "free basing" the drug.

Latest figures showed 61 deaths in 1976 and 272 deaths in 1980.

Marijuana hits the roof

FORT LAUDERDALE, Fla. (UPI) — A man and his wife were sound asleep in their mobile home when they became the first known victims of a new form of fallout from the war on drugs — a marijuana bomb.

"It sounded like a hot water heater blew out," Robert Banta said. "We came running out of our bedroom to see what had happened. The place was eight inches deep in brown weeds. There was this jagged hole two feet across in the roof."

Banta's mobile home had been bombed by a 100-pound bale of marijuana, jettisoned from a smuggler's plane fleeing airborne customs agents yesterday.

The plane dumped 100-pound bales of marijuana throughout the area, but no one was injured.

"It's tough enough living near the airport, anyway," Banta said.

Another bale damaged a van near the mobile home. A third crashed through the roof of a home under construction several miles away and a fourth hit a city utilities building but caused little damage.

By the time police reached the home under construction, only residue of the marijuana remained.

"Somebody got the bale," a police spokesman said.

The smuggler's plane landed at Fort Lauderdale-Hollywood airport, police said, and two men were seen running from it. Four hours later one was arrested.

Police continued recovering bales of marijuana until the search was halted by darkness. Thirteen bales were recovered, but officers thought the plane probably had 24 bales aboard.

'We were making love' Leary says

LOS ANGELES (Special) — Timothy Leary said yesterday Beverly Hills police were mistaken about the drugs he and his wife were accused of having when they were arrested on Wednesday and about the moans neighbors thought they heard coming from the Learys' apartment.

"My wife and I were making loud love," Leary explained. "There were a lot of moans and groans and ohhs and ahhs and oh my gods. We regularly take extremely strong aphrodisiacs."

Explosives case goes to pot

LOS ANGELES (UPI) — Sheriff's deputies told that a man "armed with explosives" was barricaded inside his apartment surrounded a block in South Los Angeles and ordered the suspect to surrender.

Moments before the officers shot teargas into the dwelling, Willie Polk came walking down the street and asked the deputies: "What's all the excitement about?"

The officers failed to find any explosives. But they discovered what they thought might be marijuana plants, and booked Polk on suspicion of cultivating pot.

Acid eyedrop scare spreads

LOS ANGELES (UPI) — A scare over acid-spiked eyedrops has spread to a second U.S. supermarket chain, which ordered squeeze bottles pulled from the shelves in 17 area stores.

Von's supermarket chain took eyedrops off the shelves in the areas where bottles of Murine eyedrops, contaminated with sulphuric acid, were found at a rival chain, Alpha-Beta.

Alpha-Beta has removed all eye, ear and nose drops from its market shelves in 158 stores after finding three doctored bottles, Vice-President Esther Cramer said.

"We don't know if we'll ever put the product back on the shelves again," Cramer said. Unless manufacturers produce "tamperproof" bottles, the market chain may have to sell the products from behind the pharmaceutical counter, she said.

Bill Davila, Von's senior vice-president, said there were no reports of contaminated bottles at the supermarket, but the removal order was a precaution.

Detectives from Los Angeles are investigating.

Pupils paid to turn in drug users

LEWISVILLE, Texas (UPI) — Officials say paying high school informants up to $100 to turn in classmates who use drugs is not fostering a class of "Hitler youth-type" spies, but civil liberty groups blasted the nationally publicized program as unconstitutional.

Educators across the U.S. said they were looking to north Texas and studying the Lewisville High School system of using paid informants to help fight the epidemic of youth drug abuse. Fourteen students have been expelled so far, and all face criminal charges.

"Lewisville is doing what works in Lewisville," said Jim Parcell, PTA coordinator for the Texas War On Drugs, a campaign founded and largely funded by Dallas computer magnate H. Ross Perot.

"There are 2,200 kids in school in Lewisville," he said. "Their right to go to school in a drug-free environment must be protected. In this case, the principal has been courageous and concerned. It seems like a good program for the situation in that city. A lot of educators are looking at it."

Said Doug Killough, principal at Lewisville who founded the program: "Somebody has to do something and this is working.

"I have no patience for people who call our system un-American," he said. "This is not a snitch campaign."

Yet it is the use of informant money that inflames critics.

Company has plans for "natural" cigarette

By H. Carlisle Besuden
Herald Farm Editor

Americans have had natural cereals and natural snacks for years. Now, make way for "all-natural" burley blend cigarettes.

A Santa Fe, N.M., company hopes to market the new blend of cigarettes this fall, but it's counting on Kentucky and Tennessee farmers to provide the essential ingredient: naturally grown burley tobacco.

"We are looking for growers who have not used any pesticides, suckering agents or other agrichemicals — other than commercial fertilizer — to grow their crop," said W.D. Drake, marketing manager for Natural Smokes Tobacco Co. of Santa Fe.

Drake said his company's offer would probably apply more to the small-plot grower who uses his family's labor to chop weeds and hand sucker the plants. Most large growers now use chemicals for this purpose to save time and labor and to reduce costs.

"We are, however, interested in contracting with anyone for any amount of burley grown to our specifications up to 100,000 pounds," Drake said.

Natural Smokes has been marketing a cigarette blended from native American Indian tobacco and herbs for the past five years. Most of these sales have centered on the California market, Drake said.

"We have been using the same tobacco — N. (Nicotiana) rustica L. — in our blend that was used by all the great Indian tribes, especially in the Southwest, and was taken back to England by Sir Walter Raleigh in the late 1500s or early 1600s," he said. "Now, we want to introduce an all-natural burley blend."

Most individual varieties of tobacco are too strong or harsh to smoke by themselves, according to cigarette manufacturing officials. Cigarette companies blend burley with flue-cured and Oriental leaf for a mild and even-burning smoke.

Drake, however, said the objectionable harshness can be reduced by soaking tobacco — including burley — in a combination of herbs that the company has produced.

Drake said the natural burley blend would be marketed in a roll-your-own package and in the form of snuff. He said his company is willing to market the natural burley cigarette under a specific name from the same general area if growers prefer.

"Our company is prepared to offer above-market prices for the naturally raised tobacco if the grower is willing to certify it as chemical-free, except for fertilizer," Drake said. "In addition, we will arrange pickup at the farm with payment on the spot for amounts of 100 pounds or more."

Only producers who have a government quota will be allowed to grow and sell burley tobacco to Natural Smokes, said Cecil Buckingham, production adjustment specialist with the Kentucky Agricultural Stabilization and Conservation Service.

Buckingham said that the contract would constitute a non-auction sale and that the company would have to apply for a dealer's number and file appropriate forms to buy burley from producers.

He said the amount of tobacco sold to the company would be deducted from the producer's quota.

Drake said people interested in producing natural burley can obtain additional information by writing to him or Robert Marian, chief buyer, Natural Smokes Tobacco Co., 106 Malaga Road, Santa Fe, N.M. 87501.

Whole world in his stein

ELDERSBURG, Md. (AP) — He once fell to his knees at the sight of Toronto's Molson brewery.

Now beer lover Gordon Matulonis is travelling the globe — not on land or sea, mind you, but on foam.

Matulonis and the boys have been getting together in his den every Tuesday night, trying out beers from all over the world.

So far Matulonis and his pals —Eddie Budelis and Casimir Razulis — have sipped 1,244 beers from 62 countries. The 53-year-old drinking buddies are aiming at eventually tasting 2,000 beers from 100 countries.

Sometimes there is sadness at the get-togethers, when the gang learns that another of the world's breweries has closed.

"We stand and we salute another brewery gone," says Matulonis, who once startled Torontonians when he got down on hands and knees to pay homage outside the Molson brewery.

The men log their evaluations of each sip in notebooks and index all the beers they taste.

They have tasted Stork beer from Senegal, Beer Sheba from Israel, Marathon from Greece, Prestige from Haiti and Rosy Pelican from India, not to mention brews from Fiji, Gambia and the Azores.

At 7 p.m. sharp, Matulonis calls the meeting to order at the bar in his den.

His wife, Elinor, who serves as bartender and referee when the scholarly discussion becomes heated, produces three tall tasting glasses — each containing a few inches of beer — and the research begins.

Matulonis, Budelis and Razulis, who have nicknamed each other Sip, Gulp and Evaluate, start sipping, pausing now and then to discuss the merits and demerits of the brew in question.

Only Mrs. Matulonis knows what they're drinking — she brings out the empty bottle only when the tasting is over.

The three, born in Lithuania, say in a rare display of harmony that German beer is tops.

And they agree that Russian beer is not.

Dead mouse in stew no tasty morsel

NASHVILE, Tenn. (UPI) — A man who found a decomposed mouse in a can of beef stew is suing Campbell's Soup Co. for $100,000, claiming he has "lost the ability to enjoy eating such food" as a result of the experience.

Lawyer Wayne Detring filed suit on behalf of Barry Martin, who said he had to pay medical bills, lost wages and suffered mental pain and embarrassment as a result of discovering the rodent in a can of Bounty Brand Beef Stew bought from a vending machine at work.

Detring said Martin, who is requesting a jury trial, ate a portion of the stew and then "noticed it didn't taste exactly right. Then he noticed a tail and then he noticed the body of a whole mouse. It was not a rat but a mouse."

Detring said the mouse was "partially decomposed."

JIM WHITE/TORONTO STAR

Regional delicacy: Yup, it's true; deep fried turkey testicles are popular in Portland, according to stand owner Marilyn Armstrong, above. In fact, they were one of the hottest items at this year's Festival of Roses carnival. They taste a lot like sweetbreads and a skewer of five costs $2.50. Armstrong says 'the rodeo crowd' loves them.

Hungry? Just reach for a 'wormburger'

CHICAGO (AP) — The owner of Earthworms Inc. is adding "Wormburgers" to the 100 recipes he has for using protein-rich dried worms as food supplements.

A fast-food chain has denied rumors it used ground red worms in its hamburgers. But Darrell Richards, owner of Earthworms, said it's a "question of time before dried worms will take their place on the diet."

People already eat snails, oysters, octopus, squid and shrimp, and dried worms will mix with any kind of cooking, he said. Richard, 43, said he cooks worm cookies and worm cakes at home about once a week.

"For dinner tonight, I'm going to mix one-tenth cup of dried earthworms to a quarter pound of hamburger and call it a 'Wormburger.' "

(Hic!) officer, it's only 7-Up

SAN JOSE, Calif. (UPI)—Teenagers cruising the city streets lift their cans of Coke in a friendly salute to passing police cars. It's the real thing — or is it?

Police say the hottest new item among San Francisco Bay Area underage drinkers is a fake soda pop label that can be wrapped around cans of beer to camouflage them.

Thin wraps of vinyl are designed in the pattern of the familiar Coke, Pepsi and 7-Up soft drink cans but careful examination reveals the labels say "Caco-Calo" instead of "Coca-Cola" and "1-Up" instead of "7-Up".

The wraps cost less than a dollar, are reusable, stick to any moist surface. Some are being advertised in stores as insulators "to keep your beer, colder longer."

One novelty store owner commented: "I think we sell more to adults than to kids. Some parks don't allow beer and some people just don't want to be seen in public with a beer can."

Big Mac tries to de-worm

ATLANTA (UPI) — McDonald's Corp., the nation's largest hamburger chain, reported Tuesday that sales at some of its southeastern stores nosedived dramatically because of a rumor worms were being used to enrich its beef.

Company officials, concerned over a steady two-month drop in sales, called a special news conference in a new effort to quash the lingering rumor. They described their product as 100 percent beef with no additives.

As many as 50 McDonald's stores in the metropolitan Atlanta area have reported lagging sales since the rumor surfaced nine weeks ago, some affected by as much as a 30 percent drop in sales.

For McDonald's, the largest user of beef in the country, it was the second potentially damaging rumor to hit the chain this year. In recent months the company had to combat rumors that founder Ray A. Kroc was linked to a California Satan-worshipping cult.

Escargot got up and went

SAN DIEGO (UPI) — A woman has filed a $350,000 suit against a restaurant, charging the snail she ordered for dinner survived the chef's preparations and tried to make a getaway at the table. Nancy Tattoli filed a Superior Court suit yesterday charging she was "disgusted and distressed" by the sight of the crawling snail. As she left the restaurant, the suit said, Mrs. Tattoli fell down the stairs, breaking her ankle.

Now smokers can puff on puffed wheat

SAN FRANCISCO (AP) — A new non-tobacco cigarette made of puffed wheat, cocoa bean husks, citrus and molasses has gone on the market in the United States this week with the blessing of a medical expert who says it may help curb heart disease.

"There are 50 million smokers in this country, and we can certainly help a lot of them quit or greatly reduce their consumption of cigarettes," said Lee Danna, board chairman of the manufacturer, International Brands Inc.

The new smokes — called Free — do not carry a health warning because they contain no tobacco.

Dr. Donald Harrison, chief of cardiology at Stanford University School of Medicine who is a consultant to International Brands, said: "I'm against smoking in its fullest extent but I have patients that won't quit."

Harrison said nicotine-laced tobacco causes cardiovascular disease that kill about 200,000 people in the United States a year.

"Ninety per cent of the smokers want to quit, but only 20 per cent do — about the same percentages as for heroin addiction." Harrison said.

The new cigarettes still have about three to four milligrams of tar, about the same as low-tar tobacco cigarettes, Harrison said. That means that they still pose a cancer hazard.

Gutline unravels mystery of what ails the stomach

WASHINGTON (UPI) — Gutline, a medical hotline for digestive problems from diarrhea to diverticulosis has opened here.

The free telephone service, operated by the Washington branch of the American Digestive Disease Society, a non-profit health organization, resulted from recent studies on the extent of digestive disorders.

"No one wants to talk about all the diarrhea in this country," said Miriam Ratner, vice-president of the society, "but it is the No. 1 cause of industrial work absence."

Digestive illness, often chronic and debilitating, afflicts more than 20 million North Americans. It is the leading cause of hospitalization and costs more than $35 billion annually, according to a congressional study.

Despite the magnitude of disorders, "the digestive tract and its functions are viewed through veils of ignorance, embarrassment and inappropriate humor," the study said.

Part of a new approach to medicine, Gutline will allow callers to discuss anonymously general and personal digestive problems with a doctor or specialist.

Snakes alive! Omelet has a wiggle

MINEOLA, N.Y. (UPI) — Ursula Beckley, a 36-year-old housewife was preparing to make an omelet.

"She cracked three eggs into a bowl — and a 6-inch snake dropped out of the third egg," her lawyer, Ralph Franco, said yesterday.

He said the eggs were among a dozen Mrs. Beckley bought a few hours earlier.

The following day, Mrs. Beckley, mother of four children, went to her family doctor who prescribed tranquilizers, Franco said.

"She becomes nauseous at the sight of eggs and suffers from psychic trauma, headaches, loss of sleep and loss of appetite," Franco said. She is undergoing psychiatric treatment.

Mrs. Beckley is suing Dairy Barn, supplier of the eggs for $3 million damages. Her husband is claiming another $600,000 damages for the loss of his wife's "comfort, cohabitation, and happiness."

"I have been told that a snake of that size in an egg would have to have come from a mother snake at least 6 feet long," Franco said.

He claims the egg was not properly examined before it was sold.

'Now I may suffer from bone cancer in 10 years'

Toronto Star special

HARRISBURG, Pa. — Reaction to the nuclear power plant accident here could be summed up by this comment from Saul Kohler, executive editor of the Harrisburg Patriot.

He said when he gets up in the morning, "I don't eat bacon because it contains nitrates.

"I don't eat eggs because of the cholesterol.

"I don't eat white bread because it doesn't have fibre.

"I don't drink coffee because of the caffeine.

"I don't smoke cigarettes (he gave up four months ago) because of the tar.

"Now when I walk outside and take a deep breath I may suffer from bone cancer in 10 years."

Kohler said in an interview yesterday he is not opposed to atomic power "or anything that will force the Arabs to drink their own oil."

But he does resent Metropolitan Edison, owners of the power plant, for "fouling the air and then lying about it."

Kohler said most people are going about their business as usual although some of them are finding time to crack jokes like, "Hey, do you see the mushroom cloud?"

The China Syndrome, a film about a cover-up of a near disaster at a nuclear plant, is playing at local theatres but business hasn't been booming, a spokesman for one movie house said last night.

And now shrimp flavored popcorn

Special to The Star

DALLAS — Little puffs of popcorn are exploding into a big business across the U.S., and the Corn Popper, based in Dallas, is grabbing a sizable share of that market.

Nationwide sales of popcorn — in forms ranging from pounds of unpopped kernels at food stores to tons of popped corn in movie theatres — exceeded $1 billion last year, according to the Popcorn Institute, a Chicago-based trade group.

While about $231 million of that is still munched at the movies, popcorn is starting to go the way of McDonald's, Kentucky Fried Chicken and Baskin-Robbins — it's being franchised.

Touting 60 flavors that range from shrimp to watermelon, Charles and Marie Bird of Dallas have in three years transformed one local store into the nation's largest gourmet popcorn chain with 35 stores, each featuring 32 flavors, in 21 states.

By the end of September, the Birds say, their firm, The Corn Popper, will have grown to 70 stores selling what the industry calls "gourmet flavors" that include ketchup, dill pickle and New England clam chowder, which is aimed at the growing market in the Northeast.

With Americans becoming more diet conscious, unadorned popcorn with between 25 and 55 calories a cup (with oil and salt it's 40 to 60 calories a cup) can fill the urge and stomachs of snackers who once might have turned to jelly beans at 416 calories a cup.

In fact, the per capita consumption of candy has dropped from 21 pounds a year in 1946 to less than 14 pounds a year today. By contrast, popped popcorn consumption has risen from 33 quarts a year per person in 1978 to 42 quarts a year, or 9.7 billion quarts last year.

With popcorn surfacing in more between-meal snacks, more popcorn emporiums are popping up to quell the hunger.

The Birds are not alone in their success. Jack Klugman, star of the television series Quincy, has started Jack's Corn Crib in New York city and plans to expand to 36 franchises. Karamel Korn of Rock Island, Ill. — started in 1929 and the nation's oldest popcorn chain — has 270 stores in 44 states. The Birds, however, are the biggest in the so-called gourmet field.

Each of their eight stores in the Dallas area, as well as the 27 franchised Corn Poppers from Washington State to Washington, D.C., offers 32 flavors, selected for regional taste from the 60 possible.

PAMPA, Texas (UPI) — A 29-year-old plumber has eaten 100 hot jalapeno peppers in less than 15 minutes to gain a world record and a giant stomachache. "I'm burning up," said Ronnie Farmer. "It's hurting but I think I'll make it. My whole body is quivering. I've got the shakes — I'm burning up and it feels like a small campfire in my belly." The old record was recorded by a Michigan man who ate 94 peppers in 1 hour and 51 minutes.

They gobble up gatorburgers

BATON ROUGE, La. (UPI) — Fast food fans bored with the burger, taco and chicken routine are bypassing the golden arches and Kentucky colonels these days for an exotic new taste — fried alligator meat.

In south Louisiana where people eagerly devour tons of frog's legs, crawfish and virtually anything that swims or crawls, fried gator is invading the fast food market.

One of the first commercial gator meat outlets in operation is a fried chicken franchise whose owner thought it might be a good idea. Diana Rice, manager of Danny's Fried Chicken, thought it was weird.

"I'm from Colorado. They don't eat gators in Colorado," she said. "That's why when my boss called me up and asked me if I wanted to sell alligator, I said, 'What?' I've been here seven years but I'm still strictly a meat and potato girl, but once in a while I try something else."

She tried the gator and declared, "It's delicious. Very good."

The meat is cut in strips and marinated in a special seasoning and dipped in a batter that is a little bit thicker than used on the chicken. Fried gator meat has a texture similar to pork, and a delicate fish taste like frog's legs.

The first shipment of gator meat arrived from southwest Louisiana less than a week ago. Free samples were given to chicken customers, and a notice on the outdoor marquee announced fried gator for sale.

Within five days the meat was sold out.

Louisiana's coastal parishes provide a home for 350,000 alligators. Each year just before the start of the gator hibernation period, a strictly controlled hunt is carried out to keep the population down. An estimated 15,000 alligators were killed this year.

Natural food fans feast on worms

PARKERSBURG, W. Va. (AP) — Anyone who gets the heebie-jeebies over things like fried ants and chocolate-covered grasshoppers probably wouldn't want to know what Edelene Wood and her friends cook up for their gourment spreads.

A newcomer to one of their Sunday afternoon feasts could unwittingly end up with a mound of rattlesnake salad on his plate.

What may appear to be an ordinary hamburger party could be fried posum sausage.

Earthworms

And get your bearings: For dessert, you could wind up swallowing a slice of earthworm cake. It could be bathed in caramel or chocolate icing.

"We don't encourage the amateur who has never tried anything like this to eat any of these far-out things," says Miss Wood, who gives her age as "past 50." But for a growing number of West Virginians and others across the United States, wild food dishes are a connoisseur's delight.

and others across the United States, wild food dishes are a connoisseur's delight.

"It definitely is a growing thing," says Miss Wood, a clerk for Monogahela Power Co.

The Parkersburg woman recently travelled to Roanoke Island, off Cape Hatteras, N.C., where she organized a Wild Foods Weekend for 75.

Eel, squid

The gathering spent the day ferreting out roots, plants, game and seafood.

At dinner, they sat down to eat 14 wild ducks, a wild goose, yellow tuna salad, steamed oysters, wild grape chiffon pie, sauteed eel, yucca flower-blossom salad and batter-fried squid.

Nature abounds with such fare, Miss Wood says. And depending on the season, and the location, you can have an almost endless variety if you're not squeamish about the bounty of the wilds and know what you're eating.

Assaulted by deadly french fry

ROCHESTER, N.Y. (UPI) — Wayne Monagan got arrested yesterday for assault with a greasy French fry.

And arresting officer Ray Mosher ended up with a catsup-splattered uniform.

Rochester police said Mosher entered Triangle Diner's all-night eatery about 3 a.m. to call his dispatcher because his portable radio was broken.

The next thing Mosher knew, a soggy, greasy, catsup-soaked French fry bounced off the wall near him.

Mosher eyed the offender and told him to stop.

But a fry flew again, this time as Mosher saw the man pull back a fork, "using it as a catapult" to launch the oily fry.

It hit Mosher on the left shoulder, the catsup splattering his uniform.

"The subject was arrested while reloading," the police report said.

Monagan, a 26-year-old resident of suburban Greece, N.Y, was charged with harassment and resisting arrest after Mosher wrestled him to the floor and sprayed him with Mace.

Monagan told police he launched the fry fight because Mosher had given him tickets.

Kennedy's quiche was just garbage

WASHINGTON (AP) — Senator Edward Kennedy and five members of the House of Representatives lunched yesterday on quiche, fruit salad and assorted other foods that had been scrounged from garbage cans of food wholesalers and supermarkets.

"Very good," said Kennedy, adding that the luncheon demonstrates the "enormous waste" of food in the United States while thousands of people go hungry. The event was designed to promote a congressional measure urging federal agencies to share surplus food with the needy.

"Good," said Ohio Congressman Dennis Eckart of his lunch of mushroom quiche, cheese, beans and potatoes au gratin.

"It underscores the point that there is a terrible over-concern about the appearance of food (in stores)," he added. "Some of this food was ready for destruction just because the package was damaged."

The Washington-based Community for Creative Nonviolence, which prepared the luncheon, says its volunteers feed 750 to 1,000 needy people a day with food that is discarded by supermarkets and food wholesalers because it is slightly damaged.

Starving sisters ate newspapers

COLUMBUS, Ohio (UPI) — Two elderly sisters who starved to death in their home apparently ate rolls of newspaper in a futile attempt to stay alive, police say.

The bodies of Naomi Schreiner, 76, and her sister Ruth, 74, were found in their home on the north side of the city.

"An assistant coroner gave a tentative cause as starvation and dehydration," Det.-Sgt. John Shawkey said yesterday.

"There was absolutely no food in the house and there weren't even any ice cubes in the ice trays in the refrigerator," he said.

Police found little rolls of newspaper on plates as if they had been eating newspaper.

"It appeared from the way it (the paper rolls) was sitting around it appeared they were eating the paper," said Shawkey.

Ruth was found lying on the floor of an upstairs bedroom and Naomi was found in a bed, covered with paper and a rolled up newspaper under her head.

Shawkey said the sisters had been dead several days.

Neighbors described the Schreiner sisters as "eccentric" and two "proud girls, but odd."

Baker's dozen sexy delights
Now it's the not-so-humble pie

NEW YORK (Reuter) — Erotica has taken a new, deliciously sinful yet tasteful form here.

A new bakery makes succulent sweets in a variety of intimate shapes. Various parts of the anatomy are sculpted in marzipan, fudge and chocolate. Gingerbread men and gingerbread women biscuits, and his and her breads, are also hot items.

The Erotic Baker shop strives to "keep a fine line between erotica and pornography," says one of the owners, Patrika Brown.

She refused one request to do a very graphic orgy cake, although she has made a "vague, happy orgy" one.

"There's a difference between a fun cake and a dirty cake," she explained. "We draw the line at being exceedingly explicit."

But for the most part, "If there is something meaningful to you and your loved one, we are happy to do it. We ask no questions," she said.

For weddings the bakery offers, instead of the commonplace bride and groom in traditional attire, a smiling couple reclining — under the covers — atop a cake.

In ornate Valentine boxes subtly lurks a private part of chocolate amidst the ordinary sentimental bon bons.

Prices at the bakery, located on a quiet street on Manhattan's upper West Side, range from a $1.50 biscuit to a six-tiered, art deco cake at $500.

The cost of their cakes begins at $12 which is comparable to other made-to-order bakeries.

★★

Cold a boon to dieters?

SPRINGFIELD, Mass. (UPI) — If you took the excess fat from 120 million North Americans and turned it into energy, it could supply the electrical demands of all residences in Boston, Toronto, Montreal and Washington for a year.

But cold weather isn't an excuse to sit idle and let those pounds pile on, says Dr. Frank Katch, chairman of the U.S. Department of Exercise Science at the University of Massachusetts at Amherst.

In fact, exercising in the cold environment can help people lose weight faster than usual.

"If you are fat, the best place to go and exercise is where it is continually cold," Katch said. He also said people should exercise while naked or in little clothing, so they'll shiver.

When you shiver, you use up 10 or 15 per cent more energy, said Ketch. He estimates the body naturally gains from 2 to 3 per cent in weight during the winter. In the summer, you lose this, he said. "People like to use this as an excuse to get fat."

★★

This meal takes back seat to none

SEATTLE, Wash. (AP) — Eaten any good chairs lately? Here's your chance.

The Pacific Science Centre is sponsoring an edible chair contest on March 15 in conjunction with a chair design exhibition.

Rules state the chair must be 90 per cent edible — composed of vegetables, bread, cake or candy held together by toothpicks, glue, wire or rubber bands. No chairs of ice or meat products will be allowed.

The chair doesn't have to be lifesize or capable of supporting weight but must have four legs and a back.

★★★★★★★★★★★★★★★★★★★★★★★★★

It's the mustard

A psychiatrist in Brooklyn, New York, Dr. Leo Wollman, has undertaken a study "of personality differences between people who habitually order hamburgers at fast food counters and those who religiously stick to hot dogs."

After dieting hard for five years, **John Lang** has shed pounds — 800 of them. But he wants to be slimmer for he still weighs 387 pounds.

Lang, 46, of Clinton, Iowa, had to take to his specially reinforced bed 14 years ago when he weighed a mere 800 pounds. By 1970 — with a food intake of 10,000 calories a day — he had eaten his way into the Guinness record book as the world's fattest man, at 1,187 pounds.

When he started dieting he cut down to 1,200 calories a day. Now he is to undergo an operation in which surgeons will remove about 100 pounds of excess skin and fat.

Says John: "I'm tired of lying around."

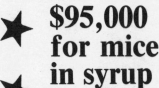

$95,000 for mice in syrup

WILMINGTON, Del. (AP) — Three dead mice in the bottom of a bottle of syrup were worth $95,000 to a man and his daughter who said they kept getting sick whenever they ate pancakes.

Wilson Bozman, 62, of Bear, Del., and his daughter, Susan, 24, of Lindenwold, N.J., could not understand why they were getting nauseated by pancakes or French toast. Then Bozman noticed the dead rodents in the syrup.

When Bozman contacted General Foods Corp., about the problem, the company offered him $100, he said. He refused that offer and a top offer of $1,500.

A court decided Tuesday that Bozman and his daughter should receive $95,000 in damages.

Miss Bozman testified that she and her father used the syrup on six different occasions during a three-week period in December, 1978, and January, 1979. Each time, they suffered cramps and diarrhea, she said.

Chapter 7

Sports & Entertainment

BILLY BOB'S STATS ARE IMPRESSIVE... MULTI-MILLIONAIRE... RESTAURANT CHAIN... LINE OF MEN'S CLOTHING... CONSTRUCTION... AND PRESENTLY NEGOTIATING A LARGE COSMETIC CONTRACT...

Rudy Tomjanovich got more than he asked for yesterday from a federal court jury in Houston, Tex.

The star forward with Houston Rockets of the National Basketball Association was awarded $3.3 million in damages for the injuries he suffered when struck by former Los Angeles Lakers' player Kermit Washington during a 1977 game.

The five-man, one-woman jury gave Tomjanovich $1.8 million in actual damages and $1.5 million in punitive damages. Tomjanovich had asked for $2.65 million.

The jury found that Washington, now with San Diego Clippers, committed a battery on Tomjanovich; acted with wreckless disregard for the safety of others and did not act in self-defence.

The jury also ruled the Lakers were negligent in training Washington and were negligent in keeping the player on their roster when "they became aware that he had a tendency for violence while playing basketball."

Washington was fined $10,000 by NBA commissioner Lawrence O'Brien after the incident and suspended for 60 days.

Lakers' troubles aren't over yet. The Rockets are suing the Lakers for $1.4 million for the loss of Tomjanovich's services during most of the 1977-78 season. That phase of the trial will be heard by the same jury next week.

Daredevil describes his death

ZEPHYR COVE, Nev. (UPI) — In an interview two days before his death, speedboat daredevil Lee Taylor described himself as a man without fear, but said there was virtually only one outcome in an accident at over 300 m.p.h.

"The boat just disintegrates . . .," he said.

During at attempt to recapture his world title yesterday, Taylor's $3.5 million rocket-powered speedboat roaring across Lake Tahoe at 304 m.p.h. veered to the right, flipped three times and shattered, spewing debris 40 feet into the air.

Trapped in cockpit

Taylor, 45, was trapped in the cockpit of the 40-foot aluminum boat, U.S. Discovery II, which sank almost instantly to a depth of more than 300 feet. His family and hundreds of spectators watched from the shore in horror.

"Oh, no, oh no," screamed his wife, Dorothy. She and other family members were taken immediately to a secluded place.

Before the run, Mrs. Taylor said she knew the dangers, but "You can't tell a man what to do. He may not be here tomorrow."

In an interview Tuesday, Taylor said, "I have totally no fear. I'm well aware of what could go wrong but I'm also very concerned with what I am doing. I'm very cautious . . .

"Any type of accident related to speed and water is almost always disastrous," the California race said. "The boat just disintegrates at high speeds. Water is 800 times more dense than air and the friction created at 30 miles an hour is unbelievable. The smallest problem becomes a real problem."

Early today, as sonar-equipped rescue boats probed the depths hoping to find Taylor's body, the cause of the accident was still unknown.

"It was a super run and everything went perfect," said Roy Seikel, the back-up pilot who watched the speedboat from a cliff high above Lake Tahoe.

Taylor had close calls before, but he never talked about the danger or possible death, Seikel said. "He was confident he was going to set the record."

It was the first run of the day for Taylor, who wanted to top Australian Ken Warby's record of 317.60 m.p.h. Taylor held the speed record for 11 years before Warby's run in 1978.

Tricky waters

While going through the check-off, Taylor said there might be a leak in the hydrogen peroxide fuel system. But later he said everything passed inspection.

He waited an extra 15 minutes to allow the tricky Tahoe waters to settle. His last words referred to the readiness of the rocket-powered craft: "It's cooking like hell."

The futuristic red, white and blue craft entered the speed trap at 230 m.p.h., and reached an estimated speed of 304 m.p.h. by the end of the 1-kilometre run. But when Taylor shut down the engine, the boat veered out of control.

In 1964, Taylor bailed out of a jet-powered boat at 200 m.p.h. He skipped across the water, hit land and bounced back into the water He suffered severe head injuries and was pulled from the water by a U.S. army helicpter.

Minutes later, the rescue helicopter crashed and Taylor suffered multiple injuries. He was in a coma for 18 hours and had to learn to walk and talk all over again.

Seikel, president of the company that built the Discovery — the world's first rocket-powered speedboat — called Taylor "a breed apart."

Spinks mugged in Detroit hotel

DETROIT (UPI) — Former heavyweight boxing champion Leon Spinks told police yesterday he was attacked on a city street and later woke up in a motel to find he had been robbed of $45,000 worth of clothes, jewelry and other items.

His assailant or assailants, who left him naked on a motel bed, even took his gold dental plate, the ex-champ told authorities.

Spinks, who bought a house in Detriot a few years ago, told police he was leaving a west side bar Wednesday night when he was struck on the head. He told police he did not see who attacked him.

The next thing he remembers, Spinks said in a police report, was waking up at about 1 p.m. yesterday in a motel about five miles away.

Missing, Spinks said, were his jewelry, his removable front teeth, and all of his clothes — including an expensive blue fox coat. Spinks estimated the value of the missing items at $45,000.

Spinks told officers he called a friend to pick him up, then reported the incident. He apparently was uninjured and requested no medical treatment.

Bid's jockey fined $100 for kicking his horse

BALTIMORE (UPI) — Jockey Ronnie Franklin, who rode Spectacular Bid to victory in the Preakness Stakes last weekend, was fined $100 for kicking a horse that did not race as well as the winner of the first two legs of the Triple Crown series, officials at Pimlico Race Course said yesterday.

Franklin was fined for hitting Big Vision over the head with his whip and kicked him in the stomach after Monday's eighth race, said steward J. Fred Colwill.

"I guess the horse didn't run kindly for him," Colwill said.

Franklin kicked the horse after the race in the unsaddling enclosure, Colwill said.

Nyad planning Cuba swim

JUNO BEACH, Fla. — Diana Nyad, exhausted but in good condition after a record Bahamas to Florida swim, is already looking ahead to another marathon attempt — from Cuba to the Florida Keys through the swift-running waters of the Gulf Stream.

Miss Nyad's record swim, 89 miles from North Bimini Island to Jupiter, Fla., came as another American swimmer, John Erikson of Chicago, failed in a bid to become the first person to make a non-stop, triple-crossing of the English Channel.

Erikson, a 24-year-old schoolteacher, was pulled from the water 11 miles from the French coast yesterday on his final lap across the 22 mile Channel.

Miss Nyad, who will be 30 tomorrow, said another attempt to swim from Cuba to Florida would be "pretty outrageous, but I think it's possible."

She attempted to swim from Cuba to Key West last August, but failed after battling the Gulf Stream current for more than 41 hours. She was only 40 miles from the Cuban shore when she was taken out, 50 miles from her goal.

Good weather and light seas aided Miss Nyad on her record swim from the Bahamas. She made good time, averaging 3.7 m.p.h. during the 27 hour, 38 minute swim. She failed on a similar attempt Aug. 4 because she was severely bitten by a Portuguese Man-of-War jellyfish and had to be removed from the water.

This time, she covered her body with a yellow latex preparation and had escort swimmers cl jellyfish from her path.

Stunt man's 'wildest ride'

WADDINGTON, N.Y. (AP) — Stuntman Kenny Powers says an attempt to fly a rocket-powered car across the St. Lawrence River, landing him in a hospital, was "the wildest ride of my life."

The attempt to fly the winged Lincoln Continental from Morrisburg, Ont., to Ogden Island in the United States ended last week when the car crashed in a few feet of water.

Powers said the jump took place in secret for safety reasons. "If it (the car) had gone off course, with a large crowd watching, and people were injured, it just would have killed me."

Skydivers collide, one dies

STATESVILLE, N.C. (AP) — Two parachutists collided in the air, sending one of them plummeting to his death.

The two jumped from separate balloons and had planned to grab hands, then open their chutes. Instead, they collided and Jay Curlee of Chapel Hill, N.C., fell head-over-heels to his death.

The accident occurred during the final day of the annual U.S. National Balloon Rally in Iredell County. More than 100 balloonists from around the world attended the event.

TOP FROG HOPS AWAY WITH TITLE

HARTFORD, Conn. (UPI) — For the second year in a row, an out-of-stater has hopped away with the Hartford Frog-Jumping Championship.

Canasta, owned by Carrol Castle, 14, of Brattleboro, Vt., copped the frog world's Preakness by covering 105 inches (266 centimetres) in three hops — not considered an outstanding performance.

SPIT'N' IMAGE OF SUCCESS

CHARLESTON, W. Va. (UPI) — Kevin Minear, an 18-year-old cattle farmer, is the winner of West Virginia's tobacco spitting contest.

Wearing a straw hat, he shot the juice 19 feet 8 inches on his third try at the opening of the Governor's Food and Agriculture Exposition.

★ ★ ★

Dominoes tumble to a record

WILMETTE, Ill. (UPI) — Two high school students have toppled a chain of 135,000 dominoes in 27 minutes, 40 seconds, apparently breaking the world record.

Erez Klein and John Wickham, both 17, expect their feat to be recorded in the Guinness Book of World Records.

The youths spent 10 hours a day for three weeks setting up the dominoes in different patterns, including numbers and words. One of the students mothers even examined all the dominoes for flaws that could have hampered the chain reaction.

★ ★ ★

SUNNYSIDE, Wash. (UPI) — A sky diver who plunged 6,500 feet to earth, hit the ground at a bone-crunching 80 mph and miraculously survived after his parachute became entangled says he still loves skydiving. "I would love to do it again," Don Hagert said from his hospital bed. He miraculously suffered only three broken ribs, a cracked rib and internal injuries in his stomach and chest area in the fall although his helmet made a six-inch indentation in the unplowed field in which he landed, 15 feet away from an oil derrick.

She loves her Dodgers - but almost too much

Toronto Star special

LOS ANGELES — It was the final game of the playoffs Saturday, Dodgers against Philadelphia Phillies at Dodger Stadium.

Sitting in the box seats near home plate were Andrea and David Morse.

Mrs. Morse, although pregnant, felt she had a week to go and wasn't about to stay at home while her beloved Dodgers clinched the league championship.

Contractions began

"But just before the first pitch I began having contractions," she recalled. "My husband started timing them. They were very close together."

Every time her husband pleaded with her to leave, she replied:

"Let's wait just one more inning.

"I made it to the seventh inning," she remembered. "During the stretch I sang 'Take Me Out To The Ball Game,' and then David convinced me we should at least call the doctor."

But when they climbed to the pay phones they discovered long lines in front of each one.

"My wife's having a baby!" Morse shouted.

Everybody stepped aside. Some of the fans even offered the husband change for his phone call.

"The doctor told us to leave right away," Mrs. Morse said. "He was afraid the game would end and we would be stuck in the traffic."

When the couple arrived at their Cheviot Hills home, they made another call and the doctor advised the wife to check in immediately at Cedars-Sinai Medical Centre.

"A few hours later in the delivery room," Mrs. Morse recalled, "the obstetrician said: 'I know you're excited about the Dodgers, but listen to what I'm trying to tell you.'"

She did, and a son weighing seven pounds and 11 ounces was born.

Named Russell

"My husband and I had been thinking that if we had a boy we would name him Dustin, so that we could call him Dusty, after outfielder Dusty Baker. But when Bill Russell got that hit to drive in the winning run, we decided to name our child Russell."

Yesterday, the Morse family — including the newest member — left the hospital.

Safe at home, just like the Dodgers.

Bird-in-one golfer to be disciplined

WASHINGTON (AP) — Officials at a select golf and country club are considering disciplinary action against an honorary life member who battered a Canada goose to death with his putter.

The officials at the Congressional Country Club in Bethesda, Md., say the disciplinary action against Dr. Sherman Thomas will be decided upon once a federal court case is completed.

Washington newspapers reported yesterday that lawyers have accepted a plea bargain under which Thomas would pay a fine but would not serve any time in jail.

The proposed settlement requires approval by District Judge Joseph Young, who is presiding over Thomas' trial in Baltimore today.

The Canada goose is protected under the Migratory Bird Treaty Act. Thomas could be sentenced to six months in jail and be fined $500 if convicted of each of the two original charges against him — illegal possession and killing of a goose out of season.

DOWN WENT PANTS OUT GOES PLAYER

WASHINGTON (UPI) — North American Soccer League commissioner Phil Woosnam announced yesterday that he has suspended Washington Diplomats forward Paul Cannell for 10 days for dropping his pants in disgust at a referee's call.

Woosnam said the suspension was imposed for conduct unbecoming a member of an NASL team and stemmed from an incident during a Diplomats' home encounter with Tulsa May 13.

"This is the third such suspension I have had to impose this year and I will continue to take action against anyone in the NASL whose conduct is detrimental or offensive to the league," Woosnam said.

Cannell was given a yellow caution card after he dropped his pants at a referee during the Tulsa game. Cannell had disputed a call by the referee, who claimed he ran into a goalkeeper and made a foul.

GOLFER BURIED WITH HIS CLUBS

COLUMBUS, Ohio (UPI) — James McConnell loved golf so much he asked in his will to be buried with his golf equipment. The wish was honored.

McConnell died Dec. 3 at the age of 92. His will was admitted this week in probate court here.

"It is my desire and request that my golf equipment, including golf bag, golf clubs and golf balls, be buried with me," his will read.

When McConnell was buried his golf glove was on his hand and he was wearing his favorite golf jacket.

Detroit fake sued by Cowboys for hot-pants, go-go frolic

The Dallas Cowboys, unamused by the antics of a Michigan man impersonating a Cowboy cheerleader during last Sunday's Dallas-Washington game, have gone to court to have him banned for life from Cowboy Stadium in Irving, Texas.

The National Football League team is seeking to have insurance agent **Barry Michael Bremen** of Detroit declared a nuisance and is asking for $10,000 in damages.

Bremen, 32, wore a replica of a Cowboy cheerleader's uniform — hot pants, go-go boots and open blouse — onto the sidelines during the third quarter and managed a brief frolic in front of cameras before security guards took him away.

He said the suit was unnecessary as his stint as a cheerleader was a once-in-a-lifetime project.

"It was tough shaving my legs once and dressing up like a woman," Bremen said. "I wouldn't go through that again."

Cowboy vice-president **Joseph Bailey III** said the team's main concern was the cheerleader image, but there was also fear of a repeat performance at the Super Bowl. If, of course, the Cowboys play the Super Bowl.

But Bremen said his imitation was a sincere form of flattery.

"I chose the Cowboys cheerleaders because they're the most famous in the country," he said. "The organization is so uptight about wanting a conservative image that they were a good target. I'm not really kinky. I was just having fun."

Fill 'er up — anytime!

Toronto Star Special

SAN DIEGO — Johnny Rodgers doesn't like waiting in line.

So when the former "ordinary superstar" of the Montreal Alouettes, now toiling for the San Diego Chargers of the National Football League, was caught for 45 minutes in a line-up outside a local gas station, he decided enough was enough — and then bought his own station.

It's a luxury very few gas-hungry Californians can afford.

"I stood in line one time," Rodgers said. "That's when I realixed something had to be done."

But he also belives in sharing.

"I bought it for my friends' convenience too," he laughed.

"I don't need it that often, because I only have four cars."

★ ★ ★ ★ ★ ★ ★ ★ ★ ★ ★ ★ ★ ★ ★ ★ ★ ★ ★

If Phils win title look out

PHILADELPHIA (UPI) — Attack dogs have been rented, security forces have been increased and auto insurance premiums paid up in anticipation of the biggest celebration in this city since Ben Franklin and his buddies hoisted a few following the signing of the Declaration of Independence.

Philadelphia Phillies, long the epitome of the city's reputation as a cradle of losers, can nail down their first World Series championship in history tonight when they meet Kansas City Royals in the sixth game (channels 2, 9, 13 and 25 at 8 p.m.).

If Phillies win the Series, the city is expected to turn into one gigantic New Year's Eve party. Fans who have suffered through the years of Phillies' frustration will be eager to exorcize the demons once and for all.

In anticipation of the celebration, security will be beefed up at Veteran's Stadium in hopes of reducing the vandalism caused by souverin seekers. NBC-TV, which is televising the Series, has hired attack dogs to protect its valuable equipment.

"It's going to be rough," predicts one native Philadelphian. "They'll probably try and tear out the artificial turf and the seats for souvenirs. Your car won't even be safe. They'll do a lot of damage."

What sits in Lake Erie and can't catch flies

CLEVELAND (UPI) — With memories still vivid of a river that burned, a mayor who set his hair on fire and a city government that went into default, the last thing Cleveland needed was another Cleveland joke.

And then the softballs fell.

The incident occurred at a ceremony marking the 50th anniversary of the 52-storey Terminal Tower Building, Cleveland's most distinctive downtown structure.

The Cleveland Competitors professional softball team was trying to duplicate a feat of 42 years ago, when Cleveland Indians catcher Hank Helf caught a ball tossed 700 feet from the Terminal Tower spire.

The players had mitts ready when the softballs rained down travelling at about 144 m.p.h. (232 km/h) when they reached street level.

The first ball struck the hood of an automobile; a second ball struck the shoulder of Russell C. Murphy.

Another ball struck Gail Polinsky; she was taken to hospital with a broken arm.

Finally, outfielder Mike Zarefoss caught a ball and a crowd of about 2,000 cheered wildly.

Custer videoporn irks Indians

Star special news services

NEW YORK — Sensing a big payoff, a small army of home video game manufacturers is feverishly working to bring sex and mayhem to the placid world of Pong and Pac Man.

It appears the first game to hit the market will be Custer's Revenge, in which a lumpy-looking stick figure, wearing only a hat, a bandanna and boots, rapes a naked young Indian woman tied to a tree.

Custer's Revenge is to be released early next month in time for Christmas giving.

At least seven companies, all located in California, are designing or manufacturing sex and violence-related games, according to Barry Jacobs, associate editor of Video Review, a national magazine.

Last Thursday, more than 150 feminists and members of New York's American Indian community turned out to protest the official unveiling of Custer's Revenge and two other pornographic home video games at the National Music, Sound and Video Show at the Hilton Hotel in Manhattan.

A spokesman for the company, who asked not to be named, said; "When you see the game, you'll see it's the most ridiculous thing to get upset about. It was intended strictly as a joke."

The object of the game is to get Custer from the right side of the screen to the left side, where the woman is tied to the tree, without getting hit more than three times by an arrow or pricked by a cactus.

If the player reaches the goal the woman's legs slide up and the two figures lock.

The longer the simulated intercourse lasts, the more points the player scores. The female figure smiles.

"She is not violated," the company spokesman insisted. "He does not rip her clothes off. It shows an enjoyable, fun act."

It's not fun for feminists and Indian groups. They claim the game promotes violence against women and minority groups and degrades Indians.

"They make women a target to be sexually violated by men," said Robin Quinn, a spokeswoman for Women Against Pornography.

Rudy Martin, a spokesman for American Indian Community House, a group that represents Indians in the New York area, said: "As American Indians we are vehemently opposed to the exploitative use of our race for the titilation of the public.

"We see this disgusting video game for what it truly is — a sexist, racist, sadistic expression, the sole purpose of which is to fill the pockets of its creators and promotors."

The suggested retail price for Custer's Revenge is $49.95 (U.S.), about $15 more than most home video games. KNIGHT-RIDDER

A step-by-step guide to being Bo Derek

It sure is a lot of fun being Bo Derek, and you can be Bo Derek too if you follow the simple diet her husband has designed for her: From morning till night, Bo sucks *ice cubes* — but only until she gets to her main course — two celery sticks, a carrot and maybe — maybe, if her husband John Derek is feeling especially munificent — a slice of cheese. Follow this regimen and *you* might look like Bo Derek. Then again, you might not ... Yoko Ono has been offered $3.5 million by Putnam publishing house to write her unexpurgated life story. She said Oh no ... The latest TV trend seems to be offering big bucks to movie stars to appear on nighttime soapers. First it was Burton and Taylor, now it's Sir Laurence Olivier, who has been offered $1 million to make a series of appearances on Dynasty. That's twice what Liz got ...

And a pool for Fido the dog

Okay, let's get right to the really big news of the day — **Barbra Streisand's** swimming pool.

Word's out that when the Funny Girl had a new guitar-shaped pool installed at her Beverly Hills estate, she didn't want her dog to feel left out.

So she's had another pool built for Fido — in the shape of a bone.

John Travolta would've been horrified. Because anti-disco fever struck at Chicago's Comiskey Park Thursday night, American League baseball president **Lee MacPhail** yesterday stuck the White Sox with only the third forfeiture in league history.

It was between games of a doubleheader with Detroit Tigers that an estimated 7,000 young fans from a crowd of over 50,000 stormed the field — an unscheduled segment of an "anti-disco demolition" sponsored by a local radio station. A deejay was supposed to blow up a bunch of disco records between games.

Instead, records and assorted other debris started sailing onto the field during the first game and, during the intermission, groups of fans lit fires in the outfield, destroyed the batting cage and tore up the infield.

More than 50 were arrested and 39 were charged with disorderly conduct. At least six people suffered minor imjuries.

Cocaine doesn't get anyone's dudgeon high in filmland

BY ALJEAN HARMETZ

LOS ANGELES — Robert Evans, the 50-year-old movie producer who will face sentencing in New York on Oct. 7 for possession of cocaine, spent a week recently giving Paramount and Disney executives their first look at the rough cut of his $18-million movie, Popeye. Starring Robin Williams and Shelley Duvall and directed by Robert Altman, Popeye is a co-production of the two studios and is their big Christmas movie.

"If the movie's a success, nobody will care about Bob Evans' arrest," said one Hollywood executive who asked not be identified. Then he shrugged. "If the movie's not a success, probably nobody will care either."

The executive's view reflected a report released in June by the U.S. Department of Health and Human Services. The report said that one-third of all Americans between the ages of 18 and 25 had tried cocaine or other hard drugs such as heroin. In 1962, according to the report, 3 per cent had experimented with such drugs.

In some circles of Hollywood, cocaine replaced the after-dinner drink four years ago. Occasionally, the drug has moved from the privacy of being snorted in Beverly Hills living rooms onto police blotters. Charles Evans, Robert Evans' 54-year-old brother, bought five ounces of cocaine for $19,000 from undercover narcotics agents in New York on May 2.

Although Robert Evans was 3,000 miles away in California at the time of the sale, he pleaded guilty on July 1 to possession of cocaine. The authorities said he had agreed in a telephone call to split the cost with his brother and his brother-in-law, both of whom also admitted the charge. For the misdemeanor, they can be given a $5,000 fine and sentenced to up to a year in jail.

Michael Eisner, president of Paramount, gave a carefully worded "official" response. "Bob is not an employee of Paramount and has not been an employee of Paramount for four years," he said. "We have a relationship with him as a producer, and nothing that has happened changes that relationship. Paramount does not condone what he did, nor does it harshly deal with something that has no bearing on his professional relationships."

"Will it hurt his career?" another studio president asked, laughing. "It sure hasn't hurt the careers of the actors who use it."

"I was very concerned that my arrest would affect my career, but I don't think it has," Stan Dragoti, director of Love at First Bite, said. He was arrested in May, 1979, at Frankfurt airport in West Germany for possession of cocaine.

"Nobody makes any moral judgments about cocaine because it's so widespread," said Dragoti, who has development deals for movies with Chartoff-Winkler Productions at United Artists and with Filmways. "People are afraid to hire you only because they're afraid you're out of control. After my arrest, I went into health — into tennis, jogging. I had a lot of meetings where people could see I was okay. I proved my dependability by doing CBS promo commercials. And I made some other commercials that got a very good response, especially one for Olympus Cameras in which my wife took pictures of Italian bike riders."

Neither Dragoti nor Evans thinks that cocaine, which costs roughly $100 for a 20-minute high, is exclusive to Hollywood. "It tracks affluence," Dragoti said. "It's no more widespread in Hollywood than it is in any other affluent area."

Three actresses, Louise Lasser, Gail Fisher, and Mackenzie Phillips, who at the time was 18 years old, were arrested on suspicion of cocaine possession a few years ago and allowed to go into drug-diversion programs.

In Hollywood, the most fashionable drug is still "free base" cocaine. Free base is usually extracted from street cocaine just before using by putting the cocaine in a chemical base and adding a solvent such as petroleum ether. The crystals of base that are left when the solvent evaporates can be smoked rather than snorted, and the high is said to be sharper.

"The high from free base," says John Randall of the Century Institute of Living, a Los Angeles psychiatric and drug-addiction treatment centre, "is similar to the high from heroin. It's typical to chase the high, to free base for three or four days straight."

How prevalent is cocaine use in Hollywood? "Patients say to me they don't know anyone who doesn't do illicit drugs," Randall said. "None of my patients will believe I have never been offered cocaine socially."

A producer tells of a large Beverly Hills party at which thousands of dollars worth of cocaine was accidentally spilled on a white rug. The guests, he said, ended the evening lying down and snorting the rug.

Woolworth heiress recovers in hospital

LOS ANGELES (Reuter) — Woolworth heiress Barbara Hutton, 66, is recovering from pneumonia in a Los Angeles hospital.

Miss Hutton, who has been married seven times, entered Cedars-Sinai hospital eight days ago. Friends said she had been on a strenuous diet, consisting mainly of soft drinks, and had lost a lot of weight.

The department store millionairess, who has been in poor health most of her life, has homes in many parts of the world.

The joys of being a star

So you think it's fun to be a movie star? Let's check via writer Rex Reed with actress Shelley Duvall, who hasn't had much fun on her two latest films. Tell us, Shelley, how were things on The Shining?

"I cried 12 hours a day for nine months. I developed cramps, anemia, my blood sugar dropped. I lived on 30 cups of tea, 15 Coca-Colas and hundreds of cigarettes per day as well as the horrible English food.

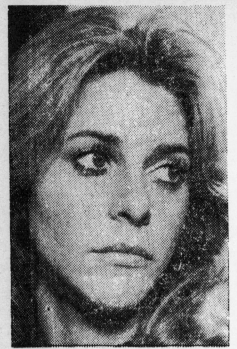

"Bionic Woman" Lindsay

Wagner helped talk a young woman out of leaping to her death from the roof of a 20-storey Hollywood hotel last night. Police flew Miss Wagner to the hotel roof by helicopter after the woman said she would jump unless she could speak to the actress.

Communists doped our kids, U.S. dancer says

First, a little straight talk from a surprising source — Ann Miller, tap-dancing star with Fred Astaire and others in movie musicals such as On The Town and Kiss Me Kate. Tell me about your theories on drugs, Ann.

"I think the country's drug problems were casused by the Communists, who doped the young to make Americans easier to fight."

Hmmm. And how would you deal with drug users?

"The best way to treat them is to beat the hell out of them with an old-fashioned brush. If they're too big for that, I think they should be sent to psychiatrists. If by that time they can't deal with their problem, they should be let go to reach rock bottom. I wouldn't give them money, because that would be paying for their habits."

Uh huh. And how do you think society should deal with Socialists?

"Do you know what I really think? I think they should pick up al the Communists and all the limousine liberals in the business, eject them from the restaurants where they spend half the day waiting to be photographed, and send them to Russia so we could see they like it."

Sometimes it's nice to be ill

Most hospital patients with minor ailments would consider themselves lucky to get a private room.

But with **Elizabeth Taylor**, you always have to figure on a little extra.

During her confinement at the Washington Hospital Centre for treatment of a salivary gland infection, Liz has occupied a special penthouse room, complete with:

☐ A dining table for eight, where she can offer her dinner guests a wide range of gourmet treats prepared by a special chef;

☐ An oversize Grecian orgy-style bath, where she can while away the hours amid the bubbles;

☐ And a panoramic penthouse window, offering a sweeping view of Washington and the surrounding countryside.

All this for just $328 a day, plus $200 for private nurses.

To his thousands of fans (and two 'lovers') Elvis lives on

By WAYNE ROBINS
Special to The Star

NEW YORK — *On Aug. 16, 1977, the Shelby County, Tenn., coroner concluded that Elvis Presley, 42, expired of a heart ailment, possibly irritated by dietary and pharmaceutical carelessness. To his fans, however, Elvis Lives.*

In Memphis, where Presley spent most of his adult life, a billboard 44 feet long and 14 feet high towers above Elvis Presley Blvd. It is diagonally across from Graceland, the mansion where Presley lived his semi-reclusive life. The billboard, known as The American Trilogy, depicts three phases of Presley's career.

Across the street from the billboard, the Meditation Garden at Presley's Graceland mansion is visited by 7,000 people every weekday, and more than 10,000 people on weekends.

Memphis officials estimate that at least 100,000 Elvis fans will make the pilgrimage to Memphis this week alone.

Chapter 8

Religion & Racism

Santa pinched

A sherriff's deputy in Akron, Ohio, frisks Hare Krishna member John Kaufman, 30, who was charged with assault after a complaint that a man dressed as Santa sought a donation downtown "in an aggressive manner."

"Nectar of the gods"

Claude Nowell of Salt Lake City displays a bottle of a beverage called "nectar of the gods," which is made and distributed by Summum, a church based in Salt Lake City. A federal judge ruled Thursday that the drink must be regulated as a wine.

Minister faces slavery charge

DURHAM, N.C. (AP) — Nine members of the Church of God and True Holiness were beaten, whipped and threatened by the church's minister who kept them in slavery, authorities charge.

The indictments charge Rev. Robert Carr and three others with nine counts of violating slavery laws and one count of conspiracy to violate laws against involuntary servitude.

Watergate plotter enters the church

NEW VERNON, N.J. (UPI) — Jeb Stuart Magruder, convicted and jailed in the Watergate scandal but now a divinity student, will assist at services in a Presbyterian church starting in September.

Magruder, 44, served seven months in the federal penitentiary at Lewisburg, Pa., after he pleaded guilty in the break-in at Democratic National Committee Headquarters in Washington. He was deputy director of former president Richard Nixon's re-election committee in 1972.

Holy profits! Parable nets his parish $5,000

WESTERLY, R.I. (AP) — A Roman Catholic priest who gave $2,000 in $5 bills to parishioners to illustrate a parable has received $7,000 back.

Rev. Norman Guilmette of the Church of the Immaculate Conception passed out $5 bills at a service last November to illustrate St. Matthew's Parable about a landowner who gave a large sum of money to each of three servants. Two doubled their money by investing it. A third servant buried his and earned nothing but the landowner's wrath.

This time, a family of four invested the priest's $5 in jute and wound up making $425 by selling macrame plant hangers.

Two women who used the money to start baking and selling pies brought in $185. A girl who sang carols at Christmas and turned over $50. One man bet $5 at poker and won $17.50.

Half the earnings will be distributed among the poor and the other half will be used to pay for repairs to the parish centre.

Guns seized from sect

WOLF POINT, Mont. (UPI) — A cache of weapons, including semi-automatic rifles, was seized by police in the arrest of three members of a religious sect charged with beating to death a 4-year-old boy, police say.

The three are among nine members of the River of Life Tabernacle accused of deliberate homicide in the death of James Gill, who prosecutors say

was repeatedly beaten as part of the group's practice of harsh discipline of member's children.

His body was found Saturday at the home of one of the defendants, who was also caring for three other children.

The leader of the group was James DeLorme, 44, an ex-convict who said Christ convinced him to give up a life of crime.

Dial A for atheist

DALLAS (UPI) — To counter recorded dial-a-prayer telephone messages sponsored by religious groups, an atheist group, the Dallas Chapter of the Society of Separationists has instituted Dial-An-Atheist.

"Atheism is a life philosophy which accepts the facts there are no gods, devils, angels, heavens or hell, or life after death," a voice says in the atheists' message. "We don't believe in miracles, myths or magic, whether it's Mother Goose or the Holy Ghost."

Holy relic

PHILADELPHIA (UPI) — City council is considering a proposal to sell pieces of the platform on which Pope John Paul II celebrated mass last week to help defray the $196,000 cost.

$2 million award against church

PORTLAND, Ore. (UPI) — A jury has awarded damages of more than $2 million to a 22-year-old woman who claimed she was damaged psychologically by participating in Church of Scientology programs.

God may be a woman church says

CINCINNATI (UPI) — Leaders of the 1.2 million-member Christian Church (Disciples of Christ) are not ruling out the possibility that God is a woman.

The church's 200-member general board yesterday recommended disapproval of a proposed resolution that the church mandate use of male language — "the father, His, He and Him" — in reference to God.

The board's recommendation goes to the church's general assembly

Ex-panther now a 'moonie'

OAKLAND, Calif. (UPI) — Eldridge Cleaver, a former convict and founder of the Black Panthers, is now a supporter of the Unification Church, headed by Dr. Sun Myung Moon.

Cleaver declared in an interview he was impressed by the "Moonies".

Atheist files suit against Pope

AUSTIN, Tex. (AP) — Atheist leader Madalyn Murray O'Hair says she has filed suit to stop Pope John Paul from saying an open-air mass in Washington.

She also accused the Roman Catholic Church of arranging the papal visit to the U.S. to enhance Senator Edward Kennedy's political future.

Ms. O'Hair and her son, Jon Garth Murray, said they had filed two lawsuits in federal district court in Washington yesterday to stop the Pope from conducting mass on the mall between the Capitol and Washington Monument.

Mr. Murray, director of the American Atheist Centre in Austin, and his mother also said at a news conference they will lead a demonstration against the Pope at Chicago's Grant Park on Oct. 5.

Their suits, they said, detail that a permit has been granted for the Pope to say mass on Washington mall Oct. 7. They say such use of public land is unconstitutional.

The Roman Catholic Church owns land worth more than $162 billion, the Murrays said, and "if the Pope wants to say a Mass, he has (other) places to do it."

Ms. O'Hair said the Pope's visit has been timed "to interfere with the political process — to make Kennedy (D- Mass.) a more favorable candidate."

Ms. O'Hair led the 1963 battle to block prayer in public schools in the U.S.

Phil's ungodly gamble runs into a roadblock

SAN FRANCISCO (UPI-AP) — Every Saturday for 14 months Philip Sanders, 32, donned a Greyhound busdriver's uniform; went to a San Francisco depot, stole a bus and took church members on a round-trip gambling foray to Reno, Nevada.

He charged about $200 for the trip and made about $10,000 before he was arrested. His joyriding has cost him two years in jail.

Sanders was arrested after he had dropped off his passengers and was apparently returning the stolen bus.

But, it wasn't his first spree. In March, 1979, he was convicted of stealing a Greyhound bus from the San Francisco bus depot and was nabbed as he took tickets from passengers in the front seats.

Meanwhile, in Niles, Ohio, three church members were charged with disorderly conduct after burning a five-foot-high Easter bunny on the church lawn as a pagan idol.

Police said the edler of the Truth Tabernacle and two others set the stuffed rabbit ablaze in a bizarre ceremony.

They sat the bunny on a chair on top of a table that had been decorated with colored eggs and flowers.

When police tried to make an arrest, the three men ran around the table chanting and decrying anyone who had Easter bunnies as "heathens and dummies who worshipped pagan gods."

Cleric's protest bore fruit

OGDEN, Utah (UPI) — A crusading minister threw himself on the railroad tracks to protest the arrival of a trainload of homosexual activists but he was removed by police before the train showed up.

When the train arrived, Rev. Robert Harris shouted, "The power of God is against you; repent of your sins."

The homosexual men and women stopped briefly yesterday in Ogden as part of a transcontinental trip to a demonstration in Washington.

"You shall know the tree by the fruit it bears," the minister told the passengers.

"We are the fruit," responded one traveller.

Thousands of homosexuals from across the United States are expected to converge on Washington this weekend for three days of events that will be highlighted Sunday by the first national homosexual rights march.

ALBUQUERQUE, N.M. (UPI) — A building that once housed a notorious x-rated motel will be blessed today in an ecumenical religious service designed to purify the building in advance of its opening as a shopping centre. A Catholic priest and a Presbyterian minister are to lead the service at the former Zuni Lodge which, with its bars and ceiling mirrors in guest rooms, was once the scene of numerous knifings and vice squad operations.

Offended by hand, cut it off

LAS VEGAS (Reuter) — A 21-year-old woman was reported in satisfactory condition here last night after doctors successfully sewed back a hand she severed with a machete, saying she had sinned against God.

Police quoted witnesses as saying the woman was taken to a hospital reciting the biblical passage from the book of Matthew: "And if thy hand offend thee, cut it off."

They said they did not know the nature of the "sin" she had committed.

SAN MATEO, Calif. (UPI) — A U.S. air force policeman who says he was charged with disobeying orders because he refused to stop carrying his Bible to work has been given an honorable discharge after the charges were dropped.

Steven Ristau, 20, a born-again Christian, said: "If found guilty and sentenced, I'd be the first person ever to go to jail for carrying a Bible in this country."

MARSEILLES, Ill. (UPI) — Police are asking women to come forward if they were approached by a man claiming to be a photographer for Playboy magazine and asking them to pose in the nude. Police put out the call after Patrick Quigg, 25, an associate First Methodist minister, was arrested for posing as a Playboy photographer and offering to pay a woman $1,000 each time her picture appeared in the magazine.

TV coverage angers soap addicts

NEW YORK — Thousands of television viewers in the United States were outraged by the shooting of Pope John Paul II — because it interrupted their daily soap operas.

In Kansas City, Mo. a viewer "threatened to come down and do bodily harm to the people at the station unless the Pope story went off the air by 1.30," a station official said.

Irate viewers in Washington state said coverage of the assassination bid was "drivel" and demanded no interruptions to As the World Turns and other soap operas.

"After 25 years in the business, I'm amazed and shocked," said one television executive. "Some ardent fans are really oblivious to everything else that is going on in the world."

SAN ANTONIO, Texas (UPI) — In what is billed as a "booze bust for Jesus," Don and Pearl Langdon will destroy hundreds of bottles of liquor Sunday to signal the end of alcoholic drinks at their chain of restaurants. The couple have been converted to a sect called the Ministry of Light in a World of Darkness. A pop group called Tudy and The Holy Rollers will sing during the booze bust.

$1.05 million suit filed against local preacher

A Lexington evangelist and his wife have been sued for $1.05 million by a Tennessee couple over an incident at a Tennessee revival service, but the preacher says the confrontation "is just a hoax."

Arnold Staton, 53, was accused in the suit with striking a woman at the service after saying he would heal her stomach ailment. After the woman was struck, she fell on Juanita Embree, who suffered a broken hip, the suit says.

The complaint, filed in Sullivan County, Tenn., also says that Mrs. Embree's husband, Ronald, has lost the marital companionship of his wife because of her injury.

But Staton says he never struck the woman, Louise Gillenwater. Instead, he says he told the congregation to stay back as Mrs. Gillenwater approached the altar because he was afraid she might faint.

Staton also disputes the claim that he asked Mrs. Gillenwater to approach the altar to be healed. He says his religious denomination, the Assemblies of the Church of the Lord Jesus

Christ, does not believe in healing, except through the direct intervention of God.

"I don't believe man can do healing — if I did, I'd heal myself first," said Staton, who is a disabled truck driver. Staton, who says he's not sure how he will defend himself in the suit, says he nevertheless expects to be vindicated.

Several religious groups and the estate of the Tennessee church's former pastor were also named as defendants in the suit.

Humbard under fire

Rex Humbard

CLEVELAND (UPI) — Evangelist Rex Humbard, who last year said his television ministry was strapped for funds and appealed to viewers for more cash, admits he and his sons recently purchased a home and condominiums in Florida for $650,000. "My people don't give a hoot what I spend that money for," Humbard said. Humbard, 60, said last September his ministry was $3.2 million in debt but purchased a home and condominiums near Palm Beach, Fla., with his sons for the $650,000 sum, using $177,500 in cash as down payments.

Protest pray-in

AMARILLO, Texas (UPI) — More than 700 people gathered outside the civic centre here last night for a "pray-in" to protest a concert by Kiss — a rock group the demonstrators said advocates demon worship, sexual perversion and promiscuity.

EFFINGHAM, Ill. (UPI) — Rev. Garth Pybas preached his Sunday sermon shortly after having seven stitches put in his toe. He had been mowing the lawn when he saw a $5 bill nestled in the blades. He reached eagerly to pick it up but the mower moved and the blades tore into his foot. His sermon: The Evils of Greed.

LANSING, Mich. (AP) — It took a jury four hours to convict three sisters who went joyriding clad only in sneakers and mustard. The three divorcees were found guilty yesterday of joyriding and indecent exposure and could be jailed for 90 days to two years. Doshaline McCuin, 30, Charlene Roper, 27 and Sandra Lewis, 26, who share a house here, claimed they were seized with religious fervor caused by intense devotion to a TV religion show.

1,600-mile crawl ends in rebuff

WASHINGTON (AP) — A Baptist lay minister from Marshall, Tex., ended his 2½-year, 1,600-mile (2,560-kilometre) crawl to the gates of the White House yesterday, only to be told that President Jimmy Carter was too busy to see him.

"I just wanted to shake his hand and tell him I'm praying for him," Hans Mullikin, 39, told White House aide Phillip Spector, who had explained about Carter's "very tight" schedule.

"I understood from the start that the president was a busy man and couldn't see everyone who came into town," Mullikin said.

After pulling a small, two-wheeled trailer decked with orange caution flags along with an American and religious flags to the site, Mullikin led his parents, brother and sister in prayer at the White House gates.

The group then yelled "Praise the Lord!" and Mullikin reached into his trailer and gave his 64-year-old mother a bouquet of flowers and a kiss.

To the obvious question "Why?" Mullikin replied: "I just wanted to show America that we need to get on our knees and repent . . . This is something I had in my heart and wanted to do for my country."

Mullikin got on his knees and began his journey outside his East Texas home March 1, 1976.

"The hardest part of the whole trip was getting down on my knees the first morning," he said. "Counting the lost time on the job, I guess it cost me between $8,000 and $10,000."

A pair of bulky, well-worn goalie pads were strapped to his knees with 10 layers of padding underneath, a gift of the Dallas Blackhawks hockey team. As he crawled, he gripped a bar with two tricycle wheels on each end. Each night, he jogged back to his truck to sleep.

"Outside Chattanooga, Tenn., a couple fellows in a pickup were running me through the mill," he said. "One of them asked me where I got the money to do this and I looked down in the grass along the road and saw a crumpled up dollar bill and told them, 'Every now and then I just reach down and pick up a dollar. The Lord takes care of me.' "

Officer beaten to death by zealots, police say

MEMPHIS, Tenn. (UPI-AP) — A policeman held hostage by seven religious zealots and found dead after officers stormed the house had been beaten so badly that colleagures didn't know him.

"I've known Bob Hester for years, and after what they did to him I couldn't recognize him," said one of the officers who found the 34-year-old's manacled and disfigured body early yesterday.

"We waited too long."

Hester apparently had been dead several hours before authorities decided to try to rescue him, assaulting the north Memphis house with rifles and tear gas and killing the seven zealots who thought of police as "anit-Christ" agents. They had held Hester for 30 hours.

Several officers bitterly denounced the delay in raiding the home.

"He was screaming for help. They (police higher-ups) let him die. That's just the bottom line," an officer said.

Hester could be heard "a half-block" away, shrieking, "Please, oh God, help me!" the policeman said.

Photographs taken after the raid show Hester's colleagures crying and clinging to one another as they left the house.

Hester was married but had no children.

Authorities refused to be specific about his injuries. Police spokesman Bob Graham said only that "the preliminary autopsy indicates a blunt trauma to the head" was the injury that killed Hester.

"It was not a mutilation-type death," he said.

"The battered body of the police officer was found just inside the front door," police director John Holt said. "His hands were cuffed behind his back. There were indications he had been dead for a number of hours.

Trapped inside

"There were seven male blacks inside the house, all of whom were fatally shot," he said. "The medical director has determined that all seven of these persons were killed during the assault."

Hester and another officer had been called to the house Tuesday night and were attacked when they arrived. The other policeman, who suffered a bullet wound to the face, managed to escape but Hester was hit on the head and trapped inside.

Holt said officials held off on assaulting the house at first because they believed a pistol was being held at Hester's head and he would be shot. They tried to negotiate with Lin-

dberg Sanders, leader of the unnamed religious cult inside, but he only shouted obscenities at them.

The decision to move, Holt said, came about 3 a.m. local time after police with electronic eavesdropping devices heard someone inside the house say: "The devil is dead."

Police said they were met by gunfire from at least two rooms of the three-bedroom house.

Found dead inside were Sanders, 49, an unemployed construction worker and a psychiatric patient since 1973, and his 26-year-old son, Larnell Sanders.

The other victims included Michael Delane Coleman, 18, Earl Thomas, 20, Andrew "JuJu" Houston, 18, and Cassell Harris, whose age wasn't available. The identity of one victim was not released.

Authorities said the victims were members of a Bible-reading cult that believed police were the anti-Christ, and thought the Bible forbade the eating of pork to end last Monday.

Sanders' wife, Dorothy, who left her husband one week ago, said he believed the world was going to end last Monday.

The victims' families, held in a school across the street, could be heard screaming and sobbing after the raid.

"You didn't have to kill them!" one woman cried.

Born-again tycoon trashes $1 million

FORT WORTH, Texas (AP) — Shattered religious artifacts worth $1 million are "swimming with the fish" at the bottom of a lake after a wealthy, born-again Christian businessman destroyed them because he thought they displeased God.

Television evangelist James Robison said he and industrialist Cullen Davis used hammers to smash the gold, silver, jade and ivory objects — mostly figures associated with eastern religions that Davis had collected — after Robison found a Bible verse that called them "abominations."

Davis, who is in the oil equipment business, has said he turned to religion after two sensational murder trials. He was acquitted of killing his 9-year-old stepdaughter during a 1976 shooting spree at his

mansion and found not guilty of trying to buy the death of a judge hearing a bitter divorce case.

The two men smashed the carvings in a parking lot outside Davis' Fort Worth mansion, Robison said yesterday.

Dumped into lake

"We went out into the garage and he got hammers and we went out there in his parking lot and destroyed $1 million worth of jade, ivory and gold — all of it," Robison said.

The shattered remains were then swept from the lot and dumped into a local lake, said Jim Rogers, executive director of Robison's ministry.

"They're swimming somewhere with the fish at the bottom," Rogers said. He would not identify the lake.

"We so disfigured it, I don't think it would have been worth much," Robison told a local newspaper.

Davis had donated the art objects to Robison in September to pay debts that threatened to end Robison's national television ministry.

But Robison said he and Rogers saw a verse in Deuteronomy which read:

"The graven images of their gods shall ye burn with fire: thou shalt not desire the silver and gold that is on them, nor take it unto thee, lest thou be snared therein: for it is an abomination to the Lord thy God."

The evangelist said Davis started crying when he said he could not accept the objects.

It's bleak world for black kids in U.S.

By Herbert H. Denton
Washington Post

WASHINGTON — A black child in the United States today has nearly one chance in two of being born into poverty, and is twice as likely as a white baby to die during the first year of life.

If the black child survives that first year, the odds are against his growing up healthy, wealthy or wise. American black children are more likely to be sick and without a regular source of health care than white children. They are three times as likely to be labeled mentally retarded, twice as likely to drop out of school before 12th grade and three times as likely to be unemployed.

A black teenager in the U.S. has a one in 10 chance of getting into trouble with the law and is five times as likely as a white teenager to be murdered.

This bleak portrait, based largely on U.S. government surveys drawn together in one report, was presented by the Children's Defence Fund, a Washington-based lobbying and advocacy group for children.

Rage, despair

The statistics "show why millions of black children lack self-confidence, feel discouragement, despair, numbness or rage as they try to grow up on islands of poverty, ill health, inadequate education, squalid streets with dilapidated housing, crime and rampant unemployment in a nation of boastful affluence," said the fund's president, Marian Wright Edelman.

There is passing acknowledgement in the report that the last two decades have been years of progress for some blacks. Because of affirmative-action programs, government scholarships and court-mandated desegregation, about one-third of all black children who graduate from high school go on to college, about the same proportion as among white youths. But, Edelman contended, if the black middle class has grown, the black poor have increased at even a faster rate.

Clearly, the economic ravages of the last decade have had a particularly devastating impact on the black poor of the United States. Income for black households, adjusted for inflation, declined. In the '60s, the unemployment rate for black youth was twice as high as for white teenagers. Today, it is three times as high.

And the family structure of blacks appears to have been under even greater assault. Four of five white children live in two-parent families; fewer than half of all black children do. Only one white child in 38 lives away from both parents; one in eight black children does.

Black boyfriend ruled grounds for expulsion

ALEXANDRIA, Va. (UPI) — A U.S. judge has ruled that the principal of a Christian school had the right to expel a white girl because he thought she had a black boyfriend.

Judge Oren Lewis said the decision by Alek Lee Bledsoe was protected by constitutional guarantees of religious freedom.

Bledsoe, a fundamentalist preacher, expelled Melissa Feidler, 14, because he thought she was having a romantic relationship with Rufus Bostic III, also 14.

Her sister, Charlotte, 11, was expelled when her parents complained to the American Civil Liberties Union.

The Feidler family accused the school of violating Melissa's civil rights and sought $70,000 in damages.

But Lewis ruled that the friendship violated Baptist tenets against close interracial relationships and that Bledsoe had the right to expel the girl, regardless of the merits of the church's doctrine.

Nazi parade to go ahead court rules

WASHINGTON (AP) — The United States Supreme Court has cleared the way for a demonstration by American Nazis in the Chicago suburb of Skokie, Ill., where 7,000 survivors of World War II Nazi concentration camps live.

Voting 7 to 2, the justices yesterday turned down a request by Skokie officials that the rally planned for June 25 be postponed.

Crackdown on 'Surf Nazis'

VIRGINIA BEACH, Va. (UPI) — Police are cracking down on bicycle-riding youths they call "Surf Nazis" who are terrorizing pedestrians along the resort's boardwalk.

More than 75 summonses have been issued for reckless bicycle riding since the weekend, they say.

The youths ride in bicycle lanes and then swoop onto the adjacent Virginia Beach boardwalk to hit, kick and run over people, police say. An officer was injured when he tried to avoid a rider who tried to play "chicken."

Police say they don't know where the term "Surf Nazi" originated, but they've seen the words painted on walls and sidewalks in the oceanfront area.

One officer issued a ticket to a teenager who stuck his foot out from his bicycle and kicked a 6-year-old boy.

"I asked him why he did it," the officer said. "He told me, 'For the hell of it.' "

4 dead in gun battle at anti-Klan march

GREENSBORO, N.C. (UPI) — Four people were killed and 10 wounded yesterday as Ku Klux Klansmen leaped from a van and began shooting at a group staging an anti-Klan march through a black neighborhood, officials said.

Greensboro Mayor Jim Melvin called the shooting an "isolated, senseless, barbaric act of violence and it will be dealt with as such."

The shooting occurred as about 50 people, blacks and whites, assembled for an anti-Klan march by the Workers' Viewpoint Organization, which police identified as a Communist-affiliated group.

Seven of the injured were treated and released.

Twelve people who identified themselves as Klansmen and two members of Workers' Viewpoint, including march organizer Nelson Johnson, were arrested.

The Klansmen will be charged with first-degree murder and assault, police said. Johnson was charged with inciting to riot.

"I was standing about 50 feet from the demonstrators and had just directed my photographer when I heard what sounded like a firecracker going off," said newsman Charles Travis of WGHP-TV in High Point.

"I looked down the street and I saw two carloads (of whites) stop and individuals jumped out shooting shotguns and automatic weapons."

Police break up Nazi rally in Michigan city

ANN ARBOR, Mich. (UPI) — Thirty uniformed Nazis clashed briefly with anti-Nazi protesters at a rally outside city hall before police broke it up and arrested nine of the protesters.

The members of the Nazi SS Action Group, wearing swastikas and military gear, were escorted out of town by police after the protest yesterday, police chief William Corbett said.

The Nazis were from the Detroit area, he said.

The rally had been publicized to begin at 1 p.m., but when the Nazis showed up about noon more than 200 counter-demonstrators were already on the scene, Corbett said.

Police said bats were confiscated from anti-Nazi demonstrators, but some objects were thrown and a police officer was treated for minor injuries.

The Nazis threw flashlight batteries and "some sort of liquid," Corbett said.

At least two dozen police, some in riot gear, were posted outside city hall in anticipation of a similar demonstration a year ago, when 2,000 protesters showed up.

This year, "we think that the event went down quickly," the police chief said. The nine demonstrators arrested were held for felonious assault, interfering with police, and assault and battery.

Clean sheet for 'unbiased' Klan

PHOENIX, Ariz. (AP) — The white supremacist Ku Klux Klan claims to be an equal-opportunity employer — not discriminating on the basis of color, creed or sex.

So the state of Arizona has allowed the racist group to advertise for workers, on a one-time basis, to sew 500 bedsheets, the traditional Klan robes.

The sheets are to be used in the Klan's robe-selling campaign now under way in Maricopa County, says the Phoenix chapter of the white-supremacist group. The Klan placed the listing with the state's job services division in order to make sheets before October.

The local Klan organizer hired five recruits, including one "minority lady."

Asked if the Klan had assented to equal opportunity in this particular employment, the organizer said, "On a one-time basis, yes."

Leftists charged

GREENSBORO, N.C. (AP-UPI) — Four people were arrested as about two dozen leftist demonstrators scuffled with police at the start of the trial of six Ku Klux Klansmen and American Nazis charged with murdering five members of the Communist Workers party. Chanting "we are the victims," the demonstrators had gathered in a courtroom hallway to read a statement denouncing "capitalist kangaroo courts." The scuffle broke out when police, searching spectators as they entered the courtroom, blocked the demonstrators from entering.

Chapter 9

Armed Forces & Politics

The men are restless. If we don't come up with a war pretty soon, we're going to have a real morale problem.

Deadly war games

HEIDELBERG, West Germany (UPI) — Three American soldiers huddling in their broken down tank retriever to escape a freak cold wave died from carbon monoxide posioning after leaving the engine running to keep warm.

The deaths were the latest tragedy to result from U.S. winter "war games" in the Rhineland. Earlier, a runaway car struck and killed a U.S. serviceman and a West German tank crushed to death a West German policeman.

Women cadets forced to bite off chickens' heads

WEST POINT, N.Y. (AP) — Women cadets at West Point Military Academy were forced to kill chickens with their teeth in a cadet hazing ceremony, officials have confirmed.

The chicken-killing was done by biting across the chickens' necks, the academy's superintendent, Lt.-Gen. Andrew Goodpaster, said yesterday.

"They would pick out the woman in the platoon who seemed to be the most squeamish and call on her to do it," he said.

In previous years, both male and female cadets had been required to bite chicken's necks, Goodpaster said.

In the traditional hazing ceremonies, freshmen are forced by other cadets to perform unpleasant tasks.

Cadets interviewed at the academy said learning to kill chickens was taught to cadets as a survival technique.

"It's not hazing, and they asked for volunteers," said one cadet who asked that his name not be used. "Nobody is forced to do it."

"It's true that when they asked for volunteers, most everybody calls out a girl's name," another cadet added.

Goodpaster conceded there were "still some pockets of resentment" among the men over the presence of women, who were just admitted to West Point four years ago. But, he said: "Such foolishness will not be tolerated." He said no cadets had been disciplined by demotions and demerits.

Of the 4,200 cadets at the academy, 326 are women.

In other hazing incidents involving male cadets, one was stripped naked and hogtied and another was thrown into the shower by colleagues dressed as Ku Klux Klansmen.

Pilot says U.S. bombed hospitals 'bigger the better'

WASHINGTON (AP) — Three Viet Nam war veterans told a Senate committee yesterday that Viet Cong or North Vietnamese hospitals were often considered targets rather than areas to be avoided as required by the Geneva convention on warfare.

"The bigger the hospital, the better it was," one witness said.

The testimony came before the Senate armed services committee which is looking into secret air and ground operations of the Indo-China war from the mid-1960s to 1972.

Alan Stevenson, a stockbroker from San Francisco and former army intelligence specialist, said that while in Quang Tri province in 1969 he routinely listed hospitals among targets to be struck by U.S. fighter planes.

Army wins 'fleece award' for $6,000 study of sauce

WASHINGTON (UPI) — Sen. William Proxmire's monthly Golden Fleece Award goes to the U.S. Army for a $6,000 study on how to buy Worcestershire sauce.

U.S. gets new false alarm

WASHINGTON (AP) — For the second time in a matter of days, a computer malfunction gave a "false signal" that the United States was under attack by Soviet missiles, the Pentagon says.

"The engines of some planes of the Strategic Air Command were turned on, since SAC responds automatically to any warning signal," Pentagon spokesman Thomas Ross said yesterday.

The computer malfunction Friday was similar to one that occurred Tuesday and again last November.

"The same computer which gave off false signals on June 3rd had another malfunction and gave off another false signal," Ross said.

"The computer readout indicated an ICBM (intercontinental ballistic missile) and SLBM (submarine-launched ballistic missile) attack, but of a smaller nature than the June 3 event," Ross said.

"Within three minutes, it was positively determined that it was a computer malfunction."

The computer has been taken out of service.

Pentagon bans 'do it' slogan

DULUTH, Minn. (AP) — A recruiting slogan for the U.S. Army reserve — We Do It on Weekends in The Dirt — has been banned by the U.S. Army.

Sgt. Bill Jackson, a recruiter for the 367th Engineers Battalion at Duluth, came up with the slogan. It was printed on signs and placards and had been in use in the Duluth area since June.

Jackson said the slogan referred to the unit's construction work.

But a colonel at army headquarters at Fort Sam Houston in Texas detected sexual innuendo in the slogan and made his feelings known to Pentagon officials.

Jackson complained about the decision, saying he has seen bumper stickers proclaiming — Navy Divers Do It Deeper, and Army Airborne Does It In The Air.

Drowning Marine 'laughed at'

SAN DIEGO (UPI) — A Marine swimming instructor and an officer laughed at a drowning recruit as he screamed and thrashed in the water and the instructor kicked him away from the side of the pool, an ex-Marine recruit testified.

William Donaldson, 18, said Friday a drill instructor and an officer laughed as Pvt. Randall Christian, 18, of Dallas, drowned during a water survival test on Aug. 27 and called him a "big baby."

Donaldson said at the formal inquiry into the drowning death that he had given false testimony in an earlier investigation in order to get an early discharge and because he was coerced.

Donaldson testified that he witnessed the drowning from five feet away where he was treading water during a water survival test at the Marine Corps Recruit Depot.

He said Christian was "screaming, thrashing around, having problems staying above water." He added, "Every time Pvt. Christian would try to get to the side of the pool, Sgt. (Rudy) Rodriguez (an instructor) would stick his foot in Christian's chest and kick him back."

"They laughed as he went down," Donaldson said. "He just kept going down and he threw up on the way down and hit bottom."

After the incident, Donaldson said, his senior drill instructor took him aside and said, "You are just going to forget about that; aren't you?"

He said he answered "Yes."

Donaldson said that the captain who conducted the original, one-man, informal investigation told him before taking a sworn deposition:

"I want you to tell me how Sgt. Rodriguez just accidentally neglected the boy and that it wasn't his fault."

He said, "The captain told me to say that it wasn't the sergeant's fault that Christian drowned . . . that it was just a judgment call."

That investigation concluded that Christian's death was a blameless accident. The present formal inquiry was ordered by the Marine Corps Commandant at the insistence of two Texas congressmen.

Donaldson said he received his discharge 10 days after signing the false statement.

"I lied on the statement so that they'd let me out of the Marines," he said. "I knew I wouldn't get out unless I lied."

New York drafts plan for Doomsday

NEW YORK (UPI) — There's a "Doomsday Plan" to evacuate nine million people from the New York metropolitan area in the event of a nuclear attack, but there's a hitch — civil defence officials would need a few days notice.

It would take more than two days to get everybody out — assuming everything went as planned.

Buses, trains, planes, cars and boats would be used in the evacuation — described as the largest mass movement of humanity in history, the New York Daily News said in a copyright story yesterday.

The plan includes a series of maps, charts and documents detailing procedures for the evacuation of 9.7 million New Yorkers to emergency shelters.

But the evacuation could only come off if officials knew about a nuclear attack a few days in advance.

Even with advance notice, the evacuation would take two days and 43 minutes to complete.

Gunfire used to sink coffin

NORFOLK, Va. (UPI) — The navy honor guard at a burial at sea ceremony was ordered to fire M-14 rifles at the coffin of a veteran so the casket would sink.

Lt. Cmdr. Michael Cherry, at the Norfolk Naval Base, said the July 14 incident was being investigated "to determine if there was any other means of sinking the casket, other than use of firearms."

The casket was dropped off the destroyer USS Farragut as part of the ceremony 66 miles off Virginia's coast. The coffin flipped over when it hit the water and holes cut on the bottom to allow it to sink were then on top and the casket stayed afloat.

An unidentified crewmember of the Farragut was quoted as saying: "It never did sink while we were out there. The body was coming out of the casket when we left. It was gross."

SAN FRANCISCO (UPI) — The doomsday clock of the Bulletin of the Atomic Scientists has moved from 9 to 7 minutes to midnight, symbolizing what the journal's editor says is the world's movement closer to nuclear disaster.

U.S. MISSILE HITS OWN HELICOPTER

MANILA (AP-UPI) — A heat-seeking Sidewinder missile from a United States Navy F-4 Phantom jet accidentally hit and destroyed a navy helicopter yesterday.

All six men aboard were killed.

The missile did not follow its expected track and downed the helicopter 70 miles from the Subic Bay naval base in the Philippines, the navy said.

U.S. bomb errors kill, wound 700 in Cambodia

PHNOM PENH (UPI-Reuter) — U.S. air force planes in their second bombing error in two days today hit Cambodian government military positions only four miles from Neak Luong, damaged in an accidental bombing yesterday, military sources said.

They said initial reports showed four persons killed and another 12 injured. An immediate investigation was launched.

This Cambodian capital already was stunned by yesterday's accidental bombing in which as many as 700 people are feared to have been killed and wounded. U.S. officials said the bombing yesterday was the worst such disaster of the Indo-China war.

Inventor claims laser downs planes

ROSWELL, N.M. (UPI) — A man who claims to have invented a hand-held laser pistol that can shoot down an airplane at 5,000 feet says the device may be manufactured outside of the United States because the Pentagon is apparently uninterested in it.

Gene Robbins, 27, said he has been contacted by several foreign governments about the untested weapon.

He said he probably will accept an offer from Saudi Arabia to produce the device there, although he is also considering an offer from an American firm to manufacture it in the West Indies.

The device has not yet been demonstrated because Robbins is still waiting for delivery of a lens, but he claims it will be the most powerful hand-held weapon ever made.

Navy rocked by charges of bisexuality

VALLEJO, Calif. (UPI) — Half the 250 men and women sailors at the Skaggs Island intelligence and communications base are bisexual and use drugs, a female sailor says.

The scandal at the classified base near San Francisco is creating rough seas for the navy.

Two other scandals have stemmed from investigations into homosexual activity by female sailors. A third focused on two navy women who posed in — but mostly out of — uniform for Playboy magazine.

In 1978-79, the navy discharged 76 women and 778 men among 579,000 sailors for homosexual activity.

The problems at Skaggs arose from an investigation into the sexual activities of Seaman Carole Schultz, 22, of Rochester, N.Y., her roommate, Karen Bender, 20, and Tina Queen, 20. All three are being given honorable discharges.

Ms Schultz, a galley worker, was reported to authorities when a male sailor came to her room last month and found her naked in bed with another female sailor. The male sailor had come to the room for a wallet he lost during a party the night before, she said.

"I would rather he jumped in bed with us," she said later. "Three's better than two."

"I'm not kidding," she said. "If I had to sit down and mark off people who smoke dope on the base and are gay — that includes lots of men, too — you wouldn't have a base. You wouldn't have a navy.

Sub plot charges dropped

ST. LOUIS (UPI) — A 22-year-old Kansas City man has been dropped as a suspect in a bizarre plot to steal a nuclear submarine.

Kurtis Schmidt, who had been in custody since Oct. 4 in lieu of $250,000 bond, appeared before a federal grand jury and the government dropped all charges. His court-appointed lawyer, Ronald Vails Sr., said

Schmidt was not offered immunity in exchange for government testimony.

Edward Mendenhall, 24, of Rochester, N.Y., and James Cosgrove, 26, of Geneva, N.Y., are still in custody.

Cosgrove is scheduled to appear today for a preliminary hearing.

Mendenhall and Cosgrove are charged with

conspiracy to steal the USS Trepang from its mooring at New London, Conn. Cosgrove was a Navy clerk aboard the submarine for 14 months in 1973 and

1974.

The government said the plot was to sell the sub for $150 million to an unknown buyer in the Atlantic Ocean.

RALEIGH, N.C. (UPI) — Military recruiters want Agatha K. McGhee so badly they have sent her more than a dozen brochures asking her to sign up with the army, navy, air force and Marines. But she can't figure out why they want her. She is 64.

GI claims $5 million damages in atomic 'guinea pig' suit

NEW ORLEANS (AP) — A $5-million damage suit has been filed by a former GI who claims he was used as a human guinea pig during an atomic blast in Nevada.

Ellis Gaspard, 51, says he was in an army company sent to test the effects of atmospheric atomic detonation, but had no idea he was being used as a human subject in a dangerous experiment and did not consent to it.

Gaspard claims that as a result of the blast's radiation, he contracted melanoma and leukemia. The suit, filed yesterday, says his wife Opal, who is also a plaintiff, suffered two miscarriages attributable to her husband's exposure.

The suit alleges that Gaspard and other soldiers were marched to a point about 2 miles (3 kilometres) from the detonation point or "ground zero," placed in open trenches and told to put their heads between their knees and keep their eyes closed. Then the atomic bomb was exploded.

Immediately afterward, the suit adds, the men were "ordered out of the trenches and in to a distance of approximately half a mile from ground zero."

"The test structures and equipment were destroyed, twisted and molten. The ground around was fused."

The suit claims officials directing the experiment knew the hazards involved at the time but chose to proceed to obtain data they wanted, "despite foreseeable risks to the human life involved.

"Such actions are not justifiable as legitimate military activities sanctioned by the constitution and the laws of the United State or International Law."

The suit seeks $3 million for Gaspard, and $2 million for Mrs. Gaspard. Defendants are the former Atomic Energy Commission, now known as the Nuclear Regulatory Commission, the defence department and the United States.

The date of the blast is not revealed in the suit. Gaspard served in the army in 1954 and 1955.

New bomb to blast dud nuke

YUCCA FLAT, Nev. (UPI) — A nuclear bomb will be exploded tomorrow to destroy another nuclear bomb, which was buried but would not go off.

A bomb, code named "transom," has been sitting 2,100 feet (640 metres) under the desert at the Nevada Test Site for 16 months. It did not detonate when tested on May 10, 1978.

Another nuclear weapon, code-named "Hearts" — packing a power equal to 150,000 tons of TNT — has been buried 100 feet (30 metres) away from "Transom."

No more false alarms: NORAD

WASHINGTON (Reuter) — The false alarm that put the North American defence network into a "nuclear war" alert on Nov. 9 "couldn't happen again," says the Pentagon.

The cause was a "war games" test tape accidentally getting into the main computer, triggering the six-minute alert, and action has been taken to make sure it can't happen again, officials said yesterday.

Investigation of the incident, during which 12 jet fighters were scrambled from U.S. and Canadian bases when it was erroneously reported that a Russian missile was approaching, has been completed and the results reported to the White House.

The incorrect signal, which flashed through the North American Air Defence Command (NORAD) communications system was caused when the wrong tape was fed inadvertently into the main alert computer system.

As part of the alert, some of the 20 air traffic control centres in the United States went on emergency standby.

Convicted for sewing sailor's ear to bed

VIRGINIA BEACH, Va. (AP-Special) — The U.S. Navy hospitalman who had sewed a rowdy sailor's left ear to a bed has been convicted of assault, reduced in rank and fined $200.

But the Navy decided yesterday to punish the victim as well for "disrespect to a petty officer and assault on our corpsmen."

Fireman Anthony Russell, 19, was taken by ambulance April 12 to the Navy hospital here after he had passed out from drinking.

Hospitalmen James Ashley and Ronald Dionne were on duty at the emergency room.

Russell claimed he was tied with straps to a bed, that gauze was stuffed in his mouth, that he was beaten with fists and that his ear was stitched to the bed.

$131 billion defence

WASHINGTON (AP) — The U.S. Senate has given final approval to a record $131 billion defence spending bill that includes money for a nuclear aircraft carrier and development of the MX mobile missile. The measure includes $2.1 billion for a fifth nuclear aircraft carrier and funds for two nuclear-powered attack submarines, as well as a nuclear missile-firing Trident submarine.

NORAD drug probe

COLORADO SPRINGS (Reuter) — The North American Air Defence Command (NORAD) is investigating use of LSD, cocaine, marijuana and other drugs among more than 100 service personnel. None was in a position to make decisions involving national security.

TWENTYNINE PALMS, Calif. (UPI) — The U.S. Marine Corps has given an honorable discharge to a 22-year-old woman sergeant who posed nude for Playboy magazine.

Sgt. Bambi Finney is featured with six other service women in the Playboy April edition.

No secret now -- spies spent $25,000 on porn calls

WASHINGTON (UPI) — The secret's out — America's super-secret military spy outfit rang up an estimated $25,000 a month on long distance calls to a "dial-a-porn" number, a Pentagon report says.

The Pentagon study shows the calls were made by Defence Intelligence Agency agents to a New York city number that provides 57-second recorded messages in which a woman's voice describes sex acts.

The Pentagon's inspector-general said in his semi-annual report to Congress yesterday that the cost of the unauthorized calls could have been $300,000 a year if they had not been stopped. The report did not say how long the calling had been going on.

The Pentagon has now put an electronic block on the line to prevent agents dialling that number, which is rented by the sex magazine High Society.

Cost of the block: $150 installation plus a $15 monthly charge, the report said.

A lawyer for High Society says the number "has been much more popular than the phone messages for the time, the weather, horoscopes or even sports."

Liz Ray's former boss on rebound

Wayne L. Hays, who resigned as a representative to the U.S. Congress two years ago amid a sensational sex scandal involving his secretary, Elizabeth Ray, is on the comeback trail. Hays, who Miss Ray said put her on the public payroll in exchange for sexual favors, won the Democratic nomination for a seat in the Ohio state legislature.

★★★★★★★★★★★★★★★★★★

No wonder the South lost the U.S. civil war.

According to a recent book, one of the Confederacy's leading strategists was a certain **General Richard Ewell**, who frequently imagined he was a bird.

During these spells, he would sit in his tent for hours on end softly chirping to himself. And at mealtimes, he would accept only sunflower seeds or a few grains of wheat.

★★★★★★★★★★★★★★★★★★

'Senators, police and judge paid hookers'

MINNEAPOLIS (UPI) — In what it calls an expose of high-level hypocrisy, the Minneapolis *Star* has labeled a church lobbyist and five public officials — including a judge, two state senators and an acting U.S. attorney — as customers of prostitutes.

Acting U.S. Attorney Thor Anderson immediately admitted the alleged liaisons and issued a public apology. In Washington, the justice department said it is reviewing the matter.

Unflagging patriotism

SAN FRANCISCO (UPI) — Bob Pritkin put up 100 flags outside his Mansion Hotel today and he doesn't think it's unusual.

"I can think of 100 reasons to wave a flag on this very important day, and so I've got a flag for each reason," Pritkin explained.

To add to the patriotic fervor, he placed a "ghost" of John Philip Sousa at a grand piano in a front room. He plays Sousa tunes on request. And Pritkin's son, Scott, 16, dressed in a Uncle Sam costume, served red, white and blue Independence Day doughnuts to his guests.

Redford for president?

HOLLYWOOD (UPI) — Dustin Hoffman predicts in 10 years Robert Redford will be running for president of the United States against Warren Beatty.

Miscasting, says Redford. "I don't like myself in that role," he replies in the December issue of Penthouse magazine.

Help for dog days

WASHINGTON (UPI) — Dogs should be protected against the summer heat wave by providing them with plenty of air conditioning, fans and cool, cool water.

An Agriculture Department veterinarian says the best way to protect dogs is to keep them in air-conditioned areas.

Stuntman beats sound on wheels

ROGERS LAKE, Calif. (Reuter) — Riding his missile-boosted rocket car at 739.666 miles (about 1,183.5 kilometres) an hour, Hollywood stuntman Stan Barrett has become the first man to break the sound barrier on land.

Barrett said he felt as though he "hit a wall" when the vehicle, powered by a 48,000-horsepower rocket engine and an 8,000-horsepower Sidewinder missile, crashed through the sound barrier at top speed.

There was no sonic boom, but observers at the track across the dry lake bed here heard a two-second gentle roll of thunder as the blazing red rocket vehicle flashed by.

The run was timed by U.S. Air Force radar monitored through computers.

"I was 12 seconds into the run when I hit the Sidewinder," Barrett said. "It was incredible. It was over 612 miles (979 kilometres) an hour when I hit the missile. There was some turbulence, then quiet, and then it felt like I hit a stone wall.

"I had no idea when I went through the sound barrier. I felt a lot of resistance and then everything went smooth and then there was a large jolt like hitting a brick wall."

Barrett topped the sound barrier by just over seven miles (12 kilometres) an

hour. With the air temperature at 20 fahrenheit (minus 7 celsius), he had to exceed 731.9 miles an hour to break the barrier.

Barrett, a stuntman to Burt Reynolds, Paul Newman and other movie stars, hugged Hal Needham, owner of the $800,000 vehicle after heaving himself from the tiny cockpit.

The run across the coffee-colored lake bed took only seconds to cover 5¾ miles (9.2 kilometres).

Barrett flicked a series of switches, gently pushed the accelerator with his right foot, and the vehicle blasted off in a cloud of dust with a giant flame from the tail.

★★★

Four sail into a storm as military protests strip

SAN DIEGO, Calif. (UPI-Special) — Four U.S. armed forces personnel — three women and a man — are in trouble with top brass . . . for taking their clothes off.

Petty Officer Jeff Bandy, 23, faces possible discharge for his striptease act at a Fremont, Calif., nightclub.

His plight is something like that of Lisa Ann Woolf, Bambi Lin and Susan Gage, who are in trouble for posing for Playboy magazine.

Bandy, who has been in the navy for six years, says he'll take a discharge if commanders insist. But the navy says it won't do that, so long as he stops wearing his uniform when he begins his strip act.

Meanwhile, a row continues over the April edition of Playboy, in which six women representing the U.S. Navy, Army, Air Force and Coast Guard appear nude.

Last week the marines discharged Sgt. Bambi Lin, 22, (real name Lynn Finney) for posing.

And the navy announced yesterday that machinist Lisa Woolf, 21, and electrician Susan Gage, 22, were being investigated for possible violation of mili-

tary codes because of the spread. Neither has been formally charged.

The photo layout is billed as honoring "Women in the Armed Forces."

"I didn't do it to make the navy look bad," Seaman Woolf said.

"I called my parents before I posed and they told me to go ahead. It was an exciting thing to do, an adventure, an opportunity I would never have again."

Miss Woolf said she does not expect any cat-calling by male sailors when the magazine begins to circulate.

"They all know me," she said. "It won't make any difference. I'm a quiet person. I enjoy working in the machine shop on the ship with the fellas. They respect me and the job I do."

Mark Baker, public affairs officer for the Naval Surface Force, said "There are no specific regulations regarding women posing nude in publications such as Playboy," and added it would be up to the commanding officers of the women whether to bring charges against them.

The public uproar over Bandy's male strip has resulted in the club owner saying he will change his format.

Rita Jenrette defends nude Playboy poses

By Megan Rosenfeld
Washington Post

NEW YORK — "I have never sought publicity," Rita Jenrette said. "It just sort of happened."

Playboy asked the estranged wife of a former congressman to pose for them and write an article, and Bantam Books asked her to write a book. And she had nothing to do with the mysterious appearance of a few of the nude pictures in the latest Playboy.

It's a familiar ritual: Washington scandal is exposed . . . sex bomb tells all . . . signs contracts for books, magazine or performances, and announces her new career as an actress and liberated woman. She delights and appalls the public with confessions and conflicting words and actions and hints of various private peccadilloes.

Ex-beauty queen

The 31-year-old former Texas beauty queen has been holding centrestage since separating from her husband John who had to resign his congressional seat because he was convicted of taking a $50,000 bribe from FBI agents posing as Arab sheiks.

Among other things, she has revealed he made love to her on the steps of the Capitol.

"I don't see what taking off my clothes has to do with what I wrote," she protested yesterday.

To describe her Playboy pictures as "taking her clothes off," is like saying that Dean Martin has an occasional cocktail.

There are eight of her pictures across 10 pages in which her abundant breasts are prominently displayed, sometimes set off with a parenthesis of black chiffon or a swatch of red feather boa. She's wearing black stockings and a garter belt, and little else. In one, she strikes a reclining pose with her legs in the air, closed but uplifted enough to reveal more than can be described in a family newspaper.

"I don't think they're lewd," she said.

"I did it to recover my self-esteem," she said.

"Yes, I consider myself a feminist," she said.

"Maybe it was my way of assuring I would never have to be a congressman's wife again," she said.

"I should've got an Oscar for playing a congressman's wife," she said.

Wife tells of Congressman's sex romp in beach house

CHARLOTTE, N.C. (UPI) — Rita Jenrette, whose congressman-husband was convicted in the Abscam bribes scandal, says she once awakened in their home to find him drunk, nude and "lying on the floor in the arms of a woman who I knew was old enough to be his mother."

Mrs. Jenrette wrote an article titled The Diary of a Mad Congresswife which will be published Sunday in the Washington Post Magazine. A story based on the article was published in the Charlotte Observer this week.

The Observer said Mrs. Jenrette's article tells about the womanizing of her husband John, a Democratic congressman from South Carolina; her disdain for his constitutents; and the excesses of Washington.

Jenrette was convicted Oct. 7 on bribery and conspiracy charges resulting from the FBI's investigation of congressional corruption.

Ladies' man

Mrs. Jenrette writes that her husband told her he was trying to shake his reputation "as a ladies' man."

"After we were married, I began to see just how hard he tried," she said.

She tells of accidentally picking up a telephone extension in

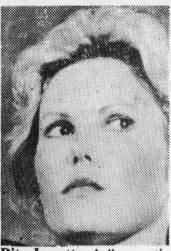

Rita Jenrette: A "romantic weekend" turned into a political sex orgy, she says.

his office and "breaking in on a suggestive conversation between him and a woman."

Another time, she writes, "I knew the honeymoon was over when I rolled over one morning to find John's side of the bed unruffled.

"After a rampaging search of the house in Myrtle Beach where we were staying, I found him: drunk, undressed and lying on the floor in the arms of a woman who I knew was old enough to be his mother . . ."

She describes some of Jenrette's associates in very uncomplimentary terms.

When she first came to Myrtle Beach in November, 1975, she writes about what she thought was going to be a "romantic" weekend on Sandy Island.

On the island, she found three middle-aged men who were there to "shack up with their girlfriends in one of the dirty, unheated cabins."

She writes that "cheap sex and making easy money were the preoccupations of some of these double-knitted, alligator-shoe boys."

Describing the Myrtle Beach women, Mrs. Jenrette says, "They were either 'nice girls' who married young and moved into big houses, surrounded by enough material distractions to ensure either their ignorance or compliance in the goings-on outside Bay Tree Golf Club . . . or they were 'wild girls' who knew about life on the 19th hole."

'Not vindictive'

"They were the women who had worked their way up from the steamy back seats of souped-up Chevies to the highway Holiday Inns and 'hunting' cabins of Sandy Island," she writes. "They had been passed around enough times not to mind any more."

She writes that her article is intended to "be candid and not vindictive."

Pigeons join air sea rescue force

WASHINGTON — The U.S. Coast Guard intends to spend $146,000 over the next two years to train a rescue squad of pigeons to find people lost at sea.

A navy report just released says that in experiments to date, the spotter pigeons strapped on a helicopter outdid Coast Guard air crews

every time in finding objects tossing on the ocean's surface.

But, in the first flight casualty of its kind, the first three pigeon graduates drowned at sea when the helicopter they were riding in ran out of fuel and crash landed off Hawaii.

WASHINGTON (Special) — The U.S. government spent several hundred thousand dollars studying how homeowners could improve the efficiency of their oil burners. The study found that a $100 expenditure could raise the typical burner's efficiency enough to reduce oil costs 25 per cent the first year alone.

So the government printed 10,000 brochures on the subject. "The only problem," one staffer said, "is that there are 19 million residential oil burners in this country. And there was no money for any more brochures."

Govt. Hires $100-a-Day Reader Who Can't Write

By DON HORINE

Where else could this happen but in the crazy, tax-bloated world of Washington bureaucracy?

A "consultant" was hired at $100 a day to evaluate a federal reading program — who was so illiterate she could not write an understandable report!

"Even a third-grade student should not use the grammar she used," declared U.S. Rep. Robert W. Daniel Jr. (R.-Va.).

The "consultant" was hired by the Dept. of Health, Education and Welfare (HEW) to judge the fitness of various educational programs for continued federal aid. Among them was a remedial reading and math course in Hopewell, Va.

Here are some samples of the "consultant's" writing:

"There is no realistically promises that addresses the needs identified in the proposed program."

"The objectivities did not specify to the quantifiable of the success of the proposed program."

"No specified services that can verify the emphasizes to an individual."

Said Dr. Charles C. Todd, superintendent of the Hopewell schools: "I would have flunked an English student for using such prose!"

Rep. Daniel said flatly: "The evaluator is a functional illiterate. This is an insult to all hardworking taxpayers, especially those with children in remedial programs. Yet I understand she was involved in decisions affecting at least 25 cities and counties!"

How did so obvious a know-nothing as this woman manage to use such fancy words in her report — even if they don't make sense? Simple. It appears she plucked the words out of the guidelines for evaluators set out on the report form, and just slapped them together haphazardly.

Her living expenses for six days in Washington, D.C., were paid, as well as her $100-a-day fee. All in all, HEW bureaucrats lavished at least $900 of the taxpayers' money on her worthless reports.

An official in HEW's Office of Education, Dr. Herman R. Goldberg, said that a superintendent of schools had recommended the woman.

Obviously, no one at HEW bothered to make sure she could at least write. Goldberg refused to identify either the superintendent or the woman, but promised she would never be hired again to rate remedial programs.

U.S. dumps bad goods abroad report says

NEW YORK (UPI) — Banned drugs and dangerous intra-uterine devices are among faulty products being dumped in Third World countries by U.S. corporations, an investigative monthly magazine charged last week.

Mark Dowe, publisher of Mother Jones, a consumer-oriented magazine based in San Francisco, said the magazine's report would be hand-delievered to every Third World embassy in Washington and to every Third World delegation to the United Nations.

Some examples

Copies also will go to the State Department, Dowie said. Findings in the 10-month investigation occupy most of the monthly's November issue.

Examples from the report:

☐ Several million children's pajamas treated with the carcinogenic fire-retardant, Tris, were shipped overseas after the U.S. Consumer Product Safety Commission forced them off the market;

☐ The U.S. Agency for International Development, "is pushing dangerous birth control devices throughout the world." This has included "encouraging and sponsoring the use in the Third World of the injectable contraceptive Depo-Provera." It was banned in the U.S. after it caused cancer in laboratory animals and birth defects in humans;

Fatal medicine

☐ Lomotil, an effective anti-diarrhea medicine sold only by prescription in the U.S. because it is fatal in amounts just slightly over the recommended doses, was sold over the counter in Sudan. The package claimed the medicine was "used by astronauts during Gemini and Apollo space flights;"

☐ After the Dalkon Shield intra-uterine device was linked to the deaths of at least 17 women in the U.S., the manufacturer withdrew it from the domestic market. It was sold overseas and is still in common use in some countries.

☐ 450,000 baby pacifiers of the type that has caused choking deaths have been exported by at least five manufactuers since a ban was proposed.

Ding-a-lings?

WASHINGTON (Special) — United Press International reported yesterday that Senator Hiram Fong (Rep., Hawaii) and William Spong (Dem., Va.) were planning to introduce in Congress a bill urging that bells be rung in Hong Kong when the U.S. table tennis team returns there.

The bill, UPI said, would be known as the Spong Fong ping pong ding dong bell bill.

The brighter side

A U.S. National Academy of Sciences panel has been investigating the best way to prevent spontaneous explosions caused by dust accumulating in grain elevators. Their recommendation, after four years of study: Cut down on the dust.

Study lacked meat

WASHINTON (UPI) — The U.S. Agriculture Department won Senator William Proxmire's "Golden Fleece" award today for "wasting" $90,000 on a study of the "behavioral determinants of vegetarianism." "This subject is just not meaty enough to warrant such an expenditure of federal funds," Proxmire said.

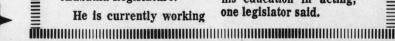

A LESSON IN ACTING

MONTGOMERY, Ala. (AP) — Actor Burt Reynolds has been invited to address both houses of the Alabama Legislature.

He is currently working on the film, The Hollywood Stuntman, in Tuscaloose.

Reynolds might "further his education in acting," one legislator said.

Just great! Granny Grimes

At 94, widow shoots for votes in Texas

Off and running: Libertarian candidate Aileen Grimes, 94, waited until her great, great, great grandchildren grew up before she ran for the Texas legislature.

UPI PHOTO

HOUSTON (UPI) — Aileen Grimes waited until her great, great, great grandchildren grew up before deciding to run for public office for the first time.

Mrs. Grimes, 94, is the Libertarian party candidate for a seat in the Texas House of Representatives.

"I have a good chance of winning next week even if those Republicans and Democrats are running," said Mrs. Grimes, ignoring poll results indicating she would be lucky to run third in a three-candidate race.

"This is the first time I'm running for office because it is the first time I've wanted to run," she said, recalling the first time she voted it was for Herbert Hoover in 1928.

The tiny, gray-haired politician, who walks with a cane following a recent back injury, spends her days at a senior citizens' centre rather than campaigning.

She is letting her friends and party workers — who mainly are interested in getting their issues aired — campaign for her.

"They are taking care of all that for me," she said during an interview. "But if I get elected, I'll hire a secretary to do all the writing for me."

Mrs. Grimes, a widow for the past 11 years whose only source of income is Social Security, was nominated for inner city state representative seat in Houston, where she has lived since 1945.

Running against her are Democrat incumbent Debra Danburg and Republican Wilmont McCutchen.

The spry Mrs. Grimes said her qualifications for elected office include long experience, including work with her husband running a grocery store. She also said she loves history, arts and common sense.

Although she thinks education is important, she has the traditional Libertarian view about parental responsibility.

"I think parents should decide how they want to educate their children and not the government," Mrs. Grimes said.

"Our government sure has gotten into a mess in the last 50 years. The Democrats and Republicans are ruining this country. We need to get the bureaucrats out of Washington."

Saudis beat Israel in arms race

Toronto Star special

WASHINGTON — The United States sold five times as much weaponry and military expertise to Saudi Arabia than to Israel in the last fiscal year, according to Pentagon figures.

Although most of the $5.1 billion in military sales to Saudi Arabia represented construction of buildings and a power plant for the armed services, rather than weapons, the record total does testify to a new relationship between the two nations.

The Pentagon figures indicate that this relationship came into flower shortly after the Arab oil embargo, imposed in late 1973, was lifted.

The Nixon administration promoted military sales to oil-rich countries to offset the higher cost of petroleum imports.

In fiscal 1973, which ended before the Arab oil embargo, Saudi Arabia spent $709 million on U.S. military equipment and services.

The next year, U.S. military sales jumped to $2 billion and kept climbing ever since.

Israel bought mostly weapons under its sales agreements with the United States, which totaled $902 million in fiscal 1979.

The Pentagon figures also dramatize the loss of one of the best customers for American arms. The shah of Iran bought $5.7 billion in U.S. weaponry in fiscal 1977, but Iran's new government purchased only $41.6 million this past fiscal year.

Chapter 10

Strange, Unusual & Humorous

Bride No. 23

Glynn "Scotty" Wolfe, 70, described by the Guinness Book of World Records as the world's most married man, took bride number 23, Guadalupe Reyes Chavez, in Blyth, Calif., yesterday. Wolfe says he will have 40 children when his 20-year-old bride gives birth to the baby she's carrying.

He is listed in the records book as making the greatest number of marriages in the monogamous world. His first marriage was 1927.

Many of his brides were teenagers, and some of his wives have been recycled. He says his longest marriage lasted five years, the shortest 38 days. He claims to have 39 children.

"This is as close to heaven as I can get," marrying all the time, Wolfe said, adding that he's "lovin' every morning and every night."

Dog lonely? Try perfume

NEW YORK (AP) — Is your dog shunned on the street by other dogs? Do you secretly fear your poodle will wind up an old maid? Do other people's dogs seem to be having all the fun?

Your dog may be suffering doggie odor.

Worry no more.

Monsieur Chien, a French perfume for dogs, is almost here. If you have the right address, that is.

"We hope to have it in the test markets by June," says Jennifer Adler. "You know, New York's Madison Avenue, Chicago's Miracle Mile on Michigan Boulevard, Los Angeles' Rodeo Drive, Southampton. Places like that."

And if this new product is snapped up in these marts of affluence, it just might be playing in the boondocks in time for your 1981 Christmas gift-giving.

You might also meet Mycroft, the English bull-dog who is the official spokesdog as well as vice-president and chairman of the board of The Gray Consulting Group of New York and London, the folks bringing us this new necessity.

Mycroft is descended from a line that includes 11 international champions but, alas, poor Mycroft lacked the chutzpah to be a class show dog.

In his youth, he received 78 out of a possible 100 points in competition. The applause was thunderous. Poor Mycroft trembled and winced at the very sound. And there went his points and his career.

"He likes the attention," says Adler. "He particularly likes to be up on a table. He thinks he's back in the show ring."

What sort of dog might want to wear Monsieur Chien?

"It's designed for the dog whose social life is the pits," says Adler. "I've noticed other dogs following Mycroft on the streets since he started wearing it," he adds.

Python crushes child to death

DALLAS (UPI) — A 7-month-old infant was bitten and crushed to death by a 8-foot-long pet python that crawled into her crib.

The child was asphyxiated in about five minutes, with the snake preventing the baby from screaming by squeezing the breath from her lungs.

The python left a series of needle-fine puncture wounds on the baby's face.

The reptile, which escaped from its glass cage in the living-room and slithered into the child's bedroom, was due for his biweekly feeding —a hamster — and was probably hungry.

Tony Lynn Duboe's 5-year-old sister, Jessie, who was sleeping in the same room escaped attack.

Mr. & Mrs. Robert Duboe had purchased the snake as a family pet a year and a half ago in California. Mrs. Duboe discovered the dead infant a short time after the attack. She called her husband, who found the snake curled up on a wooden shelf above the baby's crib.

An angry and hysterical Duboe grabbed the 7-pound python and wrestled it into his bedroom. He stabbed it with a knife, shot it with a .25-calibre pistol, then partially cut off the head with a kitchen knife and threw its pieces back into the room with the dead child.

IF THE SHOE FITS . . .

A police officer inspects the more than 60 shoes, most of them single, that police found last week in an apartment in the "shoe bandit" district of Seattle. In recently reported thefts, a man attacked young women and then ran off with one of their shoes: An unidentified man who lives in the apartment has been arrested.

This way to Planet of the Apes

NORMAN, Okla. (UPI) — Dr. Roger Fouts has been talking with his hands to a chimpanzee for 12 years and now he wants the chimp to teach her infant son to "speak" sign language.

"With the mother-son relationship we ought to see natural communications slowly develop into gestures and then signs, just like a human baby learns to speak."

Washoe is the first chimpanzee to learn American Sign Language and Fouts has been talking to her for the past 12 years. He helped her build a 240-word repertoire.

Fouts, who with graduate students monitors and records Washoe's every movement with the infant, says living with chimpanzees can prove difficult.

"I've had some very emotional arguments with her (Washoe)," Fout said.

Fouts said the toughest battle was when Washoe refused to nurse Sequoyah because "she told me she didn't like the way it felt."

"After two or three good fights, she (Washoe) gave in on the nursing bit," Fout said. He adds there has not been trouble with Washoe's

maternal behavior since the arguments.

Fouts views his animals as almost human, although "the public is probably not ready for chimp's liberation yet." He often compares their development to those of human infants.

"Chimps are non-human beings, but to think they are not individuals is just another form of racism," he said.

Puddling dog season's stupid toy most

WASHINGTON (UPI-Special) — A U.S. consumer group has singled out a plastic beagle that "puddles" in its own pan as the most stupid toy of the 1980 Christmas shopping season.

"The only gimmick with this toy is that here's a dog that urinates," said Ann Brown, head of the Americans for Democratic Action consumer affairs panel.

The toy is called My Puppy Puddles. It's made by Hasbro and is distributed in Canada.

When the dog's neck is squeezed and his snout pushed into water in his red plastic pan, the water is sucked up through holes in the dog's tongue.

Pan of water

When the dog is then placed in the back part of the tray a peg sticks the dog's underside and the water puddles into the "training pan."

"Here is a toy whose whole purpose is to make a dog go to the bathroom," the group's report said. Children who tested the toy "quickly caught on to the fact that you don't need all the paraphernalia to make him go. This toy is based on a ridiculous and questionable concept."

If the "award" is justified then "obviously people like stupid toys," responded Alan MacWillie, Ontario sales manager with Hasbro Industries Canada Ltd.

He said the toy — carried by Simpsons, The Bay, Zellers and other stores, where it retails for $19.95 or less — is "not one of our hottest items but it's selling.

"You should point out that it teaches a child how to train the puppy dog. The puppy only goes in the tray. It's well trained."

Mr. Gameways Ark stores don't stock My Puppy Puddles because when buyer Maggie Husband saw it in a catalogue she thought it was "a dumb thing to give a kid."

"I've seen some dumb toys in my life," she told The Star, "but that one took the cake.

"There have been other toys we rejected on grounds of taste, like the baby doll with the diaper rash. Such things are a part of real life, sure, but I don't think you should introduce them to kids any sooner than you have to."

Worst doll

In other "awards," the U.S. consumer group gave "worst doll of the year" honors to Baby Cry and Dry, a Remco toy that when fed water is supposed to cry until her diaper is changed.

Children, including two boys who played with the doll during the group's tests, quickly found that just pressing "activators" between the doll's legs caused her to cry even when no water was involved, it said.

"We don't see there's any play value in getting boys to press an activator between a doll's legs," Brown told reporters.

The bride wears stripes

BRIDGETON, N.J. (AP) — Instead of the traditional bride in white and groom in black, they'll both wear stripes when Mayor Donald Rainear marries two zebras at the city's Cohanzick Zoo June 28.

Zoo officials said the zebras have been living together for six weeks since they purchased the three-year-old female for their lonely male.

They said Rainear will perform the marriage ceremony to celebrate the $3,000 fund drive that resulted in the purchase of the female from a New York state animal farm.

Time's 'Man of the Year' is a computer

NEW YORK (AP) — For the first time in its 55-year history, Time magazine's Man of the Year isn't human — it's a computer. It beat out three human luminaries and E.T. for the title.

The computer beat out Israeli Prime Minister Menachem Begin, British Prime Minister Margaret Thatcher, U.S. Federal Reserve Chairman Paul Volcker and E.T., the fictional hero of the year's biggest movie, E.T., The Extra-Terrestrial.

The magazine said its editors have, since 1927, honored the indi-

"The enduring American love affairs with the automobile and the television set are now being transformed into a giddy passion for the personal computer," Time said yesterday in announcing the 1982 Man of the Year.

vidual who has had the most impact, for good or ill, on the course of events during the year. Last year's winner was Polish Solidarity leader Lech Walesa.

Alas, poor Elmer goes to turtle-tank in the sky

CHICAGO (UPI) — It started out like any other obituary call.

"Elmer Daturtle died," the caller told the Chicago Tribune city desk. "Everybody loved him and I wonder if you could run an obituary about him."

"Sure," the reporter said. "How did he spell his name?"

"E-L-M-E-R."

"No, I mean his last name."

"Are you nuts? He was a turtle. He didn't have a last name," said Harold Detienne, 67, who said his mother bought Elmer at a dime store in 1946.

Elmer died Tuesday night at the age of 36.

"When we got him, he was the size of a silver dollar," said Detienne, a retired clothing salesman. "When he died, he was as big as a dining plate."

Detienne, who lives with his brother, Walter, 69, said Elmer would let anyone play with his feet and stroke him under the chin.

"He never learned to fear," he said.

Elmer lived in a 30-gallon water tank. When he wasn't swimming or crawling he would look for flies.

"Elmer loved flies — to eat, I mean," Detienne said.

Although he called the turtle Elmer, Detienne admitted he never really determined whether Elmer was male or female.

He also never determined what species of turtle Elmer was but from the description. Ed Almandarz, the curator of reptiles at Chicago's Lincoln Park Zoo, said Elmer probably was a red-eared turtle.

"Services for Elmer will be private," Detienne said, "In fact, we'll probably have him stuffed."

They're fuzzy and they fly

LOS ANGELES (Reuter) — An American woman who entered a British competition to produce a flying saucer said yesterday she would display an interplanetary vehicle in January and hoped to take President Jimmy Carter for a ride in it.

Sue McMahon, who described herself as an artist, fashion designer and scientist, said she had entered a competition launched by a British whisky firm to produce a genuine flying saucer for a prize of $1.8-million.

In a telephone interview from her home in Carmichael, Calif., she said a flying saucer had landed through the ceiling of her hotel room while she was spending a few days in Sacramento, Calif.

"It was manned by people who looked fuzzy, as though I was looking at them through a fuzzy television screen," she said in a telephone interview.

The flying saucer took her to another planet, she said, and then brought her back through the ceiling before taking off again.

Miss McMahon, who did not give her age but said she was "now single," claimed she would produce a flying saucer on Jan. 3.

She intended to invite about 30 people, including Mr. Carter, California Governor Edmund Brown and foreign scientists, to fly with her to another planet, she said. They would be away two days.

But first, she said, she would have to teach her companions how to move out of the present time frame. "It's a simple process. People are always looking for a complicated method, but it is not complicated," she said.

"I have found another dimension. It is only our minds that restrict us," she added.

Body parts push food out of coroner's fridge

EVANSVILLE, Ind. (AP) — The wife of a deputy coroner says she's fed up with finding pieces of bodies in her refrigerator and having corpses hauled around in her truck.

Shirley Jean Cox complained at a county hearing Monday that her home is being used as an impromptu morgue because the county won't pay for a new one.

"At Thanksgiving, instead of having a turkey in my freezer, I had to clear out a space to have body parts," she said.

For the past 14 years, she said, when evidence in coroner's cases could not be sent immediately to labs for analysis it has ended up on her refrigerator, remaining overnight — and sometimes through a weekend.

Body parts, which must be preserved through refrigeration, are placed in styrofoam containers in the freezer. Blood taken from bodies is stored in the refrigerator. Other evidence must be kept temporarily in other parts of the Cox home.

Her husband, Earl, agreed that "sometimes it does get a little disgusting putting things in the refrigerator."

"When my son brings his friends over to play ball, they can't come in and get a bologna sandwich or a drink out of there. I tell them that's off limits," he said.

Babies sold for beer

ST. PAUL, Minn. (UPI) — Court records showed a woman who later turned up as a striptease performer in Florida sold her two babies to a stranger for two glasses of tap beer.

Affidavits filed in Ramsey County District Court showed the mother, who was not identified, took another woman to her apartment where her two babies, a 3-month-old girl and a 16-month-old boy, were crying in their cribs.

"I told her, 'Why don't you take the kids and give them to my mother?'" the woman said. The mother then offered to sell the children for a glass of beer apiece.

"I took her across the street and bought her two beers and she gave me the children," the woman said.

Bottom line gave the wrong impression

MOLINE, Ill. (AP) — Jodi Stutz had no idea that when she put her bare bottom on the Xerox machine, she was putting her job on the line.

"I can't believe I got fired over this," she said yesterday.

Miss Stutz, a 21-year-old secretary, said that one night after work last month at Deere and Co., she decided to "christen" the new copying machine by making a picture of her bottom.

"A lot of people were taking pictures of their hands and their faces and fooling around," she said. "So I decided I would take a picture of my bottom, thinking it would be kind of fun just to see what it would look like."

While another secretary stood watch at the door, Miss Stutz pulled down her pants, sat on the machine and pushed the "print" button.

Word got around after Miss Stutz showed friends in the office her copy.

She said her boss asked her about rumors that she had thrown a big party in the Xerox room, that three men had helped her get undressed and then guarded the door, that she had sent copies of her rear as an invitation to a birthday party.

She said she told him all the rumors were false, but when he asked if she had copied her bottom, she lied.

She chewed her way into jail

CINCINNATI (UPI) — A judge sent a woman to jail for two days because she cracked her chewing gum so loudly that the court reporter could not hear.

Judge Jack Rosen found the woman, a courtroom spectator, in contempt of court yesterday after he repeatedly asked her to quit cracking her gum so loudly.

She was still chewing as she was led away to jail.

Surgeons reattach penis severed by circular saw

ST. LOUIS (UPI) — Surgeons have reattached the severed penis of a 28-year-old laborer who fell onto a circular saw at a lumber company.

The organ was rejoined in a five-hour operation at Christian Hospital Northeast by Dr. Bela Denes, a urologist, and Dr. Wilfrido Feliciano, a plastic surgeon.

"The early surgical result looks promising," Denes said in an interview.

Denes said he knows of only two previous successful penis reattachments in this country. One operation was performed two years ago in Los Angeles and the other in Boston three years ago, he said.

"The important thing is to operate immediately," he said. "Fortunately in this case the patient was in the operating room within an hour of the accident."

Denes said the man, a 28-year-old father, slipped and fell onto a circular saw while at work.

"The penis was cut off at what we call the mid-shaft section," Denes said. "It was almost an isolated injury. He had only superficial cuts in the immediate area."

The severed section had been caught in the man's clothing and was packed in ice at the hospital. The two doctors used conventional techniques as well as microscopic surgery to connect vessels and nerves.

Denes said he hopes his patient eventually can resume functioning sexually.

Stripped over food, woman files suit

WASHINGTON (Reuter) — Caricia Fisher is suing local authorities for $800,000 after she was arrested for eating a sandwich on a subway train.

The 25-year-old, British-born Miss Fisher, a U.S. Government employee, said a transit policeman ordered her off the train in Washington and took her to jail in handcuffs where she was stripped, searched and held overnight in a cell for 31 hours. The charge of eating on the train on Dec. 26 last year was subsequently dropped.

Miss Fisher is suing law enforcement and transit authorities charging reckless disregard of her constitutional rights.

Bandit threatens to shoot corpse

FORT LAUDERDALE, Fla. (AP) — A gunman invaded a wake in a funeral home here and threatened to shoot the corpse unless the mourners turned in their valuables, a court was told yesterday.

Ronald Palmer, 25, was sentenced to 985 years in prison for robbery and weapons offences.

Witnesses identified Palmer as the man who sprang into the mourning room clad in shorts and sneakers and holding a pistol. They said he waved the gun toward the coffin and said he'd shoot the deceased if the mourners did not give up their cash and jewels.

Palmer will be eligible for parole in 42 years.

Vroom! Names give these kids racing start

LINCOLN, Neb. (UPI) — The Tonniges family likes cars. So much so that two generations of Tonniges children have been named after them.

Jaguar Ferrari, 23, Lancia LeMans, 22, and Aston Martin, 18, all were named to reflect their father Donald's intense interest in sports cars.

Now, Jaguar Tonniges and his wife, Rhonda, are carrying on the family tradition.

Their second son, born this week, was named Austin Healy. He joins 2-year-old Rory Gene Ferrari, nicknamed "Roarin' Ferrari" by his father, a University of Nebraska student who restores old cars as a hobby.

Jaguar's mother, DeLoris, who has been divorced from Donald for several years, thinks Rhonda is a good sport for going along with the family tradition.

DeLoris had to "do a little study and research" in sports car magazines to find suitable names, she said.

"The kids had no problems," she said. "The funny part of it is, (friends) always remembered their names."

Gay Bob Doll Comes Out of the Closet

NEW YORK (AP)—Forget Barbie and Ken. Gay Bob has come out of the closet.

What's billed as the world's first gay doll stands 13 inches tall, wears one earring, a custom-made flannel cowboy shirt, denim jeans and cowboy boots and costs $15. He has blond hair and, according to his inventor, Harvey Rosenberg, "looks like a cross between Paul Newman and Robert Redford."

A former New York City advertising executive, the 37-year-old Rosenberg developed Gay Bob last September. To date, he has made 10,-000 of the dolls, which he has sold through mail-order ads in magazines aimed at the homosexual community.

But Gay Bob is beginning to catch on in respectable retail stores, Rosenberg said.

"It doesn't matter if you're gay or not," Rosenberg says. "Gay Bob can help you come out of the closet."

Gay Bob (who is "anatomically correct") comes packaged in a closet. He also has a wardrobe, clothes catalogue, songbook and book about his life.

"Hello, boys and girls," the narrative reads. "Gay people use the expression 'coming out of the closet' to explain the fact that they're no longer ashamed of being gay."

Rosenberg says everyone from business executives to construction workers needs to come out of the closet, an expression he uses for being honest about what people really want to do with their lives.

"Men have to liberate themselves from traditional sexual roles," said Rosenberg, who says he is not gay. Rosenberg said the traditional male seemed to be the most attracted to the doll.

COMING OUT—Two Gay Bob dolls stand beside closet package.
AP Wirephoto

"The more macho, the more taboo, the more exciting homosexuality is," he said, adding that the first thing most purchasers do is take off the clothes of the dolls.

"People are fascinated by homosexuality but they're afraid of it," he said.

Rosenberg, president of Gizmo Development, spent $10,000 to develop Gay Bob. He was so pleased with the result that he promptly designed a whole family of "permissive dolls."

"Each doll comes in his own space," Rosenberg said.

Straight Steve, for example, comes in a powder-blue leisure suit and sits in the living room in front of the television set. Liberated Libby sits in a bedroom.

SEX, BOOZE FILL SCREEN IN KIDS' TV WEEK

EAST LANSING, Mich. (AP) — In a typical week, North American children may see their favorite prime-time TV characters engage in as many as 40 intimate acts and drink alcohol up to 50 times.

A study by the U.S. Office of Child Development of 4th, 6th and 8th grade pupils found most said their favorite shows were on at night.

Between 7 p.m. and 9 p.m. in a typical week, there are 2.7 instances an hour of intimate sexual behavior between adults, and alcohol is seen on the tube almost 3.5 times an hour, as many as four times during crime shows.

Most surprising, he said, was a finding that children see or hear seven times more references to sexual intercourse between unmarried adults than between husbands and wives.

Brother's birthday gift got his goat. . . his goat. .

CHICAGO (UPI) — The 45 goats on the lawn at John Matar's house didn't surprise his neighbors — they were a welcome improvement over the birthday gifts he has received in the past eight years.

Each year, Matar, 42, exchanges ever-more-outlandish birthday surprises with his brother.

The custom began when Sam — who is seven years younger — sent John two female models wearing micro-mini bikinis, Sam said.

"On my birthday, I got three ladies over 70 — one had Miss World, one had Miss Universe, one had Miss America banners. They sang to me and he (John) said that's all he could afford.

"I sent him an elepnant.

"He sent me a marching band.

"I sent him a 4,000-pound pet rock.

"He sent me a sign saying the rock was pregnant and I could have the kids — he sent me 26,000 pounds of pebbles.

"I sent him a sign saying the baby rocks weren't housebroken and you can have the results."

Sam sent John 8,000 pounds of "rock" manure.

"So he retaliated by sending me a diaper. It was huge — the biggest diaper in the world — that said: 'I've been taking your — all year. You can have it all back.'" He got manure.

Sam got his revenge with a never-ending supply of manure — a herd of cattle.

"I must have scared him and he sent me a nice present ... a hot air balloon. When it got up a few hundred feet, she (a woman accompanying the balloon) took all her clothes off and I had a mile-high strip show.

"I thought I'd be nice to him. So I gave him a car. But it was all cut up in pieces and he had to put it together himself.

'Nowhere but up' hard-luck Steve tells the world

CHARLESTON, W. Va. (UPI) — Steve Noetzel's troubles began when his car was hit by a truck.

He suffered serious back injuries as a result.

Not only was his car wrecked, but Noetzel lost $2,000 worth of camera equipment and $440 cash was stolen from the wrecked vehicle.

That wasn't all.

Noetzel lost a court case in which his building business was ordered to pay $35,000 damages, leaving him no choice but to declare bankruptcy.

At the time, his marriage was crumbling. While lying in a hospital bed divorce papers arrived.

But Noetzel was able to relish a sense of humor. He turned to the readers of the local Sunday paper with a special ad.

"I'm 39, just lost my family, my home, my business and my car," the advertisement said. "But not my sense of adventure."

Appearing in the newspaper's personal column, the ad wondered whether anyone would "consider providing room and board . . . and possible future partnership in mutually beneficial ventures."

Noetzel has since received several telephone calls to his hospital room.

"Most of them are women and they all sound sympathetic," said Noetzel, a civil engineer and a Viet Nam veteran.

But lady luck hadn't finished playing tricks. While he was in the hospital, thieves drove a truck to his house and stole furniture, appliances and other items. The loss was estimated at $10,000.

Reflecting on his misfortune, Notzel decided he would put another ad in the newspaper — headlined "Nowhere to go but up."

Talk about biting the hand

MOUNT VERNON, Ohio (UPI) — Bob Grimm, 52, Columbus, has a fish story to end all fish stories.

Grimm was fishing for muskie recently in Knox Lake in Knox County when he hooked a 15-pounder.

Grimm, who was alone, said he reached down to pull in the fish and it bit clear through the middle finger of his right hand. And it wouldn't let go.

"I thought he had about 40 teeth in me, but it was only one," Grimm said.

Grimm, with the muskie still on his finger, went to his car and drove left-handed for 10 minutes until he arrived at a doctor's office in Mount Vernon.

Grimm said the doctor "kind of thought it was funny" but helped remove the fish and put six stitches in the finger.

The doctor kept the muskie.

"I was never so glad to give somebody a fish in my life," said a grim Grimm.

This joke wasn't funny

LOUISVILLE, Ky. (AP) — The billboards blazed Beat Your Wife in huge letters. In smaller letters, the signs added, Go Bowling.

The Bowling Proprietors Association was trying to catch the eyes of potential bowlers. But, what it generated instead was a controversy with the Spouse Abuse Centre, which provides shelter and counselling for victims of abuse.

Carole Morse, director of the centre at a YWCA, said that when she saw the billboard, "I almost cracked up my car.

"This is just the sort of humor we have to stop," she said. "I think it is just the kind of mentality that makes this (wife abuse) the largest unreported crime."

FAIRFIELD, Calif. (UPI) — Steve Bauer and Brigitte Perdoni were "high" for their wedding — they exchanged vows in a tree. Bride, groom, best man, bridesmaids and judge were all hoisted aloft by a construction crane. Bauer owns the Longbranch tree service.

$500,000 thief now a toymaker

YUBA CITY, Calif. (UPI) — A Brink's employee who stole $500,000 from an armored car and spent it on women, nightclubs and gambling four years ago is now making wooden toys, including a model of an armored truck.

Arrested by FBI agents in New Mexico with only $400 in his pocket, after he had spent the half-million dollars in an 11-month spree, Richard Rees went to federal prison.

He was paroled in July after two years and three months.

Today, the 31-year-old Viet Nam veteran is president and sole employee of Goodwood Toy Corp., which he operates from the garage of his parents' Yuba City home.

"This is it," Rees told a reporter recently. "I'm doing what I want to do."

Rees said the wooden toys are fashioned to appeal not only to children, but to adults who want them for desks and coffee tables.

One of the items is a solid oak replica of an armored truck. Rees said he sent one of them to Brink's officials but they failed to see the humor. Instead, they complained to federal parole authorities and Rees is not making any more armored trucks.

He worked for Brink's for three years as a mechanic before opportunity came one day in San Mateo.

"I always knew I was going to rip them off someday," Rees recalls of the day in February, 1977, when he stuffed $500,000 in Brink's receipts in a champagne case and disappeared.

He spent most of the next year in Texas, where he owned a topless nightclub and a jet-set spa, spent extravagantly on women and made $2,000 horse bets.

As his money ran out, Rees wrote San Francisco newspaper columnist Herb Caen, who nicknamed him "Champagne Rickey" — now the trademark for Rees' designer toys.

Outlets for the toys are expanding, Rees said, and he has filled orders for personalized gifts for such Hollywood celebrities as the late Steve McQueen and "Jaws" director Steven Speilberg.

Bionic man would cost $1 billion

NEW YORK (UPI) — The Six Million Dollar Man could be built today — but it would cost $1 billion, says Dr. Eli Friedman.

Making the Bionic Man "would be easier than putting a man on the moon. The people who could do it are attending this meeting," he said at the opening of the International Society for Artificial Organs' annual meeting here.

Beware latest peril -- beds

Toronto Star special

WASHINGTON — Chairs, sofas and — believe it or not — beds are getting more dangerous every year.

In its annual listing of the 10 most dangerous consumer products in the United States, the Consumer Product Safety Commission (CPSC) says that while skateboards and swimming pools dropped right off the list, beds jumped from 10th spot in 1977 to seventh last year on the injury index.

Chairs and sofas leaped from 11th to eighth.

The rise baffled many CPSC officials. Most of the 100,000 injuries related to chairs and sofas last year involved people — mainly small children — bumping into them or falling from them.

For no apparent reason the number was 24,000 higher than the year before.

There was no explanation as to why beds are suddenly more dangerous either.

Swimming pools and skateboards dropped right off the list. But before parents breathe too easily, CPSC officials warn, they should look at the figures for the latest fad — roller skating.

"Roller skating injuries are sky-rocketing," an official said.

The following were the 10 most dangerous consumer products in 1978. The number in brackets is their 1977 place in the index:

1. Bicycles (1)
2. Stairs (2)
3. Footballs, related equipment (3)
4. Baseballs, related equipment (4)
5. Playground equipment (5)
6. Non-glass tables (9)
7. Beds (10)
8. Chairs and sofas (11)
9. Liquid fuels (17)
10. Power saws (6)

Mysteries helped her flee car

RICHFIELD, Minn. (UPI) — An 11-year-old girl who wiggled through a taillight to escape imprisonment in a car trunk is recovering at home and police are holding an 18-year-old suspect.

About 3 a.m. Sunday, the girl was put into the car trunk with only a shirt and a blanket to keep her warm. She escaped nine hours later by taking apart the taillight of the suspect's car and crawling through the 12-inch-by-6-inch space.

The girl had read scores of Nancy Drew mystery novels, a police spokesman said, and "that seems to have prepared her mind to deal with the situation and escape."

Animal show at the zoo stars parents

COLUMBUS (UPI) — A zoo official was astonished to see thousands of adults storm rope fences and scoop up chocolate Easter eggs placed in plain sight for a children's egg hunt.

Columbus Zoo director Jack Hanna and his 40 volunteers had expected throngs of children for the Zoo's first Easter Egg hunt. But what they saw was a rampage of adults.

Nearly 2,000 adults stormed rope fences to grab the marshmellow-filled chocolate eggs strewn on the ground.

"The adults . . . they tore down the ropes," Hanna said.

"It was like watching 5,000 rats that haven't eaten in weeks. You wouldn't think that the adults would go out and hunt eggs."

The dirty T-shirt people talk back

By Bob Greene

"I wear two of the T-shirts you wrote about," the woman said.

Yes?

"I'm 33 years old," she said. "I'm married. I have two children. And I don't see anything wrong with wearing the T-shirts."

What do your T-shirts say?

"One says, 'My Body Belongs to Me, But I Share.' The other says, 'If I Said You Had a Good Body, Would You Hold It Against Me?' "

And what does your husband say when you wear these T-shirts out on the street?

"My husband doesn't say anything. The T-shirts are just in good fun. I'm not advertising for someone to come up to me and proposition me."

But what if they did?

"They would be foolish."

It's puzzling

That, if you have not already guessed, is one of the responses to the column that appeared here recently about T-shirts with obscene words or sexual references on the front.

In the column I readily admitted that I didn't understand the phenomenon. And I quoted Dr. Roy R. Grinker Jr., an eminent psychoanalyst, as saying that people who wear such T-shirts may have certain . . . problems.

Since the column appeared, dozens of people who wear the dirty or suggestive T-shirts have written or called to defend their attire, to try to explain to me why they do it — or, in some cases, to commiserate with me and say that they, too, are a little puzzled by the whole thing.

"My mother is 47 years old," said a 22-year-old man. "She wears a T-shirt with a picture of a breast on the front."

A breast?

"Yes, a picture of a breast. She likes it and thinks it's funny. I'm a little concerned about her wearing it, but I don't know what to do."

Why don't you tell your father to ask her to stop wearing it?

"I would, but my father wears a T-shirt that says, 'I choked Linda Lovelace' on the front."

Feeling of freedom

Most of the people who called or wrote me could not understand why anyone would think twice about wearing T-shirts with obscenities or sexual innuendoes on them. Typical of the people I talked to was a woman whose 16 year-old daughter wears (to school) a T-shirt that says, "I'm So Happy I Could Just (obscenity)."

The mother said, "It's okay with me I use that word, too. It makes you feel free to talk that way. It's dumb to get upset over words. Why should words shake you up?" And then she went on to tell me that war was the real obscenity, that no one should be bothered by a T-shirt with a synonym for excrement or love-making on it when there are people out there killing one another, etc.

Well . . . I don't know. Maybe it's just me, but there's something a little disconcerting about being confronted with some of these phrases when you're out doing your daily routine.

Take the man who wears the T-shirt saying, "Don't Drink the Water — Fish (obscenity) In It."

Or the suburban plumber who shows up for house calls wearing a T-shirt that says, "Your (obscenity) — My Bread and Butter."

Or the 14-year-old girl who wears a T-shirt that says, "I Was Having a Nice Day Until You Came Along and (obscenity) On It."

Or the 42-year-old woman whose favorite T-shirt says "Go (obscenity) Yourself."

Those are all real examples, from the people I talked to. And I suppose that I'm hopelessly behind the times when I confess that, yes, I realize that those phrases exist, and yes, I realize that they are in common usage, and yes, they have passed my own lips — but that somehow it's one thing to know that the words are out there, and it's quite another to have your plumber walk into your house wearing that T-shirt.

I feel very out of fashion to say that I find this distasteful, but that's a fact. The words, after all, have been around for years. Only recently have people decided that it's okay to display them on the front of a shirt.

No personality?

And I have another theory. It's about the personal makeup of people who wear these shirts. They say they wear them because the shirts are clever and funny, but there's a different way to look at it. Namely, that it's a lot easier to wear a T-shirt than to have a personality.

Oh, well. Some of the people I spoke with gave interesting reasons, like the woman who wears a T-shirt that says, "Better Small Than None at All" because she wears the same bra size that she did when she was 13, and she figures that she'll say it before someone else does. And some are truly frightening, like the 16-year-old girl who wears a T-shirt that says, "Kill Me, Kill Me, Cuz That Would Thrill Me."

I have saved my favorite piece of correspondence for last. It is from a young woman who wrote:

"I am a normal 19-year-old bisexual woman with no inhibitions or hostilities like your shrink friend thinks. I prefer older married women as lovers, but turn on with guys also. My breasts are my best feature and the T-shirts I wear call attention to them, and have started conversations which often lead to deeply fulfiling relationships."

The woman then turns to the subject of Mr. Greene:

"I don't want to insult you — but are you a typical, neurotic, uptight, middle-class male unsure of your own sexuality? . . . I bet you went to a Catholic school."

Turkeys fall from heaven

YELLVILLE, Ark. (UPI) — Despite protests by the humane society, live turkeys will be dropped from a plane to hundreds of spectators this weekend during the annual Yellville Turkey Trot.

Bill Moore, organizer of the event, said a plane will glide in low over the courthouse square and drop four turkeys at a time.

'Love Bug' mating device leads you to Mr. or Ms Right

MILWAUKEE (UPI) — Carlisle Dickson and his single buddies were sitting around a restaurant table lamenting their love lives when Dickson came up with the idea of the Love Bug — the computerized society's answer to Cupid.

It will work like this: The lonely guy buys a Love Bug, which will probably look very much like a wristwatch. He also buys a computer chip on which he pro-then to 2, 3, 4, and finally, when they are only feet apart, 10.

Micro-chip mating is still just an idea, but Dickson has a United States patent. Others are pending in Australia and Canada, and he insists he will have his gadget on the market by Christmas 1981.

Dickson does not yet have a working model of his invention.

He says it would sell for about $50, a price he does not consider high, compared grams his own characteristics and traits and those of his ideal mate.

Next he walks into a party, onto a bus or into a church meeting and turns on the gadget. If there is a woman with a Love Bug in the room who fits the traits of his ideal woman, he begins to get a number reading from his unit.

As the two get closer and closer the numbers on their bugs rise, starting at 1 with the price of some toys or other matchmaking systems.

"Consider the cost of computer dating services — $50, $100, some even cost $500," Dickson said.

Dickson is associate director of the criminal justice training centre for the University of Wisconsin-Extension, and a part-time Presbyterian minister. He said he knows little about business or marketing and hopes to license the Love Bug.

Aerospace firm prefers pigeons

FELTON, Calif. (UPI) — When it absolutely, positively has to be there tomorrow, one of the United States' most sophisticated space and computer technology companies uses carrier pigeons.

"The first reaction to using pigeons was just what you would think — laughter," said Lockheed research chemist Werner Deeg, who volunteered to train the birds.

But Lockheed Missile and Space Co., best known for its other "birds" such as the Trident missile, has found a profitable niche for the feathered communication system at the company's 4,000-acre mountaintop site outside Santa Cruz, Calif.

The Felton test base, 160 kilometres (100 miles) south of San Francisco, uses pigeons to fly daily microfilmed prints of graphic design projects 48 kilometres (30 miles) over the mountains from Sunnyvale.

Punker put out parrot's eyes police claim

TUCSON, Ariz. (UPI) — A man who claims to be a punk rock performer has been accused of ripping open the chest of a valuable parrot and drinking the dead bird's blood, authorities said yesterday.

Pima County sheriff's deputies identified the suspect as Charles Horn, 22, who claims to be a punk rock performer using the name of "Charlie Monoxide."

Deputies said they found the parrot with its eyes plucked out after they investigated a weekend burglary at the residence of a 17-year-old Tucson youth.

Rednecks see red at switch

HOLLYWOOD, Fla. (UPI) — "The rednecks saw red" when radio station WGMA switched from country music to "music for single adults" — the station ended up with a dented building and a scared program director.

The station broadcast a satirical, three-hour farewell to country music Sunday night, but program director Dave Denver found that listeners didn't react "in a lighthearted way."

First, the station began getting profane telephone calls.

Then three pick-up trucks and a van pulled up about midnight. Twenty men carrying pipes and sticks piled out and began beating on the building.

"Our control room has bulletproof windows, thank God," said Denver, "because they were beating on the window with pipes.

"I was underneath the console calling the police. I'm chicken."

After he called the police, Denver grabbed the microphone and broadcast an appeal for listeners to call police. The irate country music fans apparently heard the appeal and left, only minutes before police arrived.

Later, Denver said, the vandals called the station and promised to return. So he spent the remainder of the night in a back room, while the station broadcast country music star Mel Tillis' song, Coca Cola Cowboy — over and over.

That's carrying love too far

HAMMOND, Ind. (UPI) — Prosecutors say Gayhart Goddard, 33, mailed up to 100 letters to women telling him he wanted to kiss their toes, lick the bottoms of their feet — and slit their throats.

Goddard faces state charges of intimidation and confinement, harassment and criminal mischief.

Billy's beer for sale at six for $9,000

The price of beer is skyrocketing in the United States. A Massachusetts man, **Russ Kempton**, is offering a six-pack of brew for sale at the bargain-basement price of $9,000.

Kempton says his six-pack of "Billy Beer", purchased at the garage of former President **Jimmy Carter's** beer-swilling brother **Billy** in Plains, Ga., is in "no dents . . . mint condition" and worth the price. Kempton says he has heard of sales of "Billy Beer" six-packs for $6,300, $7,000 and even $10,000.

People don't buy the brew for its taste, however. Kempton says the beer "was terrible. I bought it on speculation, I figured it might be worth something some day."

Oh yes, Kempton keeps his beer warm in a bank safe deposit box.

Franks for the memory

SEATTLE (UPI) — This is a tale of two Franks and one busy blonde named Betty.

Both Franks, in their 50s, were frankly surprised this week when they discovered they married the same Betty.

Frank No. 1 was awakened by a late-night knock at the door. On the doorstep was Frank No. 2, who said he was looking for his wife. He'd spotted her car outside.

His own wife was inside and nobody else, Frank No. 1 told Frank No. 2. Furthermore, he said, the car outside belonged to his own wife.

Frank No. 2 begged to differ, Frank No. 1 called police.

When an officer arrived, he found Betty, 44, who appeared to be very ill, trembling in the back room. He asked her to come to the door.

When Frank No. 2, still waiting at the doorstep, finally saw Frank No. 1's wife, he exclaimed: "Betty, why did you do this to me?"

Betty replied: "I'm sorry, but I don't know you." Then she fainted.

The policeman called an ambulance for Betty while the two bewildered Franks looked on.

Frank No. 2 told police he married Betty 10 days ago in Mississippi and travelled back to Seattle with her and her daughter, Frank No. 1 said he married Betty in Alabama two years ago.

Finally, Betty's daughter spilled the beans. Her mother married both Franks.

Not in America? Pity!

COCOA BEACH, Fla. (UPI) — Manager Jim Cheves said his pier almost toppled into the sea from the weight of people craning their necks to see the topless sunbather floating on a raft below.

"Everybody here was all shook up," said Cheves, who was not unaffected either by the charms of Helle Brun, 20. "Us old east Texas boys aren't used to that.

"For the last two days my pier almost turned over from people standing on one side of it."

Mrs. Brun and her husband, Sven, ended a Florida vacation Friday to return to their native Denmark. Both were surprised to learn that an ordinance bans nude bathing on Cocoa Beach. American movies had led them to believe such practices were tolerated.

"We were very astonished," said Brun, a Copenhagen business executive. "You Americans are very free. I'm sure in five years you will see a lot of girls walking along the beach without a top."

Brun said topless bathing is commonplace in Denmark. In fact, "At home, if a man from a newspaper had come and seen Helle with a top, he would have taken a picture."

Desk drawers reveal secrets of office life

NEW YORK (AP) — Executives and secretaries store a lot more than paper clips, memo pads and ballpoint pens in their desk drawers.

Leonard Itkin, vice-president of the Itkins office furniture company, recently compiled a partial list of items left inside rented desks returned to the firm's Manhattan warehouse. They included:

☐ A leather whip and matching mask.

☐ A Barbie doll, dressed in Ken doll clothes.

☐ Three pairs of bright red men's bikini briefs, found in the drawer of a female advertising executive.

☐ A pair of boxing gloves.

☐ Twinkies. Lots of them.

☐ A video cassette featuring what company president Lewis Itkin described as several men and women "engaged in acts of extreme friendship."

☐ A live turtle (immediately adopted by the warehouse supervisor).

☐ A complete set of 1971 Playboy magazines, in mint condition — except for 12 missing centrefolds.

Madonna and Child stamp called obscene

GARDEN CITY, Kan. (UPI) — A Christmas stamp showing a fully clothed Madonna and Child is too voluptuous for some residents.

Postmaster Bob Winn said yesterday that on three separate occasions, women have purchased the 15-cent stamps and later demanded their money back because they consider the stamps obscene.

The sculpture depicted on the stamps is by Andrea DellaRobia, a Florentine sculptor whose work is displayed in the U.S. National Art Gallery.

BOSTON (UPI) — Time is running out for James Vardaman, who is trying to spot 700 different kinds of birds in a single year. He has 697 so far.

"I have a chance. It's slim as hell, but I still have a chance." "I'm not a great birder by any means, but I'm able to do it and can't resist the challenge," he said.

Miracle of sight

Lucille and Philip Hitchuk proudly hold up their two and-a-half-month-old son, Paul, yesterday after a crucial operation that allowed the baby to see for the first time. The child was born without any pupils in his eyes and the operation was carried out last month at the United Hospitals Medical Centre in Newark, N.J. Thanks to the surgeons' skill, Paul can now expect to live a normal life.

Six-inch drunk!

Sunday Star special

NEW YORK — A dog owner didn't know his pet chihuahua drank until he saw it perched at the family bar barking for another round.

Animal psychologist Daniel Tortor said the owner believed the dog staggered to get attention. He thought it was funny.

But the little animal was getting smashed on Grasshoppers (a cocktail of creme de menthe, creme de cacao and cream) and had a serious drinking problem.

However, Torotra dried the canine tippler out and gave him a drug which causes vomiting when combined with alcohol.

After a few miserable drinking bouts the six-inch-high alcoholic quit for good. It was not known whether the owner took to the bottle when he got the bill. Tortora charges $45 an hour.

Heroine admits she's a klutz

WASHINGTON (UPI) — The 105-pound woman who recently stopped a mighty runaway subway train by picking the cab's lock is a self-proclaimed klutz who failed repeatedly in efforts to duplicate the feat.

I couldn't do it, no matter how hard I tried," said Kilena Loveless after trying to repeat the accomplishment for a photographer.

I broke my fingernails trying."

Ms Loveless gained fame earlier this month when she pried her way into the cab of a driverless train and brought it to a halt.

But she says her life with machines has been less than successful.

"I once sewed my hair into a sewing machine," she said.

She broke into jail for love

HOUSTON (UPI) — A woman was arrested yesterday for scaling a 6-foot chain link fence topped with barbed wire in an attempt to break into the city prison farm to visit her boyfriend. The regular visiting day is Sunday.

PARKING COSTS HIM AN EAR

NEW YORK (UPI) — Police said Peter McKenna, 20, and Arthur Morris, 50, began to argue when they both tried to park in the same space.

Morris, police said, pulled a hatchet from his car, lunged at McKenna, and struck him on the back with the blunt side.

McKenna bit off Morris' ear, police said, and put it in his pocket. McKenna was later persuaded to return Morris' ear, which was stitched back on in hospital.

Both were charged with assault.

Gunman forces teachers to strip

JACKSONVILLE, Fla. (UPI) — Two professors who were accosted by a naked gunman carrying scissors were forced to strip as the gunman began talking to his watch.

"I was scared to death," said math prof Stephen Powers, 35.

Powers had been driving through the Jacksonville campus before dawn when he saw someone who looked as though he needed help. But when Powers pulled over, he noticed the man had a gun and no clothes.

"He told me to get out of the car and take my clothes off, which I did," Powers said. "Then he started talking to his watch, saying, 'Come in, Fred. I've got him' and 'Okay, Mom. Okay, Mom.'"

"He asked me if I had any dynamite in the car and I said I didn't," Powers said.

A little later, Traynham jogged by them and the naked gunman ordered him to also remove his clothes.

Powers and Traynham persuaded the man to seek a friend and accompanied him to an apartment where the nude man banged on several doors.

Police arrested Albert Smith, 29, on a charge of aggravated assault after he accompanied the two teachers to a hospital.

A deuced way to win an election!

SHOW LOW, Ariz. (UPI) — Joy Harding and Brendt Wilcock tied for the seat on city council, so they settled it in true Western style — with a draw at high noon.

Harding won, without any shooting. She pulled the deuce of clubs after 14 cards.

Harding and Wilcock each had 188 votes in last week's election and agreed that whoever picked the deuce of clubs in a draw from a full deck would win.

The card has historical significance for the mountain community of Show Low, 150 miles northeast of Phoenix.

Back in 1876, two ranchers decided to end their partnership in a game of cards. Whoever could "show low," or pull the lowest card from the deck, would win all the property.

The town drew its name from that event.

Another election tie was settled in a similar manner two years ago, when Robert Pitman drew the deuce of clubs after three tries to oust David Foil from the mayor's chair.

A hot new number
Dial-a-service:

By Bruce Ward Toronto Star

"How about that TV color? I watched the Kentucky Derby and the horses stood still — the colors ran."

"But I'm still trying to get a TV series. I've made more pilots than the Luftwaffe."

That's the patter delivered on Dial-A-Joke recently in Buffalo. About all that's missing from comedian Lou Jacobi's string of terrible one-liners is the canned laughter.

Maybe you wouldn't drop a dime to hear those lousy gags, but thousands do it daily. And U.S. telephone executives are giggling and tittering all the way to the bank.

The dial-a-service business is booming. Last year, U.S. phone companies realized gross revenues of $18 million.

The schemes started back in the 1930s with the "speaking clock." Now the nation's phone freaks are becoming compulsive dialers of disembodied voices.

Too early

American Telegraph and Telephone (AT&T) has just launched a national "Dial-It Sports" program.

For 50 cents, you can a New York City number with a new 900 prefix and get a 60-second rundown on who's playing and who has won. On slow days, you get a few sports "features" thrown in free.

Ed Langsom, a public relations spokesman for the company, says it's too early to gauge response.

It's on hold in Canada, but ringing up big bucks in the U.S., even though calls can cost extra

"We're going to give it time to grow," he said in a telephone interview. "If it takes off, we'll be adding some of the more popular New York services nationally."

What, for instance? Well, there's Dial-A-Plant for people who have a black thumb, and Dial-A-Lullaby for insomniacs and Dial-An-Atheist for those dissatisfied with Dial-A-Prayer.

So what's in it for the phone companies? In Canada, nothing.

Canadians pay a flat monthly fee for the use of the instrument. You can make as many local calls as you like at no extra charge.

In the states, subscribers pay a monthly fee for a fixed number of local calls. Beyond that, a charge is assessed for each "message unit."

The more Americans use the phone, the more they pay. And that'

why the phone companies are pushing the dial-a-services — to use up message units.

Last year's Manhattan directory lists 17 dial-a-services. That's a distant second to San Francisco, whered 30 numbers are listed, everything from the weather and driving conditions to Dial-An-Earthquake.

Dial-An-Earthquake connects the caller to the University of Berkeley's Seismographic Station. Recently, a soothing, recorded voice advised that the most recent earthquake had happened 6,000 miles from Berkeley.

Dial-A-Star

In California's Bay Area, stargazers can Dial-A-Star and receive (for a buck) a packet from the Pacific Astronomical Society that elaborates on a mini-lecture by telephone on black holes.

Dial-A-Toupee will send you "a small sample" and Dial-A-Foot will chat about your bunions and discuss how your piggies may suffer "brittle skin, swelling, numbness, pain, burning, cold, clamminess, a crawling sensation, itching or limping."

In Toronto, religion leads the dial-a-something field. There are three numbers to call for prayers, little sermons and spiritual advice.

But there's nothing to match San Francisco's Dial-A-Meditation. The caller is greeted by weird flute music followed by the fruity voice of cosmic guru Sri Chimnoy moan-

Rape suspect trapped by $50 cheque

BALTIMORE (UPI) — A $50 cheque demanded from a victim by an alleged rapist has led police to the arrest of an 18-year-old Baltimore man.

Charles Merriweather was arrested by Baltimore police and charged with raping a 34-year-old woman, police said. They said the woman told them a man ransacked her house after raping her. After finding only $11.50 in her purse he asked her

how she paid her bills.

When she answered, "By cheque," the man ordered her to write him a cheque for $30, then corrected himself and said: "Make it $50."

"He said it better not bounce or he would be back," the woman told police. Police traced the name the woman said was on the cheque and arrested Merriweather.

Shooed away

CAPE MAY, N.J. (UPI) — With temperatures soaring to 100 degrees F in the U.S. yesterday, two thirsty women — one bare-breasted — went to the local chamber of commerce for a drink of water. They were turned away — because they weren't wearing shoes.

Boy who found Skylab bored with U.S. tour

CAPE CANAVERAL, Florida (Reuter) — The 17-year-old Australian boy who found remnants of Skylab in his backyard and won thousands of dollars and a free trip to the United States with his parents and girlfriend is bored and ready to go home.

Stanley Thornton, who lives in the Western Australia town of Esperance, said he was never interested in space and only read about Skylab a week before it fell to earth on July 11.

Asked if he would like to live in the United States, he said yesterday: "Never. It is too big." He also did not like the fanfare, and his girlfriend, Jo Motzel, chimed in that the United States was "too crowded and polluted to live in."

"I'll probably get married sometime and want to go back to my job as a trucker's helper," he said.

The Thornton family and Miss Motzel are staying near Walt Disney World in Orlando, and plan to leave for home tomorrow.

Teen kills himself over dad's TV ban

BRENTWOOD, Calif. (UPI) — Genaro Garcia, 13, shot himself in the head after his father removed a television set from his room, saying it wouldn't be returned until the boy quit complaining of being sick and went to school, a coroner's jury has been told.

The teenager took his father's .38 revolver to his bedroom, wrote a suicide note and killed himself on January 26, coroner's records showed. "In my heart I will take my TV with me. I love you," the note read in part. "I can't stant another day of school and especially another day without television."

Quick, think of a number!

LIVERMORE, Calif. (UPI) — The largest prime number known to man has been discovered by the computer experts and it contains 13,395 digits, creating a numeral many times the number of atoms in the entire universe. A million, for example, has only 7 digits. Even a billion billion has only 19 digits.

The discovery by scientists Harry Nelson and David Slowinski eclipses the last largest prime number recorded last February by Curt Knoll, a student at California State University at Hayward.

That number had only 6,987 digits. .

A prime number is a number that cannot be divided by any other whole number except itself and the number one. Two, for example, is a prime number. So is 3, 5, 7, 11, 13, 17, and 19, among others.

The scientists used a computer capable of performing 75 million multiplications a second. And it took them three months.

The actual number would fill almost one-third of a page of The Star.

Bride wears wig

TOWN CREEK, Ala. (UPI) — A beaming bride, wearing a wig to cover ragged locks hacked off by her groom's irate ex-wife, says she was not about to let a tar-and-feathering interfere with her wedding plans. Elizabeth Jamieson was wearing a short, brown wig during her exchange of vows with Dr. John McElwey in a brief ceremony yesterday. McElwey's ex-wife, Marietta, who tarred and feathered her Wednesday, is charged with assault and kidnapping.

Not snow nor mother's milk stops the mail

POMPANO BEACH, Fla. (UPI) — An unusual dispute over mail delivery versus time off for breastfeeding confronts Postmaster Wilton Banks and mail carrier Jean Durkin.

Banks says the mail must go through and if Mrs. Durkin, 26, wants to keep her job, she must end her six months of maternity leave and return to work. Banks says he cannot afford part-time help to replace a regular mail carrier.

But Mrs. Durkin and her husband Michael, also a mail carrier, want her maternity leave extended for another six months so she can continue to breastfeed 4-month-old Sarah every two hours, which they say is essential for the child's good health.

Christmas gift makes its point with Khomeini

NORTH LITTLE ROCK, Ark. (UPI) — An Arkansas businessman is manufacturing what could be the perfect Christmas gift for anyone frustrated at Iran's hold on the United States — an Ayatollah Khomeini dart board.

"We call it the Cock-O-Maniac Dartboard," John Gorman said yesterday.

It is designed to help Americans vent the anger they may feel at Iran, where Moslem students have held Americans hostage for more than three weeks with the Ayatollah's blessing.

"It would give people a way to say something — even if it's just hanging a picture of the guy up on the wall with a thousand darts in it," Gorman said.

Baby found in manger

LONGVIEW, Texas (UPI) — A baby no more than 2 days old was found lying near the manger of a church Nativity scene in freezing temperatures and promptly christened "Timothy Christmas." A note with the child said: "I'm Timothy — please take care of me."

SPARKS, Nev. (UPI) — A $1 million pet shelter with a tree-lined cat recreation room and bathing and drying salons, has opened in this Nevada city. It has 82 kennels, a dog pool and exercise yards — and a "visiting room" where prospective owners can get acquainted with the pet of their choice.

HELENA, Ga. (CP) — A kindergarten teacher asked her pupils to bring the thing they liked best to school to show their schoolmates. The children brought their teddy bears, toy cars and dolls. But one child brought his grandfather, 83, and introduced him as his most prized possession.

★★

Riches-to-rags silent movie queen now lives with her pets in two rooms

LOS ANGELES (UPI) — One time silent screen star Mary MacLaren, 79, leading lady to Douglas Fairbanks Sr., appearing in a soiled coat, torn dress and slippers, in court to describe how she was hypnotized into selling her $100,000 home at a giveaway price.

The once beautiful actress, who played the queen to Douglas Fairbanks' D'Artagnan in The Three Musketeers, now lives in two rooms of the house with five dogs and five cats.

She was cited by the Animal Regulation Department which wants her to reduce the number of her pets, and the Fire Department which say her residence is a hazard.

She is to appear in December to answer charges of health code violations.

Her address is listed as a church and rescue mission. She occupies two rooms.

Since 1947, she has owned the Los Angeles home. She told the court, however, she had been "hypnotized" into selling her house for $40,000.

Her attorney, Larry Bryant, said she had signed a contract to sell the property to a man identified as Rev. James Griffis and added, "There are strong suggestions of exploitation and fraud."

The house was believed to have a value in the current market of about $100,000, the court was told.

She said the hypnotist, who identified himself as a "bishop," had "cut off the hot water. Can you imagine that?" she said.

The Department of Social Services also took Miss MacLaren to court saying she lived in "sub-marginal" conditions and needed a conservator.

After Bryant said he would try to get full title to her house back for her, the judge rejected the application.

She told the court that "the so-called bishop advertises himself as a hypnotist and magician. He has destroyed my furniture, burned up my bed and my beautiful TV set."

★★

Baby, 2, gagged in car as parents go dining

MONTGOMERY, Ala. (AP) — A couple left their 2-year-old daughter bound and gagged in a stifling, locked car while they dined at a restaurant, police say.

"The child had a washcloth-like piece of material stuck in her mouth as a gag to keep her from crying out," a police spokesman said yesterday.

John Luter and his wife, Jeanie, both of Hampton, Va., were charged with child abuse and are being held in the Montgomery city jail, with bail set at $20,000 each.

The child was taken to hospital, then released to the custody of the Alabama pensions and security department.

BEAUMONT, Texas (UPI) — The young man, wearing a Santa suit, parachuted from the plane, but struck its rear stabilizer, went tumbling and landed at a construction site 1.5 miles from hundreds of children waiting at a shopping centre.

The young man was admitted to hospital with a broken collar bone. He signed in as "Santa Claus."

Lab Monster fear allayed

CAMBRIDGE, Mass. (UPI) — Genetic engineering research has dispelled fears that organisms created in the laboratory could run wild, the director of a congressional panel on genetic research says.

"The scare scenarios have been dispelled," Zolst Harsanyi told a panel discussion on genetic engineering yesterday. Existing guidelines regulating genetic research have been effective, he said.

SAN FRANCISCO (UPI) — Todd Sherratt, a 17-year-old high school student, is recovering from his leap off the Golden Gate Bridge in an apparent suicide attempt. He swam to shore, becoming the 12th person to survive the 230-foot (70 metre) drop since the bridge opened in 1937. Nearly 700 people have died from the leap.

Genetic watchdog urged in U.S.

WASHINGTON (UPI) — Genetic engineers aren't likely to "remake human beings, like Dr. Frankenstein's monster," a U.S. presidential commission concludes.

But it called yesterday for a group to watch over new gene-splicing techniques anyway, saying religious groups have expressed "well-founded" fears over the lack of control or consideration of ethics.

"The new knowledge is a celebration of human creativity and freedom, and the new powers are a reminder of human obligations to act responsibly," the commission's report said.

Genetic engineering or gene-splicing involves rearranging DNA, the genetic material in all living things.

Notch up another for black cats

BANGOR, Maine (UPI) — Two Bangor men learned the old adage about black cats and bad luck the hard way. Alton Hamm was stranded on a river bank by rising tide while trying to rescue a black cat caught on an icefloe. Alton Cole later spotted the same cat floating down the river and climbed down a stone wall to help it. While trying to coax the feline into a wooden crate, he lost his grip and fell into the river. The Fire Department was called to the river four times — twice to save the cat, both times unsuccessfully; twice to save Cole and Hamm. The cat was last seen floating around a bend in the river.

That little miss is me, woman, 40 tells Coppertone

CALDWELL, Idaho (UPI) — An Idaho woman claims a barebottom photograph of her taken on a San Diego, Calif., beach in 1941 was used without her permission and has made Coppertone Corp. "a fortune" as its trademark since 1954.

Jacquie Callaway, 40, who has suddenly decided to seek royalties, said her father took a photograph of her when she was 2 years old and entered it in an amateur photography contest sponsored by Popular Photography magazine.

The photograph bears a striking resemblance to Little Miss Coppertone.

Mrs. Calloway said she is uncertain how Coppertone acquired the photograph.

"The Little Miss Coppertone illustration came from an artist's composite drawing," insisted a spokesman for the company.

Thaw in relations?

BALTIMORE (UPI) — Two California firms are threatening to thaw the bodies of a Maryland couple, Katherine and Ray Mills, who died more than four years ago. Their bodies were preserved by 'deep freeze' cryonic techniques. But two years ago a relative, Shirley Workman, refused to pay $169,000 for storage.

One man's power trip

VIOLA, Del. (AP) — The high cost of electricity hasn't dimmed one man's enthusiasm for decorating his home with thousands of Christmas lights. Olin Dill's at it again, even though his December bill last year was $1,182.30.

Please adopt me

A 76-year-old Florida man who says he is lonely and misses children has put himself up for adoption.

Jim Donovan, a retired electrician, put an ad in a Miami-area paper this week looking to be adopted into a "normal, lively, happy family."

Says Jim: "I can cook, keep house. I would be the same as a nanny. And I can fix things, like the screens or toaster."

He's brilliant in college — at age of 12

AMHERST, Mass. (AP) — On most mornings, 12-year-old Miller Maley, like millions of other school children, feeds the cats, eats his cereal, hops on his bicycle and heads for school. Only his school is Amherst College.

School officials say Miller, a freshman, is apparently the youngest student in the liberal arts school's 158-year history.

He takes advanced mathematics and physics courses, introductory German and a required freshman humanities course.

After school, he spends a lot of time at the college's computer centre.

Oh chute! He fell off

MASON CITY, Iowa (UPI) — Skydiver Jim Templeton leapt from a plane at 5,000 feet and landed dramatically in the saddle of Pinto Bean, a blindfolded horse at a rodeo at North Iowa County Fairgrounds.

Then as he was about to acknowledge the crowd's cheers — he fell off. Only his pride was hurt.

Death ends drinking contest

WIND LAKE, Wis. (AP) — Teryl Barth tried to beat a record for drinking liquor, but instead he drank himself to death, authorities say.

The 19-year-old man collapsed and never regained consciousness after a four-hour marathon in which he drank 46 shots of whisky, brandy and rum while about 50 tavern customers watched, police said.

"He heard somebody had drunk 45 shots, and somebody said it was a record," police said. "He told other customers he was going to break the record."

Barth lined up shots and gulped them down until midnight then passed out. Friends took him home, where his parents discovered the body the next morning.

A medical report said alcohol comprised .441 per cent of his bloodk close to the .5 per cent level considered lethal by the medical examiner's office.

RANDY DOESN'T RILE NEW JERSEY RUNTS

OCEAN TOWNSHIP, N.J. (AP) — Randy Newman has gained support from high school students here for his satirical song, Short People, which has been banned on several radio stations around North America although it's a current Top 10 hit.

The Short People's Club of America was formed two weeks ago by a group of sophomores at the township high school here, in response to the song. The club's only membership requirement is for a person to have a maximum height of 5 feet 6 inches.

"We realize that the song isn't really against short people," says club president Mike Marchetti, 15, of Wayside. "It's really mocking people who mock short people."

Unlike other short-statured persons offended by Newman's hit record, club members like the song so much that they've adopted it as their theme song.

Ape goes bananas

FORT WORTH, Texas (UPI) — A 54-year-old man was attacked and mauled yesterday by a 100-pound ape he kept to guard his downtown poster shop.

Police said they did not know what prompted the attack against Ballentine Cortez, who was in serious condition in a Fort Worth hospital with severe lacerations of his left arm.

As news of the attack spread throughout the city, animal control spokesman George Brackeen said the humane society reported many telephone calls from people wanting to adopt the animal.

Animal control officials boarded the shops's windows and placed the building under quarantine until it could be determined whether the animal was rabid. The officials said they would not try to remove the ape.

Something escaped him

DALLAS (UPI) — Gun-toting hostage-taker Jim Skelton has lost his faith in women.

Having held his wife and another woman at gunpoint, he eventually asked them, in turn, to run errands for him.

Neither came back.

"He apparently hadn't thought this thing out too well," said police spokesman Ed Spencer.

Now, 33-year-old Skelton, who fired at police during a 2-hour standoff, is charged with attempted murder.

Apparently drunk and upset about his home life, Skelton had stomped into a credit union office brandishing a .38-calibre revolver. He seized his wife, Kay, 31, and another employee, Alice Brock.

After a time, he ordered Mrs. Brock to get a cup of coffee and bring it back to him. She never returned.

Then he asked his wife to go talk to the police and come right back.

She didn't return either.

Disillusioned, Skelton surrendered.

Sleeping man in garbage crush

SPRINGFIELD, Mass. (UPI) — A man who was sleeping in a garbage bin that was emptied into a hydraulic rubbish compactor is in fair condition today.

A resident raced to stop the truck after he spotted Edmund Croteau, 55, struggling to get out of the bin as heavy hydraulic doors began to crush the load.

Truck driver Joseph Sarneili said he halted the compactors when he heard "someone screaming a man was trapped inside."

Croteau was pulled from the truck by firemen and rushed to a hospital intensive care unit. He has internal and back injuries.

Robs bank for arrest

GALVESTON, Texas (UPI) — Santos Casarez Rios, 74, walked into a bank, laid his cane threateningly on a counter and ordered a teller to fill his brown paper sack with money.

But, he wasn't really looking for money. He just wanted to be arrested.

He even walked over to sit beside a security guard until police arrived and arrested him.

"He flat made a statement: 'I'm old, I'm sick, I'm going blind, I took the money, I want to go back to the penitentiary and die.' He said . . . he was all alone," reported a bank official.

"Just looking at his record, he probably spent a good portion of his life there (prison)," prosecutor George Cooley said. "I'm just assuming he can't make it out in the real world."

House wrecked

LOS ANGELES (Reuter) — A train engineer gaped when he saw a two-storey house across the railway tracks ahead of him. The train hit the house and scattered parts of it for half a mile along the tracks here, police say.

Man sells baby

ONTARIO, Calif. (UPI) — A father who tried to sell his 8-month-old daughter for $10,000 has been ordered to undergo psychiatric care and his accomplice has been sentenced to jail. Steven Curci, 24, the father, and Kenneth Floyd, 30, sentenced to six months in jail, tried to sell the baby in 1979 to a couple who had negotiated in good faith to adopt the little girl. But when Curci asked for $10,000 and indicated there would be no legal adoption proceedings, the couple called police. The prospective "buyer" was a retired police officer.

OCEAN CITY, N.J. (AP) — Before anyone could tell Janice Ball "Gesundheit," four cars were mangled. Ball, 20, sneezed as she was pulling her car into the parking lot of a fast-food restaurant. The sneeze caused her car to hit a parked car, which jumped a median in the lot and slammed into another parked car, police said. Ball's car then swerved backward, hitting a third parked car before coming to a halt. The parked cars were unoccupied and no one was hurt. Policeman John Werley listed the sneeze as the official cause of the accident and no charges were filed.

BELTON, S.C. (AP) — Troy Wall expects to use his coffee table for a long time — eternally, in fact. The table someday will be his coffin. Wall, 72, saw a television program about a California man who built his own coffin, and decided he wanted one. He then commissioned a local cabinet-maker to build it. The hand-made coffin, now used as a coffee table in his living-room, will save his family money, Wall said. "I just can't see putting a lot of money in the ground."

Beautiful people need not apply

Maynard Glenn's flooded by entries for his Ugliest of the Ugly pageant

By David Miller Toronto Star

Maynard Glenn, 70, to put it mildly, was in an ugly mood.

Reached by telephone in Knoxville, Tenn., Maynard ("everybody calls me Maynard, even my mother who hates me, and you can too unless I decide you're not ugly") was talking — at length — about the Ugliest of the Ugly Pageant he is running May 11, the night before the Miss U.S.A. Pageant.

"We are," he said in an ugly accent, "flooded by entries for our contest. We have more than 500 people who think they qualify, but we've whittled them down to 28.

"We have three categories: Semi-ugly, ugly and extra-ugly and we're not taking anybody below extra-ugly. It hurts to tell people they don't qualify — ever try to write a letter and say to someone you're not ugly? — but we've decided to be extra tough. We're cuttin' this contest off at 35."

Having said this, Maynard warms to his task. He admits he is "pretty damn ugly" and tells a lot of would-be uglies that: "There's no use trying and no use comin' unless everybody agrees you're as ugly as a board fence. No, make that even uglier than a fence."

Glenn, who is also recreation director for the City of Knoxville, has formed a committee ("all ugly as hell") of four of his peers to select the ugliest people in the world.

The snapshots sent to Glenn are judged on merit and the lucky contestants are invited to fly to Knoxville for the pageant — all expenses *not* paid. The winner — judged on talent ("as long as he or she don't fall down"), dress ("gotta be real ugly") and swim suits ("like to throw up"), gets a plaque.

"We got a budget of $6 and that's it. The Miss U.S.A. folks — and boy are they ugly about us — have a budget of $600,000."

Since word of the pageant leaked out, Glenn has been inundated with entries from around the world, but many don't qualify.

"First, you gotta tell your folks up there in Canada that we don't take no politicians. That's why we turned down (Prime Minister Pierre Trudeau) — and he was a late cut — because to take him would have opened the doors to others."

Glenn says the committee is looking for "ugly folk" from all walks of life, but is not interested in stars, politicos or TV personnae. "Everyday ugly folks is what this is all about. No ringers."

The pageant will be held in a 1,500-seat theatre downtown and Glenn has two bands ("and they're ugly!") lined up to play. The MCs are two ugly radio announcers and the judges are Glenn and his committee.

The contest will have an international flavor despite Trudeau's disqualification. Glenn has received an entry from Lebanon and says the candidate is the "ugliest person I've ever seen."

"He's a sergeant or somethin' in the army and he's got li'l pointy ears like the good ole boy on Star Trek. Damn, is he ugly."

But competition is bound to be stiff.

"We got a woman up in Massachusetts who was entered by her kids. She didn't know if she qualified, but when we saw her picture, we had to turn away. That's extra-ugly and we're proud to have her."

For would-be entrants, Glenn says, the contest is still open. Simply write to him, in care of the Recreation Department, City of Knoxville, and include a recent picture.

"We define ugly as someone so ugly that everyone else in their town or village turns away when they walk by. We have opened this contest to males or females 'cause ugly knows no sex barrier."

Maynard says the competition will parallel the Miss U.S.A. pageant, finally getting down to five finalists. When a winner is selected, he or she will get a plaque. The runner-up will get two plaques.

The pageant has been such a hit that Glenn is planning to copyright it to ensure it endures after Miss U.S.A. has been forgotten.

"I gotta retire in seven or eight years so I wanta ensure things keep going. Before this pageant, I was just another ugly guy. Now I'm ugly, relaxed and irritable.

"It's a great, great feeling."

★ ★ ★ ★ ★ ★ ★ ★ ★ ★ ★ ★ ★ ★ ★ ★ ★

JESSOP, Md. (Reuter) — The owner of a pet cemetery here is seeking approval from the county council so people can share plots with their pets. "There has been a tremendous demand for it," said William Green. Applicants include one couple that has 10 cats and a dog.

★ ★ ★ ★ ★ ★ ★ ★ ★ ★ ★ ★ ★ ★ ★ ★ ★

Inebriated granny a hot seller

SAN FRANCISCO (AP) — One year it was chipmunks. Another year it was singing dogs. This Christmas the big hit record just might be by the Shropshires, whose recording of Grandma Got Run Over By A Reindeer is selling like hotcakes around San Francisco.

"When we found her Christmas morning at the scene of the attack. She had hoofprints on her forehead and Claus marks on her back."

Those are sample lyrics from the tale of an inebriated granny who gets trampled by Santa and his sleigh when she staggers outdoors against the advice of her family.

"She'd been drinkin' too much eggnog and we begged her not to go, but she forgot her medication and she staggered out the door."

Sonoma County ranchers Elmo and Patsy Shropshire, who recorded the song written by a friend, Texan Randy Brooks, couldn't give the discs away at first. Record executives wouldn't give the Shropshires the time of day.

"They wanted to be rid of us so fast," Shropshire said. "I don't think they even listened to it. We got all those printed rejection-slips, you know? We were just picking names out of books and sending the tape around."

But their bluegrass band, The Homestead Act, kept performing the song, and they finally spent $2,000 recording the song and having 600 copies printed.

"We were just selling them off the stage," Shropshire said.

Then came a bit of Christmas magic — a fan gave a copy to a disc jockey, he played it on the air, and a record store which had taken 200 copies on consignment sold out in one day.

Suddenly the record moguls woke up, and now there are plans to push the catchy tune up and down the West Coast and across the United States — at 98 cents a copy.

The Shropshires — he's from Kentucky, she's from Tennessee — are overwhelmed by what's happened to their tune.

"Things have been so wonderful," Mrs. Shropshire said. "We just can't believe it."

Mike Cogan, president of Bay Records, says 6,000 copies have been printed so far, and "we can print 100,000 a day if we need to."

"If anybody doesn't believe in Santa Claus," Shropshire said, "what happened to this song is proof that he exists."

Record attempt runs dry

KINGSTON, R.I. (UPI) — University student Greg Martin was in the 70th hour of his attempt to beat the world record of 202 hours for the longest shower when officials turned off the water. They said the idea was totally irresponsible, citing energy waste and potential health problems.

Judge outdraws Lone Ranger

LOS ANGELES (Reuter) — A Los Angeles judge has done what no bandit has ever dared — ordered the Lone Ranger to take off his mask.

Superior Court Judge Vernon Foster also ordered actor Clayton Moore, 64, to stop advertising himself as the Lone Ranger.

Moore, who did not appear in court because he refused to take off his mask and white cowboy hat in public, said he was astonished at the decision.

Lone Ranger Television, Inc. contends Moore is too old to portray the cowboy.

Battered women's home rejects strip-show cash

CHEYENNE, Wyo. (AP) — It was a hard decision, but when directors for a home for battered women were offered proceeds from a benefit, they said they couldn't accept.

The decision came after they learned the benefit show would feature male dancers who stripped to their G-strings for an audience of women.

At first, the directors accepted the offer of money to be raised by a "ladies night only" show Nov. 12 at Caesar's Den, a Cheyenne nightclub, said Safe House spokesman Julia Yelvington.

Then news of the nature of the entertainment got out.

"It was one big rat's nest," Yelvington said of criticism levelled at the shelter by churches and other groups.

"It was hard for us. These people with black eyes, bruises and shattered arms aren't as concerned where the money comes from."

But Safe House directors decided to decline the offer and issued a statement disclaiming any part in sponsoring the affair.

It's a sad, sad day when you win a contest

ELGIN, Texas (UPI) — A pregnant woman whose husband won't take her out and a woman whose son left her to live with his father are the saddest people in town — they've won the Sad Day competition.

Elgin radio station KELG solicited letters from people who thought they had the saddest lives anyone could live. The winners will be treated to a night on the town in nearby Austin, compliments of the station.

"My husband thinks just because I'm pregnant that I shouldn't go anywhere," Donna Howard's letter read. "He won't take me dancing."

Students in U.S. play new 'killer' games

By William Lowther
Toronto Star special

WASHINGTON — As 17-year-old computer genius James Dallas Egbert III remained critically ill with a gunshot wound to the head, today police were investigating the incredible fantasy world of wizards, monsters and wraiths in which he lived.

And they warned of the dangers in the new wave of role-playing games sweeping U.S. universities.

Egbert, a curly headed, baby-faced boy with an IQ to rival Einstein, may have shot himself. He was found on Monday sprawled over a sofa in the apartment he shared with another boy in Dayton, Ohio. A .25-calibre automatic pistol was lying near him.

"It appears that his great mind led him into a tortured and twisted existence that is very, very hard to understand," said one of the investigating police officers.

Egbert made headlines last year when he mysteriously disappeared for 28 days from Michigan State University where he had become involved in a bizarre cult that played a live version of the board game Dungeons and Dragons in an eerie labyrinth of steam tunnels below the campus.

Mysterious gap

It is still not known what happened to him during the period he was missing.

Among the student games that police are particularly worried about is one called Kaos — short for Killing As An Organized Sport. Players wear sinister disguises and sneak around after dark armed with plastic suction dart guns.

The idea is to "assassinate" each other by shooting the plastic darts from the shadows. The Kaos craze started last year at the University of Michigan and Egbert may have played it at the nearby state university.

It has since spread to the University of Florida, to universities in the Chicago area and to the University of California at Los Angeles.

Administrators are worried. A typical reaction comes from UCLA security chief John Barber. He says: "This game involves a lot of very suspicious-looking people creeping around in the dark with real-looking guns.

"If there was a crisis on the campus and police were called in one of these guys could very easily end up getting shot by mistake."

After Egbert went missing last year and police failed to find him, private detective William Dear of Dallas, Texas, was called into the case. His investigations led him to a group called the Tolkien Society. The characters in Dungeons and Dragons are taken from J. R. R. Tolkien's books.

The group demanded that Dear agree in an affidavit not to seek prosecution of the Tolkien group and negotiations for Egbert's release began.

Remains silent

After Dear returned the boy to his parents he said: "This is the most bizarre case I have ever been involved in. I don't know when, if ever, the veil of secrecy will be lifted on this case. Perhaps, for the good of the boy, it shouldn't ever be. The boy has undergone a tremendous ordeal."

Egbert himself has refused to discuss what happened.

But his mother, Anna Egbert has spoken out about her son's extraordinary imagination. He was reading full-length books at age three. He moved rapidly through school and ended up teaching a course at his high school when he was 14 years old. It was about this time that his vivid imagination took over from reality.

"He read science fiction in great quantity," his mother said. "He would not read the garbage, the sleazy adventures, but only the ones that were complicated and elaborate. He became deeply involved in the game of Dungeons and Dragons and with some secret groups that acted out the parts.

"Wizards and monsters and other fantastic creatures — they all became very real to him."

Coaches show cheeky reply to school jeer

MARKSVILLE, La. (UPI) — School officials refused to turn the other cheek and temporarily suspended three football coaches for responding to the jeers of alumni by dropping their pants.

The coaches bared their behinds after being provoked by several members of the 1971 class during Marksville High School homecoming activities last week.

It was "an act unbecoming school employees," school superintendent Ron Meyeau said.

He made an ass of himself

SALEM, Va. (UPI) — An animal control officer trying to capture a wayward donkey accidentally stabbed himself with a tranquilizer dart and lost consciousness.

Authorities said Don Kelly was in hospital for observations, but they did not believe the tranquilizer would cause any lasting effects.

Kelly was filling the dart with Rompun, a horse tranquilizer, when it slipped out of his hand. When he tried to catch it, the needle stuck in his ring finger and injected the tranquilizer into his bloodstream.

A tall jail tale

CLARKSBURG, W. Va. (Special-UPI) — Nicholas Arthur is 7 feet 4 inches tall, weighs 335 pounds and takes size 15½ shoes. But these are the least of his problems.

Arthur, serving a one-to-10 year stretch for grand larceny, has to sleep in a 6-foot long bed in a 7-foot-wide prison cell in nearby Moundsville.

He's filed a petition in court claiming cruel and unusual punishment, and has demanded a bigger cell, plus the right size in clothes and shoes.

ORLANDO, Fla. (Reuter) — Bulldozer operator Doug Miller's car was stuck in the mud at a building site so he tried to use a bulldozer to push it out. But the machine's throttle stuck and the bulldozer went over the top of the car and flattened it. "I guess I might have misjudged things a bit," Miller said.

He's got a head start on a new life

LOS ANGELES (Reuter) — Want to wake up one day in a brave new world, with the bad old times of 1980 just a memory?

If so, you'll have to spend some time after you die hanging in suspension in a stainless steel capsule in a temperature of -196 Celsius.

But it could be another life for you, says Laurence Gale, president of the Alcor Life Extension Foundation. He said an associate organization, of which he is a vice-president, already has nine bodies in capsules.

He intends to take a new route — he will have only his head put in a capsule when he dies. The people in the new world will have to find him a body, but storing a head is much cheaper than storing a body.

"The idea is that all the information on my body is locked up in the genetic code of my cells," he said. "There would be cloning or a similar process and I would have to have a new body made.

"The idea is that if you can save the information that is locked up in you when you die, there will be some technology later that will allow you to be put back together."

Gale's organization moves into operation the moment someone is pronounced dead. The body is moved in a box of ice to a laboratory at Emeryville, Calif. A life-support machine keeps the heart and

In the laboratory, the body temperature is lowered and the blood is removed and replaced with chemicals which act as an anti-freeze and also prevent cells being ruptured, Gale said.

The body then is placed in a bath and the temperature is lowered to that of dry ice. The body can stay there for a week or so until a capsule — "a large stainless steel Thermos bottle" — is built to store the body.

The temperature in the capsule is reduced to -196C with liquid nitrogen. The capsule is usually topped up with the liquid nitrogen every two weeks.

Gale, a computer consultant, said he got into cryonics — the technique of freezing bodies in order to bring them back to life later — because of an insatiable curiosity.

"We have considerable confidence we are preserving the memory, the personality and the sense of identity of the person because the parts of the brain are well preserved.

"Scientific evidence points to our being correct, although we do not have definite proof. But single cells and sperm have been frozen for many years.

"If I come back as a body that has no memory or sense of identity and my personality no longer exists, then I have failed."

How far away is the new world? Gale said he should wake up feeling young and vigorous in 50 or 100 years.

"Biologists are building up life systems. Biochemists are tearing cells apart. The whole thing will come together and we will know the whole story," he said.

One of the problems is cost. Gale said preparing a body, placing it in a capsule and storing it for a year costs $12,600. From then on, storage costs are about $2,000 a year.

"A few people in capsules are still being paid for by relatives. But something happens to the relative and the body has to be buried," he said. "That is what happens to the majority of the people who are frozen."

Turtle rehoused

LUTZ, Fla. (AP) — A tiny turtle that had its shell crushed in eight places when it was hit by a car, was rushed bleeding to an animal hospital to be put out of its misery. Instead, veterinarian Mary Leisner called in a body shop technician and between the two of them, they built the turtle a shiny new shell out of fibreglass.

Attacker goes ape

BUFFALO (AP) — A Buffalo Zoo caretaker was charged at the weekend with beating an ape senseless with a stick.

Guy Shelton , 21, was accused of beating Tanga, a Celches ape, last week while the animal was in a holding cage of the zoo's hospital.

Patriotism isn't flagging

LONG BEACH, Calif. (Special) — Bumper sticker baron Ski Demski always wanted a flagpole in the front yard of his home so he could fly Old Glory.

After years of planning and spending $16,000, 50-year-old Demski's 125-foot-tall flagpole arrived this week, complete with a stars and stripes flag 30 feet by 50 feet and a gilded metal eagle (wingspan 4 feet) to preside at the top of the pole.

But some neighbors are upset. They feel that wrapping the pole in red, white, blue and gold reflective tape is rather overdoing patriotism.

BRIDE LEFT A WIDOW

ST. LOUIS, Mo. (UPI) — Less than half an hour after Richard Ising, 19, and his bride left their wedding reception yesterday, the couple got into an argument in their car.

Ising, enraged, leapt from the car on to a busy highway where he was struck by three vehicles and killed.

Dad bilks cripple

RIVERHEAD, N.Y. (Special) — When Peter Steen received $215,000 damages after an accident in 1979 left him paralyzed from the neck down, he asked his father Robert to bank the money for him. But instead of managing the money, the father used the trust account to live in "high style" — and even bought himself a $50,000 yacht. He is in jail facing a charge of stealing $233,000.

Why won't alien beings use airport provided?

LONGMIRE, Wash. (AP) — So far, alien beings have snubbed an airfield built by believers in extraterrestrial beings near Mount Rainier.

So people who believe flying saucers are flitting all around the mountain have decided an extra attraction is needed — an antenna to transmit thought energy and impulses of friendship to jittery outerspace persons.

Members of the New Age Foundation, which built the spaceport 13 months ago, are now building the signal tower. At the top will be a pyramid-shaped metal device to transmit thought energy provided by group members, says Wayne Aho, New Age Foundation leader.

The group will gather in a circle around the tower and clasp hands to form a giant battery, Aho said. The friendly thoughts will then soar skyward and can be received by whoever is up there, he explained.

"They are afraid of us. They know about the earth's great stock of nuclear weapons."

He said the entire universe was shocked when the United States used the atomic bomb in war in 1945. "With this signal tower, we can convince them of our friendly intentions."

What will the group do when the first flying saucer lands? Aho says it will start questioning the aliens about energy.

"When we learn the secret of their energy sources, gas station lines will end on planet Earth."

The UFO landing field is on the 14-acre headquarters of the New Age Foundation near the entrance to Mount Rainier National Park. It was above Mount Rainier in 1947 that an airline pilot reported the first flying saucer sightings on record.

MADISON, Wis. (AP) — Julie Caswell, 25, didn't just walk the aisle yesterday. She ran. "We're runners and most of our friends are runners, so we thought it would be nice if everyone went running," Miss Caswell said.

After the ceremony, Julie and her new husband, Rich Rogers, 28, climbed into a Chinese bicycle rickshaw for a 2½ mile (4 kilometre) ride to the reception, with the rickshaw powered by a friend who is a bicycle racer.

WASHINGTON (UPI) — There are lots of Avon Ladies — but why are there no Avon Gentlemen? That's the question a minority stockholder in the cosmetics firm is asking. Evelyn Davis has complained to the federal Securities and Exchange Commission that "Avon Ladies" publicity and recruitment practices discriminates against men. Avon has until May 1 to disclose how many — if any — Avon men sales personnel it employs.

$6 million bubble bursts

PHILADELPHIA (UPI) — Topps Chewing Gum Inc. has lost its 14-year monopoly of the bubblegum baseball card industry — and been ordered to pay triple damages of $3 to a Philadelphia competitor.

Fleer Corp., of Philadelphia, filed a lawsuit in 1975 against Topps, which since 1966 signed exclusive contracts with virtually every major and minor league baseball player to appear on cards tucked in with a sheet of pink bubblegum.

Judge Clarence Newcomer ruled that Topps and the Major League Baseball Players' Association unfairly edged Fleer out of the market.

But he balked at what he called "guesswork" at determining the extent of Fleer's losses. He awarded Fleer a nominal $1 damage award which, under anti-trust laws, is tripled to $3.

Topps is the largest U.S. manufacturer and seller of baseball cards, selling $6.6 million worth in 1978.

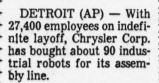

Robots will man the line

DETROIT (AP) — With 27,400 employees on indefinite layoff, Chrysler Corp. has bought about 90 industrial robots for its assembly line.

The $6 million purchase is reported in this week's edition of Metalworking News.

"They (the robots) don't displace people," a Chrysler spokesman said.

"We've had them in other plants without any loss of workers. Because of the attrition due to deaths and retirements of workers, we just move the people to other jobs."

The robots will be equipped with welding guns that automatically weld chassis and body assemblies and installed at plants in Detroit and Newark, Del., the newspaper said.

"They're much more precise (than workers) and they never miss a weld," the spokesman said."

All you need is cash . . .

SAN DIEGO (AP) — You may not be able to buy love, but if your bid is high enough, you can get rid of it at a San Diego charity auction.

Two lawyers have donated divorces to the upcoming annual Combined Arts and Education Council auction.

One uncontested divorce valued at $750 has been put on the auction block by Philip Andreen. Lawyer Mark Dodge is offering eight hours of office work and the filing fees to the unhappy couple.

The something-for-everyone auction catalogue also features a vasectomy, valued at $150, donated by an anonymous urologist.

Mom behind 8-ball

ST. PETERSBURG, Fla. (AP) — The ambulance was waiting. Her labor pains were less than three minutes apart. But 24-year-old Kathy Haddon wouldn't leave the pool tournament. Her son-to-be just had to wait. And he did.

At stake was the women's championship of the city's Tavern Pool League. Kathy was the top shooter in the league and the heart of the team from Mastry's Bar and Grill.

"I've been waiting all year for this," she said. "Everybody wants me to leave, but I'm not leaving for anything. There's plenty of time."

By 11 p.m. the baby was four days overdue and the pains were 2½ minutes apart.

"She stayed in bed for two days to rest up so she could come to this," said her husband, Dan, shredding a plastic cup with his teeth. "She went into labor two days ago, but she kind of talked herself out of it."

In the seventh game, Kathy sunk the 4 and the 8 ball to give her team a 4-3 lead. But before long, Mastry's was back in a neck-and-neck race, tied at 5-5 with Nell's Lounge.

By 11.15 there were only two balls on the table — the 2 and the 8. Kathy had to sink them and Mastry's would have its second straight title.

The pains were insistent, but Kathy made short work of it.

Dan was waiting. So was the ambulance. So was the doctor at St. Anthony's hospital. By 11.30 she was on the way. And soon afterwards Dan called the celebrants with the news — Kathy had given birth to a son.

Rat bites saved baby from death

LEBANON, Tenn. (UPI) — The rats that tried to eat 9-month-old Valerie Hearn may have saved her life, a doctor says, because she was on the verge of death from malnutrition.

The child is in serious condition at McFarland Hospital today. Authorities picked up her sisters, aged 2 and 4, to have them checked for signs of neglect or abuse.

Valerie was apparently attacked by the rodents at her dilapidated home. Her mother called an ambulance.

"Her body was really bitten bad. She was nearly eaten alive," said Dr. Bernard Wiggins, who examined the baby. "But tragically, you could say that the rats might have saved her life since she surely would have died of malnutrition very shortly."

Wiggins said the child was also suffering from carbohydrate and protein deficiencies, anemia and cerebral palsy.

The pediatrician said the child had rat bites on the arms, legs, lips, ears, body and hands. "The rats nearly bit out the palm of her left hand," Wiggins said. "It must have been several rats and they had to be big ones.

"This is the worst case of rat bites and child neglect that I've ever seen in my 10 years in pediatrics," Wiggins said.

Nurse cut off man's air for a joke, court told

BILOXI, Miss. (AP) — A nurse has been charged with shutting off the oxygen to an elderly patient — to show military technicians how the man would turn blue.

Elizabeth Coyle, 52, a civilian nurse, was charged with assault for depriving the patient of oxygen at Keesler Air Force Base Medical Centre.

Coyle is charged with assaulting Jessie Mashburn, a 62-year-old patient, on Jan. 14, 1978. Mashburn died the same day, but the indictment doesn't claim his death was a result of the nurse's actions.

Court documents say Coyle had asked enlisted air force personnel "whether they wanted to watch the patient turn blue."

One source close to the case, who asked not to be identified, said the incident occurred as Coyle was removing excess fluid from Mashburn's lungs and continued the procedure longer than was safe.

The documents allege that between October, 1977, and February, 1978, Coyle "engaged in a scheme and plan to assault and inflict further injury upon seriously and terminally ill patients in the intensive-care unit."

Child was kept in witches' den father charges

Special to The Star

ALTADENA, Calif. — Take a little girl named Purdy, add an alleged coven of witches and a mysterious old mansion and you cook up one of California's most bizarre child custody cases.

The story began — on a Friday the 13th — when Laura Tran walked out of her husband's house with 2½-year-old Purdy and moved into the mansion, which is filled with satanic paintings and guarded by fierce pit terriers.

It came to a halt this Hallowe'en, when Tony Tran persuaded a judge to award him temporary custody of Purdy.

Before it ends — with a hearing for permanent custody this Friday — Tran's lawyer will try to prove that the mansion is home for part of a huge satanic cult presided over by a former convict.

"It's definitely the most bizarre, the weirdest child custody case I have ever been involved in," said the lawyer, Henry Koehler.

"She (Purdy) has been held prisoner in a witches' den," Tran told reporters.

The judge said the pit terriers were his main reason for awarding temporary custody to Tran, saying they "pose a significant danger" to the child.

A Los Angeles police expert on fighting dogs had testified that the dogs, which roam the house freely, are capable of being sent into a violent frenzy by a child's laughter.

Zzzzzzany Zachary has a real hang-up

Toronto Star special

SAN FRANCISCO — Zachary Zzzzra is no longer unhappy — Vladimir Zzzzzzabakov has cancelled his telephone.

It's part of the continuing zany Z battle for the last listing in the phone book.

For years Zzzzra had been listed in Guinness Book of World Records "for the most determined attempt to be the last personal name in a local telephone directory.

"It really upset me when the phone book came out last year with this name Vladimir Zzzzzzabakov below my name," said Zzzzra. "I phoned this guy Vladimir and asked him how come he put so many Zs in his name. I demanded he tell me his real name."

Zzzzra said Zzzzzzabakov responded, "That's none of your damn business" and promptly hung up.

Zzzzra didn't know Zzzzzzabakov had cancelled his phone until the new San Francisco directory was published last week.

"Had I known, I would not have changed my name — if only for the listing in the new phone book — to Zachary Zzzzzzzzzzra," explained Zzzzra — pronounced Zee-zee-rah.

Zzzzra first made Guinness when he outzeed Zeke Zzypt (zipped) of Chicago, who had pushed aside Zero Zzyzx (rhymes with fizz) of New York, who replaced Vladimir Zzzyd (zid) of Miami.

Nobody's a sure winner

AUSTIN, Texas (UPI) — Nobody's perfect.

The Nobody for President campaign charmed a crowd of 500 at the University of Texas, offering an alternative to the somebodies on the presidential ballot.

Working the crowd for Nobody was a character called Wavy Gravy, Nobody's chief aide, a position he calls Nobody's Fool.

"Who was president before George Washington?" Gravy, dressed in a clown suit, asked the crowd.

"Nobody!" responded the crowd.

"Who honored the treaties with the Indians?"

"Nobody!"

"Who will free the hostages?"

"Nobody!"

"Who do you want to run your life?"

"Nobody!"

The address was so stirring — it was obvious Nobody cares — that one man stepped forward and said, "I've never voted for anybody but this year, I'm going to vote for Nobody."

Curtis Spangler, Nobody's campaign manager, went on to explain Nobody knows how to dispose of nuclear waste, Nobody has brought peace, Nobody fed the hungry and the destitute and Nobody keeps all his campaign promises.

The campaign is financed by the sale of bumper stickers, T-shirts and campaign buttons. It is the second campaign for Nobody.

In fact, Spangler argues Nobody actually won in 1976 although Jimmy Carter was permitted to take office. Spangler says only 40 per cent of eligible Americans voted, leaving 60 per cent voting for Nobody.

New Yorkers take nude laws sitting down

NEW YORK (UPI) — One law bans swimming in the nude and another bars strolling in the nude. But there's nothing on the books about sitting in the buff.

In the eyes of some New York city council members, too many sun worshippers are taking advantage of the loophole and some sections of city beaches have assumed a decidedly "natural" look.

The opponents of nude sunbathing have set out to close the legal gap. But the issue has proven as prickly as a beach thistle.

City councilmen say they have been receiving an increasing number of complaints from constituents objecting to such exposure. One councilman, Leon Katz, proposed a law banning nudity on any beach, dock, shore, pier or other structure adjacent to city waters.

Meanwhile, Parks Commissioner Gordon Davis says he goes to the beach every weekend and had yet to spot any nude bathers, "But I will continue to be vigilant and look for them," he said.

FRANKFORT, Ky. (UPI) — Waldo Wecker, an English sheep dog belonging to Kentucky Post staff writer David Wecker, is the first animal to receive a commission as a Kentucky Colonel. Only later did angry officials learn they had honored a dog. Tom Loftus, Frankfort bureau chief for the northern Kentucky newspaper, nominated Waldo for the colonelcy recently and last week it was awarded. Loftus said he "fudged a bit" on Waldo's application, listing the animal's age in human — not dog — years. The animal is 42 years old in human years. He also listed Waldo's profession as "security guard."

★ ★ ★ ★ ★ ★ ★

A stop sign for fuel waste?

CHICAGO (UPI) — President Jimmy Carter, told by an engineer that the United States could save millions of barrels of oil by eliminating one-third of its stop signs, has agreed to investigate whether unnecessary signs waste fuel.

Larry Kast told Carter during a town meeting yesterday he had studied kinetic energy and its effect on wasting energy.

"When you see these automobiles, a two-ton vehicle, coming to an unnecessary stop sign, and stopping," he said, "to get that car going 30 miles again requires an awful lot of energy — not to mention a 78,000-pound truck."

Kast has calculated the U.S. could conserve 7 million barrels of oil a day by eliminating one-third of the stop signs.

"This is the one area that we have not adequately addressed," Carter replied. "I think that that is a very worthy suggestion."

Carter said he would relay Kast's idea to Transportation Secretary Neil Goldschmidt.

Robin's a little smasher and dad has bills to prove it

GRAND RAPIDS, Mich. (UPI) — Robin Hawkins could be the little girl they had in mind when they named it the "terrible twos"— she has left a trail of nearly $2,300 in damages in two months.

First it was the plumbing, then the dishwasher, the refrigerator and the family car. None has escaped the rampage of policeman Rowlf Hawkins's 2-year-old daughter.

Robin's trail of terror began at the toilet. Alice the cat got dunked, drowned and flushed.

Rowlf, who kept track of Robin's exploits, tallied the expenses: $62.75 for the plumber, $ 2.50 for Alice.

That was only the beginning.

Robin's decision to give teddy bear a bath — atop the heating element in the dishwasher — cost her father $375 for repairs, $25 for smoke damage and $8 for a new teddy.

Then there was the refrigerator. Robin stuck some magnetic noteholders in the vents just before the family left home for the weekend, burning out the motor. The cost: $310 for the refrigerator, $120 in spoiled food and $3.75 for the noteholders.

"That evening, we sat down to watch TV," said Hawkins. "Robin had twisted the fine tune so far that it broke inside."

The repair bill: $115.

The next day Mrs. Hawkins went to pick her husband up from his second job as a part-time policeman in Sparta. She left Robin sleeping in her safety seat, with the keys in her purse inside the car.

"We heard the car start down the street," Rowlf said. She ran into a tree. Cost: $1,029.52 in repairs.

Holes in wall

A few days later, Robin tried to play some tapes in the family stereo. Cost: $36 for tapes and $35 for tape deck repairs.

Shortly after that, the Hawkins parked their car halfway in the garage after a shopping trip and left Robin strapped in her safety seat while they unloaded the groceries.

"My wife had the keys, so we figured everything was okay," Hawkins said.

Everything was okay — until they heard a loud noise and ran outside to find the automatic garage door bouncing off the hood of the car with Guess Who locked inside the car, pushing the remote control. The bill: $120.

Robin also lifted $620 out of the cash register at a supermarket, drilled 50 holes in the walls of a rental property owned by her parents, painted walls with nailpolish and slipped the garden tractor out of gear so it rolled down the driveway, narrowly missing a neighbor.

"Some day when she comes and asks me why she isn't getting any allowance, I'll show her this," Hawkins said, waving the list of Robin's damages.

★ ★ ★ ★

Grad invites public to tell her what to do

MANHATTAN, Kan. (AP) — Patty Pinair says she can't decide what to do with her life when she graduates from Kansas State University on Saturday — so she has asked 500 strangers for advice.

Mrs. Pinair, 29, an art major, said she set up a card table in front of the student union and passed out 500 questionnaires to students and faculty.

"I did it because I don't know what to do after I graduate and neither do many of my friends," she said. "I thought maybe I could get some suggestions from the general public."

Among the 292 suggestions she received:

☐ Shoot herself for majoring in art.
☐ Invent a new color.
☐ Try working for a paint company.
☐ Join the Navy.

"Someone told me to find a new major and start over," said Mrs. Pinair, the wife of a lawyer. "I told the person art was my third major. I have degrees in English and French and have taught both."

Scorned woman driver stages demolition derby

TULSA, Okla. (AP) — A woman apparently scorned in an argument with her boy friend staged a "demolition derby," ramming her car into 18 vehicles, five street signs and two fences, causing damage estimated at $20,000, police say.

"I have never seen anything like this in my entire life," traffic officer John Storms said. "I checked the records and there has never been this many points of impact from one single incident."

Storms said that Mary Glynn Boudreaux, 37, stopped by police after the rampage here Monday, told police she had a quarrel with her boy friend.

Storms said the woman snapped off traffic signs at an intersection and headed for a church parking lot.

"This is where she really started the demolition derby," Storms said. "Most of the cars there belonged to church staff members. She just went to it. Bam, bam, bam."

Some of the cars were hit with both the front and rear of her car, he said.

Big day for Deborah was really 'the pits'

KEENSBURG, Ill. (UPI) — Deborah Burnes' wedding didn't include the traditional "something borrowed and something blue," — unless you count her blue jeans.

Deborah, 23, was married to miner Roger D. Knew, 27, of Francisco, Ind., yesterday 800 feet below the earth's surface in AMAX Coal Co.'s Wabash mine.

The bride and groom were decked out in matching outfits — steel-toed boots, jeans, safety glasses and hard hats.

"I think it's kind of exciting," said Deborah, of Oakland City, Ind., before the wedding.

"I won't miss the traditional wedding finery at all. Most brides get a new veil, I got a new hard hat. I'll probably never use it again, but then, brides never use veils again either."

The Knews are fairly sure their underground wedding was a first. Company officials said it was certainly the first wedding in one of their mines.

"We talked and joked about it for three or four months, and then just decided to do it," the new Mrs. Knew said. "There have been others in strip mines, but none underground."

About 20 friends and relatives attended the ceremony. For many, however, the two-minute elevator ride to the mine's working level was nothing new.

"Just about everybody either works at AMAX or has worked here." Knew said of the guests. Even the minister, Rev. John Whitten, spends most of his time at the mine.

Deborah's two sisters, Julie White and Cindy Masters, were bridesmaids.

"I really had to talk to get them to agree to it," she said.

Dirty work foils Dracula

LOS ANGELES (UPI) — Get out the garlic, sharpen a stake! Dracula's dirt is missing!

The dirt from Romania, where a real-life inspiration for Dracula was born, was imported by a theatre here but disappeared at the Airport.

The Broadway hit "Dracula" has recently moved from New York to Los Angeles, and the producers thought actor Jeremy Brent, who plays the vampire count, would be more comfortable on a layer of cushiony soil in his coffin.

So they arranged for a shipment of dirt from the region where Vlad Tepes was born. Tepes was prince of Walachia — just southeast of Transylvania, the count's fictional homeland — from 1456 to 1462. He was famous for his capricious cruelty, executing an estimated 20,000 people in six years, most of them by impaling them upright on vertical stakes.

The missing soil had been treated to sterilize it of any organisms barred by the U.S. Department of Agriculture, the theatre producers said. They did not say whether it had been exorcised.

Sterilization was nationwide, says U.S. doctor

LYNCHBURG, Va. (UPI) — The director of a Virginia hospital which sterilized 4,000 people to rid the state of "misfits" and "race degeneracy" believes that similar programs were carried out throughout the United States.

Dr. Ray Nelson, director of the Lynchburg Training School and Hospital where the 4,000 sterilizations were carried out under a 1924 law to combat hereditary mental illness, said the facility was a model for other states in the 50 years until 1972.

CHICAGO (UPI) — Darryl Curby is a cut below the rest when it comes to hairdressing. His customers hang upside down for a trim.

"My whole technique is based strictly on gravity," says the 32-year-old barber. "When a designer cuts hair, he pulls it up 90 degrees from the point of origin.

"By inverting the person, gravity pulls the hair straight down. So we cut the inside lines of the haircut in the inverted position."

KEY WEST, Fla. (UPI) — Martin Laesig downed 10 beers in 10 bars over 1.8 miles in 22 minutes to win Key West's St. Patrick's Day "Suds Run." He broke his own record, set last year when he did the same feat in 27.2 minutes. More than 360 competitors paid $10 for the right to take part.

Rumbles of the rich: Last December, William Kurt Busch, 25, heir to the brewery giant Anheuser-Busch Cos. Inc., was charged with biting off a man's ear in a tavern fight. Now, Busch has been charged with assault after punching a teenaged employee of a drive-in Mexican restaurant.

He used mirrors for self surgery

CHICAGO (AP) — An emotionally troubled young man performed a complicated 8-hour abdominal operation upon himself in an effort to reduce his sex drive, a medical journal reports.

Dr. Ned Kalin, a University of Wisconsin psychiatrist, describes the case in the current issue of the Journal of the American Medical Association. He said he believes it was the first such case in medical history.

The 22-year-old man, using mirrors and professional surgical equipment, opened his abdomen and tried to sever the nerves to his adrenal gland, which influences sexual and aggressive feelings. He did this two months after removing his own testicles, the report said.

The man spent many hours studying books on surgery and learning about the most recent research on the adrenal gland and its hormonal secretions, the report says.

Kalin said the man made an incision with a scalpel and used retractors to keep the wound open as he tried to reach the adrenal gland. He applied a gelatin powder to control bleeding and sewed the larger vessels with sterilized cotton thread.

Air crash ghouls go on orgy of plunder

By JOE HALL
Star staff writer

SAN DIEGO — The stench of still-burning bodies hung in the air as looters went on an orgy of plundering.

Ghoulish thieves began stealing wallets, jewelry, watches and anything of value torn from mutilated bodies after the worst air disaster in North American history.

They were stealing as firefighters tried to put out blazes at pleasant, middle-class homes on the fringe of the city block that was devastated by the crash of a small Cessna and Boeing 727 jetliner.

Police Chief Bill Kolender said today nine people were arrested for looting, including one man caught trying to wrench the upper dental plate from a body. It is believed dozens more looted bodies that rained down from the sky before some 700 police were drafted into the area.

Thousands of sightseers streamed toward the crash site, and the bizarre, southern California-flavored atmosphere continued at the crash scene through the day and into last night.

Young women wearing bikinis — with the temperature even after nightfall in the 90s — sprawled on the sidewalks.

Whole families — some with picnic baskets — journeyed to the scene ignoring pleas to stay away from the disaster area. Traffic snarl-ups stretched for miles along freeways and streets around the area.

Willie rests his case -- what's left of it

ATLANTA, Ga. (AP) — Willie B, the television-watching gorilla at the Atlanta Zoo, went up against a piece of American Tourister luggage in a re-creation of a television commercial. The suitcase lost.

In fact, he found that half a suitcase makes a great cup.

As part of a consumer report on luggage yesterday, a local TV station gave the 450-pound gorilla a suitcase made by American Tourister. That's the brand advertised in a commercial showing an ape bashing, but not being able to break, a suitcase.

Willie B, who may have seen the commercial on the TV set that was installed just outside his cage to fend off boredom, threw the case around, slid it across the floor of his cage and pummelled it.

He ripped the leather-like cover off the hard-sided luggage, tore it open and ripped the halves apart at the hinges.

Then he took one of the halves over to his water fountain, held it under the spigot and drank from the water-filled wreckage.

Officials of American Tourister, a division of Hillenbrand Industries, could not be reached for comment.

John Weatherford, the reporter who did the story, said spokesmen for American Tourister had told him they thought the ape in their commercial was a gorilla.

But he said he found out after checking that the ape in the commercial was a large, male chimpanzee — also a great ape, but about 300 pounds lighter than Willie B.

★ ★ ★ ★ ★ ★ ★

HIS FRIENDS HAVE HIS NUMBER

MINNEAPOLIS (UPI) — Michael Dengler wants to be called 1069. Pronounce it one-zero-six-nine, not ten-sixty-nine.

Dengler, 31, appeared yesterday before a county district judge to ask that his name legally be changed to the number 1069. The judge said he did not know when he would make a decision. "This is the first time that I've had anyone want his name changed to a number."

The telephone company gave Dengler a telephone number under the name 1069 but won't list it in the directory. And if it does, the company isn't sure where you put a number for a number. But he is firm in the pronunciation of his name — one-zero-six-nine — although he allows those close to him to use the nickname, "One-zero."

Late? Phone in phoney alibi with new sound effects gizmo

ATLANTA (AP) — Coming up with the appropriate excuse — when you're somewhere you shouldn't be — may be easier now, thanks to the Excuse Machine.

Stuck at the airport because of a delayed flight? Push the button and jets scream in the background.

Car broken down? Push the button and you hear the sounds of busy mechanics at a garage.

The machine, with a selection of 10 excuses why the caller isn't home on time, is housed in an elaborate telephone booth in the discotheque-lounge of the Ladha Continental Hotel in midtown Atlanta.

Atop the machine is a pink neon sign which flashes the word "excuse" when someone is using it.

Among the excuses programmed into the machine are: "I'm at the airport; I'm in the supermarket; I'm stalled on the expressway; I'm at a garage; I'm in a casino, I'm at the racetrack."

Callers can even push a button to make it sound like they're playing racquetball.

Dale Robertson and Mort Epstein, the machine's creators, say the machine is simply entertainment for patrons. "Everybody wants to be somewhere else anyway," said Epstein.

Mob hitmen get professors — with a pie in the face

EAST LANSING, Mich. (AP) — Michigan State University students can put out a contract on any professor who displeases them, and a clandestine mob will make a hit — with a pie in the face.

Members of an organization called "the chefs," with pseudonyms like Riboflavin, Thiamine and Niacin, boast they have splattered 25 professors with fruit and cream pies this year.

"What we do has been called random insanity," said Thiamine. "But pie-throwing is an art and we are merely the artists. The pies are our brushes. The professors' faces are our canvasses."

The pie-throwers have eluded authorities so far, even though one attack was captured on videotape during a lecture that was being recorded.

TV bricks for those you love to hate

By JERRY BUCK
HOLLYWOOD (AP) — Attention, all you TV critics out there! Now you can do something about all the things on television that annoy you.

It is called the TV Brick and is made for you to throw at your set when you want to let off steam. Don't worry, it's only foam rubber and won't really hurt the set — unless you pick up your Pet Rock by mistake.

Jim Christ dreamed it up and is turning it out in a small factory near San Diego with the aid of Greg Schredder. So far they have made 150.

"I've seen so many uses for it," said Christ, a freelance design artist and part-time cook and waiter. "TV can be so frustrating at times. I enjoy TV a lot more now that I have a TV Brick handy."

Christ suggests the brick can be thrown at such things as sickening commercials, politicians who pre-empt your favorite shows, and bad calls by the referee.

"There's a real need for this," said a viewer who participated in an impromptu poll of the most annoying things on television.

Tying for first place in this unscientific survey were Howard Cosell and "happy" newscasters.

"I don't want to just tell Cosell to shut up — I want to throw a brick," said one person. Another said, "He may be a walking book of knowledge, but he just makes me so mad."

Those happy, jolly newscasters who act like they are sitting in the living room swapping stories made just about everyone's list.

Programs mentioned as most annoying were The American Girls, Charlie's Angels, Mork and Mindy, Gilligan's Island reruns and anything connected with Chuck Barris. One said: "I want to throw a brick every time Boxey loses his mechanical dog on Battlestar Galactica, which happens about six times a show."

Other "Brickable" offenses mentioned:

—Old movies so badly edited (to fit in all the commercials) that they no longer make sense.

—Jiggle shows that exploit women, and sexist comments, particularly in commercials where the male announcer has all the answers and the women are concerned only about a whiter wash.

—Repulsive commercials for laxatives, stomach soothers and feminine-products, which usually come on at dinner time.

—Predictable situation comedies with no basis in reality. Kids who talk like adults, as in such shows as Who's Watching the Kids and Good Times.

Diamonds are (swallowed) forever

WICHITA, Kan. (UPI) — A robbery suspect who apparently swallowed a $100,000 diamond ring rather than surrender it to police is fasting in an attempt to keep the jewel in his stomach, police say.

Sheriff's deputies armed with bedpans have waited in Bobby Carr's special cell for the past three days in hope that the 5- to 6-carat stone set in gold would routinely pass through his digestive system.

But so far the 41-year-old Tulsa, Okla.,

man has thwarted every effort to induce him to eat or drink, despite his being a diabetic.

Carr and Billy Hill, 43, also of Tulsa, were arrested Sunday following the weekend robbery of a fashionable Wichita home.

All of the loot was recovered except for the ring, but x-rays indicated it was in Carr's stomach.

COLUMBUS, Ohio (AP) — When four workers at the city zoo asked a supervisor how they could keep their Australian goose from pecking people, the supervisor replied: "Feed it to the cheetahs." So they did. Now they have to shell out $300 to replace the bird. Said zoo director Jack Hannah: "The supervisor was joking, but they took him literally."

No regrets but not again says surrogate mother

NEW YORK (UPI) — The first known surrogate mother in the U.S. has no regrets about bearing a child for another couple, but says she wouldn't go through it again.

Elizabeth Kane — a pseudonym — was impregnated by the semen of a man whose wife was infertile. She gave birth to an 8-pound-10-ounce boy Nov. 9 in Louisville, Ky.

Kane, 38, of Pekin, Ill., who has three children of her own, said she and her family had no regrets about having the baby.

Kane said, "All of us — my husband, my children and I — would do it again, but we won't. We fought for what we believed in and won."

The adoptive parents, whose names have not been made public, were present when the baby was born, Kane said.

"I felt good," she said. "I knew this was the most important day for his new parents and I went home with no regrets at all."

NOT TONIGHT, FLORENCE IT'S AGAINST THE LAW

FLORENCE, Ore. (AP) — The city of Florence has inadvertently passed a law banning sex.

A new ordinance approved recently by the council says it is illegal to have sexual intercourse "while in or in view of a public or private place."

What the city fathers (and mothers) were trying to do was ban lovemaking in public places — and in private places that can be seen from public places.

But nobody figured out until a few days ago that the wording of the new ordinance rules out sex in public and in private.

JUST A DOMESTIC TIFF – BUT 2 CARS TOTALLED

FAIRFIELD, Calif. (UPI) — Both their cars were wrecked when a man and his wife got into an argument in a tavern, then drove into a muddy field and rammed each other repeatedly.

But Mr. and Mrs. Roger Thompson, both 31, are reported reconciled.

Mrs. Thompson angrily left the tavern in one car and her husband pursued her in the other. Police said the cars ended up ramming each other repeatedly in a field until both, a 1968 Dodge and a 1968 Chevrolet, were total wrecks.

Two children riding with Thompson complained of a bumpy ride but neither was injured.

Pac-Man ate away lad's life

GRIFFIN, Ga. (UPI) — A Pac-Man enthusiast has been banned by a judge from playing video games for 10 years after he set fire to his future home because he didn't want to move away from his favorite arcade.

Judge Ben Miller yesterday said video games were the downfall of Eric Lewis McGill, 18.

McGill had dropped out of school to play Pac-Man, and was convicted of arson last week in an Aug. 30 fire at a country home where he was to have moved with his aunt and uncle.

It was the second time a house on the site burned. No one was injured in either blaze.

The judge ordered McGill to pay the $13,000 damages to the house, to seek counselling, and placed the youth on probation for 10 years, during which he can't play video games.

PHILADELPHIA (AP) — The Procrastinators Club of America will hold its annual July 4 picnic Jan. 20 at a site yet to be picked. "My goodness, it's much too early to say where it will be," Les Waas, the club's president said. "This is kind of early to announce the date, let alone where it will be." The club has over a half a million people as members, he said. "But only 3,800 have joined so far. We're still waiting for the rest to come in. Unfortunately for a club like us, it's the people who haven't joined yet who are probably the better procrastinators."

CLEVELAND (UPI) — A Greyhound Bus driver who thwarted a bus hijack attempt by alerting police with his citizens' band radio has been suspended for 10 days without pay for violating a company rule banning CB radios on the firm's coaches. "I can't believe it," said Wayne Thompson, 53. "I'm in more trouble than the hijacker." Company officials refused to discuss the case.

★★★★★★★★★★★★

SMASHING BARBARA'S HAPPY NOW

BURIEN, Wash. (UPI) — Barbara Smith has suffered in silence for years over her unreliable old car. But yesterday, when it failed to start for the umpteenth time, s h e finally lost all control.

Barbara, 2 8, took a baseball b a t from the trunk, smashed the windows and headlights and pounded the bodywork. She even offered policeman Jim Fuda a turn with his nightstick when he arrived to find her standing with a broken b a t a n d a "satisfied smile."

He declined, but Barbara told him: "I feel good. That car's been giving me misery for years and I killed it."

★★★★★★★★★★★★

MAN LOST HIS TOES — TWICE

SPRINGFIELD, Mass, (AP) — A man whose three severed toes were packed in ice and sent to one hospital while he was taken to another after a power lawnmower accident has complained to authorities.

"You shouldn't send a man's toes to one hospital and him to another," Paul Rannenberg wrote to the city fire department.

Fire officials say they do not know whether the toes could have been successfully grafted if they had been immediately available.

ALIVE AFTER DROP

Arrow points to 29th floor of Transamerica building in San Francisco from where Harold Brown, 22, plunged down an air shaft. He broke thighbones, kneecaps and a heelbone, but escaped internal injuries. "He was screaming 'whoopee' all the way down," witness said.

Santa drives bus boss sees red

MINNEAPOLIS (AP) — When driver Gary Van Ryswyk got behind the wheel of his city bus wearing a Santa suit and carrying $20 worth of candy, he was just trying to bring some Christmas cheer to his passengers.

"The passengers loved it," he said. "When I got to intersections all sorts of little kids would come up smiling."

But when he got off the bus on Christmas Eve, the bus commission told him to stay off. He was suspended indefinitely for violating the dress code — dark green uniforms — and refusing to doff his costume.

"A Santa Claus suit has a big floppy hat, long sleeves and a beard that gets in your eyes," said Gary Abel of the Metropolitan Transit Commission. "There's a big safety factor involved."

But not everybody's a Grinch.

In Darlington, S.C., Raymond Sansbury's seven children yesterday happily tore the wrapping off dozens of Christmas packages that poured in from around the country after the $112-a-week garbageman was arrested for taking discarded items from a dump for Christmas gifts.

"It's restored my faith in people," said Sansbury, 33.

Hundreds of Christmas cards were piled around the house in several boxes,

SANTA CRUZ, Calif. (AFP) — A young woman parading in a chocolate-layered Easter outfit found sweets were not enough to seduce the man she was after. After his complaint, police arrived at the man's home and saw the woman hopping through the backyard like a rabbit, wearing nothing but chocolate. The chocolate rabbit, whose identity was not disclosed, will spend Easter under psychiatric examination, police say.

WEDDING UPLIFTING EXPERIENCE

NEW ORLEANS (UPI) — Just for the fun of it, Phil Gurian and Karen Rosa chose a hotel elevator instead of a wedding chapel for their marriage ceremony.

"Church weddings are so boring," Gurian, 28, said yesterday before his marriage to Miss Rosa. The ceremony took place as they rode a glass elevator to the top of the Hyatt Regency Hotel.

"We wanted an outdoor wedding, but you can't predict the weather here," he said. "So we just decided to have it in the elevator that overlooks the city while it's going up."

Bride's fatal bed-spring

NEW YORK (UPI) — An Uruguayan rancher's bride of 10 days fell to her death from the 20th-storey window of her hotel suite while she was bouncing on the bed.

Silvia Irribar de Manini Rios, 20, died yesterday outside the Hotel Taft in midtown Manhattan.

Her husband, Bruno, 29, said his wife was "frolicking" when "she was bouncing on the bed and bounced right out the window."

NEW YORK (AP) — The Pen and Pencil restaurant in mid-Manhattan, which claims to have enjoyed a "celebrity patronage" since its opening 42 years ago, said yesterday it would "no longer exhibit photos of married show business couples. This is to avoid possible embarrassment when the stars involved arrive at the restaurant with their current escorts and might find themselves pictured on the wall accompanied by their mate of three marriages ago," the statement said.

WASHINGTON (UPI) — Another candidate has jumped into the 1980 presidential race: FUBAR, a red-eyed, glass-headed robot that bills itself as "the ultimate political machine." FUBAR — Fouled Up Beyond All Recognition — cited leadership as the biggest issue in the campaign. "The time has come for the many robots already in government to have a leader," FUBAR said.

'Disco Sally, 80, weds dancing partner, 28

NEW YORK (UPI) — Amid swirling petals and pounding music, 80-year-old "Disco Sally" Lippmann was married last night to a businessman more than 50 years her junior.

To the tune of Pink Floyd's Another Brick in the Wall, the diminutive Mrs. Lippmann — escorted by her bodyguard and carrying a bouquet — marched across the floor of the Magique Disco.

There she joined the bridegroom, importer Yiannis Touzos, 28, and the bridal party, who were dancing while they waited for the wedding to begin.

As thousands of petals and feathers were released from the disco's upper floor, the two — dressed in matching white satin jumpsuits — exchanged vows before a civil court judge.

Then, amid cheers from the 1,500 spectators, the couple took to the floor for their first dance as husband and wife.

Mrs. Lippmann, a lawyer, used to make ceramic figures before she caught disco fever.

A friend, hoping to cheer her up after her husband's death, suggested that she go to a disco. She liked dancing so much that she quickly became a figure on the New York disco scene. Undeterred by her age, she has jokingly suggested that Ain't Gonna Boogie No More will be played at her funeral.

The couple, who met at the now-defunct Studio 54, will take a one-week honeymoon trip to the Caribbean. After that they plan to go on a "disco tour" of the United States.

Parents kept boy in closet for five years

CHATTANOOGA, Tenn. (UPI) — A 16-year-old boy whose parents kept him locked in a closet for much of the past five years has been placed in a foster home, a judge said yesterday. Authorities refused to identify the child or his parents.

The blond youngster was picked up by police as a runaway about six weeks ago. He told investigators he ran away from home "because I want to go to school."

Juvenile probation officers said the boy was taken out of school when he was in Grade 4 and locked in a closet at his home, after he was "accused of doing some very small delinquent acts."

Oh, brother! Twins have double trouble

LIBERTY, N.Y. (UPI) — People kept telling Robert Shafran he looked just like a guy named Eddy who went to Sullivan County Community College last year.

Shafran, 19, was approached by Eddy's ex-girlfriend, best friend and dozens of other strangers who refused to believe he wasn't Eddy Galland, a 19-year-old who had attended the school the year before.

Galland's best friend, Michael Domnitz, told Shafran that his double was born on July 12 and had been adopted.

Shafran was also born on July 12 and was adopted. So, he phoned his double.

"Eddy," Shafran said, "you won't believe this, but I think you're my twin."

Within a few hours, Shafran, holding a speeding ticket he'd received for racing down the highway to Galland's Long Island home, was at his door.

The two discovered they'd been born within 27 minutes of each other at a Long Island hospital and had been adopted through the same agency six months after birth.

There were other similarities.

Both young men wrestled in high school, favor the same kind of music and food and date older women. Each claims the same IQ, admits to smoking too much and says he lost his virginity at the age of 12.

Both had a history of trouble in school, have been in therapy and were told their problems related to being adopted.

Well, officer, it sure wasn't termites

Police in Tulsa, Oklahoma, thought they had a weirdo on their hands when James McEachern walked in to report that someone had stolen his house.

After investigating, it was discovered that someone, indeed, had made off with the two-bedroom frame house, condemned because it was in the path of a proposed expressway. It wasn't taken by mistake, McEachern laments . . . "You don't accidentally move a house . . . it takes two or three days." At last word, police had no suspects in mind.

Kids locked up for two years

SCOTLANDVILLE, La. (UPI) — Police entered a house where a family of 15 lived yesterday and rescued two children who had been locked in a filth-encrusted room and virtually ignored for two years. The children, both 7 years old, had the physical development of 3-year-olds, deputies said.

16,045 gators nabbed in hunt

NEW ORLEANS (UPI) — Hunters in 12 south Louisiana parishes have caught more than 16,000 alligators during a one-month season and the hides are now drawing record prices.

The stories of a win

WHEELING, W.Va. (UPI) — Terry Ryan was named a finalist in the Miss West Virginia-United States Teenager Pagent — but that was before he started growing his moustache.

Terry entered the contest as a lark when he got a letter from pageant organizers stating: "As an outstanding teenager in your community, you have been recommended for competition in the pageant."

Nowhere did the application have a place to mark gender. But it did ask for height and weight — to which he dutifully reported as 6-feet-1 and 160 pounds.

In the space marked "hobbies," he listed touch football and basketball. The long-haired youth even sent a picture, as requested, but it was after that he decided to grow a moustache and trim his hair. To his surprise, he got a letter from pageant officials saying he had been selected as a finalist in the competition. All he had to do was mail in his $200 fee. "I was tempted to see it through," he said, "but $200 is still $200."

HE FLAPPED AND FLAPPED AND FLOPPED

PHOENIX, Ariz. (UPI) — An unidentified young man was arrested on Sunday when he ran nude down the main runway at Phoenix Sky Harbor International Airport, flapping his arms and trying to fly.

The man, who shed his coat as he ran onto the runway, was first noticed by an aircraft refuelling attendant.

He was arrested on suspicion of "unauthorized entrance into the airport operations area" and was taken to a hospital for a psychiatric examination.

Marriage may end up in rut

TUCUMCARI, N.M. (AP) — Among the classified ads in the Quay County Sun was the following: "Farmer with 160 irrigated acres wants marriage-minded woman with tractor. When replying please show picture of tractor."

FLASHER ZIPS BACK TO JAIL

SAN FRANCISCO (UPI) — Larry Burnstin, 27, was so overjoyed when indecent exposure charges against him were dismissed by a judge that he dropped his trousers in the hall of justice, police said.

Because of his exuberance, Burnstin was rebooked in the city jail on indecent exposure charges.

Burnstin was originally arrested for standing nude at a street corner. Less than five minutes after having the charge wiped out because of insufficient evidence, police said, he was found standing by the hall of justice elevators unzipping his zipper. His explanation to police was that he was "merely expressing his joy."

He should try walking home

DOBSON, N.C. (UPI) — George Queen has been charged with driving his bicycle while under the influence of liquor after swerving in front of a police car.

Dentist makes snap decision

IDABEL, Okla. (UPI) — Dentist Curtis Brookover, angry with a 53-year-old patient's refusal to pay for her dentures, took the matter into his own hands.

He went to her southeast Oklahoma home and yanked them from her mouth.

Since the scuffle last week, Brookover said several dentists have called. "They admire my guts," he said.

The Idabel dentist was bitten on the finger during the struggle for the $600 dentures, and Lee Ann Stoval of Bethel contends the fighting dentist bruised her kidney. She is taking her case to court.

"She bit as hard as she could," he said. "When I pulled my finger back out, the teeth came out."

★★★★★★★★★★★★★★★★

FORT WAYNE, Ind. (UPI) — People thought it was bad enough when Tom Porter pleaded guilty to having two wives in Fort Wayne. But when Porter, 26, walked out of court he told reporters and police they hadn't heard anything yet. "Heck, this is nothing," said the one-legged man who has suffered two heart attacks. "I've got three more in Alabama." When officers arrived to arrest him last month, they were met by a shower of glass and a crutch flying out of a second-story window. Police said his second wife had thrown the crutch at Porter, complaining she found him in a "compromising position" with the first wife.

★★★★★★★★★★★★★★★★

NEW YORK (UPI) — The robber had a choice: Grab the wallet that was thrown hastily to the floor of the fast-food store, or his finger that he had accidentally shot off with a shotgun. He picked the wallet.

Police found the finger, and when Paul Miller, 20, sought medical attention for his bleeding hand, he was arrested and charged with robbing a McDonald's outlet in Brooklyn yesterday.

FORT LAUDERDALE, Fla. (UPI) — A laundromat that has tried to take the drudgery out of doing the wash by selling beer and wine has added a new treat — topless dancers.

The Helpy-Selfy laundromat doesn't have a cover charge but the cost for draft beer jumps from 40 cents to 75 cents while the go-go show is on.

Nutty way to catch squirrel

PATERSON, N.J. (AP) — A judge has ordered an exterminator to refrain from fraudulent practices after a woman complained he charged her $30 to talk a squirrel into leaving her house — and the squirrel refused.

Thomas Jenkins, who operates the A-AAA Pest Control Co. in Clifton, N.J., was hired by Rosemary Sammarco of Bogota to rid her home of an extremely pesky squirrel.

Sammarco claimed in an affidavit that Jenkins got her to sign a contract and then demanded immediate payment of $30. The statement alleged he then said he had to go alone into the house to talk to the squirrel. Sammarco was instructed to stand outside and see if the squirrel departed.

The squirrel did not leave.

The affidavit said Jenkins told her he had talked to the animal, but it refused to leave because it liked being in the house.

Jenkins then offered to go back in and talk to the squirrel again for an additional $20. His offer was declined, and the squirrel finally left of its own volition when a ringing telephone scared it away.

Chance for sore losers

HAVELOCK, N.C. (UPI) — Taking a cue from Debbie Shook — who kicked her crown after being stripped of the Miss North Carolina title — local Jaycees will sponsor a "Miss North Carolina Crown-Kicking Pageant."

The Oct. 7 contest "allows each beauty contestant, especially the losers, to fulfil her fantasy and kick the crown," the Havelock-Cherry Point chapter said.

The contest is open to any woman aged 18 or older. The women will kick crowns while wearing swimsuits and evening gowns, and the kicker with the best average will be declared the winner.

Bob Dale's got a grave habit

CIBOLO, Texas (CP) — There are stamp collectors, antique collectors, coin collectors and butterfly collectors. And there's Bob Dale, a coffin collector.

Dale has 14 antique coffins and he's looking for more. That's difficult, since most old coffins are underground — and occupied.

A newspaper cartoonist and noted Western artist, he needed an old coffin for a project several years ago. He put out the word. One coffin arrived, then another, then another. "Before I knew it," he said, "I had a coffin collection."

Occasionally, at antique shows, Dale has a little fun. When people ask him where he got them, he'll say, very straight-faced, 'Oh, I dug them up here and there.'"

Chicken flying high as foe lays an egg

SAN DIEGO (UPI) — The original San Diego Chicken jumped into the air, flapped his wings, wriggled his huge orange beak and shook his tail feathers in a victory dance.

Ted Giannoulas, 25, who parlayed a $2-an-hour job wearing a chicken outfit into an internationally recognized money-making symbol, won court permission yesterday to continue performing in his funny suit in San Diego.

Judge Raul Rosado proclaimed: "Let's put this case to nest once and for all."

Giannoulas was sued for contempt of court by his former employer, radio station KGB.

The station fired Giannoulas as its mascot last year and put someone else in the suit. Giannoulas developed a new chicken outfit and won lucrative contracts to perform at nationally televised sporting events.

The radio station sought to stop Giannoulas wearing the costume in San Diego, claiming the outfit was "substantially similar" to its own.

After the verdict, the chicken jumped from his roost and let out a sigh. Well-wishers rushed up to him, clapping their hands and cheering.

"Whew! Whew!," Giannoulas sighed outside the courtroom. "I feel like a free bird. You don't know what a relief it is. I think I'll go to the Padre game and pop open a few bottles of champagne."

PET PIG SHOT, POTTED

HUNTINGTON, Mass. (AP) — An animal-control officer who gunned down a pet pig for munching on apples in a neighbor's yard faces criminal charges because he allegedly cooked and ate the pig.

Police said Richard Castle, the city's dog officer, will be arraigned on charges of cruelty to an animal.

Castle allegedly shot the white Yorkshire pig — named Meme — while she was eating apples in the yard of her owner's neighbor last August.

Man who swallowed salamander ill

LANGLOIS, Ore. (UPI) — James Sikole, 29, who swallowed a salamander on a bet with friends, was reported in critical condition at a hospital. Sikole became unconscious a short time after the incident Sunday night.

He has date with the law

DAVENPORT, Iowa (UPI) — Police had given up hope of finding escaped prisoner James Sheldon — until they spotted him on the television show The Dating Game.

Sheldon, serving time for larceny, walked out of a minimum security institution a year ago and never came back. Police found no trace of him until last week when — under his own name and calling himself a clothing designer from Chicago — he appeared on their screens trying to win the superdate on The Dating Game.

But Sheldon is still free because the show had been taped two months earlier.

An official of the correctional institution said: "Appearing on the show certainly took guts. The irony is that another contestant was a probation officer."

P.S. Sheldon didn't win the superdate.

April Fool wins two divorce suits

ATLANTA (UPI) — Jearline McCullough of Atlanta has been granted two divorces at the same time — one from the man she married on April Fools' Day, 1971, and the second from a man she married on April Fools' Day two years later.

The 27-year-old Ms McCullough obtained the divorces to clear her status, both legally and morally, her lawyer said yesterday.

Time on his hands

LOS ANGELES (UPI) — When Dick Winslow appeared at a local hospital, complaining his throat hurt, an x-ray found a Mickey Mouse watch lodged in his esophagus. Doctors removed it with forceps. Winslow, 63, said he figured the watch must have been in a glass of vitamin pills he swallowed days earlier.

Police hot on the trail

LANSING, Mich. (AP) — Police say they arrested three naked women smeared with mustard inside a stolen delivery truck.

The women are being charged with truck theft after police spotted a truck cruising down a street — with a uniformed deliveryman running after it.

They were smeared with "regular old mustard like you put on food," said Sgt. John Draganchuk.

Underwear underworld

LINCOLN, Neb. (UPI) — Police say they are looking for an undercover thief of sorts.

The robber broke into an apartment and got away with 13 bras, three slips and three nightgowns estimated at $100, police said.

In another case, a 37-year-old woman said an intruder stole a pair of panties from her bedroom dresser and left an older smaller pair.

The naked truth

FALLS CHURCH, Va. (AP) — When a woman suspected of stuffing a leather jacket under her skirt was stopped in a clothing store, she said she wasn't a shoplifter. To prove it, she took off her clothes. The woman, asked by employees to open her handbag, refused and said, "All right, damn it. I'll prove it to you." With that, and with customers and clerks staring, she proceeded to take off everything except her bra. She then dressed and left.

Ding, don't dong bell ringer told

DENVER (AP) — The city hall bell ringer has quit because he didn't like the tone of an order by city officials.

Robert Gift was told to ring his bells more slowly because officials feared PCBs, suspected of causing cancer, were contained in lubricants in the bells' electrical circuits and contaminated oil might be sprayed around the bell tower if he played too quickly.

Gift was told he could only play one note a second and one note at a time.

He resigned saying the experience would be "unmusical" and a "painful experience."

Escapers have swinging time

SALEM, Ore. (UPI) — Two prison escapers were captured riding children's swings in a playground, police said.

The two, aged 18 and 20, kicked out the glass on the fourth-floor window, separated the bars and slid to freedom on bedsheets tied together.

Speeding? Don't try these tales

CEDAR RAPIDS, Iowa (AP) — Caught speeding? Don't try to get off with a feeble excuse about an urgent need for a washroom.

And the old rotten potatoes excuse also isn't likely to wash with police here.

But if you're speeding — and wearing a chicken suit — you just might get away with it.

Police here say they've heard just about every excuse there is — and most of them just won't work.

"The most common is 'I was speeding because I have to go to the bathroom,' " police Capt. Louis Stepanek said.

Then there was the guy who had bought a bag of potatoes. Some were rotten, he said, so he was speeding home to get them out of the bag before the others spoiled.

And what about the woman who claimed she had been holding a cup of tea between her legs. It spilled and — ouch! — she stepped on the accelerator.

Another speeder claimed his wooden leg had jammed the gas pedal. None of those stories worked, Stepanek said.

But then there was the "chicken."

One Hallowe'en night, officers pursued a speeding car that failed to pull over. Suddenly, the lights and motor died and the car rolled to the shoulder of the road. Stepanek said the officers found a man in a chicken costume sitting behind the wheel.

"He was on his way to a Hallowe'en party and told the officers he'd gotten his chicken foot wedged in between the brake and accelerator. The only way he could stop the car was to turn off the key and let it roll to a stop," Stepanek said.

"It took both officers pulling to get the chicken foot unwedged."

Feeling jaded? Join the club

SEATTLE (AP) — It's easy to join the Dull Men's Club of the North-west. Even the most fascinating people can qualify.

"Belonging doesn't mean you can't be interesting," said Gerald Cutler, club president. "It just means you can't flaunt it."

The group accepts members "who have done it all and who now, slightly jaded and balding, wish to be in a situation where there is nothing left to prove."

Atoms turn metal to gold

BERKELEY, Calif. (AP) — Like Rumpelstiltskin, scientists at Lawrence Berkeley Laboratory have found a way to turn base metal into gold — the alchemist's dream.

The only problem is that it costs more than a million billion — a quadrillion — dollars an ounce.

The gold — a few billion atoms worth — was "the trivial result" of an experiment on Berkeley's BEV-LAC accelerator in which a target made of the metal bismuth was bombarded with charged atoms travelling near the speed of light.

Scientists, including Nobel Prize-winning physicist Glenn Seaborg, conducted the experiment at the lab here and will deliver a report on their findings tomorrow at a meeting of the American Chemical Society in Houston.

"In all our work we produced gold that was worth less than one-billionth of a cent," said scientist David Morrissey.

"It would cost more than one quadrillion dollars per ounce to produce gold by this experiment," said Seaborg, who is co-author of the paper to be delivered to the Houston meeting.

★★★★★★★★★★★★★★★★★★★★★★★★

Woman gives newborn baby to childless sister

LONDON (AP) — A woman has given her newborn daughter to her childless twin sister, the Daily Mirror reported yesterday.

The newspaper said that Lynda Elson, 30, and her husband, John, made their "priceless gift of love" because they already have two children.

The twin, Jean, who lives in the Shropshire County town of Market Drayton, is unable to have children and plans to adopt the baby.

"I was absolutely stunned speechless by Lynda's sacrifice," she said.

"Not in my wildest dreams could I imagine anyone making this kind of sacrifice for my happiness." ·

The Daily Mirror reported that the baby, Jodie, was born in a Shrewsbury hospital Oct. 5 and given by Mrs. Elson to her sister 30 minutes later.

However, a spokesman for Britain's National Adoption Society warned the proposed adoption might cause problems for the child.

"Naturally enough, you could have a situation where the natural mother gets upset about the way the child is being brought up," the spokesman said.

"It could cause all sorts of problems."

HOW BOSSES CAN BECOME TOO BOSSY...

HARTFORD, Conn. (UPI) — Second place in Hartford's Petty Office Procedures contest went to the divorced boss who ordered his secretary to fill in for him on "visiting day" with his children.

Third place went to the employer of the pet store bookkeeper who lost her job because she couldn't count live worms accurately.

And top prize? That went to the enterprising bank executive who required his clerks and tellers to also pitch dishware and towels.

Mayor George Athanson handed out the dubious distinctions in a contest sponsored by Hartford office workers for the most outrageous demands made by bosses.

★★★★★★★★★★★★★★★★★★★★★★★★

Fit for a duck

A veterinarian in Raleigh, N.C., says he'll try to fit a crippled duck with an artificial webbed foot to keep the duck from going in circles when he tries to swim.

Dr. Ivey Smith said the foot probably will be mad eof leather or wood and tied in place.

The wild mallard, found last week at an apartment complex, apparently lost its foot in a trap.

★★★★★★★★★★★★★★★★★★★★★★★★

Driver's disgust ties up traffic

CHICAGO (UPI) — Abraham Johnson Jr. was apparently disgusted with the way morning rush-hour traffic was just crawling along.

So he stopped his car on the busy Dan Ryan Expressway, locked himself in and refused to move — blocking thousands of motorists for three hours.

After pleading with Johnson to give up his one-man crusade — he responded by passing them obscene notes — police towed away car and driver.

He was charged with disobeying police, obstructing traffic and resisting arrest. Police said the first thing he asked when he stepped from his car was, "Where's the washroom?"

There's oil in that thar mud

PROVIDENCE, R.I. (AP) — A University of Rhode Island scientist says there's almost enough oil in the mud in the Providence River to make recovery profitable.

Dr. Eva Hoffman, an ocean chemist, says the oil is the result of do-it-yourself mechanics who wash it into sewers after changing the oil in their cars.

She said only 20 per cent of the oil is removed from the sewage at the treatment plant, estimating about 42 tons of oil reaches the river each year.

Next he'll visit the middle

Man walks 20,000 miles around the borders of the United States

PROVIDENCE, R.I. (UPI) — He began by walking down the east coast of the United States to Florida. Then he turned right.

Once he got to California, it was an easy jaunt up the west coast to the Canadian border. Then he walked east along the 49th parallel and around the southern shore of the Great Lakes and — yesterday — arrived back home again.

After an unprecedented 20,000-mile, three-year trek around the borders of the continental United States, the main thing Bill Gormally had to say when he tromped into Rhode Island yesterday was: "It's great to be home."

The 31-year-old former schoolteacher from Warwick, R.I., set out on a scorching July day in 1975 "to follow a dream." One thousand, two hundred and one days later, he strode into India Point Park, the starting point.

"It was a chance to step back and see America from a different perspective," he said.

But when asked what he had learned from the trek, he appeared baffled. "I don't know. I'll have to put it all in perspective and write it down."

Gormally had already made it to Florida in 1975 when he realized something was missing. He flew home and asked Pat O'Connell, a former fourth grade teacher in Warwick, to marry him. She walked the last 17,000 miles with him.

The Gormallys wore out 20 pairs of hiking boots through blizzards, heat waves and 40-m.p.h. headwinds, but they said it was well worth the effort.

"We're just going to take it easy for a few months and party," Gormally said. "And write hundreds of thank-you notes to all the friends we made along the way."

Giovanni married 100 times because 'he's in love with life'

PHOENIX, Ariz. (UPI) — Giovanni Vigliotto married more than 100 women not to swindle them, but to treat them as "queens" and help them escape "the humdrum of life," his lawyer says.

"He is in love with life, in love with women and in love with marriage," said public defender Richard Steiner. "He created an aura of excitement that allowed these women to join in his fantasy. He offered these 100 or more women a chance to withdraw from the humdrum of life and an opportunity to be treated as important people — as queens."

Vigliotto, 53, a convict and former mental patient who allegedly used 51 aliases, is accused of bigamy in marrying Patricia Gardiner, 41, in 1981.

Ms. Gardiner said she married Vigliotto Nov. 18, 1981, eight days after meeting him, and he convinced her to sell her house. Two weeks later, he vanished with $36,500 from the sale.

"This case is about the violation of the human spirit," said Deputy County Attorney David Stoller. He said he would call three witnesses — Gardiner and Susan Clark, both of whom Vigliotto allegedly married without prior divorce, and a third unnamed person.

★★★★★★★★★★★★★★★

Peanut butter rescue

MIAMI (AP) — U.S. Coast Guard planes dropped bread, peanut butter and jelly yesterday to 209 Haitian refugees stranded on two barren islands in the Florida Straits. The Haitians were heading to Florida, seeking a better life than that in their homeland. The coast guard didn't have enough high-protein survival kits to feed all of the stranded people — hence the peanut butter.

Son lived with corpse of mom

DETROIT (UPI) — In a scene right out of the horror movie *Psycho*, police say a man, 45, lived for a year with the partially-mummified body of his mother.

A neighbor discovered the body of Laura Travis, 64, clad in a rotting nightgown. The body was on mattresses in a bedroom laden with dust, cobwebs and the excrement of 24 dogs.

Her son, Martin, had moved out of the house Saturday because the bank was foreclosing on the mortgage.

Police Sgt. Barbara Weide found Travis at a welfare office, where he was signing up for aid.

Travis was being held in the city jail, pending results of an autopsy performed on his mother. It is believed the woman died of natural causes.

Student playing clown has place in classroom

GAINESVILLE, Fla. (AP) — Teachers should appreciate having a class clown because they make "a significant contribution to the classroom with their humor," a behavioral scientist says.

"Clowns get a negative aura attached to them and some are disruptive," said Dr. Sandra Damico. "But others may be making a significant contribution to the classroom with their humor acting as a tension-breaker and relief."

Ms Damico, a faculty member at the University of Florida, says she came to that conclusion after making a state-wide survey.

"Groups with clowns in them tend to be more productive," she said. "Humor has a place in the classroom. It's a shame that teachers don't use it more."

She found that most class clowns are "very positive about themselves. They seem themselves as leaders and are very confident."

Latest duds finally arrive: 63 years late

GARRETSON, S.D. (AP) — Mathilda Hermanson ordered two frilly dresses for her daughter and two dresses for herself from the Sears-Roebuck catalogue.

The dresses arrived last month. That was fine — except that they should have been there for the Easter parade in 1916.

The dresses, still in the original packaging with sales tickets and spring sale catalogue intact, were found in the railway depot at Sherman, S.D., as it was torn down last fall.

The package was sent to an antique shop, where a friend of the Hermansons spotted it. And it finally found its way to the hands of Virginia Hermanson, daughter-in-law of the woman who ordered the dresses.

"We don't know for sure when the dresses were ordered," Virginia said. "But since the sale catalogue says credit is good through 1917, they must have been ordered about Easter 1916."

One of the little girls' dresses is pink with short sleeves, a low-waisted pleated skirt and white embroidery. The other is a lacy, white voile with pink ribbons. According to the catalogue, the dresses probably cost between $1-2.

The dresses for the mother include a fancy, black organdie dress with a black petticoat and a gold and white sailor-style dress with 25 buttons wrapped from the nect to the waist. The dresses cost close to $4, the catalogue said.

"I suppose the dresses are quite valuable now but we couldn't sell them," the daughter-in-law said. "Their sentimental value is so much more."

The serfdom of retarded Betty

PONTIAC, Mich. (UPI) — A 50-year-old retarded woman subjected to macabre abuse for 13 years has won $1.5 million in damages for what a judge called "a shocking example of human serfdom."

Trial testimony revealed that Betty Pelletier was released from a Lapeer mental hospital in 1961 and was placed under the foster care of Dr. Alvis Finch and his wife, Kathleen.

The Finch house became a place of unending torture, abuse and humiliation for Betty. Housework spanning 12 hours a day, seven days a week, earned her $1,630 in the entire 13 years. But the Finch couple forced her to sign that money back to them.

Betty said she was often beaten, choked, and forced to sleep in an unheated garage during winter. Complaints were punished by forcing her to pose for pictures with a chicken tied to her head.

In 1974, the Finches moved to Australia and Betty moved to the guardianship of Dr. Richard Lenaghan and his wife. They learned of the abuse and filed a compaint seeking back wages.

But the judge, after hearing of the woman's ordeal, decided far more was due her. "She has been treated worse than an animal," he said. "This is a shocking example of human serfdom."

She was awarded $1 million for false imprisonment and punitive damages, $500,000 for assault, and another $55,000 as her salary for the 13 years of work.

The marshmallow spies

NEW YORK (AP) — The U.S. Central Intelligence Agency held secret experiments to develop new espionage methods using trained otters, electric stun guns, calibrated blackjacks — and marshmallow barrages — the New York Times says.

The agency was also interested in the secret life of plants, peace pills, "bioplasma fields" and electrosleep.

The story was obtained from 3,000 heavily censored pages of studies and documents related to CIA activities from 1965 to 1975, the newspaper said. The information was made public as a result of a request under the Freedom of Information Act.

Which ideas were developed and which were discarded is not known, the Times said, because the agency refused to comment on the documents. Many details were deleted from the papers, leaving very general descriptions.

In one project, the CIA tried to teach seals, otters, dogs, cats and other animals to carry explosives or microphones to places humans could not reach. Otters seemed to be the favorite since they travel well on both land and in water, the newspaper said.

Other projects included "a study of incapacitating darts," and "a flash blindess incapacitator," using a bright light source to blind a subject.

The Times said nearly all details were deleted for projects involving "a hand-held calibrated blackjack," plastic cocoons, taffy pellets and marshmallow barrages.

As in past documents, there were references to Project OFTEN, which the agency jointly started in 1968 with the U.S. army at Edgewood, Md., to study the effects of rare drugs.

In studying bioplasma fields, or extremely weak electrical forces surrounding both inanimate objects and humans, the agency apparently tried to find out whether extrasensory perception existed and could be used to "read" enemy agents' thoughts.

Missing husband dead with wife in house fire?

NASHVILLE, Ind. (AP) — For 10 years, Gerald Roberts tried in vain to persuade insurance companies that her husband had died in a fire in the family garage.

Now a house fire has claimed her life and authorities say that a man who died with her is believed to be her long-missing husband.

Dr. John Pless, a forensic pathologist, said early indications are that the body of Clarence Roberts, missing 10 years as his wife tried to claim $1.2 million in insurance, was found with the body of his wife in the charred rubble of her house.

A fire destroyed the Roberts' garage Nov. 18, 1970, and authorities found a fire-blackened, limbless body inside.

Roberts' wife tried to collect $1.2 million but insurance companies balked, saying there was no proof that the body was that of Roberts.

Medical experts agreed that the bone structures of Roberts and the body did not match. The body never was identified.

Sheriff Rex Kritzer said the Roberts' house had been under surveillance for some time. "We had reason to believe someone was living there," Kritzer said. "We kind of thought that it might be Clarence. But we didn't have proof."

Other detectives said Geneva Roberts, a 59-year-old diabetic, was described by neighbors as a recluse who allowed no one in her home except her four sons. None of them could be reached immediately for comment on the latest developments.

At the time of the 1970 fire, Roberts was more than $200,000 in debt.

His oink's worse than his bite

EL PASO, Texas (AP) — "Canadian Pig" doesn't have the lean snarl of a German Shepherd. But if you meet the young porker in the company of his trainer Marcel Leblanc, show some respect — he's an attack pig.

Leblanc, 42, who's from Vancouver, says he has trained attack dogs for Canadian police departments for 17 years. He bought Canadian Pig "to fatten up and slaughter for a friend's party."

But he noted that the 150-pound, six-month-old, pink and white Yorkshire pig learned tricks quickly. "We have given him basic training. He attacks and charges," said Leblanc.

Leblanc left Vancouver in July with his prize porcine protector and two smaller pigs trained to perform in circuses. They passed through El Paso yesterday on their way home.

The four-legged travellers are not hard to feed. "They love Kentucky Fried Chicken, steaks and ice cream," said Leblanc. The trainer said Canadian Pig also loves bubble gum, but spits it out when the flavor's gone.

Wolves in campaign to save their species poisoned in New York

NEW YORK (CP) — Two wolves, brought back from a month-long tour of Canada as ambassadors in the cause of saving their species from extinction, were killed in Brooklyn by poison.

The animals—a 7-year-old, 88-pound Canadian timber wolf named Jethro, and a 4-year-old, 110-pound Alaska tundra wolf named Clem—were apparently fed chicken laced with strychnine as they spent the night in a van that had served as their den-on-the-road.

The wolves had been taken throughout Canada and the United States during the last three years by John Harris, president of the North American Association for the Preservation of Predatory Animals, and Anthony Nocera, the association's east coast co-ordinator.

Returning Saturday night from a tour, the men decided to leave the animals overnight in the van outside Nocera's Brooklyn home.

"John Harris and I feel as if we both had just lost two sons," said Nocera.

Cleveland Amory, president of the Fund for Animals, has offered $1,000 reward for information leading to the arrest of the poisoner.

Don't get cross at duck crossing

EDMONDS, Wash. (AP) — Ducks have been given their own specially marked crosswalk across a busy street — but it's still questionable if they'll survive this city's mushrooming development.

"When the traffic hour coincides with the ducks' feeding hour, things get a little sticky around here," said city engineer Fred Herzberg.

The duck crossing, marked with a full-size traffic sign, began because Jan Cornwell was tired of looking at dead ducks.

The fowl were being killed while trying to cross the street between Lake Ballinger and the marsh on the other side of the road, Jan said.

She drafted a petition to the city council for a duck crosswalk and gathered 1,854 signatures in nine days.

That leaves only one problem — the danger of rear-end collisions when cars stop for the ducks.

'I could hear rats -- coming for me'

CHICAGO (AP) — Dave Holman's memory of the ordeal is not all clear. But he recalls the rats with chilling detail. "I could hear them coming through the garbage — coming for me," he says.

Holman, a vagrant, was found in a cold, dirty West Side basement March 3 — two weeks after he'd taken shelter there from the bitter winter.

Rats that feast on litter there had turned on Holman, a sickly man too weak to fight back. They gnawed on his legs as his fingers and feet turned black from frostbite.

'Blessed sleep'

"I didn't see them in the daytime. There was some light from a window," he says.

"But as night came, I could hear them coming throught the garbage — coming for me. Then blessed sleep came and I felt nothing until the next day."

Holman, 46, once weighed 180

pounds, but today he is an emaciated 95 pounds as a result of his ordeal. His legs had to be amputated below the knee. Fingers on both hands also were removed.

"I remember lying on the floor and getting weaker. It was awfully cold and it got so I couldn't feel much. But I could hear those rats."

Holman tried screaming, but neighbors ignored him. Policeman Sam Cozza said residents who finally called police claimed they were afraid authorities would think they were crazy if they reported the groans.

"I would try to get up to reach the door for help, but I couldn't stand. Something was wrong with my legs. I tried to crawl, but I couldn't. Something was wrong with my hands," Holman recalled in an interview at Cook County Hospital.

Holman says his parents died when he was young and he has since lost touch with other family members. He was divorced in the late 1960s and has lost contact with his three daughters.

He worked in a factory and became an electrician specializing in elevator control panels. But he says he drank, mostly beer, and eventually lost everything.

"I was living in a room on the West Side, but several years ago I even lost that," he says. "I started sleeping in basements. The doors were usually open."

Gnawed legs

Even he is surprised that he survived the ordeal. "I don't know how I made it," he says. Still more amazed are hospital attendants who note that Holman beat starvation, intense cold and the risk of rabies and blood poisoning.

"The rats had gnawed the fat off the calves of both legs to the ankles," said Dr. Richard Pearson. "His feet were black — frozen. The rats had not got to them. He probably had his shoes on. His fingers also were black and had to be amputated. The rats had not got to them, either."

Ambulance kills man it came to save

ODELL, Ill. (UPI) — A man was killed when he was run over by an ambulance that had been called to aid him.

Coroner Keith Von Qualan said James Ritchie, 30, was lying on a rural road awaiting aid when the ambulance skidded on snow-slick pavement and ran him over.

Ritchie also may have been hit by a pick-up truck that was following the ambulance, the coroner said.

A sheriff's spokeswoman said no one knows why Ritchie initially needed medical help.

★ ★ ★ ★

Fast cars, fast girls

SHADY POINT, Okla. (UPI) — D. B. Benson, who lived in mountainous seclusion in the United States for 36 years, on the run from military officials, spent his first day in civilization getting reacquainted with relatives. He said his biggest surprise upon leaving the mountains was "fast cars, jet airplanes and fast girls."

Surprise mom is really game!

BELLE GLADE, Fla. (UPI) — Glades Central star forward Mary West wasn't quite herself the night her team beat Hallandale in the playoffs.

There was a good reason. Just 31 hours after the game, she surprised herself by giving birth to a 6-pound, 2-ounce baby girl, named Cassandra.

Bit chubby

Athletic director Graham Frost of Glades Central said no one at the school, apparently including Mary herself, was aware she was pregnant, although "she wasn't quite as sharp that night."

About a month ago, school officials had noticed the 6-foot-1 forward was getting a bit chubby and Frost suggested she see a physician. Miss West went to a nurse instead, and returned with a note saying she was in good health.

She said a pregnancy test she had taken was negative, and she was unaware she was pregnant until the baby arrived March 2. She and her 11-year-old sister delivered the baby at their home in a housing project.

The brighter side

A household pet helped catch two burglars, but left Cleveland police with a different problem. The thieves knocked over a cage holding Charlotte, a pet tarantula, so "they split," said Patrolman Walter Meyke. Meyke and his partner arrested two suspects later — but Charlotte is still at large.

Texas gal takes a poke at punk rocker's nose

DALLAS (UPI) — Sex Pistol Sid Vicious accepted a female fan's punch in the nose the other night as a tribute of the highest kind to punk rock.

Shortly after the Sex Pistols started their show at the Longhorn Ballroom, one of Texas' most well-known country and western dance halls, a woman jumped on stage and landed a mighty punch on Vicious' nose.

Vicious bled profusely for the remainder of the 45-minute concert, but he used the blood to add to the show for the 1,800 fans who attended the fifth stop on the English group's American tour.

The bass player smeared the blood over his face and chest and also spat blood toward the audience.

Later, Vicious, blood still spattered on his bare chest, leaned against the bar and swigged a beer.

"Some bitch banged me in the face," he said with a smile. "Any bitch who bangs me in the face is someone I like."

Most of the audience seemed pleased with the show.

Say it with flowers -- via gorilla

PHILADELPHIA (UPI) — One man wanted a talking robot to deliver a marriage proposal to the woman he loved.

Another devilish soul sought a horse to leave in a friend's apartment as a gag Christmas gift.

A mother wanted a marching band to strut down the street on her son's birthday.

All these people were customers of Whims for Rent, a Philadelphia firm that caters to those flamboyant people who love jokes and crazy parties.

"Our motto is we fulfill your fantasies, just so long as it's legal," said Joseph Ball, president of an advertising firm that created Whims for Rent.

The 4-year-old service has contacts to supply a belly dancer for a club picnic, a football star to serve as a butler at a dinner party, or a man dressed in a gorilla suit to deliver a bouquet of flowers.

Whims for Rent has so many requests for girls to jump out of cakes that the company built its own cardboard cake, 6 feet in diameter. "Sometimes we can't get it through doors," Ball said.

"Another common request that we have to say 'no' to is the pie in the face," Ball said. "That's assault. A lot of people want to do it as a joke to people they like. They think it's funny."

Sports celebrities usually work for $500 an appearance. Performers such as jugglers, an organ grinder and monkey, or a Richard Nixon look-a-like can cost anywhere from $100 to $300, Ball said, as will rental of a Rolls-Royce or horse-drawn carriage.

It's the same 'old' story

CHICAGO (UPI) — An 85-year-old man was charged with aggravated battery yesterday in the "love triangle" stabbing of another elderly man and woman.

Police charged Charles Compton in the woundings of Nathaniel Riley, 70, and Margarite Richi, 67, who lived in the same South Side apartment building.

"It was just a typical love triangle," one investigator said.

Dead pet on ice cold comfort

WEST UNION, W. Va. (UPI) — Zelleth Stephens is keeping the "evidence" — her dead dog — in the freezer.

"I know people think I'm crazy for keeping him in the freezer," the 70-year-old woman said of the dog, Cocoa. "But I just thought the investigators might need him for evidence."

She claims the six-pound Chihuahua — her constant companion — was shot June 2 by a state trooper who said the dog had been chasing deer. The trooper, E. F. Young, has been dismissed.

Mrs. Stephens said she will keep Cocoa in the freezer for a little while longer "just to see what happens." She has written state police about the incident.

"I knew this little fellow (Cocoa) couldn't have hurt a deer. He was only 7 inches tall," she said.

Mrs. Stephens said that on the night of June 2 she heard three shots, saw a trooper drive past her house and turn around, then heard another shot. Two of her dogs returned that night but Cocoa did not.

Mrs. Stephens said she and her son-in-law found Cocoa's body, shot in the left side, the next day.

"So I brought the little fellow home and wrapped him up real good in plastic and put him in the freezer."

State police said Mrs. Stephens' allegation appears correct, but they won't say whether there'll be an investigation.

Shelves bare as nude beer kept under cover

LOS ANGELES (UPI) — Nude Beer was still under wraps today and apparently won't be titilating beer drinkers for some weeks, according to a U.S. beer industry spokesman.

The beer, to be marketed in bottles decorated with the upper half of a naked woman, has run into trouble with the California Alcoholic Beverage Control Board, which has banned the labels as "contrary to public welfare and morals."

The beer was to be shipped to Tennessee and Maryland yesterday, but James Prenza, president of the New Jersey company that brews and bottles the beverage, says it may take another two weeks to get the necessary permits from authorities in the two states.

William Boam, the head of a Tustin, Calif., marketing firm, who thought up the idea, said yesterday: "I don't feel the naked body is obscene and this is an illegal restraint on my business."

"I got the idea when I was going through a divorce three years ago and stopped by a store to pick up a six pack and a copy of Playboy magazine. I walked out thinking 'Gee, I could combine these two things.'

"I'd never been in the beer business but I just decided to get into it. That's what America's about, making your dreams and fantasies come true."

He had plans to change the picture monthly, "so the beer will be just like the centrefold in a magazine — we're going to run a nationwide contest and put the winner on the label each month."

Boam was denied a California permit by Manuel Espinoza, assistant director of regulatory affairs for the alcohol agency.

"I contacted Ezpinoza earlier this year and he said there was nothing wrong with the plan," Boam said. "He said 'I can't wait to see the nude girl — send me a bottle.' Now he refuses to talk to me."

No pheasant, so recluse ate his neighbor's dog

LAPEER, Mich. (UPI) — A recluse who ate his neighbor's dog said yesterday hunger drove him to it.

And the judge who sent Floyd Emerick to jail for 90 days said he had more compassion for the man than the dog."

"I did him a favor by giving him a roof over his head," said Judge John Spires, who handed Emerick, 59, the maximum term for cruelty to animals.

"It's not for us to judge what a desperate man should eat. If a man's starving he has the right to do what he had to do," the judge said.

Dog's liver

When animal control agents went to arrest Emerick Nov. 19, they found him busy cooking dog's liver with scalloped potatoes. They also said they believed it wasn't the first time Emerick had killed neighborhood domestic pets.

"We have enough evidence to believe he has done this quite often," said Paul Farmer, Lapeer County's chief animal control officer.

After Emerick's arrest, agents found skins and remains of several dogs and cats around the house.

Doberman missing

Emerick was arrested two days after a neighbor reported his 60-pound female doberman pinscher missing.

Emerick, who worked occasionally as a farm laborer, has lived for the past five years in a 100-year-old unheated, refuse-strewn house with no plumbing.

Before passing sentence the judge asked Emerick what drove him to kill and eat dogs.

Emerick replied that with wild game getting scarce, he couldn't find any more pheasant.

Married grandma he has

LOS ANGELES (AP) — After a year of marriage, 21-year-old Mark Goodman says his parents are "learning to accept the situation" and getting used to his new bride — his 78-year-old stepgrandmother, Ray.

A year ago today, Goodman married Ray Goodman — a former chorus girl and his father's widowed stepmother.

Many people — especially Goodman's parents — looked on the romance with disfavor a year ago when the couple, then living in England, announced wedding plans. British law forbade a marriage between a man and his grandfather's widow, so the couple came to southern California and were married secretly.

Goodman works for a securities firm selling stocks and bonds. He says he and Ray — he calls her G.R. for Grandma Ray — do some of the things young

$1.5 million left to vets

COLUMBIA, Mo. (AP) — Olive Gilbreath McLorn was so grateful to veterinarians at the University of Missouri for trying to save her dying cat she has left the school $1.5 million.

McLorn died in 1981 at the age of 96, 10 years after her cat. She left a further $700,000 to the College of Veterinary Medicine and the rest was to be divided among other university and cultural funds.

Axe-wielding artist chops off fingers

NEW YORK (Reuter) — An artist pulled an axe from a briefcase and chopped off two of his fingers yesterday after a newspaper art critic refused to see him.

Police said the artist, Henry Benvenuti, 27 later said he had chopped off his fingers "for art."

He was in satisfactory condition last night, but doctors failed to reattach the badly damaged fingers, which police brought to the hospital.

Benvenuti severed the middle and ring fingers of his right hand at the Soho Weekly News, located in the Bohemian section of Manhattan, after the paper's critic said he was too busy to see him immediately.

"It was so unexpected — there was total silence, except for the chopping sound," said Cathy Kadushin, a newspaper employee. "Thank God he didn't decide to throw the axe the other way."

★★

Woman firefighter wins

IOWA CITY, Iowa (AP) — The Iowa City fire department discriminated against a woman when officials refused to let her nurse her infant son during duty hours, the Iowa Civil Rights Commission has ruled.

"I think this is a positive step," Linda Eaton said of the decision issued Wednesday. "I'm really glad that they (the commission) see the problem and didn't just dismiss it.

"But whether the city will see the light or appeal it and go on the offensive, I just don't know."

Miss Eaton, 26, a firefighter, was suspended in January when she tried to breastfeed her 4½-month-old son during unassigned time included on a 24-hour shift.

The complaint was filed by Iowa Attorney-General Tom Miller.

Her son is still being brought in for feeding twice a day.

OKLAHOMA CITY (UPI) — A woman has filed for divorce to end her 9-year-old marriage — because her husband won't give up his pet snakes. The divorce petition, filed by Jeanette Cartledge of Del City, states her husband, Raymond, raises rabbits and feeds them to the snakes during the family dinner hour and also feeds live chickens to a 5-foot-long bull snake, which upsets her two children from a previous marriage.

Baby beer brews spat

RICHMOND, Va. (UPI) — The Anheuser-Busch brewery doesn't plan any changes in its ad campaign for Chelsea, even though Virginia groups have accused the new soft drink of "conditioning" children to like beer.

Chelsea, touted in a media blitz as "the not-so-soft-drink" — and called "baby beer" by kids — has less than one half of one per cent alcohol per bottle.

Joseph Finnigan, spokesman for the largest U.S. brewer, said the drink is safer for children than other soft drinks, many of which contain additives and more sugar.

The beverage, which began test-marketing last month in Virginia and five other areas, came under fire last week from nurses and the clergy, who said the drink is designed to lure young people into beer drinking.

OSSINING, N.Y. (UPI) — A 61-year-old woman died last week and left a good friend an unusual bequest — 57 cats. But now her frind has a problem — finding the cats good homes. Before she died, Elizabeth Morfogenis made her friend of 35 years, Marie Pritchard, promise that she would take care of the cats. Mrs. Pritchard, who spends $46 a week on cat food said: "They have to go to loving homes."

Weighty hang-up foils a lynching

SAN JOSE, Calif. (UPI) — A 90-kilogram (200-pound) boy apparently has survived an attempted lynching by three classmates because he was too heavy to hoist.

The boys, aged 10, 11 and 12 told police they were just "fooling around" when they cornered the victim behind their elementary school, and put a noose of laundry rope around his neck.

They then looped the rope over some playground equipment and tried to hoist the 11-year-old boy. But he was apparently too heavy and the boys gave up, police said.

Man wants his wife kicked out of school

SAN FRANCISCO (UPI) — A disgruntled husband has filed suit to get his estranged wife kicked out of school, saying her attempt to obtain another degree is frivolous.

Douglas Page said his wife already has a master's degree and her pursuit of a second degreen in English is useless. Society has no need for more people with advanced degrees in English, he said.

"As a California taxpayer, I resent state funds being used for wasteful and duplicate education," he said in a Supreme Court action filed this week.

Page, a 54-year-old lawyer, said he has been paying to put his wife, Nancy, 34, through college throughout their seven-year marriage. She has had six different majors but has yet to start working.

"I'm trying to avoid paying alimony for this purpose," he said, adding that by the time his wife finishes school "there will be three PhDs for every job."

ROBBER KEEPS PROMISE

MEMPHIS, Tenn. (UPI) — The robber who mugged Louis Bonicelli was a man of his word.

When the young gunman attacked him two weeks ago, Bonicelli pleaded with him to return a driver's license he had difficulty getting because of an eye problem.

"You'll get it back," the robber said

The license was returned to his office in the mail yesterday along with the stolen credit cards.

★★

HE KILLED HIS PAIN WITH RIFLE

LEHIGHTON, Pa. (UPI) — Cletus Schlier said the pain in his foot was unbearable.

So he took a rifle, went to the basement of his Lehighton home, and shot off part of the aching foot.

Schlier, 49, a former construction worker, injured his right foot three years ago in an auto accident, and arthritis set in.

His wife said their neighbors gossiped that Schlier was using the foot injury as an excuse to remain on welfare.

Slim dies dancing just as he wished

AUSTIN, Texas (UPI) — "Hackberry Slim" Johnson, a 91-year-old one-legged cowboy who staged buffalo rodeos dreaded the prospect of dying in a nursing home.

"I want to go with my boots on," he had said. "In style, by God. Dancing maybe or maybe while riding a buffalo. I don't want to shrivel up in a nursing home like some old man. Not me."

Johnson, who recently had a bit part in a Willie Nelson movie Honeysuckle Rose, being shot in Austin, attended a Nelson concert, danced a bit when Nelson dedicated a song to him, then slumped forward and died in his front row seat.

"After he died, Robbie Nelson and I played What A Friend We Have In Jesus and then the rest of the concert was cancelled," said Johnny Gimble, a fiddler on the show.

Why folks hang around

CHICAGO (UPI) — Darryl Curby is a cut below the rest when it comes to hairdressing. His customers hang upside down for a trim.

"My whole technique is based strictly on gravity," says the 32-year-old barber. "When a designer cuts hair, he pulls it up 90 degrees from the point of origin.

"By inverting the person, gravity pulls the hair straight down. So we cut the inside lines of the haircut in the inverted position."

Curby's customers hang from a one-inch tubular steel back rest — wearing attached gravity boots strapped to their ankles.

He thought of the idea last summer at home. "While hanging in the exercise room one night, I noticed that my hair was hanging straight down . . . and there was a mirror in front of me," he said.

So he designed the Curby Aero Device, which rotates clients to different positions ranging from 25 to 180 degrees "depending on what I want to do with the hair," Curby said.

His clients must sign a waiver and should not have high blood pressure, be pregnant or have any serious back injuries.

'Superman' crash-lands

NEW ORLEANS (UPI) — A 3-year-old boy playing Superman dived from a third-storey window into a patch of dirt, but escaped with a bruise and a cut head.

"He was crying a little, but he wasn't crying too much," said his 18-year-old mother, Abigail Rockett.

Ronald, was listed in a guarded condition in hospital yesterday.

"He was playing with my little nephew and I went into the bathroom," said his mother. "My nephew said, 'Ronald is playing Superman and he fell out the window.'"

Miss Rockett ran downstairs and picked Ronald up. He had a bruise and a cut on his head and complained his stomach hurt.

He was afraid he would be teased by other kids when he returned home, she said.

"My momma says that's what too much TV can do. I'm going to have keep him away from TV so much."

MAN JUMPS, THEN SINKS IN MUD UP TO HIS CHIN

BOSTON (UPI) — Police said they found Joseph Mahoney, 43, stuck in mud up to his chin last night under the Broadway Bridge in south Boston.

Mahoney apparently jumped off the bridge when the tide in the Fort Point Channel was low, police said. Suffering from exposure, Mahoney was placed on the danger list at Boston City Hospital.

Leadership from the top

CLAYTON, Calif. (AP) — After weeks of worrying about a growing budget deficit in this community of 1,500, chief administrator Pete Archuleta determined someone had to go. He fired himself.

NORFOLK, Va. (AP) — The suspect came clean. Police responded to a call from Ruth Davis and found the door of her home kicked in and a man in her bathroom taking a bath. They arrested a 20-year-old man and charged him with burglary for kicking in the door. There are no statutes on the books for stealing a bath.

In the dark

Richard White of Boston has won his fight to stay in the dark as long as he wants. White, 25, was sued after he removed his electricity meter a year ago, saying he neither wanted nor needed electricity. The lawsuit has now been thrown out of court because an obscure state law says no one can be forced to take a utility they don't want.

THIS CRUDE WIRE-MESH CAGE is where Texas sheriff's deputies found three children, aged 2 and 3, last week. The youngsters' father said the children were penned up only when he and his two wives had to work in his fields.

Father kept kids penned in a cage

HOOKS, Texas (UPI-AP) — The father of three young children found nude and covered with excrement in a 4-by-6-foot (1.2-by-1.8 metre) wire cage says he kept the children penned only when he and two sisters, both his wives had to leave them to work their two-acre (.8-hectare) farm.

The two girls and a boy, aged 2 and 3, have been in the custody of welfare officials since Thursday, when they were found behind the tiny house two miles (3.2 kilometres) west of Hooks in East Texas.

"We put the babies in the pen to keep them from going on the road," James (Chief) Jake Williston, 57, said on the weekend. "When we're out working in the fields, we can't watch them, and if they ever got hurt, I know it would be my responsibility."

No charges have been filed against Williston, a full-blooded Choctaw Indian, his legal wife of eight years, Kathy, or his common-law wife of seven years, Linda.

The sisters, in their early 20s, are the mothers of the three children and four others, ranging in age from 11 months to five years, who still live with them. Both women are five-months pregnant.

The three children ordered temporarily removed by State District Judge Ben Hutchinson will remain in a foster home until their case in reviewed at a hearing July 14.

Welfare officials said the children did not know how to feed themselves or use a bathroom.

"They were deplorably dirty," said Mona Wages, who accompanied a deputy sheriff to the home after a neighbor called to complain of the situation. "They couldn't even communicate with us," she said.

Girl, 8, gets erotic prize in Cracker Jacks box

HUNTINGTON, W.Va. (AP) — An 8-year-old girl got a crash course in sex education when she found an unusual surprise inside her box of Cracker Jacks.

The girl's relatives say that instead of a trinket or some other small prize, the box of caramel corn contained a pamphlet entitled Erotic Sexual Positions From Around The World.

The family members, who did not want their names used, said the girl bought the candy at a supermarket.

The child's grandmother was present when the pamphlet was discovered. She recalled the girl saying: " 'Wow, look at this!' "

"Her eyes got great big," the grandmother said. "I don't think she even realized what it was. She thought it was an exercise book."

Detailed drawings

The booklet is a little more than an inch square and has several pages showing detailed drawings of people in various sex acts and positions. The cover states it is the first of a series of "erotic best sellers."

A spokesman for Borden Inc., which distributes the candy, said several similar pamphlets had turned up recently in Cracker Jacks boxes.

Betty Garrett of the company's Columbus, Ohio, office said officials had determined the booklets were put into the boxes during production in Chicago.

She said pranksters with "a sick sense of humor" were responsible.

"We really believe we have stopped it," she added. "We're really appalled that anybody would put something like this in a product that's intended for small children."

Video-game pair had Pac-Man wedding night

DES MOINES, Iowa (UPI) — "Mr. and Mrs. Pac-Man" were happily launched on a life-time of togetherness in the presence of their best friend — a Pac-Man video game.

Kyle Riley and Jo Linda Richardson were married yesterday at a shopping mall video game arcade and Pac-Man was everywhere.

Not only were the aisles adorned with Pac-Man popcorn balls, the 205-kilogram (450-pound) wedding cake had 1.2-metre (four-foot) high figures of Mr. and Mrs. Pac-Man kissing on a tall pedestral overlooking a simulated playing field of the popular video game.

Riley, 31, and Mrs. Riley, 17, both of Des Moines, said Pac-Man has meant so much to them they decided to exchange vows in front of a Pac-Man machine.

"We met, dated and fell in love playing Pac-Man . . ." the couple said.

Music from the single, Pac-Man Fever, entertained guests in the reception ballroom of the Marriott Hotel, which also was decorated in the Pac-Man theme.

The bride's mother, Pat Richardson, said all the media attention did not bother her.

"It was a little hard to hear, but it was a very nice ceremony," she said.

The video game also accompanied the honeymooners on their wedding night.

The hotel's management had arranged for a Pac-Man game to be installed in their room, complete with a roll of quarters.

MAFIA PRINCESS SAYS SHE'S BROKE

CHICAGO (AP) — Antoinette (Toni) Giancana, the "Mafia Princess," says she is broke and will be evicted from her $400-a-month rented house on Wednesday.

"This is ridiculous and absurd," the daughter of the late crime figure, Sam Giancana, said in an interview in Sunday's Chicago Tribune. "They used to call me the 'Mafia Princess' and now I'm broke. Me, Sam Giancana's daughter. I deserve better."

Six years ago, she asked for a separation from her husband of 13 years, Carmen Manno, and was cut off financially from Giancana, she said.

"He was so disgusted he wouldn't talk to me," Mrs. Manno said of her father. "In his mind, no Italian girl divorces her Italian husband."

She never saw her father alive again. An unknown gunman shot him to death in 1975 as he cooked sausage in the basement of his Oak Park, Ill., home.

★★★★★★★★★★★★★★★★★★★★★★★★★

Duck flown in for champagne cocktail

LAS VEGAS (UPI) — Donna Duck has helicoptered home from hospital to a red carpet, champagne-and-corn reception attended by 100 guests at the Sahara Country Club after having a three-foot arrow removed from her breast.

When the speeches and toasts were over yesterday, she was taken in a motorcade of two dozen golf carts to her home, a pond on the 13th green, and released.

Donna left the party immediately, flying straight out over the water where her mallard mate — who reportedly was unfaithful during her absence — flew up to join her. Their four ducklings stayed out of sight, and the pair sped off at tree-top level and disappeared.

At the reception, Donna was toasted as "a brave figure who has captured the hearts of people around the world" and "for the feelings of love and humanity she has inspired in all of us."

Donna became a celebrity when she was removed from the golf course May 25 by federal agents who drugged her bread.

I do, I do, I really do! Mailer picks two brides

NEW YORK (UPI) — Author Norman Mailer, whose divorce from his fourth wife recently became final, is preparing to tie the knot again — twice.

The Pulitzer Prize-winner will marry jazz singer Carol Stevens, the mother of his 9-year-old daughter Maggie, divorce her, and then marry his current paramour, Norris Church, the mother of his 2-year-old son John Buffalo, the Daily News says.

Mailer's long divorce battle with actress Beverly Bentley ended Sept. 24, and News columnist Liz Smith reports his marriage to Miss Stevens, who lived with the 57-year-old author for seven years, will occur "in the immediate future."

Miss Stevens, Miss Church and Mailer all agreed "it's best for Mailer to make matters legal for Carol and their child," the paper said.

Mailer, who won Pulitzer Prizes in 1969 and 1980 for The Armies of the Night and The Executioner's Song, has eight children. After the upcoming marriages, all would be legitimate.

A $50,000 trip to the cleaners

MIAMI (UPI) — Jay Rudnick drove his shinny new $16,000 1979 Lincoln to the car wash for a $3 wash. But the bill came to $50,000.

Alonso Small, a 16-year-old car wash employee, started to drive the car out of the tunnel but his foot slammed on the accelerator and the car shot out "like a cannon," witness said.

The car bounced over a curb, slid into a pole, crashed into two gasoline pumps, smashed into a parked car and exploded. Six other cars also were destroyed in the blaze.

Small was treated for minor burns in hospital and charged with careless driving.

10,000 gather to whoop it up

SPIVEY'S CORNER, N.C. (UPI) — This normally sedate hamlet of 50 people will swell to about 10,000 today when spectators and participants gather for the 10th annual National Hollerin' Contest.

The contest is dedicated to retaining the memory of what sponsors call "the almost lost art of hollerin'," — the yells and whoops that turn-of-the-century farmers used to call their animals and communicate with one another.

Contest organizer Ermon Godwin Jr. said every farmer had unique yells he used to call livestock, ask for water and seek help.

"If it weren't for the hollerin' contest, people wouldn't know about it, it wouldn't have been recorded," Goodwin said. "It has definitely created a revival of the art."

Usually only retired farmers know how to holler well enough to win, Godwin said, but there are some indications that once-common yells are being passed along to the younger generation.

In addition to the hollering contest, several thousand others signed up for a planned 10,000-meter run event, competition in watermelon rolling, corn shucking, whistling and conch shell and fox horn blowing. Also performances by cloggers and bluegrass musicians were planned.

Godwin says many people may come simply to have a good time, but others attend for the audible link to the past.

Woman bites dogcatcher

MINNEAPOLIS (AP) — Jill Otten admits she bit the dogcatcher, and says she'd do it again under the same circumstances.

Otten says she and her husband came home the afternoon of Sept. 5 and found their miniature poodle, Pepper, was missing from their fenced yard.

A neighbor told the Ottens she had seen a Metropolitan Animal Patrol Service Inc. truck near their property.

She stormed to the animal service and confronted a warden, who had Pepper.

"He told me to let go of my dog or he would choke him to death right in my arms. He would not let go, and so, in desperation, and fear for the life of my dog, I bit him."

ONE BEAT WITH A BAR ENDS GORILLA THRILLER

HUDDERSFIELD, England (Reuter) — Suddenly the gorilla lurched forward, bent apart the cage bars and lunged at the fairground audience.

An alert spectator grabbed an iron bar and crashed it down on the gorilla's head. Unfortunately, Mike Towell, a regular member of the fair's house of horror, was under the gorilla skin.

Police now want to question the would-be hero, who was last seen running from the tent pursued by Towell, blood streaming from a head wound which needed six stitches.

WOMAN, 100, DIVORCING ERRING HUSBAND, 103

STOCKTON, Calif. (AP) — Johnnie Lee Fegion is suing Solomon, her husband of 28 years, for divorce, because he "spends all his money on other women."

She is 100 years old, he is 103.

"I wanted to stay with him, but he wouldn't stop chasing after women," Mrs. Fegion said in an interview yesterday.

Mrs. Fegion said she filed for divorce two months ago and since that time "he's been so mean to me, always wants to fight."

"He doesn't want to give me nothin' to eat."

She and her husband have separated.

On the subject of a possible reconciliation, she was decisive:

"No, sir, I don't want no husband now."

Canine aristocrats fly first class

WASHINGTON — There are no inflight movies, no martinis and no music. But the passengers on board this airline don't mind. They get all the Milkbone biscuits they can chew.

"I guess it's an unusual business," said Maryann Waltz, owner of the Doglift — a Virginia air charter service catering exclusively to the canine set.

The company, whose planes are based at an airport 60 miles west of Washington, is one of several U.S. charter firms transporting valuable prize-winning pooches to dog shows across America.

"Only the rich can afford it," Waltz said. The dogs fly in single-engine Cessnas or twin-engine Aero Commanders for 50 cents an air mile. That's about $1,250, one way, for a flight across the country.

The idea, said Waltz, was to treat dogs as passengers — not cargo.

"Fly Your Dogs to the Shows With the Pros," says the advertisement for Doglift, whose professional pilots double as trainers for Waltz's kennel.

The idea grew out of owners' fears of flying animals in the cargo holds of commercial airliners.

"When you own a $20,000 show dog, you just don't want to take a chance," Waltz said.

WASHINGTON POST

Would drivers have a glow on?

BOSTON (Reuter) — Convicted drunk drivers would be issued car license plates that glow in the dark under a proposal being considered by the Massachusetts legislature.

A bill before a legislative committee would require cars driven by convicted drunken drivers to bear plates etched in luminous paint. The convicted driver would have to put the plates on whatever car he or she was driving.

The measure calls for only temporary use of the plates, to embarrass drunk drivers, but legal experts said such a bill might be unconstitutional.

Toenail freak still footloose

Toronto Star special

LOS ANGELES — The Phantom Pedicurist of southern California is still footloose and fancy free.

No charges will be filed against the man who was nailed after crawling under a library table and painting the big toenails of two female students at University of Southern California. The victims don't want to testify.

"I don't think they (the unnamed women) want to see the guy again, even in court," said Sgt. Bob Steele of Los Angeles police. "Besides, maybe they decided he'd done a good job."

Dubbed Leonardo da Toenail by campus police, the man's identity was not revealed, although he is neither a student nor a library employee.

No further incidents have been reported since he was caught redhanded near the library carrying 15 bottles of fingernail polish.

The toenail tinter also may have wielded his brush at California State University, Dominguez Hills. The student newspaper there said a man had daubed the toes of several women students, and described his modus operandi thusly:

"He seeks out a lone female student and sits across from her (in the library). He carries a large folder similar to a portfolio case and sets up as though working on a project.

"He causes minor disturbances, such as dropping pens and paint brushes. As he drops something, he reached under and quickly (one brush stroke will do it) paints the big Toenail. He drops something else and paints the other."

LOS ANGELES TIMES

Jailed wife-beater bites off fingers

MAYWOOD, Calif. (UPI) — A man jailed for allegedly stabbing his wife and biting off her nose sat calmly in his cell and bit off the ends of four of his fingers.

A policeman looked into Eduardo Nedilskyj's cell yesterday and found the suspect had bitten off the ends of two fingers on each hand, severing each digit at the first joint.

Nedilskyj was transferred to a hospital, where doctors planned to try to surgically reattach the finger tips.

He was arrested at his home late Wednesday night after allegedly attacking his wife, Mercedes, in bed. Authorities said he stabbed her three times in the back with a kitchen knife, and then bit off the end of her nose. She was admitted to hospital.

★★★★★★★★★★★★★★★★★★★★★★★★★★

Chainsaw divides divorcing pair's home

CENTRAL CITY, Ky. (UPI) — When a divorce court ordered Larry Everhart to split his house with his estranged wife, he took the order literally — and unpacked his chainsaw.

He said yesterday he was just about finished cutting his 30- by 35-foot house in two pieces: "It's just about done," he said, "but I've screwed up my chain saw."

Undaunted, the 57-year-old switched to a hand saw. "It's not as fast," he said, "but it's not too tough."

Everhart said he intended to keep half of the home and give the other half to his wife, Virgil, 36, instead of selling it and splitting the profits, as the court had ordered.

"The court said I had to do so-and-so and I'm determined not to do it," he added.

★★★★★★★★★★★★★★★★★★★★★★★★★★

Special to The Star
WASHINGTON — Hot dogs in Peking, and nude pageants in Dallas, A marijuana "smoke-in" near the White House and spitting contests in Virginia.

It was all part of the scene yesterday as Americans thorughout the United States and around the world celebrated U.S. Independence Day.

There were parades and fireworks displays in countless towns and cities. Sunny skies drew millions to the beaches.

In Peking, the U.S. Liaison Office, headed by former United Auto Workers' leader Leonard Woodcock laid on hot dogs, cold drinks and jazz bands for Chinese officials and hundreds of tourists.

DRESS OPTIONAL

Dress was optional for those who turned up to see the Miss and Mr. Nude contests in Dallas, but you might have needed to run for cover in Charlottesville and Roanoke, Va. where watermelon seed and tobacco juice spitting competitions took place.

Fireworks didn't produce the only smoke drifting over the U.S. capital yesterday. Thousands of marijuana-puffers celebrated America's 202nd birthday in a demonstration that was, fortunately, not clouded by violence. Hundreds of police kept their minds on the job by wearing gas masks, but made few arrests.

Mom wants 'foul-mouthed' sons ejected

DENVER (UPI) — A woman has asked a court to order her two sons out of the house because she claims they are foul-mouthed, dope-smoking and promiscuous.

Elmenia Lampley, 37, said her sons, Earl, 21, and Frederick, 18, have refused to leave the home or find jobs.

They smoke marijuana too much, engage in "unwelcome sexual activities on a frequent basis" and talk back to her in obscenities, Mrs. Lampley said in her lawsuit filed Thursday.

The brothers appeared surprised.

"If she really wanted us to move that bad, she didn't need to do this," said Earl. "She could have just come to us."

In response to his mother's claim that the home was saturated with the odor of marijuana, Earl admitted smoking the weed "every now and then."

"But when she told me not to bring it around the house, I went to the park," he said.

The lawsuit claimed Earl and Frederick were so messy that the family home had developed "a substantial problem concerning the odor and sightliness," but Earl said he has tried to help keep it tidy.

As for promiscuity, Earl said, "Everyone has friends."

Biographies

Born in Winnipeg, Manitoba, in 1930, **Gord Deval** started in radio work while very young. His father, Roy Ward Dixon, toured Canada with his radio quiz show, employing Gord as his advance man. After several years in public relations with a large corporation, Gordon moved to Toronto where he sold sporting goods, and later established his own insurance sales firm.

Trout fishing has remained Deval's avocation, and he holds 58 Canadian Fly and Bait Casting Records, as well as Canadian, International, and World Records and titles. He has represented Canada ten times in IOF-recognized World Casting Championships.

As a result of his continuing interest in writing, Deval has been the author of many outdoor articles for newspapers and magazines, including *Hunting & Fishing Canada, Outdoors Canada, Weekend Magazine, Field & Stream,* and *British Angler*. In addition, he has shown his movies on fishing in the streams of Ontario and on the Broadback River, Quebec, in eight countries.

Simon & Pierre published FISHIN' HATS (1983) and FISHIN' TALES (1984). The books have sold widely because Deval includes stream lore, advice on locations and camp cooking, as well as information on the outdoors, while using his regular fishing buddies as the heroes or victims in the humourous and sometimes poignant stories. Deval is often interviewed for radio and television as a guest expert on fishing, the outdoors, and cooking.

His many interests and activities have made Deval an avid and sympathetic observer of people's foibles and preferences. LIFE (AND DEATH) IN THE "YOONITED STATES OF UHMURICA" is the result of this interest and his amazement at the variety of human experience.

Ed Franklin moved from Houston, Texas, via New York to Canada in 1959, after serving overseas during World War II. He has become one of the country's top political cartoonists, with his observations on Pierre Trudeau, nuclear disarmament, the Conservative party, and many other issues, appearing frequently in Toronto's *Globe and Mail*.